History of Open-Water Marathon Swimming
2006 Edition

By
Captain Tim Johnson, PE
Associate Professor
Department of Electronics and Mechanical
Wentworth Institute of Technology
Boston, Massachusetts 02115

First Printing: January 2005 by Lightning Source, Inc.
1st Revision: July 2005
2nd Revision: August 2005
2nd Edition: January 2006
Print Revision: March 2006
3rd Edition: April 2007

Other Books by the Author
    Finding a Job in Tough Times, 2002
    Introductory Digital Logic Labs, 2007

Plays written by the Author
    Stud of the Hudson—A Swim in Twenty Stages, 2006

Editor: Professor Amos St. Germain, Ph.D.
       Wentworth Institute of Technology
       Boston, Massachusetts

Publisher:
Captain's Engineering Services, Inc.
Buzzards Bay, MA 02532
(www.captainsengsvc.com)

COPYRIGHT © 2005 Captain's Engineering Services
All rights reserved. No part of this book may be reproduced, in any form or by any means, without the permission in writing from the publisher.

ISBN 0-9721726-2-9

Acknowledgements

The author would like to thank the following persons who have been indispensable in the preparation of this book: Morty Berger, David S. Clark, Marcia Cleveland, Richard Clifford Esq., Ron Collins, Mary Donahue, Jim Doty, Gary Emick, Kevin Fleming, Sally Friedman, Drury J. Gallagher, Secr. Gen. Thomas Gangel of the Austrian Swimming Federation, Tommy Golden, Joan Harrison, Ben Huggard, Michael Jackson of Wentworth Institute of Technology, Jane Katz, PhD, Tony Kaufmann Esq., Skip Storch, Carl Kawauchi PE, Preston Levi at the ISHOF, Rafael Mesa, Randy Nutt, Dale Petranech, Julie Ridge, Philip Rush, George Sau PE, Caprice Schaefer, Ben Siebecker PE, Cindy Slater at the USOC, Randy Smith PE, Amos St. Germain, PhD, Skip Storch, Shelley Taylor-Smith, William Wallace, Tammy van Weiss, John Werner, John York, and Al Zamsky. Special thanks go to Captain Bob Peters for proofreading the January version of the 2nd edition.

Table of Contents

Introduction 3
Preface 6
Chapter 1 Swims of antiquity 9
   Renaissance swimming 11
Chapter 2 18th Century, the beginning of recorded swims 19
Chapter 3 19th Century, the early years of the Channel 25
Chapter 4 19th Century, English swims 39
   Austrian swimming 56
Chapter 5 19th Century New York wakes up to swimming 57
   Early Australian swimming 87
   Swim stroke transition period 88
Chapter 6 20th Century 93
Chapter 7 21st Century 139
   Professional swims 148
Chapter 8 Staged swims 153
   Other staged swims 158
Chapter 8 Early Manhattan swims 163
   Background information 164
   The first successful circumswim 168
   Pretenders 176
Chapter 10 Modern Manhattan 181
   Computer model 185
   In pursuit of the record 192
   Secrets of the Manhattan swim 199
   Doubles 219
   The reverse swim 220
Chapter 11 The Manhattan Island Marathon Swim history .. 225
   The Manhattan Island Marathon Swim organization 241
   Manhattan Island Foundation 268
Chapter 12 Cuba 281
Chapter 13 Bogus swims 289
   The ideal marathon swim using a cage 299
   Cage construction 302
   More assisted swims 312

Swimsuits	317
Water quality	318
Chapter 14 English Channel information	**325**
Precautionary aspects of Channel swimming	334
Channel training, Montauk	337
MOMS	340
GEMS	345
Chapter 15 Organized swims	**353**
Florida swims	353
Caribbean swims	356
Boston Light	358
Other New England swims	363
British Long Distance Swimming Association	366
The Channel Islands	367
Hawaiian swims	368
Irish Sea swims	371
Long Island Sound	373
Australian swims	376
Mid-Atlantic swims	381
Gibraltar Strait	383
Cook Strait	385
South Africa swims	389
West Coast swims	390
Channel Island swimming	394
Canadian swims	396
Mediterranean swims	398
Japanese swims	399
Modern records of note	400
Chapter 16 Swims, believe it or not	**403**
Appendix	**423**
Calculations	423
Swimming related injuries	428
"Swims" of Captain Paul Boyton	431
Team Millennium	438
Index	**449**
Endnotes	**491**

Introduction

The History of Open-Water Marathon Swimming will cover a number of events that happened during the past 200 years. It is not meant to be a complete history or inclusive of all swimming events. Swimming in the early years occurred out of doors in rivers, ponds, bays, and oceans. The first known swimming pool (ignoring the Roman baths) built in England was in 1828.[1] A swim in open waters has a component not seen in pool swims, the effect of currents. This text will present a summary and interpretation of these events and where appropriate, comments about the current will be included. Individuals and related developments in swimming will be included so that the particular skills which the swimmers possessed will be evident.

A short comment about times is needed to address what could be a contentious issue. Swim starts and stops are generally from the same area but not exactly. On any particular course on any particular day, one swimmer may start from shore and another when waist deep in the water. A finish one day might be a tape held on shore that a swimmer would run through after exiting the water or it could be when the swimmer stands up in water waist deep. Since the start and stop locations for the same swim can vary from year to year, times taken for individual swims are valid for that swim and only that swim. If the course more or less is the same except for these inconsistencies, then the times could be compared provide an allowance is made for these inconsistencies. For this reason, times, recording the seconds elapsed since the start, are inconsequential and in this text only the minutes are considered valid.

For example, if a swim lasts for 7 hours 10 minutes and 50 seconds and another swim over the same general course finishes in 7 hours 10 minutes and 10 seconds, the swimmers, since they were not competing on the same day against each other are virtual ties and both swims could be recorded as 7:10 (7 hours and 10 minutes) if truncating or the former as 7:11 with the later as 7:10 if rounding off. To "beat" another swimmer, the faster time should exceed the previous time by the better part of one minute. This truncating of the seconds helps resolve minor differences between swims swum at different times. There is no shame in tying an existing mark. It speaks volumes about the quality of the swim both swimmers executed. Many organizations, which maintain records, ignore the inconsistencies in the start and finish from one year to the next and record the seconds. These times are certainly valid for all swimmers on that course in that race but become meaningless over time when slightly different courses evolve and different people are validating the authenticity of the swim. A swim done at low tide in a bay is shorter than the same swim done at high tide because there is more of the shore exposed. It's not fair to compare the times to the second for different length courses.

Along this same line of thought, swim distances as reported in the media are misleading. Where the distance is checked against a chart, the distance will be noted in nautical miles. If the distance just says miles, either the course wasn't clear where the swimmer left and landed, or no chart was available to check the distance, or the distance is irrelevant, or the distance is obvious and well known (at least to locals). The nautical mile is 15% longer than a statue (land) mile so a measurement between two islands in nautical miles would be smaller than the same distance measured in statue miles. For swimmers, a meter is 9% longer than a yard so the same distance swum in a meter pool would be a lower number of laps than if you swam the same distance in a 25-yard pool. Distances swum due to current drift are irrelevant because the current is doing the work so only the straight line distance between two points matter. However, bends in rivers or course deviations around permanent obstacles do count when determining the overall distance swum.

Not every swim could be included in this book. You might say that this history of swimming contains sample representative swims from the ages. My original focus was just on New York swims but I found other swims so interesting I could not help but include them. This helped to put the context of the Manhattan Marathon Swim in focus. For this reason I would like to extend an invitation to the readers to send me information about their swim or one they know of so that future editions can be more inclusive. I would be interested in swims that are substantial, documented and that would shed some light on the nature of our world and the swimmers that inhabit it.

Some mention should be made about the source material. The New York Times provides a complete index of their newspaper from 1851 to the present. What is even nicer is that via ProQuest® online information service, you no longer have to go to the library to look information up.[2] That has some advantage when in the middle of the night you need to do some research. Much of the initial research for this book was done at the Great Neck Public Library in the early eightys.

The London Times offered a complete indexing from even earlier. Their indexes would list swimming either under Sporting or as a separate entry. Other newspapers from these periods are available but they are not indexed. Philadelphia's Free Public Library has the Philadelphia Press, Philadelphia Bulletin, and the Philadelphia Inquirer available on microfilm; all of them cover the late 1800's but none of them are indexed. In Boston, the Boston Globe was available from 1872 onwards but it too suffered from the same problem. Another paper in New York, the New York Tribune is indexed only for the years 1875 to 1906; the newspaper publishing dates encompass 1841 to 1924. Other newspapers in other major cities didn't start indexing their papers until the early 1970's. In order to find the swimming information (or for that matter, any other information) contained in these sources, someone would have to read each issue over the summer months of each year to find any entries. It takes about an hour to search the summer months for one year. It is very possible that more swims belonging to the accumulative knowledge of swimming are recorded but cannot be found. Much of swimming history is lost. The task of indexing these newspapers awaits a generous patron who is interested in obtaining the whole story.[3] History should not have to rely on the news that tweaks the interest of a New York Times editor.

Preface

Reading a book is like swimming; but once begun, there is the joy and relish of immersion. There has been a cornucopia of swimming contests and it will be your delight to learn of them, as it has been mine to discover them. It has been my privilege to participate in many contests either as a contestant or in a supporting role. It is in hope of setting the record straight as to whether a particular swim has ever been attempted that this history is undertaken. Hopefully, swimmers will be able to learn of the mistakes and successes of previous attempts so that their effort will culminate in a success. To this end, I've included as much information as possible about decisions that affect a swim and the reasons for them. While writing the history of the Manhattan Island Marathon Swim I began to realize the extent the organization had evolved over the years. The Manhattan Island Marathon Swim has had five different starting locations. Behind each one is a story and a reason. Here, through an organizational decision, a committee has affected the swim directly. For this reason, I've included as much about the organizations behind the major swims as possible.

What sort of swimmer is it that undertakes marathon swimming? Are they gluttons for punishment or simply swimmers that are not easily discouraged? Can the challenges of life be addressed by swimming? Some are physical brutes that seem to swallow the water in their path, others are the pool swimmers who have crafted their skills to a fine point and find a longer swim more to their liking. Still others are the swimmers who find the rhythm of the pace their mantra, often they are working out problems in their life and the time in the water is when they are alone and they can digest their situation. An amazing number of swimmers when asked what is their motivation for swimming mention the death of a loved one. The lost of a loved one will undoubtedly leave a person feeling helpless and useless. It's this consideration that can be overwhelming that swimmers immersed in their element find comfort while they consider the meaning of life. The mere fact that they can swim from point A to point B proves they are alive and can accomplish something. They come out of the water refreshed, ready to face life again. Marathon swimmers find the open water more to their liking than a pool with its constant turns and lane sharing. Most swimmers after their first long swim like it and then molded their style of swimming to incorporate these longer swims.

Swimmers can find a measure of peace and contentment while swimming; life is reduced to its barest essentials: taking a breath and moving their arms and legs as they slosh their way along. For the more proficient swimmer, they've taken the lessons learned in the pool and apply them continuously in a new environment. The feel of the water, the changing scenery, and the rhythmic stroking lead them on a path of discovery summarized in a goal of finishing. They all use the water as their element to immerse themselves in and when the going gets tough they evaluate, it's mankind against the elements at its most elementary level. They can control themselves and they have confidence that they can conquer the water. When their goals expand they allow themselves as much assistance in their task as possible; thus a coach and pilot roles become essential. It's in the sharing of these goals that an event such as marathon swimming has its attraction.

Since my role has always been more of a pilot I've sometimes wondered why I place myself in this role. Some days, it's because I'm just glad to be out on the water on a boat. Other days I realize I'm involved in something larger than my life or goals I couldn't imagine and lose myself in doing my part to achieve a common goal. The swimmer's goal becomes shared and even though I may not be swimming, its accomplishment or even the attempt makes me feel better about the world and my role in it. You are playing a role, an essential role, and an appreciated role. You are doing your part. If the swim is successful, you're happy you had a part and if it's not successful, you are there to console. Swimmers are very goal driven and it's helpful to them to know that it's okay to fail. If life was simple and we were always successful, we'd all be terrible bores. For me as a pilot, the best swims take place in the mind. The joy is in seeing the vision take place and be successful.

Often after a swimmer attains a particularly difficult goal their life moves off in a different direction. When you've swum to the ropes the distance buoy becomes the challenge. When you've swum to the buoy, the only challenge left is now beyond the buoy to the distance shore. It is to these many different directions that swimmers takes that I salute as the lesson that swimming teaches us. It is the discipline to *focus* on the task at hand that we learned in swimming practices. This is the lesson that swimmers bring to other disciplines. Thus it is so that we find the talents of swimmers dispersed into the story of the whole human family. For a few hours they are in the spotlight and then their swim becomes part of our story.

Finally, while this is extensively a history book about swimming, if nothing is learned by the reading that can be applied to swims of today, then the book has not accomplished it purpose. Where appropriate, suggestions and/or conclusions are provided by the author to make the lesson more pointed.

Chapter 1   Swims of antiquity

When was the first swim? How long have people been swimming? Have people always known how to swim? These are interesting questions and fortunately much simpler to answer than "which came first, the chicken or the egg?" question. Before you swam, you learned to bath and how to immerse yourself in water. Depending on the volume of water available and knowing the entertainment factor that water has, horseplay came next. I would speculate that it was when the horseplay became excessive and one person wanted to get away that swimming per se was invented. When that person stepped off into water deeper than they could stand, if not swimming then boating was invented. Because boating served a grander purpose, commerce, it was developed with more emphasis than swimming. People swam before they began recording swimming events. Once swimming entered recorded history we can date a first swim putting our own swims in context within time itself. So, what is the earliest known reference to swimming?

The answer to this question is based upon the interpretation of cave drawings. In a cave found in Egypt at Wadi Sora are drawings of figures little more than stickmen. These figures could be people swimming based on the positioning of the figures and the imagination of the viewer. The drawings date from 7000 to 5000 BC. Mosaics from early Middle Eastern civilizations and Pompeii featured depictions of swimming.

During an excavation of a necropolis at Paestum, Italy, in 1968 a painting was discovered drawn on the inside of a cover to a sarcophagus that incorporates swimming as a theme. The building dated from the Hellenic era, about the 6th century B. C.; Greeks lived in this portion of Italy. The scene drawn *in color* shows a man in the act of diving from a high stonewalls into what is obviously a river. The stone pillars are thought to be the Gates of Ade, the end of the known world, and the river River Okeanos, which the Greeks believed to be a tempestuous river, which lead beyond the grave.[4] While the spiritual afterlife is being represented here, it is the use of common examples from life that are used to depict the afterlife. Diving into a river and the subsequent act of swimming is an experience common for the ancient Greeks.

Figure 1 The Diver's Tomb from the National Museum of Paestum, Italy, circa 500 BC.

Murals are also found in the Tepantitla House at Teotihuacan in Mexico have similar scenes. An Assyrian bas-relief found in the palace of Nimrud in northern Iraq depicts persons fleeing from archers into a river. Three persons are shown in the river, two appear to be using inflated animal skins to cross but one figure appears to be swimming. From the position of the arms of the figure swimming, the stroke looks like an overhand crawl. The dates for these drawing records are from 883-859 BC.[5] At 700 BC, written references to swimming are found in Homer's *The Iliad* and *The Odyssey*. In Japan, the Emperor Suigiu encouraged swimming in 36 BC.[6] The Bible refers to swimming in Ezekiel 47:5, Acts 27:42, and Isaiah 25:11. The Acts reference in the New Testament of the Bible is a shipwreck where people survived by swimming ashore. When St. Paul was being transported to Rome to appeal his sentence, the ship was caught up in a storm and the officers aboard decide to beach the vessel inside a bay. In making to this harbor, the boat went aground on a reef at the harbor entrance. While abandoning ship a distinction was made between those who could swim and those who needed floatation assistance to reach shore. People have been swimming throughout history in all civilizations. Swimming is a natural response to the human condition.[7]

In what is possibly the first written record of swimming during the modern times, the explorer Christopher Columbus recorded in his journal of the first voyage to the New World in 1492 that when anchored two leagues off San Salvador, natives swam out to conduct trade with them.[8] The league used by Columbus is 2.67 nautical miles so the distance the natives swam could have been as much as 5 nautical miles one way.[9] The explorer came upon the New World during the night and they anchored offshore. The only real question is whether or not upon daylight if the vessels were repositioned nearer before launching the rowboat that carried Columbus ashore. If they did, the reefs on the east side of San Salvador vary from ¼ to ¾ mile offshore. There is a shelf that extends out up to 3 miles before the 100 fathoms line. Columbus did not confuse swimming with boating as he has a separate entry to record a visit by the natives in a canoe.

One story that comes out of this period of world history tells of us of a drawback that native people incurred because of their knowledge of swimming skills. The native people of the Bahamas, the Lucayans, knew how to swim and dive, as the reefs off their coastline are a natural food source. When pearl beds were discovered off the coast of Venezuela, a work force was needed to recover these treasurers. In 1508, the Spanish Crown issued an edict allowing Spanish colonists to take Lucayans as slaves to fill the need. Within four years, the entire native population of the Bahamas was wiped out or removed to Venezuela.[10]

Renaissance swimming

From an engraving in 1628 by Oliviero Gatti (Figure 2) we see the means by which people in Europe were learning to swim. The floatation is slightly improved from the animal skins of the

Assyrian seen in the relief at the Palace of Nimrud. The floatation is strapped to the back with a belt attached to an inverted bowl. Youngsters learned and novices were swimming together with no one person seen to be in charge. The location is a riverbank that includes a bank for jumping off.

Figure 2 Children Swimming In A River, an engraving by Oliviero Gatti in 1628

The figure resting on the bank indicates that the lessons would go on for some time allowing time for introspection, observation, and rest. There is an unabashed enjoyment of the occasion, which is away from settlements, and the garments worn by the figures are nowhere to be seen. The figure in the upper left is jumping off the bank into the river. The figure in the upper right is possibly in shallow water and has just possibly started forward for another stretch at swimming. The larger figure in the middle looks like they could be doing either the sidestroke or a crawl stroke. The figure in the lower right is a novice that appears to be stroking the water in a rudimentary overhand stroke with the left-hand placement directly in front of the head. The artist is using that figure to show the details of the floatation attachment. One question you could ask about the two figures learning to swim is if the swimmers were learning sidestroke, then why would the floatation be arranged to hold them out of position? The method of instruction positions the swimmer in a prone position that is adaptable to either breaststroke or overhand crawl. In this drawing, breaststoke is not represented due to the hand placements shown.

Figure 3 Wolves Swimming Across a River, an engraving by Oliviero Gatti in 1628.

Oliviero Gatti is an artist from Bologna, Italy that made drawings of outdoor events. Another drawing he is known for is *A Hunter Releasing his Dogs on a Stag*. In Figure 3, *Wolves Swimming Across a River*, he combines a bit of imagery in his subject, wolves, but it is the stroke used by the human portion of the figure that is striking. The only wolf in the water is shown swimming freestyle, or at least in a prone position that is unmistakable. The figure is prone and the arms are extended in opposite directions. The figure is not turned on the side, as it is the head that is turned to look to the left. I'd even go so far as to say that the left arm is bent at the elbow at the beginning of the recovery portion of the stroke. The hand of the right arm on the entry is shown flat as a stroke holding the head up would be.

One artist more or less would not be anything to get excited about and might even be considered a fluke. The next example, Figure 4, is from Carlo Cesio, 1626-1686, also from Italy. His drawing seen on the next page of *Leander Swimming Across the Hellespont* is purely speculative as he was not an eyewitness. He drew Leander as an idealized swimmer sometime in the mid-17th Century. In this sense, Leander is every swimmer that Cesio ever saw in his world. This is what Jane Katz, Ed. D, has to say about Leander's stroke, "It's an open-water, splash life-saving stroke with good hand placement, note the bent elbow. The swimmer appears vertical in the water." I view the stroke as the heads-up freestyle used in water polo.

These artists are the sports reporters of their day. Their knowledge of anatomy was fundamental to their work and what is being communicated in the drawing is the story of swimming as these artist knew it through the technology of the day, engraving. What this means is that Europe knew and practiced the overhand crawl stroke long before John Arthur Trudgen or Fred Cavill visited the Solomon Islands. The real question that arises out of this anomaly is why was this stroke not among swimmer's repertoire when competitive swimming began around the early 1800's?

Figure 4 Leander Swimming Across the Hellespont to Hero by Carlo Cesio.

For a while I considered that some disaster occurred that killed off all the swimmers and Europeans had to learn to swim all over again. One disaster that comes to mind would be the Black Death; but this plague occurred around 1350 and millions of people died, estimates include up to a third of Europe.[11] Another possibility is the rise of a religious fanaticism that forbids swimming. A modern example occurred recently in Bangladesh. The Bangladesh's Sports Minister, Fazlur Rahman, prevented four women swimmers from participating in a long distance swimming event in a river in Chandpur, a district south of the capital in early December of 2004 when 1000 religious Moslem adherents took to the streets in protest.[12] The only parallel to this in Europe is the Inquisition where religious authority had temporal powers and the Reformation where a sect might forbid communal bathing out of respect for personal piety. Europe had moved out of this era by the time of the Renaissance and Protestant modesty was satisfied with the invention of the bathing suit. The Moslem community is presently still wrestling with the outward displays of piety. These sources as causes for the ignorance of the freestyle stroke as modern competitive swimming began have to be discounted for the drawings occurred subsequent to the historical events.

Figure 5 Leander close-up.

The comment by Jane Katz of the swimmer being vertical in the water is the key. There is no kick seen. If you are swimming strictly by arm stroke and dragging your legs in the vertical plane, this is not a very fast stroke because of the drag created. I think we've all seen a beginning swimmer whose position in the water is dictated by lifting their head to breathe and forcing their feet down. Renaissance Europe might have known the overhand stroke but they didn't know how to exhale in the water. The head above the water approach to swimming quite possibly was a defense mechanism when swimming in rivers that served as sewers. When breaststroke was developed and then sidestroke; the use of these strokes in combination with a leg kick made immense speed improvements over the heads-up freestyle stroke. It was these advanced strokes that were used by competitive swimmers. These newer strokes were taught to younger generations and this is what I suspect led to Europe forgetting the overhand crawl. The freestyle stroke was not taught leading up to the 19th Century due to the inefficiencies of the stroke as it was practiced. A proclivity for maintaining the head above the water developed that further submerged the stroke style until the late 19th Century when speed became important and the water quality improved.

Textbooks on swimming from this era (after the invention of the printing press by Johannes Gutenberg in 1445) are derived from a Latin text by the Cambridge scholar Everard Digby, *De arte natandi libri duo*, first written in 1587. A first translation appeared in 1595 by Christopher Middleton.[13] William Percey wrote what is considered an unattributed translation of Digby's Latin for his book, *The Compleat Swimmer*, also known as *The Art of Swimming*, in 1658. A translation of the Digby book by Melchisedec Thevenot called *The Art of Swimming: Illustrated with Proper Figures with Advice for Bathing* appeared in 1699. Of these, the later provided 39 engravings while the original Latin text only had 5 engravings and Percey's book had but one engraving seen in Figure 6.[14] The subject of the books included: how to tred water, leap like a goat, swim like a dog, swim on your back and on your side, and how to float. Textually and graphically, none of the aforementioned books approached the level of instruction found in the drawings by Gatti and Cesio. Here is a case where one Renaissance drawing is worth a thousand Latin words. It could be concluded from a comparison between engravings that swimming in the Mediterranean was far in advance of English style and technique.

Figure 6 Engraving from The Compleat Swimmer by William Percy, 1658.

Chapter 2   18th Century, the beginning of recorded swims

The public history of open water swimming begins with a swimming event that took place in London on September 17, 1791. In a short paragraph in the London Times was a report of three men swimming from Westminster Bridge to London Bridge in the afternoon, a distance of just under 2 miles.[15] It probably never would have been recorded had not the victor been carried on the shoulder of the crowd to a public house to celebrate and swimming suffered its first loss. It was reported that the winning swimmer drank so much gin that he expired a half an hour after the event. One would expect that for a swim of 2 miles, you wouldn't find many takers if they were not already prepared for the exertion. Smaller swims would have been undertaken previously in private. It should also be noted that the victor garnered 8 guineas.[16] A person or organization could have sponsored the award or it could have been a wager. Seeing as how it was held in the middle of London, it probably drew the contestants from a wide area. The fact that this event was reported in the London Times is most probably due to the death of the unnamed winner than to the fact of their swimming in the Thames.

It's of interest that the swim went from bridge to bridge, a common designation of swim starts and stops. Bridges provide an easy way to designate a well-known beginning or finishing point and from the water are quite easy to distinguish. The Westminster Bridge was relatively new having been first built in 1750, the second bridge to span the Thames in London. The London Bridge the swimmers swam toward was the medieval bridge that was built in 1209.[17] Built subsequent to this swim was the 2nd London Bridge, which was designed by John Rennie and completed in 1831.[18] This replacement for the medieval bridge allowed the tidal flow along the Thames easier access to the Thames upper reaches. In 1791, the current was impeded by the many bridge footings so the swimmers made their way down stream with the assistance of a weaker ebb current than present day swimmers would encounter.

The difference between the high and low tides along the Thames today at London Bridge can vary as much as 6½ meters (20 feet).[19] The tidal range in 1791 will have differed slightly due to the medieval bridge foundations constricting the flow, so the current would have been much less than 4 knots that could flow with a twenty-foot tide range. It could be presumed that the swimmers used a variation of the breaststroke in their swim or possible the sidestroke. You could float the 2 miles downstream in 30 minutes at 4 knots; by using a stroke on a weaker current, the winning time could have been about the same.

Figure 7 The London Bride in Lake Havasau, Arizona, is still the site of a swim. During the Festival of Lights, the day after Thanksgiving, the winner of a swim the length of the bridge gets to turn on the Festival lights.

This unnamed victor could well be the Phidippides[20] of swimming, except for the fact that he died from drinking and not swimming. The oversight of not recording the name could be attributed to the novelty of the event and that sport reporting had not matured enough to include the names of the participants and the times.

Prior to this swim, which was a competition, a well-known American, Benjamin Franklin, swam 3½ miles down the Thames in 1726 in an exhibition of stunts and figures or "ornamental" swimming when he was twenty years old and living in London. He also designed for his own use a set of hand paddles and swim fins ten years earlier.[21] This is mentioned due to the stature of the swimmer as opposed to the nature of the swim, it neither being the first nor a race. While many books on the history of swimming begin with Lord Bryon crossing of Hellespont; it is Franklin who predated Bryon's poetry with his own book, an instruction book on swimming in 1781, *The Art of Swimming,* wherein he tells of this demonstration swim.

Another well-known American who swam all over the world was John Quincy Adams, the sixth President of the United States (1825-1829). It is said that his regularity in life was an obsession. One of his regularities was to take a swim in the morning if not a walk. This was before swimming trunks were fashionable. When John Quincy Adams was president, he would take nude swims across the Potomac River.[22] At age 58 he swam the width of the Potomac about a mile in an hour's time. He took his last swim at age 79.[23] Prior to that he was a Secretary of State and before that was a Minister to the Netherlands and Germany. He traveled throughout Europe, presumably observing his swimming regime and fastidiously writing in his journal.

Lucy Royall, a woman newspaper reporter had learned of his peculiar habit of swimming nude and therein devised the mechanism for conducting what is called the first Presidential news conference.[24] She sat upon his clothes and refused to give them to him until he answered some questions, which he did while immersed.[25] Press conferences are not always the most pleasant experiences for Presidents; neither was the first. Can you imagine the discomfort if Presidents were required to answer questions in the nude until the press was satisfied before giving them their clothes back?

It should be noted that in 1603 in Japan a national swimming organization is started. A three-day meet was held in 1810.[26] Little is known or available about the state of Japanese swimming, the style, the times, or its development. One influence upon swimming could be from the Japanese custom of bathing. Bathing is slightly different in Japan than in the rest of the world where the cleansing can be quite brief, the social aspect of the Japanese bath is a well-known custom. It's commonly called ritual bathing.[27] Hot springs abound throughout Japan and could well be the reason for the prevalence of bathing. Their society includes pearl divers and harvesters of seaweed who had to be able to get about by swimming in the sea. Women traditionally did these occupations.[28] In 1906, a swimming demonstration was given by a Japanese swimmer named Fuiggi at Sea Gate, New York. The swimmer performed dolphin swimming and jumping into the water at a swimming carnival hosted by the Atlantic Yacht Club.[29]

In contrast to the Japanese, bathing was rare in Europe. Louis XIV (1643-1715) was said to have taken only 3 baths, and one of those was when he was baptized. Soap was not made in England until 1641.[30] It is little wonder that the Roman Baths in Bath, England, were such a surprising discovery; yet, once adopted, these societies made great progress in swimming. Against this background, Ben Franklin's swim down the Thames must have been viewed as daring and avant-garde.

One cannot help but notice that wagering is associated with early swims. While the influence can be speculated upon, money has always been considered the distinction between amateur sports and professional sports. To entice swimmers into a competition, a wager is put up by a swimmer or their backer and may or may not be mentioned in a news report. Sometimes the wager takes the more respectable guise of a trophy by the host club and visiting teams would ante up what we'd call today the entry fee.

Swimmers would be given head starts so that the races are more interesting. The favorite would be called the scratch swimmer because after their name would be drawn a line indicating no time advantage was given. *Gambling in England* was the title of a book review in the New York Times in 1899 and it gives us a look into the world of English gambling from which I extract the following. Since gambling in America followed the English led, it behooves us to recognize this influence.

> Horse racing was considered a social cancer compared to wagers and betting yet it was encouraged by Queen Anne. Both are considered forms of gambling. The Greeks bet, as recorded in the Iliad. The Romans did also according to Virgil. Shakespeare was familiar with the giving and taking of odds and used this activity in scenes from Hamlet and other plays. Letters to the Editor from early newspapers, the Spectator August 16, 1711, mentions the prevalence of laying wagers. Social institutions were further corrupted by the practice of lotteries with even the Westminster Bridge being financed in part by a lottery.[31]

Just as today, swimmers would write books. *How to Swim* by Capt. David Dalton was published in 1899 and was said to be "…a practical treatise on the art of natation, together with instruction as to the best methods of saving the drowning and of the resuscitation of those apparently drowned. The author a few years ago won widespread fame by swimming across the English Channel in 23.5 hours…Capt. Dalton who is Chief Inspector of the United States Volunteer Life Saving Corps, has saved 281 persons from death by drowning."[32] His and other individuals mentioned later use of the title of Captain comes from their service in the Life Saving Corps, an organization for life guards, and does not necessarily mean the individual was a ship's master.

The other title that today sounds odd is the use of professor. The dictionary definition of the term professor assigns the meaning to an academic rank at a college or university. An additional understanding of the term is "an instructor in some art or skilled sport."[33] This is a usage of the term that has fallen in disuse for quite some time but during the zenith of this usage, to be called a professor was an indication of the esteem with which the instruction of a skilled sport could be attributed.

Chapter 3   19th Century, the early years of the Channel

Onto the swimming scene in the late 19th century appeared two men who by their daring, courage, and fortitude set the standards for open water swimming. The first golden era of swimming was about to begin in England. There was a general population that supported with interest the many contests held throughout the land. Local champions would be declared and crossings of great bodies of water would be attempted. The greatest of all was the crossing of the English Channel. This era began with two successful crossings and an argument as to what constitutes a swim. But first we will turn our attention to the precursors.

Preceding the swimming was a canoe crossing in 1867 from France to England, which caused a stir among the residents of Dover.[34] A Mr. Bowker, a member of a canoe club left Ambletense, a village seven miles north of Boulogne, and 11 hours later landed in Dover. His canoe, called *Octoroon*, was 16 feet long, two feet wide, and 8 inches deep. During the transit he lost his chart and his compass failed to function so he was fortunate that a steam packet stopped to point out the course. While underway some porpoises surfaced causing him some consternation but the water condition was overall very calm for the duration of the trip. The reason this event is mentioned in a swimming history is the idea of crossing the channel by human propulsion alone was not a unique concept.

It had long been rumored that some prisoners had escaped and crossed the channel years before Captain Webb. The rumor is this: some seventy years earlier, 1800 or shortly there about, three men were convicted of a political offense in France. To avoid a prison term, the men made their escape while aboard a ship in Calais and began swimming to England. One swimmer died during the crossing; another died immediately from exhaustion upon reaching shore; while the third recovered and lived in Dover for a number of years.[35] This information was from a London Time report in 1876, as background before the first ever attempt to cross the channel. By the 1970's the rumor has morphed into a French prisoner, Jean-Marie Saletti, aboard a British prison ship in Dover, escaped and swam to Boulogne.[36] It is interesting that the nationalities and direction swum changed but the venue and motive didn't. Conrad Wennerberg's book shed some light on the original of this rumor when he mentioned a swim across the Channel by a Frenchman who claimed to be one of Napoleon's soldiers. This swim is discounted as the captain's logbook shows that he took rests aboard his escort vessel. Also mentioned is the swim by William Hoskins on December 20, 1862 who floated part of the journey across on a bundle of straw.[37] The bundle of straw as a floatation device is quite plausible as that is what thatched roofs are made of and in England that was a common roofing material for the time.

    The first public announcement of an attempt to swim across the channel came from a well-known swimmer in London. Following a swim down the Thames, J. B. Johnson, age 24, announced that he would next swim across the Channel. This announcement was posted about London on placards proclaiming Johnson as "the hero of London Bridge and champion swimmer of the world." Betting immediately favored his not making a successful crossing, giving 100 to 1 odds on the day of the swim. The conditions on the bet stipulated that he was to be unaided by any appliance of any sort, that he not leave the water once begun, and it be completed in 12 hours. On the appointed day, August 23, 1872, the weather was not conducive to a Channel swim, so Johnson gave a swimming demonstration instead so as to not disappoint the crowd, which numbered in the thousands.[38] The following day, August 24, Johnson with 30 medals pinned on his chest lead the Royal Surrey Zoological Gardens band down to the piers at Dover surrounded by thousands of onlookers.[39] When the swimmer attempted to leave from the pier the harbormaster refused to let him pass the barriers due to the large crowd that was following him. Instead, the swimmer left by boat. When the escort boat was 200 yards off the piers, Johnson made his appearance on the paddle box and a tremendous cheer went up. He dove in and began his swim at 10:40 am. He managed about 7 miles in a little over an hour of swimming when he left the water.[40] Although this swim was not as billed, word of this swim propagated throughout the world via the news reports and due to the fact that J. B. Johnson made a very successful tour of the United States in the years following his attempt. I would think that it was during one of his appearances in the United States that Paul Boyton either met Johnson and learned of this exploit or read of the attempt in news reports of Johnson's exploits.

The era of channel swimming opened in April of 1875 when Captain Paul Boyton, age 26, of the Atlantic Life-saving Services of the United States announced his intention of crossing the English Channel from Dover to Boulogne. He was demonstrating his newly invented life-saving dress: Merriman's Patent Waterproof Life-Saving Apparatus.[41] His purpose was to prove to the maritime nations that the means and science were within their reach to provide for the safety of mariners upon whose efforts their own greatness derived.[42] This statement made a week prior to his attempt put this crossing in a category apart from swimming. In fact, his press release makes no mention of swimming the channel, only crossing it. The press referred to this experiment as a voyage. Capt. Boyton expressed a wish in his press release to conduct a "fair, square, and above-board" test of his life-saving dress by means of a practical demonstration. The undertaking was under the auspices of the Humane Society of Boulogne of France.[43]

It's interesting to note that in this public declaration of the event's purpose, he details some of his preparation by giving a time and current that he hoped to catch. He planned to leave Dover at night so that he might reach the shores of France in daylight so the citizens of Boulogne could welcome him. He reasoned that by catching the ebb current off Cape Gris-Nez during the day he would be able to achieve his objective. This planning for the crossing showed an understanding of the currents that all open-water swimmers need to consider in their swims. His analysis of the currents is valid today, if a swimmer reaches to within 3 miles off Cape Gris-Nez and their strength endures, they have every reason to count on success. Today, the dividing line is reaching the French inshore waters of the shipping lanes so that the swimmer doesn't drift south in the northbound shipping lane. His emphasis on the crossing being fair and square reveals how important it was to the success of the demonstration that observers verify that he completed the crossing due to the aid of the life-saving dress. His was an assisted swim.

His efforts might possible have been overlooked or receive little notice were it not for Boyton's cunning. Before his demonstration he exhibited his life-saving apparatus to Queen Victoria at the Isle of Wright[44]. The Isle of Wright served as Queen Victoria's summer residence where at Osborne house, built by her husband, Prince Albert, in East Cowes on 1000 acres she would stay for a good portion of the year. This notice in the newspapers represented a coupe of supreme marketing savvy. The press did not fail to mention the extent of the Royal interest in this event. Press coverage included explanations of who was representing the Queen at the demonstration and any remarks the observer would make. Because of the Royal interest, observers from France and Russia were expected as Queen Victoria had an influence around the world. The Queen's interest was such that she had asked to be notified by telegraph of the start of the crossing.[45] This is an indication of the Queen's interest in new technology as the telegraph has only been invented but already there were underwater cables connecting the Queen's residence in the Isle of Wright, located two miles off the shores of England in the south. Because Capt. Boyton's expressed purpose was to demonstrate a method of marine lifesaving, the Queen's concern for her subjects alerted every sailor that had ever sailed the seas under the British flag that the Queen was thinking of them and their safety. How Captain Boyton manages to arrange this demonstration is not known but it made all the difference.

What is this life-saving dress that Capt. Boyton was testing? The London Times described it as a suit made of Indian rubber that can be inflated via some tubes. The dress floated the user and allowed the use of a paddle. It was an airtight and waterproof suit. On the day of the swim, Boyton arrived at the dock dressed in his inflatable suit with a suit of blue surge underneath and large woolen stockings carrying an oar. He also carried a foghorn hung around his neck, a brandy flask in a waist pocket, and a large knife; safely ensconced under his dress was a packet of letters, "the Boyton mail for the Continent" which he intended to deliver.[46] Additionally, there were provisions for hoisting a sail about the size of a large handkerchief by means of a small mast placed in a socket attached to the foot and controlled by lanyards attached to the suit.[47] Both feet were outfitted with these sockets. Undoubtedly, this was the most unique floating contraption and it was a wonder that he could inflate it in a few minutes. The paddle was used for propulsion and Capt. Boyton would stroke along both sides, as he lay on his back in a skillful employment of the paddle. In his second attempt, a small screw propeller was brought along and could be affixed by means of hoops to his torso and thighs so that while lying prone in the water, he could propel himself. It is unclear if this means of propulsion was used in his second attempt. Most likely, it was found deficient and discarded as reports of his progress make no mention of its usage.[48] It is probably the secret dream of every distance swimmer to have a little propeller attachment by which they could facilitate their journey by any means other than swimming. Capt. Boyton seems to have thought of them all.

There were in this event, elements of controversy and confusion that is present in every other swims of similar originality that bear telling. The points of contention were the starting time, the best method to attack the course and how to call a swim off. Capt. Boyton's journey across the channel began in London, and then he visited with the Queen in the Isle of Wright before traveling to Dover. He planned to depart from the Admiralty pier at 10pm on Friday April 10, 1875 and announced it in the press.

The resident engineer objected to the presence of a large crowd on the lower promenade when the mail train from London was expected and refused permission to start from the pier. Previously, J. B. Johnson had a similar problem when he sought to depart from Dover. This issue was resolved when the starting time was changed to 11pm, after the train had departed.[49]

The Royal Cinque Ports Yacht Club whose facilities overlook the harbor hosted Capt. Boyton on the night before his departure. The enthusiastic reception toasted heartily to the success of his voyage. The Royal Cinque Ports Yacht Club[50] is still in existence today at the same location. During the day, he practiced the start from the pier. This was crucial as an unexpected current might prevent his use of the pier but the practice was successful. By doing a trial start twelve hours prior to the expected time, a similar tide will be found; thus allowing time to make changes. It proved a start from the pier was feasible.[51] Swimmers today still practice in the same harbor in front of the Yacht Club but for a different reason: to become acclimated to the cold water conditions present in the channel. Their starts are less complicated as they start from Shakespeare Beach just south of the harbor. Practice starts are normally incorporated in a well thought out training regime for channel swimmers.

Once the starting location issues were settled, the starting time became a focus of contention again. The passage was envisioned as starting at 10pm so that he might arrive in France in the daylight hours. This had now been changed to 11pm to accommodate the train schedule and still arrive in daylight. When the lugger sent over by the Humane Society of Boulogne to escort Capt. Boyton into Boulogne arrived, its pilot immediately argued for a later start after doing a series of calculations. He was joined in this opinion by the harbormaster of Dover, a Mr. Iron. Their intent was to allow Capt. Boyton to travel far enough out into the channel so that he would avoid drifting into a series of sand bars found north of Dover called Goodwin Sands.[52] Their concern over this obstacle overshadowed the desire to arrive in France during daylight. The start time was moved to 3 am in the morning.[53] This put Boyton's start on an ebb tide which means he would be carried south and that he most likely would be halfway across when the tide would switch to flood carrying him north. Tide calculations are still part of any swim strategy and early morning starts are quite common.

Support craft for swimmers, spectators and the press is always an issue. This issue arose when it was discovered that one of the vessels carrying the press, the tug Rambler, was not licensed to carry passengers. All swims need organization, a beginning, an end and a means to accomplish the journey and transmit the story. In the organizer's haste to find some support boat at reasonable cost, small details such as licenses are overlooked. The customs official and trade officials warned the passengers that they traveled at their own risk. While this was more of a logistics problem, events conspired to add drama impinging upon the expedition's success. Complicating the start was the arrival of the morning mail steamer, expected by those familiar with the vessel traffic at this time of the morning but certainly unplanned for the expedition's organizers. This caused the pier officials to ask the tug to move off. With Capt. Boyton already in the water prior to the start, the stirring of the tug's paddles created such a disturbance that he was seen banging up against the pier's pilings. The observers watched as he was tossed by the waves until his own paddling extricated him from this danger. After a few minutes, the report of a cannon and the firing of a rocket signaled the start of the demonstration. Capt. Boyton was seen in the glimmer of a torch carried in a boat towed behind the tug paddling on his back seaward before disappearing into the darkness.

After an hour, as daylight approached, while off Foreland light, Capt. Boyton raised a sail attached to his foot to catch the start of the morning breeze. He managed to use his paddle as a rudder and he made good progress under this meager spread of canvas. By 7am he was enjoying a cigar given him by the captain of the French boat, and soon his first refreshment break where he reported "All's well". At this time, Dr. Driver, of Southsea, took his temperature and found it normal. A Mr. Willis, a surgeon from London, was also on board. It was estimated that he was 8 miles off the coast of England. In the middle of the channel is a reef called the Varnes. As Capt. Boyton approached this location he blew on his foghorn to scare some fish away. Since this sea floor at this location is shallow, wave action was noticeable. The steamer was so far away from him that he was scarcely discernible among them. At 9am he hailed the vessel and requested some brandy and water. He switched the sail to his other foot and continued on paddling across the Varnes. The wind picked up, a rain started, and he stopped again to consult with his brother and the doctor. It seemed he was sleepy. He rested for about a quarter an hour holding onto the boat then set out again with the sail and paddle. The object was to cross the Varnes and get into the French side of the current that would take him down along the coast of France. At this point the on-board consultation of the physician and brother began to take on ominous tones. They worried if he should continue his efforts any longer. The physician asserted that the Captain's strength was leaving him but his brother was confident in his brother's endurance. By this time, Capt. Boyton had crossed the Varnes, was into smoother water and was inquiring of the distance to Boulogne. His inquiry provoked a cheer from those watching about the vessel. After some more brandy, he resumed his journey for another hour. About noon, the sky cleared, and Capt. Boyton began a regular schedule of hourly brandy and cigar breaks. In fact, whenever he seemed to falter, his brother would row out to him and serve him a small quantity of brandy. The regular channel traffic would come upon him, slow down, and their passengers would cheer him. He sent along a message via the mail packet *Napoleon III* to the crowd of several thousand on the look out for his arrival in Boulogne that all was well.

All Saturday afternoon Capt. Boyton paddled away but as evening began to fall, a serious discussion began again only this time it was not about his strength but the course. The pilot of the French boat and the captain of the tug disagreed as to where they were in the channel. The press was going to both asking for statements and even found a third professional seaman on board to inquire. This complicated their coming to agreement upon a course, which reveals one flaw in their organization: no one person competent in navigation was in charge. Open ocean travel requires charts, seamanship skills, navigational skills, and attention to these chores. They were out of sight of land, the wind was increasing, and there was a disagreement among the experts. The brother was consulted and he assured them that Capt. Boyton could continue paddling for another 12 hours. Finally, the French pilot stated that after nightfall he would no longer be responsible for Capt. Boyton's safety. The captain of the tug decided that based upon the raising wind conditions, it would no longer be safe for his men to be towed astern. The prospect of losing sight of Capt. Boyton during the night finally convinced the brother to tell Paul that the worthiness of the invention had been proven and to quit the crossing. Capt. Boyton could not be prevailed upon to quit and it wasn't until he was told they didn't know where he was that he consented but he first paddled around the steamer to prove that it was not due to his failing or the invention that the crossing was to be abandoned. This episode reveals the reason the expedition failed to complete the crossing began in the pilothouse, as the swimmer was perfectly happy to continue upon his course. Many times on long distance swims, the conditions are worse for the persons accompanying than for the person in the water.

Days later, interviews with two of the captains of steamers that passed by during the crossing expressed confidence that if Capt. Boyton had only been left alone, he would have completed the trip. It was just this sort of encouragement that leads to Capt. Boyton's second attempt. He didn't need to prove the usefulness of the life saving dress. Upon his arrival in Boulogne where he was transported at the conclusion of the first swim, he was met by a large number of people who had heard of his demonstration. The next night, the Humane Society of Boulogne awarded him a gold medal for his services to humanity before an overflow crowd. The Queen, the Lord Mayor of London sent congratulations and the medical exam served to attest to the success of the life saving dress.

Capt. Boyton was not finished with the channel. In late May, he arrived in France to attempt a crossing in the opposite direction. He had learned some things from his previous attempt. He changed the direction of the swim, he modified his life-saving dress to allow the attachment of a screw propeller, and he changed pilots to Captain Dane,[54] one of the captains of the steamers mentioned earlier who expressed confidence in his finishing. Capt. Boyton attributed the eventual success of the crossing to Captain Dane's complete knowledge of the tides and currents of the channel. It might seem like a small thing but this knowledge is crucial to any open water swim because the speed with which the swimmer progress is often exceeded by the current. The successful swimmers will use the current to their advantage. Capt. Boyton still attracted attention, in the press and in the public. He was sponsored by no less than South-Eastern Railway Company who placed the steamer *Prince Ernest* with Captain Danes at his services. His movements were followed by thousands of onlookers when he moved his point of departure from Boulogne to Cape Gris-Nez, the closest point of France to England. He segmented his trip into parts and since the first part was along the French coast, it made for the height of entertainment for the onlookers to move down along the coast following his movements. There were the usual breaks for cigar and brandy and at one point he was in such spirits that he wanted to start immediately for England but was dissuaded. He came ashore and rested the night at the Framzelle Inn in Cape Gris-Nez. At 3am the next morning, he began the second and final leg of his trip.

On this trip, the sea state was more favorable for crossing. Reports of his progress across the channel were made by carrier pigeons. By noon of Friday, May 29, 1875 he had crossed over half way and at 1:30pm he was reported to be 8 miles off of Dover, under sail, paddling with an American flag flying. When there was no wind or it opposed him, he would drop his sail. By 5pm, he was 6 miles in a flood tide and being carried north to Goodwin

Sands. Goodwin Sands is a sandbar built by the settling out of the sand washed away by the Thames. His regime for this crossing was under the supervision of a Dr. Howard who was feeding him green tea and beef sandwiches. As he neared the coast of England, the steamer *Victoria* out of Dover, gaily dressed up in bunting, came alongside to cheer him. A few members of the Royal Cinque Yacht Club and the Dover Rowing Club rowed out to meet him about 10 pm. Long into the night, as he approached the shore just west of South Foreland, some local fishermen pointed out a beach that he could land safely and he completed his journey in 23 hours and 38 minutes. After the finish, he went by rowboat back out to his escort boat the *Prince Ernest* with his brother aboard. As they went by the Admiralty pier at Dover at this early hour on their way to Folkstone, there was heard an 11-gun salute and cheering. After sleeping for a while, Capt. Boyton received well wishers and innumerable telegrams from throughout the kingdom as the news of his successful crossing has been well received. The Queen sent her congratulations from Balmoral. He received an invitation to pay the town of Dover a visit where he was toasted by numerous dignitaries and societies and attended a luncheon with the vice-consul of Belgium. It was here that he said he was proud to have completed such an unprecedented a feat but no amount of money would persuade him to undertake it again. After a train ride by special coach to Folkstone by the South-Eastern Railroad Company, the directors of the company hosted him at a dinner. Here he thanked the company for their support, Captain Danes for his invaluable assistance, and expressed the hope he had succeeded in showing the entire world the value of his life-saving dress whose success would be judged in the saving of thousands of lives after he was long forgotten. This was an altruistic ending for what was an adventure of extraordinary proportions. Boyton went on across Europe to cross other straits and travel incredible distances down rivers. You could say he was the spark that lit fires in the imagination of swimmers around the world.

  The Channel crossing fascinated millions of people and its events were followed closely by the news reports. Nowhere in any of the accounts was the word swimming mentioned but the desire to cross the Channel simply by swimming occurred to one Capt. Matthew Webb. In his person was the local hero who would change the event into a swimmer's Mt. Olympus. There can be no question that the publicity surrounding Capt. Boyton crossing motivated Capt. Webb. The credit for the idea has to be given to J. B. Johnson; the credit for pioneering the way to Capt. Boyton while to Capt. Webb goes the credit for the accomplishment. Just like Capt. Boyton, Capt. Webb was successful on his second attempt on August 25, 1875 completing the swim in 21:30.[55] This swim was the first big marathon swim. It was 36 years before anyone else duplicated the swim. The enthusiasm had died out with only a few hardy souls taking on the task. The Channel swim began to take on a gargantuan perspective. Onto this stage stepped Gertrude Ederle. She became the first women to swim the English Channel on August 6, 1926, only the seventh person to make the crossing and she lowered the record to 14:34.[56] Just like Boyton and Webb, it took her two tries before her successfully swim. The Channel does not give up its successes easily. It so impressed the American public that she was treated to a ticker tape parade attended by millions upon her return to the States by ship. Gertrude set the standard by which all other women athletes were to be judged and the publicity received cast the swim into a standard unlike any other.

Figure 8 Gertrude Ederle.

Chapter 4   19th Century, English swims

What was the state of affairs for swimming in the 19th Century? We've seen already that distance races were taking place. In fact, swimming pools were being built in the 1800's to accommodate the interest in swimming. Literature served to stimulate an interest in swimming when Lord Byron wrote of his swim duplicating an ancient swim across the entrance to the Black Sea at Hellespont. It was a reality check for the writer as he immersed himself in the water for the one-mile swim. The interest in this swim is not the time or technique but an attempt to replicate the swim of Leander across the straits to spend the night with Hero as related in classical literature as a myth. It would be a myth if the distance could not be swum. Byron proved otherwise on his second try; he completed the swim in a time of 1 hour 10 minutes. He wrote a poem to commemorate the occasion: *Written After Swimming from Sestos to Abydos*, and set a new standard for sports reporting.[57] How often do you have to look up words when reading a sporting column? One of the meanings of "ague", the last word in the poem, is a fit of shivering. Byron's poem is about how Leander gambled his life for a night of love and all Byron got out of it was cold. Byron's exploits were not limited to Hellespont, he would at some point after 1816 swim from the Lido in Venice and then down the entire length of the Grand Canal in 3:45. The distance is estimated at 4½ miles.[58]

As early as 1804 experiments were being conducted that tested a new design for lifesaving. In late August of that year, a half dozen people were seen in the Thames being supported by a new-fangled waistcoat. It was made of copper and strapped about the body at the neck and waist. The device was made of compartments that were hollow, about 6-8 inches round. The people were floating in a vertical position without any danger or pressure from the device.[59] This describes an early forerunner of the compartmentalized lifejacket. The Thames is the major river that flows through the City of London and could be considered the lifeblood of the city. Until the advent of sewerage treatment, it was also the backbone of the sewer system, which is a common heritage of all cities.[60] The river itself is 190 miles long from Cricklade through Oxford, Abingdon, Wallingford, Reading, Henley, Marlow, Maidenhead, Windsor, Staines, Kingston Upon Thames, Teddington, Hounslow, Richmond Upon Thames, Hammersmith & Fulham, Kensington & Chelsea, Wandsworth, City of Westminster, City of London, Greenwich, and then finally, Gravesend, the last town before the estuary leading to the North Sea. There are today 44 locks on the river. The river is tidal from Teddington to the sea, in other words, the Thames is subject to tidal flow from a suburb southwest of London, through the center of London and on out to the North Sea. The headwaters of the Thames starts at Trewsbury Mead in a meadow beneath the boughs of an ash tree and on its way to the navigable portion just mentioned, it flows through the Cotswold Water Park.[61]

Lord Byron was not the only ocean swimmer in England. In late summer of 1805, an unnamed solder for a wager swam from a point opposite his barracks in Deal to Ramsgate, a distance of 8 miles, in the ocean before considerable crowds.[62] Deal and Ramsgate are towns along the English Channel just north of Dover; between them the land is quite flat with a sandy beach; Ramsgate protruding out into the Cannel farther so the straight-line course would take a swimmer out into the ocean. On this occasion the ocean was a bit rough so from shore he disappeared from sight with nearly every wave. This kept the interest of the spectators for they did not know what was going to happen next. In 1810, Edmund Austice, an officer aboard the *Cossack*, a British ship, swam a short distance in Plymouth Sound to the Victualling Office Point in twenty minutes. He also collected a crowd of spectators not to mention the 10 guineas wagered.[63] A Mr. James Grapham, while station in Malta, on August 8, 1821, swam from Waterport Wharf in Gibraltar to Algeria, a distance of about 8 miles across the Gibraltar Strait.[64] He didn't come ashore in Algeria, stopping within 200 yards of shore, in 4¼ hours. He would swim on his back for portions of the journey. The discipline of leaving and landing from shore was not developed as of yet for marathon swimming. Neither was thinking that the swimmer might need some food and water along the route, so none was brought. When he left the water, all he mentioned was that he was thirsty. The Gibraltar Strait connects the Atlantic Ocean with the Mediterranean Sea and separates Europe from Africa.[65] In antiquity, the straits were known as the Pillars of Hercules.

Returning to merry old England, in 1822, the River Mersey in Liverpool was crossed not once, not twice, but three times in the space of under two hours by Mr. Claude, of Liverpool. On Saturday, August 3, 1822, he first swam from George's Pier[66] to Woodside, a distance of nearly a mile, in 29 minutes. He then immediately swam back across the river reaching Old Quay Pier in 40 minutes. Finally, he swam the river once again in 46 minutes landing at Seacomb Point, a bit downstream of the starting point. All together his time totaled 1:55.[67] The third trip was unplanned as he planned to swim out to a rowboat in the middle of the river, climb aboard, flex his muscles, and otherwise does a victory dance. This is the first known occurrence of anyone swimming this river much less doing a triple. The first trip was made at high tide so the current was slack, then as the swim wore on, it began going out to sea flowing downstream. This is the river made famous by the British singing group Gary and the Pacemakers in their song *Ferry Across the Mersey*. I've visited this location and while the river is not especially wide, it was a serious river with quite a bit of industry about and the current flow looked challenging. Not every swim was as successful as this one.

In 1824, two men on a wager of four sovereigns swam across the Serpentine in London and upon the return trip; one of them was seized with a cramp.[68] Assistance was offered from shore, as he was evidently that close, to no avail. The winner's name and time were not recorded as the demise of one swimmer most probably put a crimp in any celebration. This is the first mention of the Serpentine, a lake in Hyde Park located in the center of London. The name is hardly descriptive of this artificial lake formed by the damming of the River Westbourne in 1730. The River Westbourne ran through Hyde Park, London, before joining the Thames. The lake is about a half-mile long and a shade over 200 yards wide at the widest point. Many, many events were first hosted on the Serpentine before moving to baths, later to be called swimming pools. Hyde Park is easily accessible making it a popular swimming and boating area for Londoners.

Athletes like most people are opinionated and could even be biased about their own abilities. In 1827, two gentlemen from Manchester, UK, wagered a tidy sum over who was the best swimmer. The prospect of a contest over the longest swim on record to date to settle the matter attracted attention from as far away as London. Dr. Dedale and Mr. M. Vipond proposed to swim from Liverpool to Runcorn in the River Mersey; a distance of 18 miles in one tide, to see whom was the better swimmer. The Mersey is not as narrow upstream as it is at Liverpool. South of Liverpool it widens out into an estuary. At the very end of this estuary are the headwaters of the Mersey. A small stream turns east and there along the banks of the headwaters lies the village of Runcorn. The Mersey is affected by the tidal flow over its entire length. In order for the two gentlemen to even consider this swim, they must have started at low tide and swam with the tide upstream as it filled in the Mersey. The start was not far from where Mr. Claude began his swim across the Mersey five years earlier. On Wednesday, July 15, 1827, at 7:45 am they started off from Queen's dock[69] in Liverpool and began to swim up the Mersey. They stayed fairly even throughout the swim until they entered the headwaters when the doctor took a commanding lead. Mr. Vipond was only a half-mile from their designated finishing place when he got into his boat. Dr. Dedale finished the swim opposite Runcorn Church in 3:35.[70] The edifice is quite visible from the river. Because the dispute was long standing, there were considerable bets placed on this swim.[71]

While everyone endorsed learning to swim for the many reasons of health and safety, not every aspect of bathing was an acceptable practice as seen in the following Letter to the Editor published in the London Times in 1829. It was written by an unnamed owner of a home on the Regent Canal, "…Every summer we have been annoyed, particularly on Sunday, by a great number of grown-up persons bathing at all time in the day and indecently exposing themselves by running naked in the field in front of my windows and of course of others in the neighborhood. I have five sons, and take delight in teaching them to swim and think it a useful part of education which all parents should attend to, and so far as public decency permits would render every facility to the inhabitants of this great metropolis to indulge in the pleasing useful and helpful recreation of immersion and swimming. ... I have seen on the continent that it is almost the universal practice there for men to bathe in breeches prepared for the purpose but alas it is pretty well known that many of those who bathe in Bethnal-green parish can scarcely cover their nakedness any time."[72] In some ways, this problem is humorous as this location is right in the center of London.[73] When you think about it, the English really took to swimming. The canal mentioned is one of many, many canals in England. Before road transportation became prevalent; raw material and products moved by barges throughout England. Many of these canals still exist. These canals provided opportunities for swimming throughout England and as the writer of the letter stated, he taught his own children to swim and they most likely swam in the canal at his property edge.

Swimming doesn't use much technology except for stroke techniques and the occasional costume[74] improvement. This story is about a different kind of technology. In July of 1838 on the Thames was a dreadful accident that cost the life of a young child. A man named Vaughan, of the Strand,[75] was the designer of an apparatus whose purpose was to teach children to swim. The machine had to be tested and persons were contacted to bring children to the testing site on the Thames. While under the Westminster Bridge on the Vauxhall (east) side, it bumped into a barge. Everyone on board was dumped into the water. The sole victim was the 4-year old son of the carpenter who constructed the machine. There was no description of how the machine worked or why it was in the river. One can speculate that the machine floated, it was in the river because it needed a source of water, all the participants were on the machine but not all were in the water contained within to teach swimming, and it was of frail construction and unstable. Why it was not tied up to a pier is not explained. There was little information given about the machine except that it was being tested. It failed.[76]

Regular swimming competitions were held in London by 1837. The events were organized by the National Swimming Society[77] founded on June 30th, 1837 by John Strachan.[78] The first public record of this society appeared in Sept of 1838 at an event in Chelsea, England. The purpose of the society was to teach the art of swimming. In the two years of their existence, they had instructed nearly 2000 expert students. The school's professors gave instruction in three locations: on the Surrey Canal, the Serpentine, and on the Thames. On September 20, 1838, the society held a swimming match between pupils of the National Swimming Society and other persons on the Thames at the "Stadium" at Cremorne House in Chelsea.[79] The competition was for silver cups and silver snuffboxes. The course was across the Thames and back, a distance of approximately 1000 yards depending on the tide. The contestants were schoolboys dressed in flannel drawers who wore jockey caps of various colors to distinguish themselves. The match commenced at about 3:30 pm at the turn of high water. The tide took the swimmers up the river to Batterysea and at the turn of the tide brought them right back to the grounds of the stadium. This was an excellent selection of the start of the race showing a great understanding of the problem of drift when crossing a stream. No times were reported other than it took 15 minutes for the race. The paper reported the finisher's places by stating the color of the hat worn by the contestant. The spectators cheered loudly at the start and upon their finish.

By 1840, the practice of handing out silver medals had entered the swimming world for winning races. The National Swimming Society hosted at Oxford a swimming contest on Kennington-reach[80] on August 26, 1840. Twenty schoolboys competed for one of three silver medals. The distance was 400 yards down the Thames. The course was set up so that the start and finish could be viewed from both sides of the river. The arrangement for the contests is very similar to today's Olympic contests. There were five heats of four swimmers with the two top finishers advancing to the final. The final consisted of all the top finishers with a winning time of 7 minutes 9 seconds over the distance. In keeping with the National Swimming Society's previous policy of not naming the competitors, no names were published in the London Times.[81]

In England, in 1844, a large group gathered at the Holborn Baths[82] in honor of a Mr. T. Hownslow of Oxford. He had just lost a match against a Mr. Pewtress in the Serpentine.[83] They were there to demonstrate feats swimmers could perform in the science of swimming. Those attending of high regard included Kenworthy, Snelling, Paulton, Gowern, and Roberson. They performed feats of floating, diving, summersetting,[84] and other feats. The gathering featured a rematch of the two men, Hownslow and Pewtress. Hownslow was the more muscular but older by 18 years while Pewtress was of slight built but quick. The contest consisted of two laps, which was won by Pewtress for the second win.[85] From this information we learn that the ability to swim gave the person stature and were practitioners of a science.

This adherence to swimming as a gentlemanly art was further tested in 1844. Two American Indians, Tobacco and Flying Gull, were brought to England for a swimming meet. While they demonstrated their competitive skills satisfactorily and demolished their competition, there was no rush to adopt the thrashing motions with its splashing by the English no matter how much faster you went.[86] The time mentioned for the winning Native American over the distance of 130 feet was 30 seconds. This is equivalent to 34.5 seconds for the 50 yards free.[87]

An event two years earlier in September of 1842 created quite a stir in London. An American seaman, named Michael Smith, in an attempt to raise money so that he could outfit himself for sea, posted bills throughout London announcing that he would jump off the Sanderland Bridge into the Thames.[88] The bridge was designed so that sailing ships of the day could pass underneath without lowering their masts so it rose quite a distance over the river. Diving from heights was not without precedent, as sailors were long known to jump from the rigging aboard the ships of that era though it might be in a warmer clime. Many a young officer gained stature by rescuing drowning seamen who had fallen overboard. To the local populous, this was an event worthy of viewing. On the appointed date and time, he arrived only to be arrested. It seemed the Crown in the representative of the police found the crowd control frustrating and blamed him for their problems. He was released on condition that he pays the court costs, refrains from creating a disturbance, and was prohibited from diving from the bridge under pain of imprisonment. That very night at about 10 o'clock in the evening Smith returned to the bridge and mounted a street lamp from which he made his leap. His leap was estimated at 110 feet. Upon landing, he swam "as a sea bird"[89] for a barge. Here he "saluted the spectators on the bridge and on the heights in the style of a true jack tar, which was immediately returned by a round of hearty cheers from the astonished multitude."[90] When he returned to shore, people offering money besieged him; the police arrested him for "begging money"[91]. This would be the fate of many a swimmer in their quest for fame and fortune: they would be considered little more than an annoyance.

    Swimming fetes were events held to attract attention to the sport or to select a champion. At the Holborn bath in 1851, a swimming fete took place on August 5, 1851, that featured an exhibition of swimming skills given by a Mr. Harold Kenworthy. In exhibitions of this sort, skills such as swimming, floating, diving, swimming while bound, and smoking underwater are demonstrated. Mr. Kenworthy gave a grand display. This performance was common before swimming contests.[92] There were two races for adult swimmers. The first race was for the Leander Medal, six laps for a total distance of 192 yards. A Mr. Stedman won the race. The second race was at twice that distance for the championship belt of the Surrey Swimming Club. It was won easily by Mr. Beckwith[93] who it seems had won the previous year when the contest was held at the Westminster Baths.[94] Should he succeed the following year, the belt becomes his to keep and a new trophy is commissioned, a common arrangement for awards was to hand over the trophy should the same person win three times in a row. Unfortunately, there was no results published the following year to record whether he did or not.

By the end of this decade, in 1859, an editorial by a Miss Martineau promoting swimming by women was published in the London Times.[95] In it, she stated all the obvious reasons for women to learn to swim. These included the fact that Englishwomen have four limbs, live on an island, make voyages, practice sea-bathing, go out in small boats, and as a result of learning to swim, their frames and health are improved. All these reasons applied equally well to men. The biggest difference was the need for privacy. She mentioned a wealthy Quaker gentleman who built a bathing house for his daughter and obtained the necessary privacy by a fence of reeds. She called him sensible.

The Brighton Swimming Club was formed in 1860 to promote open-water swimming or, as it was known then, sea bathing. While there are records of other clubs in existence prior to this date the Brighton SC is still in existence.[96] A common distance to compete was 1000 yards.[97] An early member of the club was Frederick Cavill. While it is recorded that he attempted the channel several times subsequent to Webb, his more famous contribution to swimming was his children and the stroke he taught them. By the time the Amateur Swimming Association, a governing body, was formed in 1880, it had 300 member clubs.[98] Returning to Frederick Cavill, in 1876, at age 39 he swam 20.5 miles in the Thames from London Bridge to Greenbithe, 4 miles short of Gravesend in a time of 5:50. Two of his young sons joined him in the swim for a short time, Harry, age 6, and Charlie, age 4. The previous year he had swum from Putney to Blackwall, a distance of 13 ¼ miles in the Thames.[99]

Eton is an exclusive school for children located near the Thames upstream from London. Their swimming was done at Athens, a bathing place on the Bucks shore of the Thames, which is in walking distance of the campus. On Wednesday, August 2, 1865, a competition was held that day that lasted from noon until quite late. Reported were the times for the results of two races: the 100 yards in 1 minute 25 seconds and the 300 yards in 3 minutes 12 seconds. The college master, the Rev. E. Warre, gave a swimming demonstration of skill and dexterity. The fun event was diving for eggs throw into the water. What with an overcast, showery day, this made for increased difficulty in the retrieval as the visibility underwater was diminished. The winning of this diving contest brought up the most eggs, which was reported as six.[100]

In 1867 swimming was quite popular and annual swimming matches were being held. In Plymouth, England, on August 13 of this year, an all-comers match was held and eight swimmers competed. Participating was Henry Gurr, of London, the Champion of England. The distance was 1000 yards or two laps over the course (there and back). The winning time posted by Mr. Gurr was 13 minutes and 21 seconds. Second was another resident of London, David Pamphlio, and the provincial men were reported as "nowhere".[101]

In 1871, an annual race for the amateur championship was held on the Thames on Saturday, July 22, 1871. The swim was from Putney Aqueduct to Hammersmith Bridge, a distance of a mile and ¾. The competitors in their order of finishing were: H. Parker, London Swim Club, in first place; F. Wilson, Leeds Swim Club, in second place; G. Cole, North London Swim Club, in third; and two others who did not finish. The winning time was 24 minutes and 35 seconds, second place was 43 seconds later, and third place was 250 yards behind the leaders.[102] There was such a large flotilla of accompanying rowboats that a single small Thames Conservancy skiff was unable to patrol the swim properly which lead to charges that new standards for how not to manage a swim was established. A controversy also unfolded when it was alleged that the winner swimmer competed in the professional race held a month earlier. This was settled two days later when the paper published an extract from the rules of the Metropolitan Swimming

Association (a precursor to the Amateur Swimming Association[103]) that permitted a swimmer to compete in a professional race and as an amateur as long as the swimmer was unofficial and competed strictly for the honor in the professional race.[104] This instance revealed that as early as 1871 were established rules and an organization for standardization of swimming.

The issue of learning to swim generated Letters to the Editors in 1871 with one writer mentioning schoolboys learning to swim, races that were held as a result, and the need for more facilities.[105] This letter summoned a commentary from a member of the London School Board who stated that they have a National School with an enrollment of 300 boys. The school had a swimming club that had taught swimming for a number of years. The arrangement was for individual boys to pay two shilling each for the season. He further went on to give a number of interesting statistics, 16 boys had learned to swim that year with hopes for several more by the end of the season and all together 100 had learned to swim in four years.[106] Finally, another writer wrote about his own community raising funds for the support and establishment of a swimming bath and went into some details about the subscriptions and means to finance the building.[107] It's obvious that the English took swimming seriously and supported learning to swim.

The Swimming Championship of 1873 took place late Saturday, September 13, 1873 on the Thames over the same course as the amateur championship did in 1871. The course was described in the London Times as an open water competition. This was the first time a swim had been so labeled. No mention was made whether this was a professional swim or amateur, only that the real championship of England should be contested over the Thames tidal course of a distance not less than a mile and three quarters. It was specifically mentioned that several championships had been held previously that did not meet this standard, which harkened back to the days of Henry Gurr, the original Champion of England. The Serpentine Swim Club had subscribed their members and funds had been raised to provide for a Silver Cup valued at 30 pounds which was to be awarded permanently to a winner should that swimmer prevail over three Championships seasons. The winner of the cup was not to be compelled to defend the title more than 3 times a season. Thus the cup winner had to win nine races. There was a money stipulation that all competitions are for not less that 25 pounds a side.[108] This was the entry fee for a club. All members of a club would contribute and the club would pick a champion to compete on their behalf. Four swimmers competed: J. B. Johnson and his brother P. Johnson, both from the Leeds Swim Club; J. Collard, Serpentine Swim Club; and F. Cavill, Brighton Swim Club. This was the Fred Cavill destined to change swimming before he went to Australia and the South Sea Islands. The race was quite exciting, what follows is the description of the race:

"On plunging from the barge moored to Putney Aqueduct, Cavill was the first to show in front, and led J. B. Johnson by a length, Collard almost immediately leaving P. Johnson and steering wide towards the Surrey shore. Off the Star and Garter, J. B. Johnson drew level with Cavill, but meanwhile Collard had all the best of the tide in the center of the river, and was rapidly drawing on both of them. P. Johnson, however, followed close behind his brother and Cavill. Off Bishop's Creek Collard had been doing so well that he headed J. B. Johnson, who had in turn disposed of Cavill and led him by some five yards. In addition to the race between Collard and J. B. Johnson there was an equally interesting struggle between P. Johnson and Cavill, the pair swimming neck and neck till about opposite the mouth of Beverley Brook, where P. Johnson began to tail off. When J. B. Johnson began his shoot across to the Soapworks there was nothing to choose between him and Collard, the other pair being 20 yards in their rear. Opposite Rose Cottage J. B. Johnson made his effort, and by the time the Crab Tree was passed had, bar accidents, secured the championship. Arriving at the Soap works, he was quite 20 yards to the good, a heavy rainstorm just commencing. The real struggle now lay between Collard and Cavill for places. The former was at first then too much in towards the Surrey shore,

and next made an equally bad error of heading for the Distillery on the opposite shore. This enabled Cavill to come level, and a splendid race to the finish resulted in a dead heat and their (sic) dividing second and third money (ed.—3 pounds). J. B. Johnson won easily by 30 yards and his brother was beaten off altogether. Time (taken with a chronograph by Messrs. Hancocks and Co. Bruton Street, Bo, Bond-steer), 26 min. 26.4 sec."[109]

Captain Matthew Webb at age 27 made his first appearance in newsprint when on July 3, 1875; he swam down the Thames from Blackwall to Gravesend, a distance of 20 miles.[110] The starting time was at 2:25 pm and he finished amid a flotilla of boats at Gravesend at 7:18pm, elapsed time: 4:53. The report mentioned that in April of 1873 he jumped overboard to save a sailor from the Cunard vessel, the *Russia*. For this action, even though it was unsuccessful, he was awarded the silver medals of the Liverpool and Royal Humane Societies. The Duke of Edinburgh who was chairman of the 100th anniversary dinner of the Royal Humane Society also awarded him the Stanhope Gold medal for this same effort at that dinner. The London Daily News reported that the Channel was to be his next swim. In preparation for this swim, he swam, during a rainstorm, from Dover to Ramsgate, some twenty miles distance in 8:45.[111] He did not complain about the temperature of the water at all saying that he was as warm at the finish of the swim as he was at the start. In this report, mention was made that during the previous summer, he had swum from Dover to a point beyond the Varne, over half the channel distance. It seems that J. B. Johnson's swim in 1872 sparked a successor as soon as 1874.

Sometimes, you don't have to wait quite so long before another swimmer duplicates the feat. Once people sense the lure of publicity, it's hard to judge the real reason why people do a swim. In 1875, Miss Alice Agnes Beckwith, age fourteen, swam from London Bridge down the Thames to Greenwich at the behest of her father, Professor Beckwith. This was most likely the same Beckwith that had won the distance championship of the Surrey Club in 1851 only he was now a swimming instructor. This

51

happened on Tuesday, August 31, 1875. The distance was about six miles and she completed the swim in 1:08.[112] To test her abilities for this swim, she swam down the Thames from Batterysea to Westminster successfully on Monday, August 30. On this occasion, the swimmer and supporters, gathered from the various piers along the Thames as the steamer she was aboard pulled in to pick them up, stopped right by London Bridge. The swimmer had changed into a light swimming dress. About the bridge more spectators had gathered to watch the start. Miss Beckwith transferred from the steamer to a smaller support boat from which she dove off into the river at 4:56pm. When she arrived in Greenwich, she was "greatly cheered". Captain Webb had already done this distance and quite a bit more but the month before, however he was not a 14 year old school girl which was the interest of this swim given that the English were still discussing about women learning to swim. This swim and the following certainly settled that argument.

One family not cheering was the Parker family. It seems that Miss Emily Parker, age fourteen and only a few months older than Miss Beckwith, sister of Harry Parker, the Champion of London,[113] had been touring the towns about London making public appearances presumably with her brother. It seems that some time previous to the Beckwith swim, it had been decided for Miss Parker to swim from London Bridge to Greenwich. She, too, had made a trial trip. Because Prof. Beckwith had persuaded his daughter to make the swim a few days earlier, first honors had gone to another. Undaunted, the Parker team decided the swim would now be from London Bridge past Greenwich to Blackwall, about a mile further on. Four days later, on Saturday, September 4, 1875, Miss Parker set off along the same course as Miss Beckwith. The young girl handled this task mightily, swimming breaststroke the seven miles in 1:35 passing Greenwich in 1:08, the same time as the Beckwith girl. There was a great deal of support for this swim as nearly 70 other boats accompanied the escort boat from where her brother observed the swim bedeck with all his natatory honors not to mention the thousands of spectators afloat and on shore. Her brother joined her in the river past Greenwich and the swim finished in the dark at about 7:25pm.[114] After finishing the swim and boarding the steamer, a subscription was taken up by her supporters at the suggestion of her being awarded a gold medal.

To further remove the stain on the family fortune, Miss Parker, two weeks later on Saturday, September 18, 1875, swam from London Bridge to North Woolwich gardens, a distance of ten miles. A crowd had gathered expecting to see a race; after her last swim, talk had been of a race from London Bridge to Greenwich, presumably between the two girls. There was none of that but the crowd did get to see the start of this swim. The time for this swim was 2:35.[115] At the end of the swim, her brother gave the gold medal to her.

An open water swim across a channel not quite as formidable as the English Channel occurred on Sept 2, 1884 when Horace Davenport swam across the Solvent in the south of England from East Southsea, Portsmouth to Ryde Pier on the Isle of Wight then swam back to Southsea Clarence Esplanade Pier in Portsmouth without resting. The Solvent is a little over 4 miles wide at this point so the swim distance was approximately 8½ miles distance. The Solvent was the venue for the first America's Cup yacht race in 1851. The difficulty in this swim lie in the tidal currents which he swam across. The time taken for the entire swim was 5:25.[116] It looks as though Horace was able to take advantage of the end of a flood tide as Ryde is a bit west of Southsea to reach the spit of land that sticks out into the Solvent called Pier Head at Ryde. Then with a tide change he would be able to make it back to Southsea and not get carried into Gosport which is to the west of Southsea. Southsea is the neighborhood at the tip of Portsmouth, England.

Other worldwide news from this century included the formation of the New Zealand Amateur Swimming Association[117] in 1890. The first swim club in New Zealand was formed ten years earlier in ChristChurch.[118] An article in the Washington Post in 1892 reported that the German Army made swimming a requirement for certain departments and optional for others.[119] An

Austrian General Ernest von Pfuel recognized the need for the military to have swim training in 1810. The first Austrian military swimming school was formed in Prague using a 76 by 15 meter basin.[120] Most likely, they trained using swimming breeches. On March 5, 1898, a Lieutenant Moser of the Austrian cavalry swam across the Danube at Klosteruenber in 10 minutes 10 seconds while in uniform. The river is about 380 meters across at this point. He was carried down stream about 800 meters during the crossing. The water temperature was 3 degrees above zero.[121] One might suspect that the lieutenant was inebriated and responding to a challenge based upon the dress and the water temperature.

During the Spanish-American War, two men from the 20th Kansas Regiment were put to the test and successfully implemented their training. On April 27, 1899, while deployed in the Philippines, Ed White and Bill Trembly swam the Rio Grande de Pampanga River. They brought along with them a rope to secure to the opposite shore, the means to pull across the river floats that the remaining troops would use to cross. This swim was accomplished under enemy fire and both men were awarded the Congressional Medal of Honor for their swim. Their Colonel, Frederick Funston, accompanied them on a raft and he also got a Congressional Medal of Honor.[122] Their swim took about 45 minutes.[123] While this is not an Olympic medal, their swim is one of the few so honored by the Congress of the United States.

Rounding out the century in 1899, bicyclist Monty Holbein[124] demonstrated his prowess beyond the bicycle by swimming from Blackwall to Gravesend and back in the Thames River. The distance swam is 43 miles which he accomplished in 12:42 on July 25th. The starting point was near the West India Docks, on a peninsula carved out of the center of London[125] where the Thames snakes through London. While the Thames is completely tidal over this section, without swimming, Holbein would not have gone as far. He doubled the distance swum by Captain Webb in his 1875 swim over the same course. This swim by Webb was a training swim for the English Channel and so it was for Holbein. Two years later, Holbein chose to swim across the channel on the anniversary of Captain Webb's swim, August 24, 1901. The route was a duplicate of Webb's first attempt, starting at Cape Gris-Nez to Dover. He made it over half way but was pulled from the water after 12 hours as his eyes had swollen shut from exposure to the salt water.[126] The next year he tried the same course again on August 1, 1902 and after 13 hours was within sight of Dover when the tide changed causing the swimmer to abandon the swim.[127] At least this time he wasn't suffering from exposure. On his third attempt, August 28, 1902, he came within one mile of Dover after 22:21 when he suffered an attack of cramps. When he landed, he announced that he would not attempt to swim the Channel again.[128]

When does an athlete ever give up? In Holbein's case, not even when he announces it. On September 1, 1903 he attempted the channel a fourth time. After 17 hours and twenty minutes of swimming the tide changed again. He was 4 miles off France this time.[129] The next year on August 21, 1904, he failed again after a miserable cold swim that saw him unable to finish after over 15 hours swimming. A good portion of that time he was seasick and couldn't retain nourishment. He made his 6th attempt in 1909. The results were the same.[130] This was an instance when failure was not the best teacher. These swims are not attempted in isolation and his team needed to do some serious thinking. It only took Boyton and Webb one failure to teach them what they needed to know to get across the channel. Six failures did nothing for Holbein. On the surface, the method of attack on the channel and the style of swimming for that era dictated a swim in excess of 20 hours for success. Holbein's best effort in the water was 17 hours. Since he was a bicyclist, I suspect he was lightly framed and not of sufficient bulk to stand the rigors of the ocean waters of the North Sea. The Thames is warm compared with the Channel. Nowadays, with the right stroke, he would definitely have made the swim.

Austrian swimming[131]

The first swimming hall worldwide was built in 1581 at the Augsburg Fugger-Palast. The Fugger's were cloth merchants who branched into mining and then into financing emperors starting in the late 14th century with Johann Fugger.[132] They were the first family to have an indoor pool installed. In 1830 the first modern Hallenbad (swim center) was opened in Magdeburg. A woman's swimming school opened in 1833, the Viennese Damenschwimmschule, and a woman's swimming center, Damenschwimmbad, opened in 1840. The first men and women's swimming pool called the Ferdinand-Marienbad was opened in 1842 in Vienna. The Dianabad in Vienna open in 1843 and became a legendary Hallenbad. It opened in 1843, but the Viennese Bade-un Schwimmchronik (Bath and Swim Chronicle) used the name as early as 1806. The pool was a 36 x 12.5 meter basin with a high dive. It was a venue for the Olympics in 1936.

Distance swimming in Austria saw a 5-kilometer swim in the Danube River organized in 1881 to decide the Amateur Champion in the Danube. The race was from Nubdorf to Kommunalbad. Emanuel Bachmayr won using breaststroke in a time of 25 minutes 50 seconds. The same year Emanuel was challenged by another swimmer, Ungar Szekrenyessy, to an even longer swim down the Danube; 33 kilometers, from Waizen to Budapest. The challenger put up 50 Austrian gold pieces as a prize. The odds makers gave Emanuel a 10-minute head start. Emanuel was the winner in a time of 4:59 but Emanuel did not take the prize money as he valued his amateur status more than the money. For this noble act, he earned the name: the Golden Amateur. The following year, Dr. Cole, an Englishman who was using an early version of water wings, challenged him over the same distance. Again, Emanuel was the victor in a time of 4:56.

The first European Championships were held in 1889 at Dianabad. Representing the United States was H.T. Brown. Competing against him was Emil Lemberger. The distance was 102 meters. The American won by a full second in a time of 1:17.4.

Chapter 5   19th Century New York wakes up to swimming

In America, swimming was not the active and vibrant sport that it is today. It was not uncommon for whole families to drown while on vacation, caused by one member stepping off into deep water and dragging the rest behind as they attempted to save the first. Six teenage girls, residents of a girl's reform school, holding hands perished in the Hudson River in 1858.[133] It was not that swimming was unknown in America. In this instance, to aid in the search came a Mr. Robert B. Montgomery, an expert swimmer and diver who was a Captain of the Central Park Police. It was just that swimming was a haphazard affair, with young boys teaching other young boys to swim off a pier in Manhattan. Some were successful: in 1872, one young lad was reported to have swum across the East River on a wager.[134] He traversed from Fulton Ferry dock on Manhattan to the ferry dock on the Brooklyn side. He was accompanied by a small rowboat. The passengers aboard the ferry in the slip gathered to watch the swimmer to the extent that the ferry began to list. Fortunately, the boat did not capsize.

Drowned was a common headline for news items up through the 1870's and well into the early 1900's. There was a social need to teach people to swim that cried out to be addressed. In 1875, at the boathouse docks on the Harlem River, a member of the NYAC, J. H. Hannekamp, age 28, who could not swim decided to learn. While surrounded by capable swimmers, two of them in the water next to him and several more on the dock above him, slipped his hold on the dock and began his self-taught lesson. Despite his struggles and some efforts to save him, he was lost within feet of the dock.[135] Capable swimmers of the day didn't know lifesaving techniques and were helpless watching this life and death struggle. Oars and wood chairs were extended to the struggling man who in his panic did not know to take hold. The writer of the report was quite upset that of those swimmers present, some didn't even move to help.

In the newspapers of the day were found public discussions of the need for learning to swim,[136] the health benefits of sea bathing,[137] protection from drowning as well as lifesaving,[138] as well as articles that argued for the establishment of swimming schools.[139] New York City sought to provide the instruction with baths where lessons could safely be held.[140] In one editorial by the New York Times called *The Dangers of the Deep* the author mentioned the example of the National Swimming Association annual swim meet held on the Serpentine in London, on this occasion, August 10, 1872. The argument was if that island nation could address this need through an association whose purpose was the practice of swimming, perhaps the same was needed in this country.[141] This organization eventually became the American Red Cross forty years later. Clara Barton in Washington, DC, formed the American Red Cross on May 21, 1881. The original purpose of the Red Cross was to tend to battlefield wounded but because of Clara Barton the scope of the Red Cross was expanded to include disaster relief. Water safety and first aid were added to the mission of the Red Cross prior to World War I when it hired Wilbert Longfellow in 1914 to promote water safety.[142]

How were people learning to swim? The answer to this question lies in custom and a delicate balance between the law and youthful exuberance. As soon as it was warm enough, around the vicinity of the Fulton Ferry or at any one of the many piers of the island of Manhattan young boys gathered to swim, eschewing bathing costumes as if they were in the Garden of Eden. The manner of instruction began with dropping novice swimmers into the water, letting them sink, assisting them to the surface if needed until they can paddle about on their own. This was all under the close inspection of the older more experienced swimmers.[143] This method of instruction is capable of producing an accomplished swimmer who might be able to swim 20-50 yards if they survived their lessons. The main goal of the instruction is to produce someone who could jump off the pier and make it back to the ladder.[144] This source of training for swimmers was still producing swimmers as late as the 1920's and occasionally, an exceptional swimmer.[145] It also produced some police action because of complaints received by owners of excursion boats and public decorum regarding the scandalous nude bathing by men and boys. On Sunday, July 15, 1877, a large flotilla of police rowboats approached the docks with an even larger number of police stationed under the piers. One hundred fifty men and boys were taken into custody who spent the night in jail to appear the next day before the court to answer for their misconduct.[146]

A safer method of learning to swim in the 1850's was to visit the Peoples Wash & Bath House located on Mott Street in New York City. Besides the laundry and bath facility for public usage were large swimming tubs. Here, the youth of the city were encouraged to "...sport and tumble, greatly to their edification and amusement; and, without any apprehension of policemen to interfere... (and) may learn that most valuable and little-learned art of swimming." This was the only establishment open in the city at this time while in London there were nine similar establishments with 25 outside of London including Ireland.[147] In France we learn from an ad that appeared in 1801 that the Central Boarding School of Bordeaux offered swimming lessons to students.[148] Within a decade, the swimming tub evolved into a swimming bath.

A few words should be said about the swimming baths of this era. While the topic of this book is open-water swimming, baths are the other dimension of swimming that today's pool swimmers share as a heritage. Originally, they were for cleanliness for the poor[149] but a broader meaning for their purpose came into being. Baths came in two types, permanent structure and portable. One of the first baths constructed in New York was built in 1867.[150] This structure was located at 6th Avenue and 33rd Street. The bath, called the New York Swimming Academy, contained a 25-yard heated pool, changing rooms, ventilation, showers, and a snack bar. One bath does not effect a change on the social need for learning to swim as much as the City of New York deciding to protect the welfare of the public by going into the swimming pool business. By 1870, some public baths had been opened. One, at 5th Street, had just opened in June of that year.

The City Commissioner in charge of this bath, a Mr. Krack who had 20 years of experience from a private bath located at Grand Street,[151] was committed to free admission at least for the first season.[152]

Portable baths were tanks constructed in shipyards and towed to various locations such as a berth at piers were they would be tied up and then filled by partially sinking them in place. The baths were collected up at the end of the summer and towed to a shipyard for winter repair work and painting. The shallow end for one new bath constructed in 1882 was 2½ feet. Instruction in swimming would be given at baths and generally were promoted for safety reasons. These baths were located around Manhattan at: the Battery, Fifth, Nineteenth, Thirty-seventh, 112th Street along the East River; on the Hudson River side they were located at Canal St. and 51st Street. These baths were well attended; it was reported there were 3.4 million admissions in 1881. Washington, D. C., didn't see their first portable bath until 1903.[153] Opening day was traditionally on June 1st and hours were from 5am to 9pm. The combination of private baths[154] and public baths run by the City of New York was the beginning of a great effort that saved many lives and continues today to perform the same needed task.

The floating baths operated in New York until 1937 when only four baths remained. In 1938, under the direction of Robert Moses, the Parks Commisioner, a new gigantic bath open at 96th Street and the Henry Hudson Parkway made out of three of the remaining baths. It fell into disrepair by 1942 when the City of New York refused to fund the maintenance. In the summer of 2007, after a sixty-five year absence, a float pool will be again moored along the shoreline of New York City thanks to the efforts of Ann Buttenwiser.[155]

The YMCA opened their first bath in 1885 at the Brooklyn Central Y, one of 17 YMCA baths opened that year. Their role, while slow to start, grew until in 1984, the YMCA is collectively the largest operators of pools in the world. The initial mission of the Y was a ministry to provide a safe sanctuary for juveniles at the beginning of the Industrial age for Bible study. Now an organization over 150 years old, they have never really lost sight of their goal: to provide a place in the community to gather apart from the world of work and through recreation, physical exercise, and play on teams that develops self-reliance, leadership, and re-create a better member for society, morally, spiritually, and physically. The particular gift of the Y to the swimming world was George Corsan of the Detroit YMCA who developed the technique of first training beginner swimmers on land with exercises that mimic the swimming stroke. His methodology was the basis for the first Learn-to-Swim campaign in 1909 to teach every boy in the United States and Canada to swim. Another development was a design for filtration of the water by Ray Rayburn for the Kansas City pool in 1910.[156]

The contribution by George Corsan and its adoption by the YMCA can't be underestimated in solving the problem of drowning. In the 1904, the New York Public school system was 100 years old. There were 15 swimming pools attached to the schools and in the previous year only 1652 boys and girls learned to swim. That is only 110 students per pool. One reason for the low number is the method used to teach the students. Individual students had to lie on a wide belt that was submerged in the water during instruction. If the student couldn't swim after the instruction without the belt, they were sent back to "pound the belt" until they could.[157]

As a comparison, on the continent in 1905, German swimmers in Munich were enjoying a wave pool[158] and in France the method of instruction is seen in the next illustration. The scene of the swimming bath in Paris is from the pages of Harper's Weekly, drawn by Simon Durand. The pool is crowded, so much so that you could surmise that the engraving is a compendium of scenes the artist saw over time. Prominent is the swimming master on the left giving instruction to a young child. To his charge's left in the water is another student using what appear to be water wings for support. Directly across the pool is another instructor with his charge in the water.

Figure 9 A swimming bath on the Seine, at Paris, published 1873.

Notice the security of the rope to which their youngsters are tethered. This is one-on-one swimming instruction. Behind the swimming instructor are two children having a great deal of fun pushing each other into the water and off to their right come two other urchins running. About the tank are patrons shrouded in robes, most standing but on the right are two gentlemen evidently warming up and drying off after their bath. The diving platform looks to be about 3 meters in height and notice the forward dive captured in mid-flight indicating that this tank has some depth. Two young boys are playing leapfrog at the pool end while off over their shoulders is seen either a distant attached room or mirrors. Lap swimming appears non-existent but the one gentleman seen with the robe gathered about his waist near the child sprawled upon the deck in the foreground probably wants to go back in but finds the pool too crowded for his tastes. There are lifeguards present; they are the individuals with the kerchief tied about their neck, two of them are the instructors and a third is seen at the base of the diving platform exactly where you would expect to see one stationed. In the water the patrons are floating, swimming, splashing (one fellow is kicking with his feet) and conversing about the pool edge. And just maybe, someone is swimming freestyle on the far side approaching the steps but the image is so small that it could be sidestroke. It's hard to tell. What isn't hard to tell is that there are no women in the drawing. They come on another day.[159]

The highlight of learning to swim is competing; to this end, swimming schools promoted themselves and swimming to the general public. The swimming school of Richard Allen located at 54th Street and the East River, sponsored a swim meet on August 10th, 1872. A woman's course of a half mile in the East River was set. There were seven contestants: Misses Katie Allen, Broderick, Weber, Siegel, Cohen, Westerner, and Candidus. The paper described the various outfits the women were wearing. The most popular was a sailor's suit. The start was upstream from the school. Miss Allen, daughter of the proprietor came in first followed by Miss Broderick then Miss Weber. The winner received $75. Next was a boys' race of 1 mile won by William Foster who pocketed $35. The highlight was the men's' race of 2 miles from the school to a stake boat anchored off Randalls Island[160] for a purse of $75. Twelve men competed. The current at the start was against them and they drifted as much as ½ mile off course. The winner was a Mr. Gublemann followed by a Mr. Wolff then a Mr. Davis. Wolff was so upset that he came in second that he challenged Gublemann to another race for $250. The race had started at 2:25pm with the winner finishing exactly one hour later.[161]

In August of 1875, the Braun Swimming School at the foot of 65th street of Manhattan held a swimming match.[162] The course was from 84th street to the school so the distance was one mile. Each swimmer had their own boat and the start was from the boat with the competitors diving in at the start. The winner, a young man named Stern completed the course in 7 minutes 55 seconds. The swimmers would occasionally turn over and swim backstroke. This time includes the effect of the current, which was in ebb at the time of the swim. The large number of German immigrants that lived in the vicinity provided the spectators who watched the contest. Also held on the same day was a scratch race for boys of

½ mile distance won by a lad named Max Obright with a chap named Miller coming in second.

After J. B. Johnson, Champion of England, bailed out of his cross channel swim, he showed up in the United States. An international swimming match between him and Alexander Trautz, the Champion of America, was scheduled for Saturday, August 22, 1874, at Long Branch, New Jersey, but wound up postponed due to inclement weather when the official boat couldn't put out to sea.[163] The contestants were quite upset as $2000 and a Tiffany cup was riding on this contest. The men were to be taken by the official boat 3 miles offshore then the contestants were to swim back. The first man back to shore would win. A second date was picked for August 25th, a Tuesday and thousands of spectators showed up.[164] Again the race was postponed due to inclement weather when the official boat couldn't put out to sea around Sandy Hook. Long Branch, NJ, is south of Sandy Hook along the coast. To get to Long Branch, the official boat has to come out from the sheltered water behind the Hook into the Atlantic Ocean then travel south. It didn't help that the spectators could see other boats out in the ocean. The hotel sponsoring the race, the Ocean House, provided some diversions and saw the participants swim out through the surf a quarter mile. Another date was schedule for Friday, August 28, 1874.

Again the official boat failed to show and at this point, a steamer *Escort,* which was loaded with spectators from New York, was hired to act as the official boat. This was arranged by a French swimmer named Andre who swam out to the *Escort,* which was anchored offshore waiting for the race to start. Unfortunately, the beach lifeguards refused to put out in their rowboat. The two swimmers even offered to pay $100 to any crew to row the boat but still no one volunteered. At this point, the *Escort* left the area to return to New York. At this point, the race was moved inland to Pleasure Bay, not far from the hotel. The swimmers, trainers, and all the spectators, estimated at 5,000 took a short walk across Ocean Avenue to the new venue.

The race started in one of the tributaries of the Bay so that the swimmers traveled from north to south. The distance was approximately 3 miles. At 4:24pm the swimmers dove in from a steam launch and began swimming. Trautz took the lead right off the start. After twenty minutes, Trautz was still in the lead by twenty feet but Johnson appeared to be playing with him. Ten minutes later, Johnson pulled up even with him. The English champion was described as swimming like a dolphin, even rolling like a porpoise as he swam. Trautz's stroke by this time had increased to 54 strokes per minute yet Johnson was keeping 34 per minute. After increasing the swim stroke to 69, Trautz managed to maintain his lead over Johnson but just barely. As they neared the finish, Johnson put on a spurt and passed Trautz to win the race by 35 yards in 1:10.

The description in the press of J. B. Johnson's swimming stroke was quite vivid. He was under the water and then over it. The stroke was described as not nearly hand-over-hand as he never reached forward with his left arm. He would seem to reach forward with his right hand, grab onto something in the water and then pull himself up and over it. It almost sounds like a dolphin kick for the sidestroke and as if he turned off his side to complete the stroke.[165] In another description of his stroke, during an exhibition swim in the East River, his right hand is seen to work when his body was above the water "…he grasps the element as if he found support in it to draw himself up."[166]

August 24, 1875, in Philadelphia saw another Championship of America held on the Delaware River. In the pre-race publicity, the course was to be from Chester to Philadelphia.[167] The course used was from Lazaretto, four miles above Chester on the Pennsylvania shore to Gloucester, NJ, a distance of ten miles. This course was picked over the one taking the men into Philadelphia to avoid the myriad of boats found there. The contestants were J. B. Johnson of England and Thomas Coyle, a naturalized Irishman. This was their second match as Coyle claimed foul play caused him to leave the water early during the first race when he was in the lead. In fact, after the 1st swim on

July 22, Mr. Johnson danced a jig and attended a banquet while the doctors tended to Coyle fearing for his life.[168] With their rematch, Johnson took the lead straightaway and kept it. Coyle after 7 miles was turning blue and was pulled from the water with Johnson a full mile in the lead. The winning time for the ten-mile swim was 2:46.[169] This race like all early swims was a stakes race with money awarded to the winner and bets being placed quite freely. In this case, the stakes were for $2000 with the 1st swim scheduled to take place on July 15th but it wasn't until the 7th of the month that the final $1000 of the purse money was deposited causing the race to be postponed. The initial odds favored Johnson, the English Champion.[170] Odds on swims were common: even when Gertrude Ederle swam the Channel, the odds were listed in the newspapers, as 7 to 1 she would set a record in 1925.[171]

Not to be outdone by English reports of swimming champions or reports from Pennsylvania, a Championship of America was held in New York in mid August of 1878. The title was contested on the Harlem River over a one-mile distance starting at the Macomb Dams Bridge[172]. The winning time was 19 minutes and 50 seconds by Dennis Butler.[173] The defending champion W. R. Weissenborn, of Jersey City, was entered but scratched. Butler was a 22-year old oysterman from South Brooklyn and he had never swum a race before. One tends to wonder about the quality of the championship if a novice could win.

The year 1878 was a busy year for swimming. Captain Webb was not through with swimming having successfully crossed the Channel in 1875. On August 3, he swam 22 miles in 9 hours in the Thames between the Parade at Woolwich and Gravesend, turning to swim with the tide as it shifted.[174] In the meantime, Captain Boyton was giving a swimming exhibition in Paris on August 31st.[175] In the same year on August 13, 1878, there was an 18-mile race between Kunno Dimmers, age 31, and Hans Tuelff, age 26, for a wager of $300 and the Long Distance Swimming Championship was thrown in as well. Both men were German, Dimmers was a photographer and had swum from the Harlem

Bridge[176] to the Battery the previous summer. Tuelff worked as a swimming master at Allen's Bath, located at the foot of 55th street and the East River. The swim started at 10:15, by Mill Rock Dimmer and Tuelff were tied for the lead with Dimmer pushing ahead. They passed Allen's Bath around noon even; then, at 14th street, Tuelff had dropped 40 yards behind. Tuelff left the water south of Governors Island with a cramp. Dimmers continued on arriving at Staten Island between Clifton and Stapleton in an elapsed time of 5:36.[177]

The next year, 1879, Captain Matthew Webb brought his swimming fame to America again in a series of events that demonstrated his swimming ability. On August 13, Webb swam 10 miles from Sandy Hook, NJ, to Manhattan Beach, NY. The stipulation by the promoter of this event was that he not land before 5pm so he stayed offshore from about 2pm until 5:05pm having left New Jersey about 8:38 am.[178] A gale blew up and the launch following Captain Webb nearly had its fire in the steam boiler put out from the breaking seas. Following this, a swimming match on August 22, 1879, in Newport, Rhode Island was arranged that brought together Webb and Boyton in what could be called a grudge match. The distance to be covered was 25 miles in a ½ mile course (25 laps) laid out along Easton's Beach off Narragansett Avenue. The venue was for the purpose of viewing the contestants. Betting on the outcome seemed to occupy the spectators time and interest. In fact, when Captain Webb left the water after 9 miles due to cramps the betting switched as to whether or not Capt Boyton would be able to finish before midnight. Boyton continued on, finishing the race by 11 pm having started at 3am.[179] Capt. Webb wore bathing tights and a blue cap, while Capt. Boyton wore his life-saving dress. No mention is made if Boyton used a paddle or some other method of propulsion but paddling was the usual method.

On September 14, 1879, a race in Gravesend Bay, off the Bath Park Hotel, was held for the Championship of America and money prizes. Competing in this race was five of the top professional swimmers known in the country: Captain Webb, of

England; W. H. Daily, of California; George H. Wade, of Brooklyn; George Woerhan, of New York; and Ernest Van Schoening, of Brooklyn. The news report described the participants: Webb was red faced with a thick chest and big muscles, Wade was of similar built, Daily was long, lanky and wearing a wig, Von Schoening was well built but not of the size of Webb and Wade, finally, Woerhan was described as looking like an inflated bladder. They were to swim around two "stake" boats about a 1/5 of a mile apart so that when they complete 5 round trips from one of the stake boats to the other and back, they will have completed 2 miles. At 1:20pm the contest began and continued into the early evening. The men began dropping out one by one until only Woerhan and Van Schoening were left as night fell. Surprisingly, Captain Webb was the third man to drop out after 6 miles about 6:40pm. His manager, a Captain Harley, said that Webb felt uneasiness in his stomach much like he felt in Newport (the previous race, against Boyton) where he was taken with cramps so Webb thought it best to retire before that point. Finally, when Woerham could no longer see where he was going he withdrew from the race, leaving Van Schoening the winner of $1500. However, in the final sentence of the description of the race, the reporter mentioned that he saw no money exchanged "…but it was a very dark night."[180]

In August of 1880, Ernest von Schoening swam from Pier 1, North River to the Norton's point, Coney Island. The distance is twenty miles and the time was 8:45.[181] In 1882, a half-mile contest was held down the Harlem River for the New York Athletic Club championship. Edward A. Cone won the race even though he had a distinct disadvantage as he had only one arm. The swimmers all swam sidestroke. His opponent was given a 3½-minute head start but was overtaken by Mr. Cone who finished in a time of 14 minutes and 45 seconds.[182] Mr. Cone was such an imposing swimmer that two days later at the 100 yards NYAC club championship across the Harlem River all nine contestants were given head starts ranging from 3 to 11 seconds. He won the event with a time of one minute and 45 seconds.

How is it that a one-armed swimmer could possibly be competitive against two-armed swimmers?[183] If the able-bodied swimmers devoted a good portion of their stroke to keeping their head above water, they are losing swimming efficiency. Edward Cone was use to being submerged and as a result had to develop a kick to keep himself above the water as well as propel him forward. In the reports of J. B. Johnson's stroke, they said he was moving through the water as if he was a purpose. These swimmers were use to being submerged and utilized their strokes to pull themselves forward. For this era of swim stroke development, this was the secret for swimming speed: you put your head in the water to swim faster. As simple as this sounds to us today, it worked magic back then until other swimmers got tired of being beaten and adapted their strokes. 1882 was the year American swimmers learned to exhale underwater.

On Aug 24, 1882, Captain Matthew Webb entered a 2-mile swimming contest against Thomas Riley, the champion short-distance swimmer of America. It was a match race for the princely sum of $1000 and the title of Champion of the World. It was held in Boston. Webb won the race with a margin of 20 seconds in a time of 1 hour 4 minutes and 50 seconds.[184] One year later Captain Webb was dead, leaving a wife and two children in Boston where he had settled, when he attempted to swim through the Whirlpool Rapids just downstream from the falls at Niagara. It's a fair question to ask, what brought him to this end?

Webb had decided to do one last money swim and scouted the Niagara location in June of 1883. In July it was reported that Capt. Webb was proposing to go over the Niagara Falls in a rubber ball 4.5 feet round.[185] One can only wonder what influence betting had upon his choice of swims. It was said that Webb had solicited hotels and railroads for $10,000 to do the swim.[186] When the money didn't materialize Webb was left to do the swim because his word had been doubted.[187] The water in the river at the location of where he was to swim just below Suspension Bridge rises 20 feet higher in the middle than at the banks.[188] Capt. Webb revealed his strategy for conquering the rapids. He was going to submerge and swim under the waters when the going is tough.[189] It was heartbreaking and disturbing to read the account of his last swim on July 24, 1883, where the news report spoke of his struggle with the current in the Whirlpool Rapids.[190] He was seen disappearing under the water then surfacing a number of times and then of his throwing his hands up and disappearing for a final time under the water.[191] A cry was raised asking why the authorities didn't stop him; but this was the man with a stellar reputation, with a swim strategy for beating the rapids,[192] who could question him?[193] The search continued for several days until his body was found.[194] This fascination with death evolved from swimming through the Niagara Rapids into going over the falls in a barrel. Today, the fascination is a basis for a genre of TV shows misnamed "reality TV" in an attempt to titillate viewers with pseudo death-defying stunts.

By 1884, contests were being held in the Harlem River for 100 yards and 1-mile distances. There was no handicapping, as this was the second Annual Amateur Championship of America. By this time, Mr. Cone was no longer the swimmer to beat. This may have something to do with opening the contest up to persons outside of the New York Athletic Club. The 100-yard time was dropped to 1 minute and 21½ seconds, won by H. E. Toussaint of the NYAC and the mile race by R. P. Magee of the Baltimore Athletic Club in a current assisted 25 minutes 40½ seconds. The event wasn't particularly significant but the description of the event as reported in the New York Times was striking. Selections from the article[195] are here included so that the reader might appreciate the festival atmosphere occasioned:

"All the local natatorial talent of New York, with a great deal from the surrounding country and a little from England, gathered yesterday afternoon at the New York Athletic Club boathouse, on the Harlem, in Mott Haven, and in the vicinity, to witness the second annual competitions for the amateur swimming championships of America. There were any number of pretty girls among the spectators, and the balconies of the New York Athletic Club boathouse and the boathouses of Columbia college and the

Dauntless Boat Club were gay with bright-colored parasols, while the brilliant hues of the sun umbrella of the period decorated countless rowboats, steam launches, and pleasure craft of every description. Pretty girls in white congregated in little groups on both banks of the river and along Macomb's Dam Bridge. Small boys lined the banks and mounted aloft on lumber piles, and adult men and women were present in boats and under awnings on shore but it was the presence of the aforementioned pretty girls that inspired the swimmers to make their best efforts.

The racing began promptly at 4 o'clock, but for an hour before swimmers and divers were giving voluntary exhibitions from piers and floats. Young men in bathing costumes which displayed manly arms and powerful chests swam short races, dove under water and came up scores of feet away, or wrestled and playfully ducked each other, to the amusement of all concerned...and Magee came in a winner amid the shrieks of all the pretty girls and the howls of their brothers....Just as the race concluded the big rain storm came on and left half the spectators as wet as the contestants."

If you've never thought of bridge jumping as a sport, then you've never read the papers from the late 1880's. Of course, you'll need a platform, which was conveniently provided by the opening of the Brooklyn Bridge on May 24, 1883.[196] There was a toll of 3 cents to use the bridge. In 1885, a swimming instructor named Robert Emmett Odium, from Washington, D. C., lost his life in an attempt to jump off the Brooklyn Bridge. The man who pulled the lifeless man out of the water was Capt. Paul Boyton.[197] This is the same Prof. Odium from Washington, D. C., who opened that city's first natatorium in 1878[198] only to see it sold the next year.[199] After managing the pool for a number of years,[200] he had come north to open his own natatorium on Coney Island but sought to garner fame to attract clientele to the new proposed establishment. Odium's motives were disclosed by Capt. Boyton in an interview given the day of Odium death, May 19, 1885. It seems that Odium had visited with Boyton to propose this scheme, from which Boyton tried to dissuade him. Then seeing that

Odium's mind was made up, Boyton gave the young man some advice and Odium left in Boyton's keepings his worldly affects.[201] They had met several years prior on one of Boyton's trips to Washington; on this day, Odium died aboard the tug as Boyton orchestrated the rescue effort. Odium became known after death as Odlum with articles using both spellings.[202] Despite the numerous articles about the dead man with some even blaming Boyton,[203] the next year saw the first successful jump from the Brooklyn Bridge on July 23, 1886.

In an event that was a secretive as the dive from the London Bridge in 1842 was

Figure 10 Steve Brodie in costume.

public, a young man named Steve Brodie jumped from the Brooklyn Bridge on a $200 wager.[204] Brodie was motivated to make this jump in preparation for a dive from an even greater height having shown friends a newspaper report of a woman jumping from 235 feet from the Clifton Suspension Bridge. Steve once shined shoes and sold newspapers in the Bowery, he first was mentioned in the press when he was appointed a Lieutenant in Capt. Ayer's famous Life Saving Corp organized on the East River waterfront.[205] It was reported in the press that several sporting men and reporters were gathered by a pier near the bridge. Brodie had trained by jumping from High Bridge in the Harlem River and various masts of ships in the harbor. If fame mixed with notoriety was his goal, no doubt the two columns on the front page of the New York Times newspaper were Steve's reward.[206] Steve Brodie was the first to make a successful jump. The distance above the water at high tide is 135 feet. When he was interviewed from a jail cell we learn of his wife and child and the problems of all young families, money. We'll hear more about Steve Brodie in the chapter on staged swimming. What we learn from all this is the extent with which people will go to achieve fame and glory. The question lurking in the background is what role did Captain Paul Boyton have in this jump? Was Boyton standing in the shadows having a hand in the event but staying out of the limelight because of the press he received when Odium died the year before? Regardless, a whole host of jumpers began appearing on the Brooklyn Bridge[207] while Brodie started a career in a sideshow at Coney Island.[208] He exhibited himself in a dime museum for a while on the Bowery then opened a saloon on the Bowery. His saloon featured a mural of his jump behind the bar along with a certificate from the barge captain that retrieved him and photos of famous pugilist. Brodie went on to become an actor appearing in a play *On the Bowery* where he played himself, photo seen above. Within a month, five persons jumped, were stopped, or claimed to have jumped in an effort to, as the newspapers put it, "Meet Odlum's Fate or Share Brodie's Fame."[209]

It should not go without mentioning another character from the era, Jumping Sam Patch. The recollection was from a former child worker in a factory owned by Sam Patch when the teller of the tale, William P. Brown, was 11 years old. Sam it seems was a Cape Codder by birth and came to Paterson, New Jersey, after some time at sea. He and another man owned the factory, which eventually failed. Not having a recourse to another venture but capable of swimming and diving, Sam Patch announced one day that he was going to jump from the rocks at Passaic Falls, about 80 feet to the water. A collection was made that amounted to $50 for the event and a small crowd gathered to watch. Sam, ever the typical sailor, had jumped from mast yardarms and was quite comfortable with the jump. He tested the drop and the arc by dropping small pebbles off the ledge before he launched himself over the abyss with a short run. He cleared the rocks below by ten feet. This started him on a new career that lasted until November

13th, 1829, where he was to jump at the Genesee Falls at Rochester, New York, a distance of 125 feet. It seemed he consumed a little too much fortification prior to the jump, landing horizontal killing him instantly.[210] He was reported to have jumped into the waters at the base of Niagara Falls twice in 1829.[211] Swimmers on long distance swims in open water come upon many a bridge. Sometimes that's the only thing they can see for hours and they sometimes serve as the finishing line. I remember on a swim down the Hudson River coming upon the George Washington Bridge. It only looked like a little ways but it sure took a long time to reach even with a current. Swimming teams today are made up of swimmers and divers. This bridge jumping history is part of the story of open-water swimming. It happens in the open and after the dive (jump) the individual swims to shore.

A short swim serves to introduce the next swimmer, John Robinson. He was 25 years old, 150 pounds, and the amateur champion swimmer of the Mersey in Wales and the Isle of Man, England. On May 23rd, 1886, he swam across the Hudson River at from Nyack to Tarrytown for a purse of $500. He had to complete the swim within 1:45. Swimming sidestroke with an overhand recovery, he completed the swim in 1:36. To provide for the entertainment aboard a steamboat that was used for the spectators, two pugilists gave an exhibition match.[212] His next race was for no less an event than the Championship of the World and a purse of $250. It was being held in New York at Oak Point. Only two swimmers were competing: John Robinson and Gus Sundstrom, the coach for the New York Athletic Club. Gus was 24 at the time and similar in physique to John only with slightly bigger chest and arms. Gus had covered himself with what was called porpoise oil except for his head so he took on quite a dark complexion. The course was from a point opposite Port Morris[213], the southern most part of the Bronx that borders on the East River to Oak Point, a small marina along the western shore at the entrance of the Bronx River.[214] Gus was slightly behind at the start and the difference in their strokes seemed slight. Both were doing the sidestroke on their right side with an over the water recovery for the left hand. Robinson would submerge his head during the pulls and only appeared to take a breath every two strokes. Gus would keep his head up during the entire stroke. Eventually, Gus took the lead and near the end was so far ahead that he did a summersault in the water before finishing. The winning time was 14 minutes 5 seconds.[215] His margin of victory was 25 seconds. They had an East River flood current behind them.

Gus Sundstrom celebrated his victory with another swim within the week. This time it was from Bedloe's Island to Oak Point, Bronx. This was a swim across the Hudson River just below the Battery and then straight up the East River and out to Queens. The distance was advertised as 17 miles. Naturally, there was money on the swim; Gus had 3½ hours to complete the swim to collect $200. He finished the swim in 2:42 on a fine flood tide. The start was from the island where the Statue of Liberty was being built and it was under construction at this time. It would have its opening day on October 28th, 1886. This is one of the first swims that featured the Statue of Liberty as part of the venue and it gave the swimmers, the support crew, and the spectators aboard the yacht accompanying Gus a fine view of the work on the Statue. She was nearing completion but possibly parts of Gustave Eiffel's structural framework were visible.[216]

Turning to Detroit, a young lady, Miss Olga Dohmstreich, age 17, swam across the Detroit River on August 27th, 1886. The course was from Beller's dock on the Detroit side of the river to Belle Isle located in midstream, about a half a mile. The time for the swim was 32 minutes. There was great cheer in the eastern part of the town for her father, F. F. Dohmstreich, was the prominent German owner of Peninsular Brewery.[217]

Philadelphia hosted a professional swimming race in the Delaware River on August 25, 1887, for the Championship of America.[218] There were an unseemly number of Championships of America in this era around the time before the establishment of sporting authorities such as the AAU who would set standards for the course and officials. This championship was a stakes race for a total of $350, a handsome sum for the era. The course was a ten-mile swim from a slip opposite the Billingsport Beacon to a boat anchored 100 yards north of Ridgeway Park. Three men participated: Dennis T. Butler and William H. Blackhurst of Philadelphia and Robert P. Magee of Baltimore (the winner of the amateur championship mile swim held in 1884 in the Harlem). The referee was George Turner and each swimmer had their own pilot. The pilots for the swimmers (taken in the same order) were: Benjamin Shockley, Nimrod Albright, and Amos Baisley. Conditions that day for the race were not easy as the tide was running up the river and the wind was blowing a gale[219] down the river thus causing a sea state with steep waves of about 1 to 2 feet with whitecaps. The eventual winner was Magee, age 26, who came from behind to over take the leader. The stroke counts for the men varied from 31 to a high of 48 as Magee strove to overtake the leaders. He had held the amateur championship for three years and in a professional race held two weeks earlier, he defeated Dennis Butler and Charles Dunlay in a five-mile race. He was a painter by trade but at the time of the swim, he was employed as a clerk for the Pennsylvania Railroad Company. The winning time was 2:57. Obviously, at some point, the current switched from flood to ebb as they averaged better than 3 miles per hours to finish 10 miles in 3 hours. Additionally, they were not doing the crawl stroke, as that stroke was not popularized yet.

Swimming strokes used at this time weren't particularly fast strokes if you were swimming for time. By 1887, in a contest in the Harlem River, the 100 yard time had dropped to 1 minute17.2 seconds, winner: H. T. Braun[220] of the Pastime Athletic Club, and the mile time to 35 minutes 18 seconds, winner: A. Mefferia of the Manhattan Athletic Club against 12 contestants.[221] These times are difficult to assess because river swims have a current component and the strokes were inefficient with stroke counts as low as 25 per minute that they could even have been swimming against the tide.

In 1888, on August 25, at the Travers Island boathouse the first annual AAU championship was held. The contested distance was 100 yards along the inlet for the boathouse and it featured nine swimmers. The winner was Herman Braun who lowered his time for the 100 to 1 minute 16.2 seconds.[222] This is a significant meet because it was the start of the Amateur Athletic Union.[223] This organization was to provide a structure for all sports in the United States. With the emergence of the International Olympic Committee (1894)[224], the National Collegiate Athletics Association (1905)[225], and FINA (1908)[226] the AAU role has diminished somewhat in certain sports but it still plays a major role in amateur athletics.[227]

Another Championship of America was in 1888 at Old Orchard Beach, Maine, on July 10th between Prof. Thomas Riley of Boston and Prof. P. F. Mack, from Australia. The purse for the contest was $500.[228] The distance was 5 miles on an ebb current. The Australian, Mack took the lead initially. By the end of the first mile Riley had caught up and the race was fairly even until the last quarter mile when Riley sprinted ahead to win by a half a minute in a time of 1:26.[229]

Steve Brodie had not yet finished his tango with fame and fortune. After his swim down the Hudson River the next year found him registered under an assumed name with some accomplices at the Waverly House in Niagara Falls. He and some friends were not there to rob a bank. They were there to assist Brodie go over the falls and since he was well known as a daredevil his present might have alerted the authorities. They had brought Brodie's rubber suit, a copy of Boyton's or it might even have been Boyton's. This was no barrel or a rubber ball but it was more than just a life jacket. He had padded his body with cotton batting over which he fitted the suit. The suit inflated to 52 inches around the waist and 72 around the chest. The helmet inflated and was guarded by two steel bands.[230]

No one had ever gone over the fall and lived to tell about it.[231] At 5:30 am, on September 7th, 1889, Steve Brodie pushed off from shore and using the paddles made for the middle of the river. In five minutes, he was over. He said that once the river got him in its currents, he began having second thoughts and tried to make for shore but was unable. He began saying his prayers and passed out at the precipice. When he struck bottom at the base of the falls, he regained consciousness only to pass out again. He finally awoke floating at the waters edge. One of his accomplices, John Ledger, from the Brighton Beach Lifesaving Corps Station No. 39, had swum out to tow him into shore. He was bleeding from the mouth, most likely having bit his tongue upon the landing, but otherwise, none the worse.[232] No mention is made if he went over the American or Canadian falls; however, the common knowledge is with the rocks at the bottom of the American fall, its sure death so Steve and all subsequent daredevils have gone over Horseshoe Falls on the Canadian side.

That afternoon, as the group gathered at the Grand Trunk station to leave, he was arrested and charged with attempted suicide. In the court case held that very evening, Brodie was asked if he went over the falls by Judge Hill. Brodie said, "If I tell you I did not go over, will you let me go?" The judge said, "Yes." "Well, then," said Brodie, "I did not go over and I am off." The judge then declared that such a pronouncement was not enough. He did not believe that Brodie went over the falls and not wanting the people to be deceived and the judge wrote out an affidavit to that affect. He asked Brodie to sign it. Brodie refused and the court case continued. Several witnesses were called who testified that they saw Brodie go over the falls. Judge Hill then found Brodie to be in violation of the laws of the Dominion. The Judge then "…bound over the prisoner in $500 (Canadian) on his own recognizance to keep the laws of the Dominion for one year, especially that relating to attempts to go over the falls."[233]

Steve Brodie was accused and convicted in Canadian courts of having gone over the falls and living to tell about it. The fact that he lived is testimony to the Paul Boyton designed suit. Yet, today in Niagara Falls the first person recognized as going over the falls is Annie Taylor, also known as Minnie Taylor and Annie Edson, in 1901.[234] Steve was more a man of action who recognized the feat was more important than the pictures. Fortunately, there was not the slew of imitators that followed his leap from the Brooklyn Bridge. Perhaps, that's just as well. The cottage industry that surrounds Niagara Falls is going to have to retool as they now have a new addition for their list of daredevils.

Modern historians have not looked upon Steve Brodie kindly.[235] In an earlier era, the movie actor George Raft portrayed him in the 1933 film *The Bowery*.[236] It's disputed that he made the Brooklyn Bridge jump with detractors saying he hid under the piers and swam out to be picked up while friends threw a dummy off the bridge.[237] This poorly thought out scenario doesn't take into account the eyewitnesses to the jump who would have seen him swimming out. Were he already in position beneath the bridge, he'd had to swim for his life to stay in one spot because of the current. Other detractors site a computation of the velocity and leave you to conclude it is too fast for Steve to have survived.[238] These calculations[239] ignore wind resistance, which puts an upper limit of the rate of fall and common sense given other daredevils have made successful jumps.

Figure 11 Brooklyn Bridge in 1900. If you swam out to pretend to have landed from a leap, you would be seen thus disproving the scenario the detractors of Steve Brodie have concocted.

Even today, his actions are astonishing, so much so that his detractors concoct fairly reasoned and plausible accounts of how he could manage a hoax. There is a reason for this reaction. In 1898, Steve was reported to have died on March 30th when returning from the Midwest for a theatrical performance of *On the Bowery*. A train conductor was unable to rouse a sleeping Brodie. The New York Times printed his obituary the following day based on the report from his wife of the news given her by the railroad. Steve had the pleasure of reading his obituaries when he arrived back in New York.[240] One cannot help but notice that his death was timed so that the obituary appeared on April 1, 1898, generally known as April Fools Day. For a public persona who lived off his name, a publicity stunt that didn't involve jumping, leaping, or otherwise throwing yourself into mortal danger must have seemed relatively tame, especially if it attained the same results and friends had a good laugh. Shortly after this episode, he moved to Buffalo, NY, where he purchased another saloon and established himself as a leading citizen.[241]

It should be mentioned that when Steve Brodie died in 1901, his funeral was attended by State Senator Tim Sullivan, president of the Fraternal Order of Eagle, No.40, of which Steve was a charter member. A number of ex-Assemblymen attended.[242] It's hard in this era to find a saloon owner not connected in some way to Tammany Hall. Steve had grown up shining shoes at City Hall.

Steve Brodie's final swim that received notice was on February 18th, 1889, in the East River. You might suspect that the river was a bit cold at that time of year. Exactly the point of the wager, as Brodie didn't do anything unless money was on the line. Using Boyton's swimming suit, he was to "swim" from 90th Street to the Brooklyn Bridge within two hours through the ice. Setting off in an ebb current, he paddled for the center of the river where it was clear of ice, Brodie's trip was uneventful except for the part where he was rammed by a steam schooner in the ribs at about 80th Street. The incident capsized him and he was unable to rotate himself to the surface. Fortunately, the rowboat following him wasn't struck by the yacht and quickly came to his aid else he would have drowned. The rowboat had its turn around 69th Street, capsizing but the fellows in the boat climbed back in and then immediately put into shore for shelter. This stretch of the East River up through Hell Gate has turbulence worthy of a kayak river course. Brodie finished the trip accompanied by the steam launch carrying the observers and collected on his bet.[243] Every year the Manhattan marathon swim with kayak support pass along this same course in the opposite direction.

Before the end of this decade, swimming had risen to a new prominence. A six-day swimming contest was held in Boston starting on October 1, 1889, in an era where 6-day bike races were commonplace. The contestants were Clara Beckwith of Boston and Valeska Neilson from Germany. Certainly of interest to the participants was the award should they be the one who swam the farthest over the six days, a $1000 purse, a $1000 a side meaning each side had to put the $1000 up to compete. The contest was held in the Boston Grand Museum Natatorium at the corner of Washington and Dover Streets. Each day saw large crowds of spectators. The ladies would start swimming around noon and finish at 9:00pm each night. They could take as many breaks as they wanted. On the first day, the German swimmer fell ill after 3 hours and withdrew. Clara allowed the backer a substitute, Maggie Dyas, and the competition continued. This showed a considerable amount of confidence. The substitute actually pushed Clare harder as Valeska stroke must have been weak due to the illness. First day results: Beckwith, 7 miles 33 laps; Dyas, 7 miles 1 lap. Day 2: Beckwith, 17 miles; Dyas, 15 miles 19 laps. Day 3: Beckwith, 24 miles 38 laps; Dyas, 23 miles 18 laps. Day 4: Beckwith, 32 miles 17 laps; Dyas, 30 miles 17 lap. Day 5: Beckwith, 39 miles 30 laps; Dyas, 36 miles 37 laps. On the final day there was speculation that the girls would break 50 miles but they fell a bit short: Beckwith, 45 miles and Dyas 41 miles. The current event that would be a comparison to this six-day swim is the 24-hour swims. The record for that is now over 50 miles. In 1889, they couldn't even break 50 miles over six days with rest![244] Today, top swimmers will do 50 miles in one 24-hour swim.

The first Olympics were held in 1896 on April 11th. The swimming champion was Alfred Hajos from Hungary based on his winning two out of the three competitions contested.[245] The three swimming events (100 m, 500m, and 1200m) were held in *open water* in the Bay of Zea near Piraeus. His winning time for the 100 meters was 1 minute 22.3 seconds.[246] This was exceedingly slow even for the era but since it was held in open water, a current could have been a factor as the venue bordered on the Saronic Gulf.[247] Additionally, the water was particularly cold that spring day, purported to be between 53 to 57 degrees. Alfred was the 1895 European Champion in the 100 meters in Vienna. The swimmers were conveyed by boat out to an in-water start off shore with the starting line marked by two buoys. The course led to shore and was marked by floating hallowed-out pumpkins. The contest was close with Alfred winning by a half meter over Otto Herschmann of Austria.[248] Alfred also won the 1200-meter competition in 18 minutes 22 seconds. He went on to have an illustrious career as an architect even winning a third medal in an Olympic design competition in 1924.[249] Alfred began swimming after a personal tragedy in his family, when his father drowned in the Danube. Alfred has a higher winning percentage of Olympic swimming events than Mark Spitz.

There was some strategy employed by the swimmers in the first Olympics. Since Dr. Paul Neumann lived in Austria and Alfred Hajos had won the 100m European championships in 1895, Paul and Alfred most likely swam against each other at some point. The 500-meter swim began immediately after the 100-meter swim so Alfred, who entered all the events, used that time to recover for the 1200-meter race, scratching from the 500-meter swim. Dr. Neumann only entered and swam in one event, the 500-meter swim which he won in a time of 8 minutes 12.6 seconds over two Greek competitors; Antonios Pepanos was second in just under 10 minutes.[250] Dr. Neumann later competed for the Chicago Athletic Association.[251] He was one of the first great physician swimmers.

Greece entered a number of swimmers in this Olympic competition and a swimming event only for Greek sailors was also held. The only American competing was Gardiner Williams from the Boston Athletic Association[252] who appears to have come in third behind Alfred Hajos in both races. However, he did not place, as only the first two places were timed. Great Britain had only one swimmer entered, H. F. Suter, but he failed to appear at the swimming events. Likewise, the French team didn't show nor did two other Hungarians.[253]

The inconsistency of the Olympics results compared with the current world record continues to this day. Quite often, the world record is faster than the Olympic record. In 1896 the inconsistency could be attributed to the failure of the best swimmers to show up while today the reason is simply the fact that the world swimming championship are held more often making it easier for swimmer to reach their peak performance.

The Olympics traditionally held their swimming events in open-water venue until 1908. The 1904 Olympics at Paris held their swimming events in the River Seine and a small lake in 1904 at St. Louis.[254] The Olympics are returning to an open-water venue for the 2008 Olympics in Beijing, China, for one marathon swimming event, a 10 kilometer swim, after a 100-year lapse.

Figure 12 US Olympic team for 1904.

Leading up to the turn of the century, Austrians and other Europeans were also competing in swimming meets held in the Danube River either in Vienna or Budapest.[255] The Danube flows from west to east; any swim in the river is a current assisted swim. The Danube is the 2nd longest river in Europe behind the Volga. Since the construction of the Gabcikovo Dam by Slovakia, the flow of the river has been altered significantly. Additionally, on January 31, 2000 at Baia Mare, there was an ecological disaster that dumped cyanide waste water[256] into the river to the extent that 700 kilometers below the site, cyanide levels of 2 milligrams per liter of water were found; .1milligram per liter is consider a lethal dose for humans.[257] The difficulty of the cleanup of the Danube is complicated by the fact that the river flows through 10 different countries.

In the same year on September 21, 1896, Charles Cavill swam the entrance to San Francisco Harbor known as the Golden Gate. A fleet of sailboats and steamers accompanied him. The swim started when he entered the water at 3:30 pm. His time from shore to shore was 1:15.[258] He is the first man to have swum this course. There was no bridge across the strait, as the Golden Gate Bridge wasn't built until 1937.[259] Hazel Langenour became the first woman across on August 11, 1911.[260] Charles died less than a year after swimming The Gate. He was performing an underwater endurance stunt in Stockton, a town up the Sacramento River from San Francisco that went wrong. He would submerge and then to extend the time under water, he would breathe air from a submerged upside down tub. Unknown to Charles was the fact that vapors were being emitted from an underground gas deposit at this location. Evidently, the gas collected in the tub and Charles suffocated from the poisonous vapors.[261]

Charles Cavill was one of the six sons of Frederick Cavill. Frederick, who swam for the Brighton Swimming Club in the south of England, immigrated to Australia. This family literally taught America, England, and Australia how to swim fast and endowed the freestyle with the name: Australian crawl.[262] How the father, Frederick, learned to swim this stroke is an interesting story. On a visit to the Solomon Islands, he watched some natives swimming with their native overhand stoke. John Arthur Trudgen had introduced the overhand stroke to Europe in 1873 from the same source. This stroke was known as the trudgeon and consisted of an overhand stroke with a scissor kick. Fred Cavill noticed that the natives used a different kick, theirs had a vertical component to it and he developed a two-beat kick. He taught his sons what he learned; who then went around rewriting the record books in swimming competitions. Three of the sons died during some event while trying to make a living popularizing swimming. The swimming world owes a debt of gratitude to the Cavill family.

Dr. Judson Daland of New York City while investigating cholera in Italy in 1893 claimed to have swum the Messina Straits, the passage between Sicily and Italy. To the ancients this is known as the whirlpool between Scylia and Charybdia. This swim was from Sicily to Italy leaving from the town of Faro. The distance at the narrowest point is 2.7 nautical miles. The time for the swim was 2:20 and the swimmer used breaststroke and sidestroke.[263] There was no independent observer and the swim was reported in a letter to his secretary who reported the news to the papers. He did do his research for the swim having talked to several people in the village including the innkeeper where he was staying. The innkeeper had even tried the swim himself but was unable to make the distance. His research found that according to the oldest living member of the village, the Straits had never been swum. How quickly the natives forgot that Captain Paul Boyton had, sort of, swam across the Straits on March 16, 1876 in his lifesaving suit.[264]

By the end of the century, local swimming events had swept up and down both coasts and throughout the country. Some of the location where swimming meets were being held that haven't been mentioned thus far are: Asbury Park; Bergen Beach, Long Branch in New Jersey; Brighton Beach and Bay Ridge in New York; Schuylkill River at Lafayette, Grand Swimming Bath in Philadelphia, Pennsylvania; Rohn's Swimming School and the Milwaukee Rowing and Swimming Association of Milwaukee,

Wisconsin; River View, Marshall Hall, and Columbia Athletic Club in Washington, D. C.; and St. Louis, Missouri.

In San Francisco, several clubs were home to the open water swimmers: Dolphin Swimming and Boating Club established in 1877, South End Rowing Club established in 1873, and the Olympic Club established in 1860. The first two clubs share a building that sits at the east end of Aquatic Park and west of Fisherman's Wharf. Their pool was San Francisco Bay. The Dolphin Club inaugurated the Golden Gate Crossing swim in 1917[265] and the first organized Alcatraz swim occurred in 1960.[266] At one point prior to 1974 a group of six swimmers were run over by a tug with two of the swimmers being seriously injured during a Bay swim.[267]

Before closing out this century, a new fad swept the beaches at Newport, Rhode Island, kite swimming. A swimmer would be canoed off shore where they would be attached to the stout cord affixed to a box kite already aloft. The swimmer would attach the cord to their bodies via a sling and with the onshore breeze enjoyed all summer long at Newport, would be carried, nay, dragged through the water to shore. If the party swam, all-the-better as the kite carried the weight of the swimmer as it assisted them in their adventure. There were as many as 30 box kites at one time employed in this entertainment in 1899.[268] I believe this sport has evolved into board kiting at the present time, a new fad.

Early Australian swimming

Swimming history for Australia begins with the construction of swimming enclosures in Darling Harbour, Sydney, as early as 1788. This was for protection against sharks. The first enclosure was built at the bottom of Erskine Street and a second was built at Dawes Point Battery. By 1810, orders were posted by the Governor prohibiting au natural bathing at public places other than in enclosures all ready set aside. In 1834, the Sydney Gazette reported swimming as the favorite recreation of the populous. By 1854 with the growth of industry and the lack of sewerage treatment, a commission of inquiry recommended the closure of all swimming enclosures in Sydney Harbour. Bathing moved to Wooloomooloo Bay until the first inland, indoor Natatorium was open on Pitt Street in 1888 by the Sydney Municipal Authority.[269]

The first swimming competition, all male, was held in 1846 at Robinson's Baths, Sydney. In the mid-1870s, the first female swimming competitions were held at the Adelaide City Baths. Swim clubs were organized as soon as local swimming baths were built. The first swimming association for the coordination of swim competitions began in 1892 with the New South Wales Amateur Swimming Association. By 1901 there were 1,119 members in 29 clubs in the NSWASA.[270]

From a swimming resume of Arthur Kenney, an Australian studying dentistry at the University of Pennsylvania we discover that St. Kilda, his hometown near Melbourne, had age-group swimming competitions at the South Melbourne Baths as early as 1875. He competed in swimming contests held at Baliarat, Victoria; Adelaide, South Australia; and Sydney in New South Wales which hosted the colony championship. Finally, Montreal hosted an international competition in 1893 where Arthur competed in the 100 yards, winning in a time of 1 minute 11.5 seconds setting a record for the era.[271] In 1906, a rising star, B. B. Kieran, died on December 22, 1906 at age 19. He had just set the record for the 500 yards to 6 minutes 7 seconds and 1/6.[272]

Swim stroke transition period

Right at the end of the 1800's and the beginning of the 1900's there was a lot of technical improvements in the swimming stroke due to observations by Trudgen and Cavill. This eventually spills over into the open-water competition so it behooves us to take a look at what was churning the competitive waters. There was the increase in swimming speed evident in the lowering of the swimming records for the 100 yards. In the 1880's the 100-yard time hovered around 1 minute 16 seconds and it had dropped to 62.5 seconds by 1895. J. H. Thayres of England held the 1895 record. This increase in speed was accomplished by changing over from the sidestroke to the trudgeon stroke.[273] By 1900, the time had dropped to 1 minute flat held by Freddy Lane of England.[274] Then in 1902, Richard Cavill set the record even lower to 58.4 seconds using the Australian crawl at an International meet held in London.[275] However, back in the United States, E. C. Schaeffer from Pennsylvania won the A.A.U. championship for the 100 yards in a time of 67 seconds at the NYAC Travers Island course on September 20, 1902. He had won every championship event he entered that season with equally slow times.[276]

Because all of the world records in swimming were held either by Englishmen or Australians, the New York Athletic Club in 1903 decided to place more emphasis on developing faster swimmers. The NYAC, founded in 1866, noted at that time there were only twelve swimming clubs in the United States as opposed to at least sixty in England each attached to a tank. The NYAC had their clubhouse built in 1885 with the tank on the third floor![277] Besides themselves, they mentioned the Brookline Swimming Club and the National Swimming Club of Philadelphia as having the potential to be capable of generating a champion.[278] The NYAC had just been the beneficiary of an influx of top swimmers and water polo players from the Knickerbocker Athletic Club, which had changed over to a social club in 1902. One of the swimmers changing allegiance was a 16-year old swimmer named Charlie Daniels.[279] Other clubs around in 1900 were: Pastime Athletic Club, New West Side Athletic Club, Avonia Athletic

Club, Sedgwick Athletic Club, Star Athletic Club, St. Bartholomew Athletic Club, Union Settlement Athletic Club, Xavier Athletic Club, Pawnee Athletic Club, National Swimming Association, and the Avoca Swimming Association in New York[280] while nationally there was the Boston Athletic Association, founded 1887; Chicago Athletic Association, founded 1890; San Francisco Olympic Club, founded 1860;[281] St. Louis Athletic Association; Orange Athletic Club; New Jersey Athletic Club; Missouri Athletic Club, founded 1903; and the Atlantic Swimming Association and National Swimming Club in Philadelphia. In addition to athletic clubs there were teams that belonged to the Harlem Navy, a water polo league; one team, the Lone Star Boat Club, won the water polo championship in 1899 at Madison Square Garden. Other clubs in the Navy were: Union, Dauntless, Nonpareil, Wyanoke, Harlem and Bohemian.[282]

The best these athletic clubs swimmers could do for the 100 yards was 61.5 seconds by Brookline's Harry LeMoyne in 1903. Even their knowledge of the record was dated for they thought the record was at 1 minute still.[283] They were perhaps thinking of the American Record as J. Scott Leary of the San Francisco Olympic Club, a student of Sydney Cavill, did 1 minute flat in 1903 while Richard Cavill had gone 58.6 in 1902.[284] Around this time a swimmer out of Philadelphia, E. C. Schaeffer, previously mentioned, was having great success at setting records. At the AAU championships in Buffalo, NY, on July 9th, 1901, at the Pan American Exposition grounds he won the 100-yard swim in 1 minute 10 seconds against stiff competition. The American comprehension of swimming records somehow failed to grasp reality. For example, in Washington, D. C., a local swimmer named Carl Ricks was hailed as being close to the record for 110 yards, then held by Schaeffer, in winning the annual swimming contests held at Bathing Beach. He was 14 seconds slower than Schaeffer's time.[285]

The NYAC two best swimmers, C. M. Daniels and Charles Ruberi spent the next few years trying to improving their strokes without much success. C. M. Daniels, on August 19, 1903, swam

1 minute 2.2 seconds for the 100 yards on the Schuylkill River at the AAU meet in Lafayette.[286] The following year wasn't any better as he managed 1 minute 3.8 seconds in a meet at the same location.[287] Charles Ruberi best time for the 100 yards was 1 minute 8.8 seconds on August 8, 1903 at a meet in Ottawa for the Canadian swimming championship.[288] In August of 1905, C. M. Daniels swam slower still at 1 minute 3.8 seconds to capture the AAU championship held at Travers Island. He competed against D. B. Renear of the Chicago Athletic Association, Ben "Bud" Goodwin and Charlie Ruberi of the NYAC, with Marquand Schwartz of St. Louis, Missouri, coming in second. All of these swims were in rivers that had a current component. The Travers Island NYAC swim course was in an inlet between Travers Island and Glen Island on the Long Island Sound. Distance races began from the floating dock at the NYAC yacht house and extended 110 yards into the inlet toward Glen Island to a wooden barrier erected on floating marks.[289] The proposal for the NYAC to be an incubator for swimmers was not panning out through the summer of 1905.

The indoor season over the winter of 1905-1906 resulted in a remarkable change. On December 21, 1905, in a meet at the University of Philadelphia, C. M. Daniels, using a double overhand stroke finished the 100 yards in 61 seconds. Ruberi in the same meet had switched over to the backstroke and was setting records in that stroke.[290] A month later, Daniels busted loose. He finally got his entire name published: Charles Meldrum Daniels. At the close of a 100-yard race at the NYAC pool, the timing officials held a confab as they looked at their watches. Then they announced the results: 57.6 seconds for the 100 yards. It was unbelievable. It was under the world record at the time, 58.0 seconds held by B. B. Kieran of Australia. The second place swimmer, George Dockrell, the Irish champion, said Daniels' stroke was a combination of the trudgeon arm stroke and the crawl kick and was a new departure in swimming.[291] The English swimming authorities did not recognize the time, as there was a dispute about the suit he wore. On February 22, 1906, wearing an acceptable suit, Daniels tied the existing record of 58.0 seconds. Then on March 23rd, he took 2 more seconds off the record to drop it to 56 seconds flat in a match race against Marquand Schwartz in St. Louis.[292]

Daniels took 5 seconds off his 100-yard time in less than 3 months. He actually dropped most of the time between the meets in December and January. One could easily assume that he had only just developed this stoke which differed from the Australian crawl by the number kicks per arm stroke, six as opposed to two.[293] Daniels had been taught the Australia crawl at the Knickerbockers Athletic Club by Alex Meffert and Harry Reeder. Gus Sundstrom was the coach at the New York Athletic Club and after a loss to the Brookline Athletic Club in the spring of 1904 began experimenting with adaptations to his own stroke. He worked on developing a continuous kick while still using the crawl arm stroke. Gus realized he had finally perfected the stroke when in a test at 25 yards he went the distance in 11.8 seconds, which under the world record of 12.2. He was 46 years old at the time of this achievement. He then taught the stroke to Daniels and the rest of the NYAC swimming team. Daniels credited Gus with his stroke improvements.[294] Daniels was still learning the stroke and as a whole, so was the swimming community. In a description of Daniels swimming the 200 yards, in January of 1907, in which he set an American record in the NYAC tank of 2 minutes 15.4 seconds, he switched over to the trudgeon stoke from the crawl for the 5th and 6th laps, switching back to the crawl for the final two laps.[295] Daniels best performance occurred on April 7th, 1910 when he went 54.8 seconds for the 100 yards freestyle.

There have been no other change besides training techniques[296] that has so vastly improved a swimmer's ability so far-reaching as this change in the stroke technique pioneered by the these early swimmers. Once adopted, marathon swims of greater distances could be planned, tricky currents could be negotiated, and faster transit of shorter distances made for more interesting spectator viewing. Upper body strength became more of a factor in marathon swimming than tolerance for cold because you were working up a sweat and not passively sculling through the water. The development of the stroke allowed the marathon swimmer a repertoire of strokes to use depending on the ocean conditions and the level of exhaustion experienced. If a shoulder condition prevents a full stroke, the swimmer could change to a completely different stroke if needed and rest an arm. The new strokes changed the way we think about swimming and brought a whole new dimension of the mechanics and the aqua-dynamics to consider. Swimmers could finally learn about the lift portion of the drag equation. The "feel" of the water became real.

The role of the swimming club cannot be ignored in this achievement. The nurturing and encouragement a swim club provides plays a significant role in allowing swimmers to concentrate on the task at hand and explore their potential. It wasn't until the NYAC decided to go after the record that their swimmers achieved it. It was an organizational decision backed up with deeds. Neither can the role the Cavill family played in this development be ignored. Richard Cavill was not just a sprint swimmer; his time for the mile swim in April of 1902 was 21:11.4 set in a meet in New Zealand.[297]

Summary of Swim Stroke Improvement

Year	Stroke	Swimmer	Location	100 yds
1865	Breast		Eton	1:25
1884	Breast	Magee	Harlem River	1:21.5
1887	Side	H Braun	Harlem River	1:17.5
1888	Side	H Braun	Travers Island	1:16.2*
1893	Trudgeon	ArthurKenny	Montreal	1:11.5
1895	Trudgeon	JH Thayres	England	1:02.5
1900	Trudgeon	Freddy Lane	England	1:00
1902	AusCrawl	Fred Cavill	London	58.4
1904	AusCrawl	B. Kieran	Australia	58.0
1906	AmCrawl	Chas Daniels	NYAC	56.0
1908	AmCrawl	Chas Daniels	NYAC	54.8

*1st AAU meet

Chapter 6   20th Century

At the beginning of the 20th Century, the Volunteer Life Savers' Association held their 2nd annual water carnival at Far Rockaway, New York, on Aug 6th, 1900. The venue was Coffey's Pavilion and swims contested were 100-yard swims for novices, juniors, and seniors, a 65-yard swim for women, an 880-yard swim for novices, a Championship, plus a row, a swim underwater, a 30-yard tub race, and a duck chase. No times were recorded. The Championship of Far Rockaway was contested over the 880-yard distance, won by A. Reuse of the Knickerbocker Athletic Club, a summer residence. A Miss Meehan won the woman's race while her brother won the tub race. Immigration waves would bring swimmers who learned to swim in Europe to America where they would settle. One German swimmer, Hans Hole, on August 17th, 1900, swam 6 miles in Lake Winnebago in Wisconsin as a warm up for longer swims across the same lake.[298] There was no word whether he completed these other swims.

Also in 1900, two swimmers, Henry Dawson and George Chase, from Washington, D. C., swam from the Arsenal to Fort Washington down the Potomac River. The Arsenal is a historic fort, now known as Fort McNair,[299] located at the southernmost point of Washington, DC, at the entrance to the Anacostia River. Their time was 4:45 for the 13-mile distance. The previous year they swam only as far as Alexandria in 5:25, a shorter distance and longer time.[300] Fort Washington is a town located on the eastern or Maryland shore of the Potomac River south of Washington, DC, opposite North Mount Vernon. They most likely came ashore at Fort Washington Park.

The swim from the Battery in Manhattan to points south is a fairly easy swim when you catch the outgoing tide. In 1903, two lifeguards, Edward Fuller and Philip Fay, decided to settle a dispute between them by seeing who could swim to Coney Island from the Battery.[301] They each put up $25; a princely sum for those days that the finisher would collect should the other not finish. On August 21, 1903, they began their swim from the

Battery at 7:10am and right away had to dodge the local skiff traffic around lower Manhattan. Along the way, as they skirted the Brooklyn shoreline, the steamboat *Sirius* on its way to Coney Island came up upon them. Fay managed to avoid the vessel but it appeared that Fuller didn't see the approaching vessel until it was upon him. Needless to say, the pilot didn't see the swimmers either even though escort boats accompanied both. Fuller was hit by the bow wake and disappeared only to reappear unharmed. Later, as they approached Norton's Point, Fay misjudged a buoy, ran into it and wound up pinned to it by the current. The tide was rushing out so fast that he couldn't break free. His launch came alongside and pulled him off. This was a tricky operation for if they bore down on the buoy, they'd crush the swimmer, not the sort of support you're looking for on a marathon swim! At some time after 12:30, they both came ashore near the old Iron Pier, Fay first then Fuller. Both collapsed on the beach before a large crowd who had heard of the contest. Since both finished, they split the pot. An exact finishing time was not given but a reasonable estimate would be 5:40 for the distance.[302]

Another swim involving Coney Island occurred in 1904. This time the swim was from the Brooklyn Bridge to Coney Island. There were 32 contestants. It was not the first time the event was held but this was the first time that women could compete. At the starting block were Eleanor Weber of Flatbush and Florence West of Fort Hamilton. The contest was actually an endurance contest conducted by the United States Volunteer Life Saving Corps. The starting time was 11:07am, with the pack splitting into two groups. The women stayed with the slower group and by Gravesend they had moved to the front. By noon, all the contestants were still in the water. Soon lifeguards were rescuing other lifeguards with one being pulled unconscious onto a rescue launch. The drowning man recovered and wanted to resume the race and had to be restrained from jumping back in. One lifeguard swam up to the main committee boat and complained that the official on his escort boat had disqualified him for holding onto the escort boat when he paused for a drink of whiskey. The swim director told him to never mind and to get back to work. When the remaining swimmers rounded the point for the final leg, the tide was against them and the final eight swimmers retired from the race. No one made it to Coney Island that day but medals were awarded to the final eight swimmers in the water.[303]

The problem with this swim was the organizers assumed that high tide would mean the current would ebb with the dropping tide to give the swimmers an easy ride down to Coney Island. In New York Harbor, there is no connection between the height of the tide and the current flow. The ebb current wouldn't start for another 2 hours so the swimmers' progress was slow down past Governors Island. Then once they were in the Hudson River, which was ebbing, they would be able to make the westernmost tip of Coney Island. On this final leg along the south side of Coney Island would find the swimmers fighting an ebbing current out of the Rockaways.

In 1904, a young Australian girl, Annette Kellerman, age 17, who was successful in local competitions setting record marks for the 100-yard and mile distances, had completed the first stage of her swimming career. Her family held a conference after she set the mile mark and charted a course for Annette to become a professional swimmer. By going to England, they sought a large audience for her abilities. At the behest of her father, Fred Kellerman, she swam the Thames, from Putney Bridge to Blackwall, a distance of 15 miles. In order to understand the role that the family was involved with her swims consider this: her father was dressed in a frock coat and top hat in the rowboat. This brought her to the attention of Lord Northcliff, the owner of a newspaper called the Daily Mail. In exchange for an exclusive, he arranged for her to swim the English Channel in a race with six male swimmers. Thousands viewed the start. She fortunately managed to outlast all the males; but despite 3 attempts, the Channel outlasted her. She became known as the Aqua Queen from her early days in Australia when she was the mermaid at the Melbourne Aquarium; this was a title that would stick when she was invited to swim for the Prince of Wales. By the time she was

21, she was recognized as the greatest woman distance swimmer in the world. She toured the United States and appeared in two movies.[304] She popularized the one-piece bathing suit.[305] She was the silent films version of Ester Williams. The lives of these two stars crossed in real life when Ester Williams starred in the 1951 film *Million Dollar Mermaid* about Annette's life story.

Figure 13 Annette Kellerman and her one piece bathing suit.

A century later, we find its Annette Kellerman's image that adorns the letterhead of the Manhattan Island Foundation. Her career path still is valid, as three different Australian women have come to reign over this long distance event: Shelley Taylor-Smith, Suzy Maroney, and Tammy van Wisse.

A Miss Nora Stanton Blatch, a college student on summer vacation, had a minor career swimming across some lakes in the Adirondacks. On August 25th, 1904 she swam across Cayuga Lake where the width was estimated at 2 ¼ miles. Two weeks prior, she had crossed Seneca Lake a few miles south of Geneva.[306] On September 3rd of 1904 Newport, RI, was the scene of a 3-mile swimming race that featured some foreign swimmers touring America. The winner of the race around buoys through the inner harbor from Long Wharf to Coaster Harbor Island in 1:23 was Joey Nuttall, a swimming champion of England. He competed against Percy Cavill of Australia who finished in 1:24, followed closely by John McCusker of Boston in 1:25, and 3 other swimmers that included Alfred Brown. This was a professional race with first place winning $450, 2nd $150 and 3rd $75.[307] Nuttall won swimming the English sidestroke, which was considered a regular sidestroke with abbreviated but quick arm strokes.[308]

One thing can lead to another and in this case, one swimmer's boast lead to an embarrassment. A Miss Anna Fitzgerald swam across the Hudson River in 57.5 minutes in early September of 1906. Her admirers announced that she had beaten the record of another swimmer, Ruth Frank of Washington Heights, New York. The odd thing of it was that Miss Frank hadn't swum across the Hudson. The boast became so vociferous that a supporter of Miss Franks offered to put up $1000 that Ruth could swim across the Hudson faster than Anna. There was no word if the offer was matched. On September 20, 1906, Ruth Frank accepted the challenge and dove into the Hudson River in front of the Washington Heights baths, and began her swim across the river. Two male pace swimmers, Edward Tenthoff and F. P. Kellar, and two boats accompanied her. She swam using the breaststroke, English sidestroke and trudgeon stroke. She completed the task in 45 minutes;[309] thus ended a contentious episode in the early part of this past century. Arguments or accusations in the press arose often, nearly every ten years or whenever there was a new crop of marathon swimmers. The arguments were usually about which woman swimmer was the best. Newspapers love this sort of controversy and have always provided coverage.

Swims from the Battery were very attractive to race organizers as the press is able to see the start of the race. On September 8, 1907, four swimmers started for Coney Island but only one finished. There were 52 entries in this swim sponsored by the American Life Saving Society. Competing were Alfred Brown of College Point, Queens; Antonio Rossi, of Coney Island; Louis Musa of Buffalo, and Thomas M. Brennan of New York City. The swim began during a downpour. Brown held the record of 4:40 for the course set in the previous year. The other swimmers had all dropped out by the 5 mile mark with Brown a good half mile in the lead. Currents swept him two miles off course around Fort Hamilton. He finished in a time 4:53. Brown was a Commodore of the Flushing Bay Division of the American Life Saving Society.[310] A week later, on September 15, he won another race from the 84th Street Baths in Manhattan against three other men to the United States Volunteer Lifesaving Station in College Point. His time for this swim was 1:40. The newspaper report made note that the swimmers immediately began boasting that the distance they had swum was 8 miles while the reports claimed it was at most 5 miles. They did have a favorable tide for this swim.[311]

In 1908 the Battery to Coney Island amateur swim was won by Bud Goodwin of the NYAC in a time of 4:30 on August 30th The race saw only 4 finishers out of 30 starters. This race was the A.A.U. Metropolitan Long Distance Swimming Championship sponsored by the American Life Saving Society. One swimmer, F. H. James, who came in 4th place, protested the 3rd place finisher, as he believed Alois Anderley was being towed by his boat since the distance never varied between the swimmer and his boat for the entire race.[312] The 1910 race with 100 starters misjudged the tide and no one finished.[313] In 1911, Rose Pitonoff, age 17, in a solo effort swam the course with a slight modification, starting at East 26th Street, in 8:07.[314] This was a repeat of the same swim a year earlier by her on September 18, 1910, when she made the distance in 5:08.[315] Alfred Brown returned to the Battery-Coney Island course in 1912 when on August 25th he swam the course in 5:05 in a match race against Frank Radamacker of New Jersey for $100 purse that had been postponed after both swimmers pulled out two weeks earlier at the 13 mile mark.

The year 1912 saw a swim across the Hudson serve as the 3rd Annual championship swim for members of the YMCA of Greater New York. The distance was a mile and a quarter from the Columbia University boat-house on the New Jersey shore to the Cobweb Yacht Club located at 153st on Manhattan's upper west side. This location is south of the George Washington Bridge and the starting and stopping locations were almost directly across from each other. The reigning champion was J. B. Mantrell of the West Side YMCA in a time of 32 minutes in 1911. He finished the race this year around 138th street because of the ebb current. The winner for the 1912 race held Saturday afternoon, July 13th, was Ruble Capelle of the Brooklyn Central YMCA in a time of 1hour and 9 minutes.

In 1914, Elaine Golding of Bath Beach swam from the Battery to the Steeplechase pier on Coney Island in a time of 4:32. This beats the best men's time of Alfred Brown of 4:23 because their finish was about a half mile shorter. She also won the same race the year before.[316]

A young man just starting his amateur swimming career named Charles Durborow of Riverton swam from Chester to Philadelphia in the Delaware Bay on August 8, 1909, a distance of 14 ½ miles in 5:40. He hadn't learned the newer strokes yet so was limited to just the breaststroke and sidestroke without the over-arm recovery. He previously had swum from Tacony to Burlington Island in the Upper Delaware in five hours.[317] He turns out to be a steady competitor learning the trudgeon for later competitions. At some point during 1912, he lengthened this swim from Chester to Philadelphia into 19 miles possibly swimming from another departure location taking 15 and quarter hours. However, the "patent logs" which are navigational equipment that measure the distance through the water, showed he had gone 43 miles.[318] This swim got stretched into 48 miles in 14:15 in other reports[319] that established Charles as the premier distance swimmer in America. What the press didn't realize was that all the patent logs were recording was the flow of water past the boat's hull, when the tide turned and Charles was stuck in the current, the logs keep recording the current flow and showed a trip distance that far exceed the actual distance swam.

Adeline Trapp became known as the Queen of Hell Gate for just finishing a race in 1909 from east 89th Street, Manhattan to Clason Point in the Bronx.[320] By virtue of being the only woman to finish out of 40 competitors, she was bestowed this title by the press. Her abilities that day were bested but previously that summer she was the only finisher in a swim from Hastings-on-Hudson to New York City, a distance of 24 miles among 25 entries. She also set a record time of 5:07 from North Beach, Queens to the ferry landings in Staten Island on September 3, 1911.[321] Her other notable accomplishment was wearing a man's swimming suit in competition when their costumes look like today's short wet suits. The swim through Hell Gate was most interesting as it indicates that swims through this treacherous stretch of water were not uncommon. This stretch of water is by far the most difficult swim to safely transit; any swim organizer would be hard pressed to get insurance coverage today. Naturally occurring standing waves that continuously break for hours are found in this stretch of water. The millions and millions of gallons of water that pour through this "S" curve are turned back on themselves creating whirlpools and underwater waterfalls where shear forces tear at one another. In any era, this is a dangerous swim.

At the harbor entrance to New York today stands a wonderful suspension bridge, the Verrazano Narrows Bridge built in 1964 across the strait. Often, swimmers take to swimming between Brooklyn and Staten Island, which the bridge unites, a distance of nine-tenths of a mile. Currents in this vicinity average 2 knots and can range as high as 2.8 knots. When crossing the distance in a time of 30 minutes, swimmers can expect to be swept a mile off course due to these currents.

In 1909, three sisters conquered the Narrows on August 29th. Ethel, Vera, and Beatrice Due who range in age from 17 to 12 started at the foot of 100th Street Brooklyn and swam to Fort Wadsworth, Staten Island. This was the second trip for Ethel, the oldest, having swum the distance in 1908 and she lowered her time to 1:12. The middle daughter was accompanied by her mother in a boat was also carried by the tide but landed but 200 yards south of the Fort in 2:13. Beatrice, the youngest had her father swimming with her alongside, was carried out of the harbor on the tide and had to wait for the tide change to bring her back close enough to Staten Island to finish, which she did, about 2 miles south of where the bridge would go taking over four hours for the swim. The family that swims together stays together? The poor father got no credit for his part; you might say he didn't get his due?[322]

In the spring of 1911 a discussion broke out in the press about the differences between the Australian and American crawl strokes and which was the better. The first article was on the occasion of comments by Richard Cavill which caused some swimming coaches on the East Coast to even say that Richard being an instructor at the Illinois Athletic Club of Chicago wasn't in a position to criticize the stoke since he had only seen the stroke in the Midwest and all the records were held on the East Coast. There was agreement that the strokes differed but even the descriptions of the American crawl from the experts who were consulted, Sullivan, Meffert, Mackenzie, Kistler, Wahle, Cady and others differed greatly. The origin of the stroke was place around 1904 in the article. Cavill's criticism was on the use of a straight-arm position during the recover portion of the stroke by the American crawl where he favored a shorter stroke with emphasis on the arm being carried down along the center of the body and close to it. This criticism was refuted by a discussion of the bent or raised elbow that is taught by the coaches mentioned for the American crawl. Little was said of the kick in this discussion except for the Yale coach, Richards, who was studying the swordfish kick of Gus Sundstrom, the coach at the NYAC.[323] After the National indoor championships had passed in May of 1911, another article appeared that touted Frank Sullivan as the inventor of a new stroke although the article admittedly conceded that Charles Daniels was still king. Cecil Healy of Sydney mentioned the timing of the arm and leg stroke with reference to a fluttering of the feet between leg drives as an improvement he was touting after racing against Daniels in Europe. This could be the first mentioning of the flutter kick. The fact that Cavill's student, Perry McGillivray, came in second to Daniels in the 100-yard championship was attributed to the short arm stroke and wide leg thrash.[324] These were interesting articles and pointed to a need for a national swim magazine where more details and photos could be distributed and discussed in detail.

A swim that hasn't been seen in nearly a century had an interesting beginning around 1910. The swim is from the Battery to Sandy Hook, NJ, a distance of 22 miles. Charles Durborow from Philadelphia had made 3 attempts, trying both directions and even coming as close as ½ mile from finishing once.[325] Life Saving Commodore Alfred Brown began experimenting with the swim in 1913. His first attempt on August 4th wound up in failure when pollution consisting of tar, oil, other rubbish and driftwood from Bayonne prevented him from continuing the swim.[326] This is the first known time that pollution was sited as a reason to cancel a swim. He eventually was successful, completing the swim on August 28, 1913 in a time of 13:38. He was accompanied in a launch by Paul Frommlach, Charles Kaufman, James Kennedy, and John Reuschett. This was his fourth attempt in less than a month. His persistence paid off with his becoming the first to successfully complete the course.[327]

His dance on top of the marathon-swimming world, which the press bestowed upon him, was short lived. Two weeks later, Samuel Richards from Boston came to New York with a seven-man support crew from the L Street Swimming Club. They took a rowboat and scouted the swim out plotting their attack. On September 14, 1913, he dove off Battery pier at 6:40 AM and finished in 8:12, taking more than 5 hours off Alfred Brown's time.[328] This was considered a spectacular swim but what had confounded all the previous swimmers, the tides and opposing currents were second nature to Richards who did his training in Boston among the Harbor Islands. Charles Durborow felt insulted by the success of his contemporaries and issued a challenge to race Richards but his one condition was that it couldn't be in Boston Harbor.[329] So many challenges arose over this course that the next phase of the swim was a natural.

The American Life Saving Society proposed a marathon-swimming contest from the Battery to Sandy Hook, which wound up being sponsored annually by a New York newspaper, the New

York Herald Tribune.³³⁰ One reason the paper sponsored the race was because the publisher was Odgen Reid, a NYAC member who while at Yale University was captain of their swimming and water polo teams.³³¹ The first race was held July 19, 1914 from the Battery, NY, to Sandy Hook, NJ, a distance of twenty-two miles. The race was promoted by the newspaper and claimed it to be the greatest contest of its kind ever held in the country. The race was won by George R. Meehan, age 23, of Boston in a time of 7:18.³³² He was followed by two other finishers: Samuel Richards in 8:19 and Walter Dunn in 8:39 both, also, from Boston. The only other finisher of 31 starters was Charles Durborow of Philadelphia in last place; this swim settled the issue of who was the better distance swimmer.³³³ George F. Esselborn of New York led in the early stages of the race until the Narrows when Meehan challenged for the lead. Meehan was using the sidestroke when he overtook Esselborn who was using the trudgeon stoke. The start was from Pier A of the Battery at 4:55am into a weak flood tide that didn't end until 9am. In the same swim season, Nell Kenney, age 27, of Sydney, Australia, successfully swam the distance in 9:35 on September 21, 1914.³³⁴ She swam solo but had witnesses to authenticate the swim as she had arrived in the United States too late to participate in the first swimming race over this course. In 1916, a young man named Robert Dowling placed 6th in that year's marathon swim. This young man had already made his mark on the marathon-swimming world the previous year.

The town of Cincinnati, Ohio, held an annual swim on August 24th, 1914, down the Ohio River. The contest was over 8 miles. There were 34 participants. The winner was Michael McDermott a member of the Illinois Athletic Club in a time of 3:10.³³⁵

On the same tide that was taking Robert Dowling on his successful around Manhattan trip in 1915, Raymond Boyle of Pittsburgh was plotting to swim to Sandy Hook from the Battery. He was trying to beat the record at the time set by George Meehan of Boston in the Tribune marathon swim of July 19, 1914 of 7:18. His course was via the Buttermilk channel to near the Staten Island shore then past West Bank light and Roamer Shoals to Sandy Hook. He left early in the morning but he didn't finish this swim; pulling up with a cramp as he cleared Staten Island.[336]

In 1915 was a summer picnic outing by persons of Japanese descent at a lake in Monroe, New York, on July 11th. Two individuals, S. Sasayama and T. Nakamura raced each other over a ½ mile course in Walton Lake. Mr. Sasayama won that race. At the same gathering, possibly during a fishing contest on the lake, two other gentlemen, Messrs Hirai and Ito, rescued some young ladies from a Camp Fire girls' camp nearby when their canoe upset. They jumped in and pulled the young girls to shore after a bit of a struggle.[337]

The late summer of 1916 provided quite a few distance swims. Charles Durborow next swim put him in the record books alongside Robert Dowling, with a swim across the entrance to the Chesapeake Bay. His course took him on the ocean side of the present day Chesapeake Bridge/Tunnel, itself a course for a swim organized in the early 1980's by Fletcher Hanks. On June 23, 1916, at 9:25 pm, Charles left from Fisherman's Island on the southern shore of Maryland's Eastern Shore and began a night swim to the Virginia Coast some 13 miles distance. He had tried the swim the previous summer but gave up after 12 hours. This year's swim went much easier. He landed at his planned location, the Cape Henry Lifesaving Station at 6:08am on June 24th, 1916. The elapsed time was 8:43 and the distance between the start and finish is 18 miles. Charles used the trudgeon stroke for the entire swim, not taking any food or drink for the swim. A small party of residents greeted him upon his arrival.[338] This is the first recorded crossing of the Chesapeake Bay entrance and as far as I can tell, the only night swim.

Not finished with his swimming career, on September 10, 1916, Charles Durborow swam 36 ½ miles in the Delaware River from Chester up river to Penn Treaty Park opposite Petty's Island (Philadelphia), catching the ebb tide to return to Chester, and finally leaving the water on the third trip back up river at Eddystone, Pennsylvania. His time was 13:30. His stroke count was all of 26 strokes a minute and he took no refreshments during the swim, only speaking once during the swim.[339]

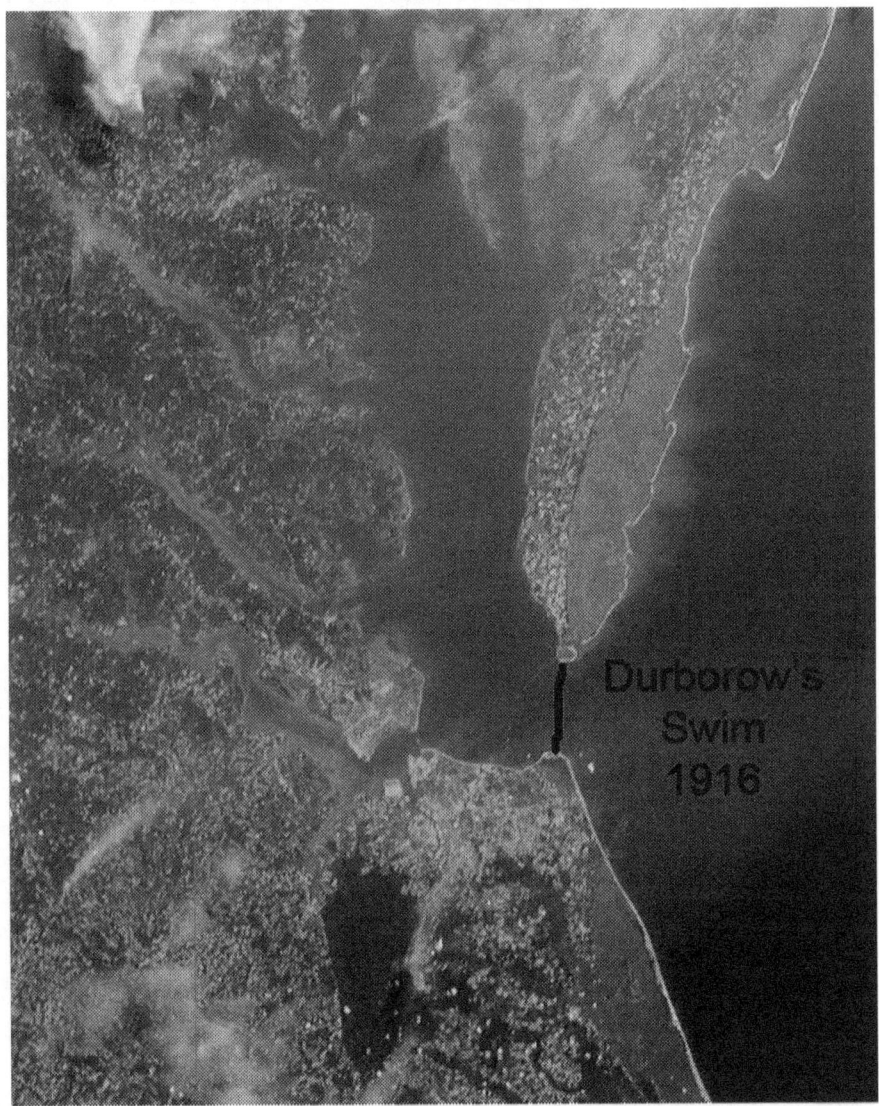

Figure 14 Chesapeake Bay as seen from space.

On August 20, 1916, two swimmers, Charles Toth[340] of Boston and Henry Sullivan of Lowell, Massachusetts, started a race from Provincetown to Nantasket Beach just outside and south of Boston Harbor.[341] Neither man finished with Toth leaving the water when a shark was spotted nearby and Henry being declared the winner after 20 plus hours in the water. On September 9, 1916, Charles Toth who swam for the L Street Swimming Club won a ten-mile swim over a one-mile circuit in the Charles River. This was a much safer venue than his last race, Provincetown to Nantasket. He competed against nine other swimmers. His winning time was 7:46.[342] Another local swimming contest of 5 miles was held in New York on September 12, 1916, over a course from the Columbia University crew floats at 116th Street on the Hudson River to 216th Street on the Hudson River.[343] Bud Goodwin of the NYAC won the race; however, the race had some problems. The newspaper reported mismanagement on the part of the organizers as there were no escort boats, no time kept of the swim, and two of the swimmers were retrieved from the middle of the Hudson River after the winner was pulled from the water opposite 247th Street.[344]

Lucy Freeman, a National AAU long-distance swimming championship for women, swam from Spuyten Duyvil to the Battery in 3:59 on September 2, 1917. This was her second attempt as the previous swim was aborted due to flotsam. She started her swim at 11:11 am when the tide was at ebb. She used a four-beat trudgeon crawl stroke even when the wind and wave increased at the end of the swim.[345] She certainly wasn't biting off more than she could chew as this entire swim was current assisted and is only part of the entire Manhattan course. The four hours is a typical time for this section of the swim when swimming Manhattan during the annual marathon. Since the tide that day was 2.6 knots, she should have had a faster transit but she started two hours before ebb began at Spuyden Duyvil.[346]

In the same year, 1917, Robert Dowling and Charles Toth of Boston competed in a 40-mile "up-river" swim in the Hudson River but both had quit the race by the time the tide turned at Spuyten Duyvil, the furthest point reached in this swim. They started at the Battery. This swim took place on September 9,

1917.[347] Someone must have forgotten to read the tide tables for this one; it would take 3 cycles of the tide to complete this swim. However, the fact that the swim would take so long might have been the point of the swim; Toth was declared the winner, as he was the last to leave the water.

World War I caused a break in swimming events worldwide. After the end of the war in November of 1918, a swimming event was held in Paris on July 20, 1919, that signaled the end of the hiatus. An American swimmer, Norman Ross from Chicago, while serving his country as a soldier, won a 4-mile swim through Paris in the Seine River. His time was 1:30 for the event and was closely followed by an Italian swimmer named Bacigalupo and an Australian named Morris. Women swimmers had a 500-yard headstart, which the men overcame. This was an event held during the Interallied Games and was watched by an immense crowd lining the banks of the Seine.[348] A 3-mile swim off Genoa, Italy, was held on August 22, 1921. Antonio Sachner won the race in 1:31 in heavy seas.[349] A swim by Pouilley, a Frenchman in training for an attempt on the English Channel, went from Meaux to the walls of Paris down the Canal de Loureq covering about 17 miles in 9:49.[350] A Russian swimmer, Indritsanov, abandoned an attempt on the English Channel on September 19, 1922.[351] An Argentina swimmer, Romeo Maciel, swam across the Rio de la Plata from Colonia, Uruguay, to Buenos Aires, a distance of 27 miles in 24:30 in 1922.[352]

On October 8, 1922, at a swimming meet in Hamilton, Bermuda, Sybil Bauer from Chicago, set a world record in the 440-yard backstroke of 6:24.8, breaking the men's record of 6:28 held by Harold Krueger of Honolulu. This was the first time in swimming history a woman had beaten a world's record held by a man in a pool swim.[353]

The Ohio River had a marathon swim in 1924. On August 23, 1924, a four-mile marathon swim down the Ohio River near Cincinnati was won by Walter Laufer, a Cincinnati YMCA swimmer in a time of 55:14.[354] Other local swimmers participated. Warren Laskowitz of the Hoosier Athletic Club placed 2nd and

Carbis Walker of the Cleveland Athletic Club placed 3rd. This is a shorter course than the 1914 course but based on the time, they were picking better currents.

On June 14th, 1925, Gertrude Ederle set a world record for the 150-yard freestyle in the Olympic Pool in Long Beach, Long Island. In a time of 1:42.6, she took a full second off the record, which she had set in February.[355] The next day, in a tune up for her English Channel attempt, she set the course record for the Battery to Sandy Hook swim of 7:11 on June 15, 1925. The next day she left for England for her 1st English Channel attempt.[356] Ms. Ederle was, also, the first woman to complete the Battery to Sandy Hook swim. She started the swim at 4:42 am at the Battery. The course took her down Buttermilk Channel on the east side of Governors Island. The current wasn't finished flooding at this point and she had a slug of it. She would occasionally switch over from the eight-beat crawl to using the sidestroke or breaststroke to talk with the crew during the swim. Conrad Hahn of Jersey City and Walter Wendt of Hoboken were the oarsmen on a rowboat accompanying her. She took no food or drinks during the swim and was slightly bothered by the salt water in her eyes.

At of the close of the 2004 marathon season, Gertrude Ederle still held the course record for the Battery to Sandy Hook swim. This is akin to finding out Babe Ruth still holds a record in baseball. What is this swim like? You leave the Battery at the beginning of an ebb current, striking out for a safe passage down through Lower New York Harbor. You pass just off shore of Governor's Island. Then you pass among the ships at anchor just off the main channel by Brooklyn. By this time the current has picked up speed and you are going so fast it looks like you are going to crash into Staten Island. At some point, you've crossed over the main channel and are now cruising past Staten Island. You go under the Verrazano Bridge high above your head and before you is the Atlantic Ocean getting wider every minute. You stay in the current and pull away from New York, on your right you see the Highlands and below them is the Hook. About this time, as you've drawn near to Sandy Hook, the tide turns and you've a two mile slug to shore. It's carrying you into Raritan Bay and you swim with everything left. You can't take a break here as the current will sweep you pass the Hook. The hours have ticked by and now the precious minutes wind down to the 7th hour and the 11th minute that a seventeen-year old girl in 1925, holder of 29 national and world records, took to complete this swim. It's been 79 years since anyone has swum this course. Except for Gertrude Ederle, interest in the swim waned when the New York Tribune stop publishing in 1924.

In 1925, President Calvin Coolidge sponsored a swimming meet in the Potomac River to decide the National amateur team championship over a 3-mile course. It was to be a perpetual challenge cup, called the President's Cup. The course ran from Chain Bridge to Georgetown and it was to be held under the auspices of the Washington Canoe Club. The first competition was held August 22, 1925. The AAU designated the event as a national championship event. Up to ten swimmers could compete from each club but only the first three finishers would score points. Since each swimmer was to be accompanied by a canoe, the Washington Canoe Club was a good choice to host the event. The winning team got to keep the cup for a year, returning to defend the title.[357]

There was no article about the President's Cup in the New York Times as this was three days after Gertrude Ederle failed in her first attempt to cross the Channel and all other swimming news was pushed into the background as the world held its breathe waiting for her 2nd attempt a few days later which also ended in failure. It also didn't help that upon her return, she accused her handler of incompetence in the press.[358] Her trainer, Jabez Wolfe who accused her of playing the ukulele instead of training, refuted these charges.[359] And so it went, a real brouhaha that wasn't settled until she finally crossed the Channel in 1926 to settle all arguments as they say, in the pool. Finally, a week after the first annual President's Cup, a photo appeared in the New York Times of Clarence Ross receiving the diamond-studded medal for the first place finish and the trophy on behalf of the NYAC for the 1st place team.³⁶⁰ This occurrence of one overriding news story stepping on another news items happens all the time. When the 14th Annual Manhattan Island Marathon Swim occurred on July 14, 1995, we had the great misfortune to compete on the day that Mickey Mantle, a New York Yankee baseball great, died. The press coverage for the Manhattan marathon swim that year was nil.

Let's look at the swim background of one star that swam on the national stage during this era: Ray Ruddy. Ray was the third of four sons of Joe Ruddy, the NYAC water polo great, all 1st class swimmers.³⁶¹ He was first mentioned in the press in 1926 for winning a 100-yard swim at Camp Ruddy run by his father at Lake Oscawana in a time of 1:08 for Boys under 16.³⁶² This swim camp was recognized nationally and many a national championship took place here including long distance swims of 4½ miles. The next year, at age 15, he was winning and making a name for himself in the 880-yard AAU championship at the Palisades Park lagoon at Bear Mountain in 11:38 held in late June, 1927.³⁶³ The interesting thing was that the day before this swim, his dad took him out of the Atlantic City 15-mile marathon swim after the 3rd hour while he was leading the field of nationally known marathon swimmers. A week later he took first in a 4½ swim in the Reynolds Channel in Long Beach, NY. The swim started at the Long Island Railroad Bridge and ended at the Atlantic City Bridge.³⁶⁴ Ruddy used the trademark NYAC six beat crawl and while at the time it was called a fast turn-over, his stroke count was only 42. In September of 1927, he returned to Atlantic City to compete in the 6th Annual Atlantic City Pageant one-mile swim between piers. His time for this swim was 27 minutes 26 seconds.³⁶⁵

When he turned 16 in 1928, Ruddy started swimming against international stars. In a meet at the Ravenshall Baths at Coney Island in a 50 yard pool, Ruddy touches out Albert Zorilla, the captain of the Argentine Olympic team, in the mile swim. The Olympics were scheduled a month later in Amsterdam. Johnny Weissmuller who was swimming for the Illinois Athletic Club gave an exhibition 100-yard swim at this meet and turned a 53.0.³⁶⁶ The next day, half the family got together for a swim meet and water polo match at the Olympia pool at Long Beach. In the water polo match, Joe Ruddy, Sr. and Ray played for the NYAC and Joe Ruddy, Jr., played for the Naval Academy in a losing cause. The star of that meet was Henry Matalene, the former Princeton captain who scored 25 points himself. Ray took first in the 440-yard freestyle in the swimming meet with a 3:40 (sic 5:40?).[367]

In the Olympics held in August of 1928, Ray placed second in his heat for the 1500 meters event with a time of 22:12.4. The other American of note swimming the 1500 meters was Clarence "Buster" Crabbe from Hawaii who in his elimination heat came in 3rd with a time of 20:17.8.[368] In the finals, Arne Borg of Sweden established an Olympic and World Record for the 1500 meters of 19:51.8 leaving Andrew Charlton of Australia in second, Buster Crabbe in third and Ruddy in fourth.[369] Ruddy made the finals of the 400 meters but came in last. In the 400 meters race, Zorilla of Argentina pulled an upset by beating Borg the favorite after trailing most of the race in second and third place and set an Olympic record of 5:01.6.[370]

A month following the Olympics, Ruddy was operated on for appendicitis successfully following a local meet where he set the metropolitan record for the 440 yard freestyle swim at New Rochelle, NY.[371] He noticed a pain and five days later he had the operation. Whether or not this affected his Olympic performance has to be judged against the effort of Dick Roth in a later Olympics. In the 1964 Tokyo Olympics Dick refused an operation preferring to use an ice pack the night prior to his swimming in the 400-meter Individual Medley. Making the start, he fell far behind in the butterfly but gained the lead in the last 100 yards of the freestyle to win the gold metal setting a new Olympic and World record. Upon returning to the United States, he had his appendix removed.[372]

After his Olympic exploits, Ray kept up a vigorous swim competition schedule and competed in the water polo trials for the following two Olympics with the NYAC water polo team. In both of these trials, the Los Angeles Athletic Club won the round-robin competition to represent the United States in water polo.[373] In a twist of fate, the NYAC played the Hungarian water polo team prior to the 1932 Olympics and lost 9-2.[374] Both Ray and Don Ruddy played in that game. Playing for the Hungarians who were undefeated in four years was Oliver Halassy, a one-legged swimmer[375] and future International Swimming Hall of Fame member. The Los Angeles AC was unable to score on the Hungarians during the 1932 Los Angeles Olympics causing them to take the Bronze metal behind the Germans who scored two points against the Hungarians.[376]

Following the 1928 Olympics, Ruddy competed for the NYAC in the President's Cup held over the Memorial Day weekend at the end of summer, something he had been doing since 1926, winning every year for six year straight.[377] The following week on September 8, 1928, he won the 17th annual Pawling marathon swim held in the Schuylkill River. The course was 3.5 miles from the Conshohocken Bridge to the Philadelphia Swimming Club located in Migon, Pennsylvania. His time was 1:01 in a current assisted swim.[378] This swim apparently was first contested in 1921.

In July of 1929, he returned to recapture the AAU senior long-distance swimming Championship he first won when he was 15. This contest was held over a 4½ mile course in Great South Bay near Massapequa along Long Island's south shore. The swim was from a point a half mile east of the causeway drawbridge near Jones's Inlet, down Goose Creek, then the Massapequa Canal, finally two laps in the Biltmore Shores lagoon. His winning time was 1:19.[379] In August, he broke five more records at the Park Inn pool at Rockaway, Long Island.[380]

Ray also began college at Columbia as a freshman in 1929. He competed for them over two semesters, was elected captain of the swim team[381] then dropped out in the spring semester of 1931 presumably for academic reasons.[382] In March of his freshman year he sets 3 world records for the 800, 600, and 550 yards swim at a meet in the Carnegie pool at Yale University.[383] Then he won the NCAA national championship for the 440 yard swim while still a freshman.[384] After leaving college, in the summer of 1931, while upstate with his family at Camp Ruddy, he and Joe Farley, another NYAC swimmer and boxer visited a dance pavilion at Lake Oscawana, NY. At some point they became involved in a fight where Joe Farley was stabbed three times. Ruddy was not injured and Farley recovered.[385]

Ruddy continued his winning way competing for the AAU championships in swimming and water polo year after year. In 1930, he again won the Metropolitan AAU senior one-mile event in 23:33 at the pool of the Lido Club in Long Beach, Long Island.[386] In September of 1931 Ray went up to Toronto, Canada, for an international competition winning the Canadian national exhibition 2-mile swim for amateurs, two years in a row. He competed against over 100 competitors in each swim. His fastest time in this event was 52 minutes.[387] For 1931, Ruddy's NYAC competition record totaled 54 first places, 4 seconds and one third.[388] For 1932, his NYAC competition record totaled 46 first places, four seconds and one third.[389]

In 1933 he won his seventh AAU long-distance swimming championship in a two-mile swim at Riis Park, Belle Harbor, Long Island in a time of 1:02 with a furious sprint at the end. He was competing against Edward Lee who was the national titleholder in this event.[390] He won the Metropolitan AAU mile swim for eight consecutive years. In the last year that he won this competition, 1934, he had stopped competing from September of 1933 until this event held at the Jerome Cascade pool most probably due to pressing financial concerns brought on by the Depression. He won the event in a time of 24:21.[391] Even in a year when didn't compete as much, he came in 4th in the NYAC annual competition totals. In 1936 during the Olympic year he came in 3rd in the NYAC competition totals. Ray Ruddy died December 4, 1938, from a fall down a flight of stairs in an accident eerily similar to the Gertrude Ederle accident that ended her swimming career.[392]

In one of the few accounts of early Japanese swimming, Setsu Mishimura, attempted the English Channel on August 28, 1925. He didn't get too far, only covering about two miles in an hour and three quarters. There was one small difference about this swim that was noticed and commented upon: Setsu wore a bathing suit and a dress that reached down to his knees.[393] Except that there was a slug of reporters over at the Channel because of Gertrude Ederle and he wore the unusual dress, this attempt would not have received any press. He was a professor at the Kyoto Law School who visited Europe quite often during the summers. His swimming resume includes a seven-day "lake tour" in Japan where he swam 25 miles daily and crossing the Yangtze River in Shanghai, China, over a distance of 20 miles in 3 hours.[394] This was as respectable an attempt as J. B. Johnson's attempt in 1872. Around this time, Japanese swimmers were quite competitive in pool swims; Katsuo Takaishi was winning numerous events over 100, 200, and 400 meters distances in dual meets with other nations.[395] Yasuji Miyazaki broke the 1928 Olympic mark set by Johnny Weissmuller for the 100-meter freestyle on August 2, 1932 at the 1932 Olympics with a time of 58.0 seconds.[396] In a look at a swimming power in the later part of the 20th century, the New York Times filed a report in 1930 about sports in the Soviet Union. A swimming club at the Dynamo, a sporting facility on the outskirts of Moscow had a pool located on the Moscow River. Pools were tanks with boards set across the pool at a regulation distance. The men's record for the 100-yard freestyle was 59 seconds.[397]

Because the author lived in Port Washington, New York, for years, the following event is mentioned. Manhasset Bay was the venue for a swimming festival in 1925 held in conjunction with a power boat race. It was not well organized. There was a four hour delay while a boat was located that could serve as the 100 yard mark before the races could begin. Plus the location wasn't measured nor did the vessel drop anchor. During the 300-yard race, the boat drifted away causing the favored swimmer to come in second in the medley race. The individual medley swim in those days consisted of 3 strokes: breast, back and freestyle, so only 3 laps were needed for this race. Nationally ranked swimmers who attended were Walter Spence and Clarence Ross. In the 100-yard race, the boat drifted again causing one end of the course to be nearer the beach, favoring the eventual winner, George Fissier.[398] The location of the swim was most likely at a private club, the Sand Point Bath Club, now closed. The club was built on a sand spit jutting out into Manhasset Bay. One feature of the swimming festival was diving. The Club was quite popular during the Big Bands era with bands appearing more often than named swimmers. Swimmers could sit in front of their cabanas and gaze out at the sailboat races with the Manhattan skyline in the distant background.

On August 27, 1925, Otto Kemmerich, who was a well-known German distance swimmer, swam alone with no escort from the tip of Fermarn Island, Staber Huk, Germany, across Mecklenburger Bay in the southern portion of the Baltic Sea toward Warnemunde, a small town in Germany along the coast near Rostock, Germany. He took with him a thermos bottle of beef tea, a compass and a watch. Swimming from west to east, after 22 hours and 36 miles, he came ashore at his destination.[399] In choosing this route, he avoided the current that plagued Jenny Kammersgaard in her swim from Denmark to the same destination in 1938. The difficulty of verifying the swim is one thing; the foolishness of swimming alone is another.

Often swimmers will swim just off shore along the beach outside the breakers unaccompanied while training. If they get in trouble, it's a short distance to shore. It's much, much safer to swim with a buddy or even have them follow along from shore. Another method is to limit the distance to just those sections of the beach where a lifeguard is available; I've done laps back and forth. There are far too many cases of swimmers swimming alone never to be heard from again. In researching old newspapers for this book, I've mentioned drowned was a common headline, presumed drowned was a close second. It means they couldn't find the body but the individual was last seen swimming.

Byron Summers, 28, of Glendale California established a new record for the San Pedro Channel on April 25, 1927 crossing in 13 hours 35 minutes.[400] He swam from the isthmus on Santa Catalina to Point Vincente on the mainland. He lowered the record set by George Young of Canada, a winner of the Wrigley $25,000 marathon, by two hours and ten minutes. His stroke count average was 46 strokes a minute.

A lake swim that proved of considerable difficulty was Lake George, New York, in the Adirondacks. In 1927 lured by a prize fund of $6500 148 swimmers registered for a 28-mile swim from The Hague to Old Fort Henry. The list of swimmers included many of the well known distance swimmers still around and competing: Lottie Schoemmell from New York, Ernest Vierkotter[401] of Germany, and Charles Toth of Boston, all channel veterans and a number of other swimmers of more recent fame.[402] The race started at 9:45am on July 12, 1927. The water temperature was less than 60 degrees. What is unusual about this swim was that only one person finished. Forty-one contestants went to the hospital, the majority for cramps. The winner was Edward F. Keating, age 24, who was a swimming instructor for the Board of Education in New York City. He literally blew away the competition in 18:47 finishing at 4:32am the next morning to the cheers of the remaining spectators. His nearest competitor was Ernest Vierkotter. They were fairly even until 8pm when Edward pulled ahead. When Ernest pulled out of the race at midnight, Edward was 3 miles ahead. The winner took home $5000 and the lure of $1500 for 2nd place keep some die-hard plugging away until William Erickson of the Bronx, the last competitor, quit the race after 29 hours but still 3 miles shy of the finish. A Lucy Diamond of Brooklyn came within a mile of the finish before dropping out after 19 hours of swimming. Edward had learned to swim in the traditional NY city method, his brothers taught him swimming off the piers of lower Manhattan. In 1923, when he was twenty, he won a ten-mile swim in the Delaware River at Philadelphia for the national long distance championship.[403] The results of this swim put a damper on future competitions in the lake.

Lake George was next swum in competition in 1948 over a 12-mile course. The competiton attracted another large number of contestants, 127 to be exact including Keo Nakama from Hawaii but this time only $6000 was riding on the outcome.[404] Jerry

Kerschner, age 23, of Ohio was the eventual winner in a time of 4:59 from Bolton Landing to Head of the Lake.[405]

In a more pleasant environment, three women crossed the Great South Bay on July 9, 1927. The winner of that race was Marion Robartes, age 17, in a time of 3:53.[406] The course was from Watch Island Hotel to Patchogue, Long Island. The Great South Bay is an inland bay of shallow depths protected from the Atlantic Ocean by some barrier islands, most notable among these is Fire Island. Coney Island is first along this chain of barrier islands along Long Island's southern shore. Using a slightly different course, from Fire Island Lighthouse to the Bayshore bathing beach, a distance of 7 ½ miles, was won on August 25, 1928 by Terry Craven of Richmond Hill in a time of 3:18. The record at that time for this course was 3:05 from an earlier swim.[407] In 1929, a 9-mile swim was arranged from Fire Island to Heckscher Island by the Long Island Parks Commission.[408]

A more unpleasant swim was across Newark Bay on July 23, 1927, when William Irvine of Newark, New Jersey, on a bet of $30 swam from Newark to Bayonne, New Jersey, starting at 10 o'clock at night. The distance is approximately a half mile. It required 5 gallons of gasoline to remove the grease that had accumulated on his body during the swim.[409]

An unimaginably cold swim for distance was undertaken by Hilda Mitz, age 18, when she swam down the Danube from Melk to Vienna on May 23, 1928. The distance was 75 miles in eleven hours in a water temperature of 48 degrees Fahrenheit.[410] There was no information if the swimmer used an early version of a wet suit. This possibly inspired the next distance swimmer, Pedro Candiotti of Argentina. He accomplished what no swimmer before has ever managed. He established a distance record and an endurance record for the ages. He swam in the Parana River more than 188 miles in 67 hours and 10 minutes. This feat was accomplished on March 11, 1930.[411] He swam from Goya to Santa Fe down the Parana River. This river is known to be a habitat for carnivorous piranha fish. While this effort was stupendous, more was to come from Senor Candiotti. The following year he made an attempt to swim from Santa Fe to Buenos Aires but gave up after 71 hours and 55 minutes. In 1933 he made a non-stop swim of 236 miles from Corrientes to Santa Fe establishing a new distance mark. Finally, in 1935, he pulled out all the stops and swam from Santa Fe to General Uriburu[412], a distance of 287 miles in 87 hours and 19 minutes.[413]

Late summer of 1929 brought a slew of swims. On July 30, 1929, Sadie Schwartz, age 19, swam from Philadelphia to Wilmington, Delaware, in 13:50 in the Delaware River. She was hailed as the first person to ever swim this far along the course, a distance of more than 20 miles. She was a Temple University student who was in training for the Wrigley marathon swim to be held later that summer in Toronto as part of professional circuit.[414] A twenty-mile portion of Savannah River was first swum on August 5, 1929. F. H. Sills, Jr., swam from the City Hall Dock in Savannah to Tybee Island at the mouth of the river in a little over 7 hours. He was able to accomplish a swim of approximately the same length as the Delaware River swim in a shorter time because he timed his swim to utilize the currents rather than oppose them. This was his third attempt so it took him a few tries to get it right. The swim started just before dusk and he finished after 3 in the morning.[415]

Lake Geneva was crossed in 1929. Corry Liebbrand, age 21, from Utrecht swam from Lausanne to Geneva on August 15th, 1929, in 35 hours. The distance was 60 kilometers, 37.3 miles. The course doesn't cover the entire length of the lake because the lake is shaped somewhat like a boomerang. Using this model, she swam from one end of the boomerang straight along one wing then to the other edge straight opposite. The entire lake distance is even longer. She started at 6:30 am on a Wednesday, August 14th, swam through the night, and finished at 5:40 PM Thursday, August 15th. They think they were lost for several hours during the night. This is believed to be the first swim of this course.[416]

Another international swim but a bit shorter happened on September 24, 1929. Two teenagers, Anita Grew, daughter of Joseph Grew, the US Ambassador to Turkey, and Duncan Elliott, age 13, along with Representative Roy G. Fitzgerald of Dayton, Ohio swam across the Bosporus near the mouth of the Black Sea. The Representative was on a tour of Constantinople. Their swim only took them about a half an hour.[417] Two years later, Anita became the first person to swim the length of the Bosporus on August 18, 1931, in a time of 5:10.[418] She began the swim just before 5am and finished just before 10am. Her father accompanied her in a boat called a caique. On September 7th, the Turkish Water Sports Federation honored her with a silver medal. In the intervening year, 1930, on August 4th, an 8-year old child named Barbara Tompkins swam across the Bosporus from Beykoz, Turkey to Europe, a distance of a mile and a quarter. No time was recorded. Her father worked for the Standard Oil at the time and was assigned to Istanbul.[419] One would venture a guess that work was slow over in this area of the world.

Going from the youngest to ever swim the Borporus to a senior citizen and around the globe, an Anna Van Skike swam 20 miles on her 70th birthday. The date was August 10, 1930 and the course was from the Venice Pier off Santa Monica, California, to the Santa Monica Canyon Lighthouse and back. She was accompanied by a rowboat with two men in it. The trip took 12 hours and 10 minutes.[420] Happy birthday, Anna! Since we are in this festive mood, let's consider what Mercedes Gleitze did on her honeymoon. After marrying her sweetheart, Patrick Carey, the first woman to swim the Gibraltar Straits went to Turkey and swam the Hellespont at its widest point in 2:45. She was married on August 9, 1930, and by August 16 she was off stroking.[421] Back home, William Sadlo established the Battery to Coney Island record of 3:39.[422]

In the same year, 1931, and on the same date as Anita Grew's swim, September 24, another swim came to a close in the Baltic Sea. Alexander Laas, age 26, from Estonia, completed a staged swim across the Gulf of Finland from Reval to Porkkala Island. Reval is also known as Revel was a fortified town along the southern entrance to the Gulf of Finland that surrendered to Peter the Great in 1710, now part of Estonia.[423] Estonia first attained independence in 1918 and after WWII and the Cold War, attained independence again in 1991. Reval has been renamed Tallinn and is the Capital of Estonia. Porkkala is a town on a small peninsula that sticks out into the Gulf of Finland just to the west of Helsinki. The total distance swam was 40 miles. The first stage on August 17th, 1931, was from Reval to Nargo Island. The next day he swam the remaining distance, 25 miles in 19 hours in 45° Fahrenheit degree waters to Finland.[424] The swim was in waters that are at 60° North Latitude. The Gulf of Finland is fed from the Neva River that runs through St. Petersburg at the head of the Gulf. The Neva River, 46 miles long, connects the Gulf and a large lake called Ladoga. St. Petersburg was founded by Peter the Great as the "Venice of the North."

The Connecticut River was the venue for an 18-mile race won in 1931 by Henry Gauthier, age 24, of the Hartford YMCA in a time of 9:44. He broke the previous record set in 1926 by Virginia Doncoes, also of Hartford, of 11:55.[425] The race goes from the State Street dock in Hartford to the Middletown Yacht Club. While Hartford is considerably inland, the Connecticut River is still tidal at this point. The ebb is considerably stronger than the flood so any swim below Hartford needs to take the current into consideration for much as a 1-knot current can occur opposing a swim. The Delaware River saw some activity in 1931 when a girl and a boy swam the ten miles between the Vine Street wharf in Philadelphia to the Riverton Yacht Club Pier. The girl, Ida Mae Berg, age 14 and crippled with infantile paralysis, completed the swim in 3:30 on July 29th.[426] Charles Holt, Jr., age 12, swam the distance on August 15th in 2:30. Norman Ross holds the record for this distance and venue of 1:59 set nearly 10 years earlier.[427] In what could be the first recorded crossing of the upper Chesapeake Bay, Sarah Harris, age 20, a student at Virginia State Teachers College at Fredericksburg and Edwin Smith, age 24, of Betterton, left from Havre de Grace to Betterton on the Eastern Shore, a distance of 7 miles in 5 hours.[428] Havre de Grace is right at the very top of the Bay where the Susquehanna River empties out into Chesapeake Bay. Betterton is on the Maryland shore nearly directly south of Havre de Grace.

Swims were happening all across the country. Before Alcatraz Island became a Federal prison, Anastasia Scott, age 19, swam to shore from Alcatraz on October 17, 1933 in a time of 43 minutes.[429] Her father was stationed at the Army disciplinary barracks on the island and the weather conditions were said to be perfect. A small boat for the mile and one half distance accompanied her. Lake Michigan saw some swimming activity during the Thirties. William Randolph Hearst newspapers sponsored a professional swim with a $10,000 purse. The winner in 7:54 was Marvin Nelson of Iowa.[430] It was his second win in Lake Michigan having won the inaugural event the previous year. The event was held on July 22, 1934. In the same year, Frank Pritchard of Buffalo was the winner of a twelve-mile professional swim between Sarnia, Ontario and St. Clair, Michigan in a time of 3:57.[431]

Another lake swim of merit would be Lake Tahoe. Lake Tahoe is a lake at the intersection of the bend in the border between the States of California and Nevada. This was first swum on August 24, 1931 and carried over into the wee hours of the 25th by Myrtle Huddleson. She traveled from Deadman's Point, Nevada, to Tahoe City, California in 22:53.[432] The distance was reported as 20 miles.

In 1935 an article appeared in the New York Times that announced everyone was swimming. Swimming was a sport that had changed; being a woman and age were no longer barriers to swimming. This was the unofficial announcement of the end of the crusade by the New York Times to teach people how to swim.[433] No longer would we see editorials bemoaning the drowning of hapless individuals or the need for women to learn to swim. The mechanism that undertook the instruction of the American public had succeeded and continues to do so to this very day. It is a very worthwhile achievement. Countless lives were saved because a child learned to swim. The Manhattan Island Foundation continues this work as their charity for city children.

The Soviet Union produced a marathon swimmer on August 20, 1935 when Nicolai Malin swam 50 kilometers in the Black Sea near Sochi.[434] The twelfth annual President's Cup was held on August 24, 1935, with Harry Tresnack winning the three mile Potomac River swim.[435] On June 14, 1936, Hazel Cunningham swam the Great Salt Lakes from Antelope Island to the shore settlement of Black Rock in 7:10. The distance was reported as 11 miles, it was her second attempt.[436] In 1937, Elwood Woodling of Ohio State University won the George Pawling Trophy. He set the course record for this trophy in a 3.5-mile distance down the Schuykill River near Philadelphia with a time of 55 minutes 6 seconds. This was a record and his second straight win.[437] The President's Cup was won by Steve Wozniak, a Canadian, in a time of 1:52.4. He beat Elwood Woodling, the defending champion by 25 yards in the win.[438]

Candiotti's long swim inspired Clarence Giles in 1939 to set a distance record and he just happened to have a river near-by that runs for 671 miles, the Yellowstone which is the river that runs through Yellowstone National Park. Clarence was a 41-year old auctioneer from Glendive, Montana. He began his swim on Friday, June 30, 1939 at Billings, Montana. Three days later, he arrived back in Glendive having swum 288 miles down the Yellowstone River in 77½ hours.[439] The swim was made during high water. He floated on his back for a good portion, smoking cigars, and his body was coated with axle grease. He'd have to swim some to make sure he stayed in the current but once he was in the current, he could relax. He, also, was bruised and quite tired when he was welcomed home by a tumultuous crowd of 4,000, possibly the entire town. You might not think of a small town in Montana as having a marathon swimmer but when he arrived, he *was* Glendive's marathon swimmer. He beat Candiotti's record by 1 mile and 10 hours. During the swim he was greased frequently to counteract the affects of the cold. He left the water once for a few minutes (estimated at a half an hour) due the escort boat having bent its prop on a rock and they stopped to attend to this matter and/or due to an eye infection.[440] This is less than Candiotti who was reported to have left the water a number of times during his swim.[441]

Swims were happening around the world. Nassau in the Bahamas annually held a 2.5-mile swim from Prince George's dock to the dock of the Fort Montagu Beach Hotel in Montagu Bay.[442] The Mississippi River was the venue for an annual ten-mile swim from Lagrange, Missouri to Quincy that started in 1931.[443]

In a swim of giant proportions in 1938, a 19-year old swimming star, Jenny Kammersgaard, from Denmark, swam across the Mecklenburger Bay at the lower extreme of the Baltic Sea from Gedser, the southernmost point of Denmark to Nienhagen, Germany, a small town just to the west of Warnemeunde. Her route paralleled the ferry service between Rostock, Germany, and Denmark. The distance between these two points is 28 miles. The Baltic Sea discharges mostly fresh water at the surface with the heavier salt water underneath. The tide was a factor in her swim. The currents took her over a 37-mile course. At one point, she took 9 hours to cover a four-mile stretch. Her diet consisted of fried eel and fruit salad. The young lady swam through two nights to reach her goal on July 30, 1938, taking 40:09 for the swim.[444] She said she could have swum even longer if needed. Her arrival so enthralled the populous that even the arrival of the Netherlands royal couple, Princess Juliana and Prince Bernhardt with their infant daughter, for a holiday at the estate of Count Ahlefeldt in nearby Ourupgaard was ignored. The municipalities of Warenmeunde and Rostock held a dinner in her honor the next night. The next year, on August 11, 1939, she swam back along the same course in a time of 34 hours.[445] In 1937 she is reported to have swum from Gniben on Zealand Island, Denmark, across the Kattegat to Klint, Jutland in a time of 29:37. Jenny uses breaststroke in her swims. In an unaccompanied swim in Ore Sound, Jenny at age 25 swam from Skodsbor, Sweden to Gilleleje, Sweden. She took 43 hours to complete this thirty-mile swim in 1943.[446]

Figure 15 The Baltic Sea swims of Otto Kemmerich and Jenny Kammersgaard across Mecklenburger Bay to Warenmeunde near Rostock, East Germany. Jenny follwed the ferry route and Otto swam SE from Fehmarn Island.

As if there was a foreshadowing of the darkening clouds of war, the reports mentioned Jenny received congratulations from King Christian and Chancellor Adolf Hitler. The first swim received a large article in the New York Times but the second was a brief sentence or two. It was as if people need a distraction in 1938 but by 1939, nothing was important. Very little happened in swimming over the next decade with the outbreak of hostilities. One swim that bears mentioning during this period of time is a swim to and from Corrigador, Philippines, by Lieutenant Damon "Rocky" Gauss, which is covered later in this book. The only other swim besides A. A. U. sponsored swim meets happened in July of 1940. John Sigmund swam down the Missouri River for

297 miles in a time of 89:49 from St. Louis. The location of the arrival is unknown according to Conrad Wennerberg's book.[447]

Back in the United States after WWII, swims were being organized on both coasts. In a tune up for an English Channel swim, 16 year old Shirley Frances of Somerset, Massachusetts, swam from the Battery to Coney Island in 5:40 on July 10, 1949. She had competed in the 1948 Lake George swim with 100 other swimmers finishing in 10th place.[448]

Tom Park was a well-regarded professional swimmer who established numerous records in marathon swimming. He was a Canadian truck driver. On July 2, 1950, when he was 26 he participated in a race from the beach at Matunuck, Rhode Island to Block Island. Matunuck is about 3 miles west of Point Judith. The race was called off after 12 of the official 15 miles were completed in a little over 7 hours due to fog. Tom was in the lead and took home $1000 for his efforts. The current had an effect in this race, as Tom should have completed over twenty miles in seven hours.[449]

In a different year, Jim Doty of New England Marathon Swimming Association swam with Horacio Iglesias of Argentina, Abdel-Latif Abo-Heif of Egypt, and others in a professional swim to Block Island. Jim dropped out as did many of the other swimmers, but Iglesias and Abo-Heif completed the swim from Point Judith Pond, Rhode Island, to Great Salt Pond, Block Island, in a tie. The tie was their means to secure an even split of the 1st and 2nd place monies, $5000 and $4000 respectively. A third man finished but he walked across a sand bar and was disqualified. When he complained, he was given place money just to keep him quiet. This was a professional race. Even the tie was something the swimmers negotiated just before the finish in Great Salt Pond. Jim Doty revealed they were discussing who felt like sprinting to the finish to win first place. After that swim, neither of them felt like it.[450]

On October 5, 1958, Greta Andersen, who by now was a housewife in California having retired from Olympic competition, became the first person to swim both ways across the Catalina

Channel in one swim. Her swim to the mainland was phenomenal, taking 10:49, breaking both the men and women's existing records by nearly two hours. Her return trip after a half hour rest was completed in 15:36.[451] On Dec 10, 1972, Kenneth Crutchlow, swam from Alcatraz to San Francisco (in 35 degree weather). This swim was a repeat of the swim by Anastasia Scott and would merit little attention as it was not the first nor was it a record except it was to publicize a running, swimming, biking trip from London to Dundee, Scotland he was planning.[452] Sounds like a triathlon to me. The triathlon aspect was so important they forgot to mention the time for the swim. Two years later, in 1974, Mike Garabaldi swam the same course in 15 minutes and 20 seconds. His finish was at the Aquatic Park at the city's edge directly south of Alcatraz Island.

The early 50's saw a slew of swims across Lake Tahoe. On August 16, 1952, Bill Long, age 27, swam a slightly shorter "across" the lake swim of 17 miles from Cave Rock to Meeks Bay in 12 hours. On June 23, 1954, a multi-talented football player named Bert Capps completed the same swim in 7:12. A young lady, Glenda Ortlip, age 18, of San Francisco swam the same course in 7:57 on August 15, 1954. The first lengthwise swim was on August 28, 1955, by Fred Rogers, age 29, from San Francisco in 19:06.[453] Ashby Harper at age 68 swam the length of Lake Tahoe, California, in 14:14, a distance of 32.7 kilometers or 17.6 nautical miles in 1985.[454] Ashby Harper had previously swum Manhattan, the English Channel, and was one of marathon swimming most loved swimmer. To put his accomplishment of swimming the English Channel in perspective, he would recall what a friend said when he mentioned that he was planning to swim across the English Channel, "I admire your spirit but I question your intelligence."[455]

Another lake swim saw a slew of swim in the early 50's and that was the Sea of Galilee. The distance is 13.5 miles down the length. An 11-mile section was first swum in 1944 by Yekhezkiel Isaac of Tel Aviv in 9:37. In another lake swim, across Lake Ontario, in 1955 a swimmer was reported lost. Snowlton was attempting to swim across the lake from Niagara-on-the-Lake, Ontario, to Toronto. Starting on September 17th, it was early in the morning on the 18th, about 3 am when his Clifford coach, Hilton Middleburgh, looked at the ship's compass taking his eyes off the swimmer. When he looked back, the swimmer was nowhere to be seen. Hilton wasn't the only one along; accompanying Clifford were two boats holding a total of six persons. A day later, they were still searching for the swimmer.[456] When I organized my first night swim, the escort boat pilot introduced me to the light stick concept marketed under the brand name of Cyalume.[457] We tried it out and were instantly sold upon its value. You could look out in the darkness and instantly spot your swimmer, provided they were on the surface. I introduced this technology to the Manhattan swim and it became a policy on all night swims. I normally pack a spare in my bag just in case a swim goes long and extends past dusk.

Swimming across national borders was Florence Chadwick, age 33, who in 1953 swam the Gibraltar Strait in 5:06.[458] She swam using a 30 stroke per minute breaststroke on September 20, 1953, from Point Marroqui, Spain to the northern most point of Spanish Morocco. This time beat the previous best time set in 1950 by Jorge Sugden of Argentina of 6:59 by two hours.[459] Her record lasted for a month before Baptista Pereira of Portugal cut two minutes off the time on October 25, 1953.[460] To give you an idea of the difference between swim eras and stroke improvement, the current record for this swim is under 3 hours. Subsequent to this swim Florence Chadwick announced that after a swim of the Bosporus, she would retire.

Another swimmer who swam across national borders was, Bert Thomas, age 29, who in 1955 swam from Port Angeles, Washington, to Victoria, Victoria Island, Canada, across the Strait of Juan de Fuca making an international swim. The distance across the Strait is 18.3 miles and he completed the swim in 11:10.[461] Bert was a former frogman for the Marines and was employed as a logger. This was his fifth try and the first time he started at Port Angeles. This seemed to make all the difference in the success of the swim. He picked up two money prizes for being the first person to cross the Strait. The next year saw quite a cluster of marathon swimmer including Marilyn Bell of Canada. Cliff Lunsden made the second successful crossing in early August followed on August 18, 1956, by Amy Hiland in a time of 10:51.[462] Marilyn Bell set the record at 10:39 a short time later.[463]

Other swims across waters bridging two land masses of the same nation included David Hart, age 22, who swam four miles across the Mackinac Straits at the site of the Mackinac Bridge near Cheboygan, Michigan, on August 18, 1956. His time was 1:57 for the swim.[464] The Mackinac Straits connect two bodies of water, Lake Michigan and Lake Huron. The bridge connects the Lower Peninsula of Michigan with the Upper Peninsula of Michigan. The other swim was by Florence Chadwick, age 36, who swam the Bristol Channel, a distance of 14 miles, on August 5, 1957, near the end of her career in a time of 6:07.[465] The course she swum was from Weston-Super-Mare, England, to Penarth, Wales at the widest part of the mouth of the Severn. The channel, an estuary of the River Severn, separates South Wales from South West England. Caprice Schaefer, a recreational swimmer, recalls swimming in the Bristol Channel near Weston-Super-Mare and coming out of the water covered in an orange residue in 1989.

In 1952, two politicians swam across the Bosporus in a demonstration of swimming prowess and political savvy: George C. McGhee, the American Ambassador to Turkey and Senator Russell B. Long of Louisiana. Not missing an opportunity for publicity, Florence Chadwick, of San Diego, California in 1953 swam across the Bosporus in a time of 1:14 shortly after her Gibraltar swim.[466] The Bosporus width is 5 miles at its widest. Interest then changed to swimming the length when Carlos Ritter, a New York native, became the first man to swim the length in 1955.[467]

Staten Island has only been swum around once. In 1961, Palmer Donnelly of Perth Amboy, NJ, completed the 35-mile swim on August 29th in 25:10.[468] The swim has four tide changes in it, making it difficult to plan and Donnelly spent some time at various points around the Island waiting for the tide to change in his favor. This was his second try having failed to complete the swim the previous year. Mr. Donnelly wore packets of shark repellant and was accompanied by armed divers in a small boat. His precautions seem extreme today but at that time, few marathon swims were being attempted. He was paced at various times by his wife, Ginny, and two brothers. The completion of the swim attracted 15,000 onlookers and a flotilla of boats. His diet for the swim consisted of hot tea, honey, and beef broth. Mr. Donnelly was a captain of the Perth Amboy lifeguards.

Hard to believe that Huntington Park, California, could generate a cold water swimmer but they did. Mary Margaret Revell on July 16, 1962, swam 10 miles through the Mackinac Straits. The water temperature ranged in the low 40's and she was in the water for 7:28.[469] A year later at age 24 she completed a swim from the Black Sea through the Bosporus to the Sea of Marmara in July of 1962. The distance was 19 miles completed in a time of 4:53.[470] The Turkish Swimming Federation recorded the swim. In he previous week she had completed a double across the Dardanelles, the entrance at the other end of the Sea of Marmara, in a time of 2:46. On this trip to the Mediterranean, she swam a double across the Messina Straits in 5:22.[471] Supposedly, the waters between Turkey on the eastern shore and Istanbul on the western shore were named after the first person to have crossed the river. Miss Revell set the bar for future performances in this region having caught a favorable tide. The series of straits and seas are the inland waterway connecting the Mediterranean to the Russian heartland and is considered the separation of Europe from Asia. In ancient classical literature, the Dardanelles were called Hellespont meaning Sea of Helle, named for the daughter of Athamas of Greek mythology who drowned there.

The early sixties saw Lake Tahoe swum lengthwise by a woman on her third attempt. On July 29, 1962, Erline Christopherson swam 17 miles from Baldwin Beach on the southern shore to Dollar Point on the northern shore in 13:17.[472] Lake Tahoe has been most recently swum in 2003 by Kevin

Murphy in a time of 13:56. His distance for the length was 22 miles. His boatman was Don Dalkin from San Diego.[473]

In 1965 the International Swimming Hall of Fame pool open to the public in Ft. Lauderdate. Three years later, the museum had it's grand opening. The Hall's first president was James "Doc" Councilman and its present president is Mark Spitz.[474]

Chairman Mao Tse-tung on July 16, 1966, at age 72 swam 11 miles of the Yangtze River's nearly 4000-mile length near Wuhan in China in 65 minutes.[475] Oddly, this information was not well published and the world only heard of this occurrence by way of diplomatic conversation regarding the health of the Chinese leader.[476] Then the Chinese decided to publicize it as an 8-mile swim before 5000 participants in the 11th annual[477] swim "Across the Yangtze" contest.[478] As proof, a photo was offered that evoked considerable discussion as to its authenticity.[479] Besides inspiring millions of Chinese to take up swimming as their duty,[480] one man chose to swim to freedom. It was reported on August 8, 1967, in Taiwan that Li Yao-sheng swam from the Amoy on the mainland of China to a Nationalist occupied island called Quemoy, a distance of about 6 miles off the Chinese coast in about 18 hours.[481]

In 1967, a 41-year-old Army Signal Corp officer, Lt. Col. Stewart Evans, swam from the Farallon Island located off the California coast to San Francisco. He was the first person to make this difficult swim. He came ashore at Point Bonita, on the northern shore of the straits leading into the Golden Gate. He completed the distance of 34 miles in 13:45.[482]

In 1972, Benson Huggard and six other fellow police officers[483] swam by relay from Montauk, Long Island, to Coney Island along the southern shore of Long Island.[484] The entire swim took 4½ days of continuous swimming starting at Montauk Point on August 9th until the 13th when they finished 150 miles away at Sheepshead Bay, Brooklyn. So serious were they about the swimming, when their escort boat at one point went aground on a sandbar in Hampton Bays, they swam circles around it until the tide lifted the boat off the bottom. This appears to be the longest continuous swim in elapsed time and distance by relay. One thing we learn from this swim is to have a 2nd support boat available.

Lake Ontario saw some spectacular swims including the first swim from north to south by Diana Nyad in 18:20 on August 16-17, 1974.[485] In a professional swim race across Lake Ontario in 1978, John Kinsella set a course record for the south to north direction of 13: 49.[486]

The Yellowstone River saw another attempt at the distance record by a young man, Joe Macaig, age 20, over July 1 to July 4th, 1976. He swam 292 miles from Billings, Montana to near the Interstate 94 Bridge downstream of Glendive, Montana in 70:42.[487] In the press leading up to the swim, his swim routine was to include stopping for 5 minutes every hour, walking around bridges and diversion dams and he planned on renting a wet suit. It's hard to affix the level of swimming done by any of these river floats but at least Macaig worked on his floating skills having managed a 35-hour float in preparation. Nor does it make sense to swim out of the current to stop and rest then swim back into the current. I think once the swim started, conditions dictated what the swimmer could and couldn't do. It was hard for the rubber raft to keep up with him and the support crew even lost sight of him for an hour. From the reports, he only held on once when a log struck him in the chest and he held on to recover his breath.

The greatest challenges are often undertaken by the "uninformed?" That doesn't mean they can't learn. Give Sean O'Connell, a lecturer in mathematics, 22 weeks and he's ready to take on a crircumswim of Bermuda, a 47-mile open-ocean journey. He started at 1.5 miles, trained in the ocean exclusively, learned the perils and challenges. Two practice swims of twelve hours and eighteen further increased his distance and confidence and his resistance to nausea. Midway through his training he started considering the shark danger. Undoubtably, he calculated the odds. His solution for jelly fish? The pain only last for a few minutes so he'd swim through the pain. In his first attempt on July 9th, during one section of the swim, the current held him in check for 8 hours. His team strategized on how to beat the current and elected for the shallow water approach. Three weeks later on August 19th, a calm day, he set off again on the swim and prevailed over currents, nausea, vomiting, and a final three-mile swim that was trance-like where he was kept awake with a torch shining in his face to guide him. After 43:27, Sean could collect on the $1000 bet that has helped raise thousands for the Bermuda Physically Handicapped Association.[488]

In a "one off" swim that parallels the Battery to Sandy Hook swim promoted by the New York Tribune in the 1920's, George Kauffmann swam from the Battery to Keansburg, NJ, on September 24, 1978. He claims to have beaten the woman marathoner, Gertrude Ederle, time of 7:11 for the Battery to Sandy Hook distance. The distance claimed for the complete swim was 16 miles in a time of 12 hours.[489] It's difficult to claim a swim from the Battery to Sandy Hook and at the same time claim a swim from the Battery to Keansburg, NJ.

In July of 1979, a group of swimmers organized themselves to achieve a lifetime goal of swimming across the Long Island Sound in what was basically a one-off event. Here is their story:

A Swim for Muscular Dystrophy Across Long Island Sound

I grew up on Long Island Sound. After becoming a proficient swimmer on the Milford High School swim team, I would look at Long Island and say to myself, "I am going to swim across this someday." Eight years later, I married into a swimming family and happened to mention this goal to my sister-in-law, Marcia Brisson. Shortly thereafter, she coordinated a swim across the Sound to raise funds for Muscular Dystrophy and I was her first entry. On Saturday July 21, 1979, eight of us dove into Long Island Sound at Eaton's Neck Point.

It was a perfect day for a long-distance swim, the weather was a bit foggy, but the water was extremely calm. We donned our bathing caps and greased up with vaseline just before diving in to protect our skin from the salt and dirt in the water. We waved good-bye to well wishers on the shore and dove in. Everything was perfect until we heard the sirens and saw the blinking lights of two Coast Guard ships bearing down on us about a mile and a half out.

They intended to enforce the one-boat-per-swimmer rule, but after some negations, said they would join our escort patrol. We swam together as a group and soon we had a small entourage of pleasure craft. The water warmed up during the day and little clear jellyfish increased in numbers until we were swimming in the equivalent of tapioca pudding.

Figure 16 Lunch break on the MDA swim. Don't touch the boat and who has the mayonaise?

As we approached Norwalk harbor, the Coast Guard swung into action, busily chasing harbor boat traffic away from us. Norwalk radio station WNLK's sent a boat to join the escort brigade. As we approached the Norwalk shore we could see people standing on the rocks, cheering us on. Five hours later we emerged, tired but triumphant, on the shores of Rowaton Point of Norwalk, Connecticut, eight miles away. My wife Jane and her sister Marcia gave a $2,000 check to the Jerry LewisTtelethon on Labor Day later that summer. Recollection contributed by Ben Siebecker, PE.

On August 20, 1979, Diana Nyad, swam from North Bimini off the Florida Coast to Juno Beach, Florida, a distance of

60 miles. The island is 7 miles long and 700 feet at its widest point. It is located only 50 miles off the coast of Florida. The longer distance swum is due to the drift caused by the Gulf Stream. Her time was 27:38. This was her third attempt.[490]

    I encountered Diana Nyad's pilot Richard Dumoulin for this swim at Hemingway Marina, Cuba, while assisting Suzy Maroney in her 1996 attempt across the Florida Strait. He was on his boat tied up at the dock in Cuba. We discussed an aspect of the Bimini swim that is little known to the general public. That is the issue of the counter current. The counter current is a remnant of the cold Labrador Current that rakes the East Coast. This current is trapped inshore of the Gulf Stream when the Gulf Stream turns to the right off Cape Hatteras. It is not really that strong by the time it gets down to Florida but it is enough of a current that south bound coastal vessels take advantage of it. I asked him how he took advantage of the counter current. He smiled and said nothing. I then went into more detail of the information I was looking for. As these two currents oppose each other, eddies from the Gulf Stream tear off and create large swirls that drift southward. If at the end of a swim across the Gulf Stream, you have an exhausted swimmer and they encounter the part of the swirl moving away from shore, that swim is over. If you put the swimmer into the part of the eddy moving toward shore, your swimmer can roll over and float into shore with little trouble.

    These minor eddy currents move slowly southward with the counter current so they are difficult to determine their location. The trouble is in detecting the part of the eddy you've encountered. Richard gave up his secret: he had three small boats out in front of him widely spaced and he watched them on radar.[491] The one that was drifting to shore clued him where the current was. The swimmer can be inserted into a particular spot by delaying their departure from the northbound Gulf Stream. They just ride that Gulf current north and break out of it when the current favors their swim ashore. The picket boats have to be positioned north of the swimmer's position.

Richard revealed his method of detecting the counter current but I haven't revealed mine until now. Boats are subject to wind drift and you could possible be mislead. I would have a lead boat or two several miles north of the swimmer position dropping oranges, my favorite current marker, and tracking their movement for 15 minutes or so. If the orange is moving north, reposition the orange closer to shore. If the orange is moving away from shore, this is the wrong edge of the eddy. If the orange is moving south, you're in the center of the swirl, and if the orange move toward shore, you've found the current and the boat can now start determining how wide the current is and its southern drift speed. It may be possible to detect the eddy currents by variation in the ocean temperature: water that has mixed with the Labrador Current should be colder than the edge of the eddy that has just torn off from the Gulf Stream and is headed for shore. If you have a strong swimmer at the end of the swim, none of this may be necessary. It's just one of the tricks up the sleeve of a good navigator. Of course, once a swim record is set, tricks like this become necessary to insure a new record on subsequent swims.

About 80 kilometers north of Cape Town, South Africa, off the coast about 11 kilometers is Dassen Island. This island is actual the top of one of 34 underwater mountain that are found along the west coast of Africa and the only one that protrudes above the surface of the sea. On May 7, 1986, Barry Cutler was the first person to swim from this island to the mainland. He completed the swim in an area known for rouge waves and cold water in 3:56. In 1993, Gordon Pugh completed the same swim in 2:35.[492]

Lynne Cox swam for two hours across part of the Bering Straits in 1987, a distance of 2.7 miles in water temperatures of 38° Fahrenheit.[493] Her time of 2:05 between Little Diomede, Alaska and Big Diomede, USSR, was an attempt at splash diplomacy initiated by an athlete. Lynn Cox was such an accomplished swimmer having held the Catalina Channel and the English Channel records simultaneously and breaking her own records for both swims in subsequent swims in the early 1970's. She has written a book, *Swimming to Antarctica: Tales of a Long Distance*

Swimmer, detailing her many swims, which I highly recommend. The author had the opportunity to meet Lynne Cox when she flew into Manhattan to swim around the Statue of Liberty on a route from the Battery to Liberty State Park, NJ.

Chris Green, a marathon swimmer from Cheshire, England attempted a swim not seen in decades, an East River swim through Hell Gate in 1988[494]. Starting in the water just off Rikers Island, he swam 10 miles on an ebb current to a point next to the Coast Guard ferry dock at the Battery, the southern most tip of New York City in 2:27. Starting just before one o'clock in the afternoon on October 26th near green buoy #1, Chris began his swim. The wind that day was blow quite strong, over twenty knots. There were occasional white caps as the swim was mostly in the shelter of the land from the wind until he arrived at Hell Gate, where the waters looked like the surf at Jones Beach. One wave near the Bronx side was a standing wave, continuously breaking as the wind pushed back the ebbing current. He would later recount that during the swim he felt his arms and legs being pulled in different directions as he swam through Hell Gate.

A resume of swim accomplished in the early 1990s by Dr. Christopher Stockdale of London is impressive because of the variety of locations. Chris swam the Manhattan Marathon in 1987 successfully finishing in 8:40. In 1989, he swam the length of Lake Garda, 32 miles in 31:10 beginning on July 21 and finishing on July 23. This is the largest lake in Italy location in the north. On August 1, 1990, he swam from Anadolukavagi, a small town near the northern end of the Bosporus to Buyukada (Big Island) in the Sea of Marmara,Turkey, a distance of 26 miles in 16:15. Buyukada is the largest island of the Prince Islands and served as an exile location for various royalty and personalities from the region and get-away for the wealthy. He next swam Lake Zurich from Rapperswil to Zurich, 26.4 kilometers in 11:24 on August 3, 1991. A month later on September 17, 1991, he swam 27 kilometers in the Cyclades from Naxos to Paros, in 9:34. In 1994, he swam from Ventotene, a tiny island off the west coast of Italy near Naples to Forio D'Ischia, a large island outside the entrance to

Naples. The distance he swam is 37 kilometers in 20:21 on July 16th.[495] He liked long, open-water swims to/from islands. He recently attempted in July of 2000 another swim in the Cyclades for the return of the Parthenon Marbles, 17 figures made of marble that once decorated the Acropolis in Athens, now held by the British Museum. The swim was from Paros to Delos islands but failed 3 miles short of the 26 miles swim. This swim shows him wearing a full length body suit.[496] The swim might have failed but the publicity was quite successful.

Another long swim of a great distance is across the Irish Sea from North Wales at Holyhead, a peninsula of Wales that sticks out into the Irish Sea to Dublin Bay, 56 miles where the water temperature might approach 58 or 59 degrees on a good day in the summer. The course is nearly due west. This swim was tackled in 1983 successfully by a six-man relay team on their third attempt. One of the members of that team, Feilim O'Maolain, went on to do more swims in equally difficult waters. He swam north from Bray along the Irish coast to Dublin in 1995, a distance of 12 miles and on August 7, 2002, he swam from Mor of the Aran Islands thru Galway Bay to Salthill, Galway, Ireland. He covered the distance of 24 miles in 14:59.[497] He also did the same swim as part of a relay.

A swim across the channel between Japan's largest island was the swim venue for David Yudovin, age 39, on July 7, 1990. He swam from northern Hokkaido Island south across the Tsugaru Channel to Honshu Island. The distance was 17 miles and it took him 11:56. He was delay 5 weeks training the boatmen to work off a swimmer and learning enough Japanese to communicate and by typhoon weather. This was a first ever crossing of this channel.[498]

Gail Rice swam around Sanibel Island which lies at the harbor entrance to Fort Meyers in Florida, a distance of 22 miles in a time of 9:37 on January 10, 1998.[499]

Figure 17 Teresa Skilton at sea off Gibraltar in twilight. In 1990 she was part of a relay swim around Jersey. In 2000, she swam Manhattan in 9:08, English Channel in 10:54, and was part of a relay across Gibraltar Strait.

Chapter 7   21st Century

You occasionally hear about blind swimmers. James Pittar, age 30, from Australia was the first to swim from Martha's Vineyard to Nantucket on July 23, 2000. These islands are 11.6 nautical miles apart and he completed a 15-mile swim from the Vineyard to Nantucket in 7:53.[500] The method for controlling the direction he swims is simple: he has a kayaker alongside him who signals him via a whistle. The second person to swim the distance and the first woman was Debra Taylor, age 36, of Martha's Vineyard only 15 minutes behind. She was the organization behind this swim and achieved a successful strategy for making the crossing by careful analysis of the tides and currents between the two islands with the assistance of the local harbormasters. Jim originally hadn't planned on making this swim but through a misdirected email that wound up at Debra Taylor's inbox, he took her up on her invitation to join her in this successful attempt. Jim has an impressive swim resume that includes Manhattan, English Channel, Cook Strait, and Gibraltar.[501]

Four marathon swims in Asia over two years took place beginning in July of 2000. David Yudovin swam across the Sumatra Straits from Pujut Beach near Jakarta (on the northwest end of Java) to a deserted beach north of Kangalan on Sumatra. The distance was 22 miles that he covered in 10:24. Using native guides and a compass, enduring jelly fish stings, avoiding sea snakes, crocodiles and whirlpools, he completed a goal that was four years in planning.[502]

Near Vladivostok, Russia, in 2001, a Japanese swimmer crossed the Tatarskiy Proliv Channel on August 1st.[503]

Another swim in this part of the world but a bit further south was held by FINA as part of their marathon swimming championship on June 5, 2002 in China. A 13.5 nautical mile swim across Qiongzhou Strait, the northern entrance to the Gulf of Tonkin, started at Haian Baisha Bay, Quangdong Province and ended at Haikou, Hainan Province on the island of Hainan. The onlookers pushed right out into the water to get a better look at the start. Twenty-six athletes competed. Yury Koudinov was the winner in 4:51.5 with the 2nd place swimmer, Anton Sanatchev less than 5 seconds behind.[504] The other location that FINA runs an open water event in China is Hong Kong.

In 2002, a relay team swam from LaJolla Cove just north of San Diego, California, to Point Loma Lighthouse located 19 miles to the south.[505] Point Loma light is at the entrance to San Diego Harbor.

Summer in the United States is winter in Australia so you don't find many swims being undertaken during their winter months. On June 6, 2004, Tammy van Wisse swam the length of Gippsland Lakes from Bairnsdale to Lakes Entrance, a distance of 21.6 nautical miles. She finished in 9:57. This is the middle of winter for Australia so the water temperature was comparable to the English Channel. This was a first-ever swim of this lake located about 185 miles from Melbourne, Australia. The swim was filmed by Discovery Channel.

A swimmer that compares himself to Lance Armstrong for good reason embarked on a swim to raise money for cancer research in 2004. Maarten van der Weijden, age 24, swam across Holland's Lake Ijsselmeer in 4:20 establishing a new record. A diagnosis at age 19 of leukemia slowed him down and brought him a new view of his life as an athlete.[506]

In another part of the world, Khoo Swee Chiow, an adventurer from Singapore who has seen the world from the top of Mt. Everest and visited both poles, swam across the Malacca Strait in 21:53, a distance of 39 kilometers on December 5, 2004. The starting point is Tanjong Medang in Sumatra and the finish is Cape Rachardo in Port Dickson, Malaysia, just south of Kaula Lumpur. He is the second swimmer to complete the swim. The first swimmer is believed to be a Japanese swimmer who swam the Strait around 1970. As part of his training, he was the first swimmer to cross the Singapore Strait on September 12, 2004, 16 kilometer distance in 8:30 hours. He had to learn to swim freestyle, thus the training swim.[507] Since Richard Haliburton, a novice swimmer and a fellow mountain climber; marathon swimming has not seen as versatile a person as Swee Chiow.

In 2003, Nelson Mandela Bay in South Africa was swum for the first time. Kyle Main swam from Hobbies Beach to Bluewater Bay a distance of 18 kilometers in 4:00. A different route 4 kilometers longer from Port of Coega to Hobie Beach was swum by Philip Kuhn in 2004 in a time of 4:40.[508]

Another swimmer that has been on a tear since before the turn of the century is Bula Chowdhury. She was awarded the Tenzing Norgay Sport Award in New Delhi in September of 2004 in recognition of her achievements.[509] These include: two crossing of the English Channel in 1989 (time 10:46) and 1999 (time 13:15)[510]; the Gibraltar Strait on August 19, 2000 in a time of 3:34 (set women record)[511]; the Tyrreanean (Tyrrhenian) Sea (water surrounded by Italy, Sicily, and Corsica and Sardinia) from Zannone to Sal Felice Circeo in 2001; the Toroneous Gulf, Greece, 26 kilometers or 14 nautical miles from Cassandra to Nikiti in 8:11[512] and the Catalina Channel in 2002; the Cook Strait, New Zealand in 2003; and the Palk Strait from Talaimanar in Sri Lanka to Danushkoti near Rameswaram in Tamil Nadu, 40 kilometers (25 miles), in 13:52[513] on August 20, 2004.

The Palk Strait is the body of water between India's southern-most point and the off-shore island called Sri Lanka. Swimmers swim along a shallow opening to Palk Bay between Danushkoti on India and Talaimanar in Sri Lanka; both towns are located at the end of long peninsulas. Presently, a ferry operates between the two countries over this strait. This east-west course runs parallel to an underwater formation called Adam's Bridge. Hindu legend has it that the bridge is man-made, built to transport Rama, hero of the *Ramayana,* to the island to rescue his wife from the demon king Ravanna.[514] The water in the strait at this point is only 4 feet deep at high tide. In the photo seen taken from space, the land bridge is quite visible. Sand bars form and disappear over time, some, such as Cape Cod or Sandy Hook, develop a geography similar to Adam's Bridge but the peninsula that forms is one-sided, not two-sided unless there is a reason. A man-made cause is not out of the question. Putting that issue aside, Bula completed her 2005 goal of swimming from Three Anchor Bay on the shoreline of Cape Town, South Africa, due north to Robben Island. She covered the 11 kilometer swim in 3:26 on April 29, 2005.[515]

Figure 18 NASA image of Sri Lanka next to India in the upper left. The light color of the water between the two countries is indicative of the shallow water in the Palk Strait.

The Salton Sea has been out of the limelight for some time. Growing up in Southern California, it was an a weekend destination for many Los Angeles families seeking a water vacation spot not as overpriced as the coastal property. Greta Anderson was said to have won a ten-mile race here in the mid-Fifties.[516] It was a middle-class dream. Some dreams turn into nightmares. Salton Sea, California's largest lake was created by an accident in 1905 when agricultural canals burst and the Colorado River poured into the Salton Basin for 18 months. With no natural drainage because it's 227 feet below sea level; agricultural run-off and salt have created the ultimate water management challenge.[517] On August 13, 2006, James Cain, age 46, from Phoenix swam 9.6 miles across the lake. His mouth and nose crusted up from the salt during the 7:46 long swim. Did I mention the odor? A week previous to the swim, excessive hydrogen sulfide gas killed 3 million tilapia fish. The tilapia is a small fish that is accustomed to brackish water and used in aquaculture farming.[518] This fish, little known, but is the fifth most popular seafood in the United States and, in 2005, Dr. Modaduga Gupta was honored as the World Food Prize Laureate for his work developing aquaculture for the poor that included tilapia fish. The prize is a $250,000 award.[519]

A new swim was initiated across Sarangani Bay in the Philippines on May 18th, 2007; swimming from Tampauan Point, Kamanga, Maasim to Barangay Tango, Glan, a distance of 15 kilometers; the longest in the country. This location is a bay on the southern coast of Mindanao, the southern-most island of the Philippines. Ten relay teams of teenage swimmers participated in the Across-the-Bay Open Ocean Swimming Competition held in conjunction with the 1st Sarangani Bay festival and attended by the 29 year-old governor, Migs Dominguez. The winning team, the Dadiangas Torpedoes of General Santos City, won in 4:05 and took home $30,000 in Philippine money. Sarangani Bay is home to 5 of the 7 endangered turtle species in the world. This is not the only swim in the Philippines. There have been swimming competitions in the Duimaras Strait between the mainland island of Davao and Samal Island over a distance of 5 km.[520]

Deke Zimmerman, age 25, has set a new standard for swimming in a harbor. Deke swam from Parramatta, the city at the headwaters of the Parramatta River, east to Sydney, through Sydney Harbor, turns left at the harbor entrance and swims north to Manly Cove outside of the harbor and then back. Total distance: 70 kilometers (43.5 miles) in 15:42 holding an average speed of

143

4.4 kilometer per hour (2.7 mph). The Parramatta River is the longest river associated with the harbor and since Sydney Harbor has as much as a six foot tidal range; the entire swim had to be timed to match the tide flow with the swim direction. In 2003, Deke swam a single lap stopping at Manly Cove. This double is impressive. Manly Cove was named by Capt. Arthur Phillips as his description of the indigenous people living there. He named the cove after the people of the Kay-ye-my clan, "their confidence and manly behavior made me give the name of Manly Cove to this place." This was a very generous gesture given that they fell into a dispute about water and Arthur received a spear in the shoulder.[521]

Carina Bruwer notched another swim on her belt by becoming the first woman to swim across False Bay, South Africa, in 10:58 on March 12, 2006.[522] The course is from Rooi Els to Millers Point, a 35 kilometer distance. During the swim, they lost their GPS signal in the fog and had to fall back on the magnetic compass. False Bay is known for its Great White shark population. On March 7, 2007, Barend Nortje, age 33, established a new record for this course of 9:17. All distance swims in South Africa monitored by the Cape Long Distance Swimming Association which uses the Shark Shield on all its swims that is attached to the support boat.[523] Well, at least the boat is protected.

Carina is not the only woman setting distance records. Twelve year old Becca Heller won the (Florida Keys Community College Swim) Around Key West title making her the youngest title holder on Saturday, June 24, 2006. The 12.5 mile swim was covered in 5:03. She took over the lead at the nine mile mark and held on after losing it to two boys at the two mile mark. Her goal is to swim the English Channel before getting her driver's license. The swim was her second trip as she competed when she was eleven.[524]

The Battery to Sandy Hook swim of 17.5 miles course has a natural ½ marathon location just as the swimmers head out of New York Harbor: Coney Island. This feature would make the Ederle swim one of the most versatile marathons in the world as it has a recognized marathon swim at its halfway point. This would mean that swimmers who sign up for the swim to Sandy Hook could pull out for any reason and get the Coney Island swim under their belts plus if for any reason the complete swim had to be cancelled due to weather or other reasons, the Coney Island swim is an alternate finishing location. The distance to Coney Island from the Battery is 8 nautical miles or 9.2 statute miles. The course was swum to a variety of finishing location since 1880.

Figure 19 Caprice Schaefer passing under the Verrazano Narrows Bridge.

The current record for swims to Coney Island stands at 3:39 set in 1931 by William Sadlo and tied 75 years later in 2006 by Caprice Schaefer, age 55, swimming mostly breaststroke on August 13th. Caprice was planning on swimming all the way to Sandy Hook but due to a delayed escort boat arrival, lost the tide and would not have made the complete distance when the escort boat with myself aboard redirected her to the long, sandy beach at Norton Point at the western end of Coney Island.

INTERNATIONAL MARATHON SWIMMING HALL OF FAME

HAS PLACED INTO THE ORGANIZATION'S ARCHIVES THE RECORD OF THE JULY 23, 1990 SWIM OF

SKIP STORCH

LENGTH OF EAST RIVER

FROM

THE THONGS NECK BRIDGE

PAST

BATTERY PARK

TO

THE STATUE OF LIBERTY

A DISTANCE OF 15 STATUE MILES

IN THE TOTAL ELAPSED TIME

OF

5 HOURS 30 MINUTES

DALE PETRANECH, SECRETARY
INTERNATIONAL MARATHON SWIMMING HALL OF FAME

15 NOV 2006
DATE

One Hall of Fame Drive • Fort Lauderdale, Florida 33316 • Tel 954.462.6536 • Fax 954.525.4031 • www.ishof.org

Figure 20 IMSHOF certicate available to swimmers.

Lake Ontario was the scene of a swim by Samantha Whiteside, age 16, on August 8-9, 2006. She swam the course established by Marilyn Bell from Youngstown, NY, to what is now known as Marilyn Bell Park in Toronto, a distance of 32 kilometers missing the record for a woman swimmer by one minute. Her time was 15:11 set in exceptionally calm waters. The record was set in 1974 by 16 year old Cindy Nicolas at 15:10. The course starts at Niagara-on-the-Lake just north of Youngstown. The water temperature started at 72° Farhenheit then dropped to 64°. The air temperature was quite similar. The swim began at 7pm. The swim strategy employed by her team was to get the night portion of the swim over first so that she would have the bulk of the day to finish if the swim went long.[525] Another attempt on the record is planned for 2007.

The eastern end of Lake Ontario was the site of a marathon swim for a young girl on July 18-19, 2006. Jenna Lambert, age 15, who despite an affliction with cerebral palsy that prevented her from using her legs in the swim showed that she had spunk enought to swim 32 hours over a 32 kilometer distance. She left from Baird Point, NY, and landed at Lake Ontario Park in her home town of Kingston where she was meet by members of her swim club, the Penquins.[526] This is the swim club that Vicki Keith has supported as the designated charity for her swims. She's had quite an effect on the this team member. See her website: www.penquinscanfly.ca. Bravo!

Another swim for disabilities occurred beginning on August 26th and ending on August 27, 2006. Tyler Patterson who had just turned 40 years old swam around Lake Washington, approximately 55 miles in 37 hours. It wasn't a totally serious swim as he'd take breaks and after the first 27 hours, got a massage before returning to his task. They had to fend off a Seattle police boat who wanted him out of the water as he approached the Montlake Bridge near the end of the swim. The charity was Experimental Educational Unit of the University of Washington, a unit set up for young children with disabilities.[527]

Professional swims

There are currently a number of open water swims held throughout the world on a regular basis under the auspices of FINA, Federation Internationale De Natation. This international swimming organization has defined open water swimming and established a set of rules for swimming. By their definition, long distance swimming is any distance up to 10 kilometers and distances greater than 10 kilometers are considered marathon swims. Unfortunately, their definitions exclude traditional swims that attracted swimmers originally to the sport and have reduced the sport to a series of moneyed competitions. The competitions are over set distances of 5, 10, and 25 kilometers and exclude swims if the currents are other than minor. Swims that originally were pioneered by amateurs, lifeguards and open water swimming enthusiasts are now swum professionally for purse money. Master Swimming, an affiliated federation of FINA, has rescued these amateur swims.[528]

Some of the swims that have been adopted by FINA are the Rio Coronda and Puerto Gaboto-Rosario in Argentina, the Red Sea and Alexandria in Egypt, Hong Kong Island in China, Atlantic City in the USA, Capri to Naples, 18 miles in Italy, Lac St-Jean and Lac Memphremagog in Canada, Abu Dhabi in the United Arab Emirates, Lake Ohrid in Bulgaria, and Sabac in Serbia and Montenegro. In one sense, these swims do establish a world champion long distance swimmer but their champion is often focused only on specific events. In the 2004 Olympics, well-known professional basketball and tennis players were allowed to compete. The surprise was when rank amateurs defeated them. Some professional races, where a cash prize award for winning is paid, are covered in this book. Conrad Wennerberg's book, *Wind, Waves and Sunburn* does a great job on professional swims as well as some amateur swims and I have tried not to go over the same ground. Sometimes, a professional swim is the impetus for an amateur swim; for example: the Catalina Channel swim.

The 2005 holder of the Marathon Swimming World Cup for men is Petar Stoychev of Bulgaria. He has stood at the top of his craft since 2001. The women's division is represented by Edith van Dijk of the Netherlands having previously won for 2000 and 2001.[529] For 2006 there are 19 venues throughout the world that will host FINA open-water marathon swimming races. The big news in the swimming world is that the Olympics will host a 10 kilometer marathon swimming event at Beijing in 2008.

FINA itself is an evolving organization that has started to incorporate the open-water swimming events by holding open-water swimming championships in between FINA pool championships. For a period of 10 years, 1986 to 1996, FINA held a biannual Long Distance Swimming World Cup championship event. After a sporadic start in 1991, there has been an annual Open Water Swimming World Championship. The odd thing is for five years, 1991 to 1996, there were two flavors of championships. Since 2000 there has been just the annual championship that is based on the accumulated points by the professional swimmers over the season.[530]

In addition to the championship, there is an effort to acknowledge individuals, teams, and countries made up of individuals representing their country. Events that have been tracked are the 5, 10 and 25 kilometers swims. This was accomplished in 1993 and 1994 by holding under FINA auspices The FINA Marathon Swimming World Cup Series of designated swims. Starting in 1997, FINA allowed the patronage of swims organized by the member countries of the Federation to make up the World Cup Series. The patronage is a guarantee of $30,000 in prize money.[531] The number of swims and venues in the Marathon Swimming World Cup Series varies from year to year.

A swim in Lake Ohrid located in the Balkans reveals the extent the political instability affects a swim. The lake is 25 miles long and is rumored to have been first swum as a competition in 1924. After a few years, instability in the region didn't permit another swim until 1954 when eight swimmers competed in a contest over a 2.5 kilometer distance. Again the swim lasted for a short time then disappeared. In 1962, a marathon swim of 36 kilometer took place along a route from Pestani to Struga then back to Ohrid in 1962. There were 22 participants. This swim occurred regularly for a few years then another lapse. In 1983, the original swim of 2.5 kilometers reappeared and has been held on a continuous basis since.

Figure 21 Lake Ohrid is the lake on the left in this view of the Balkans.

In 1992, with the backing of a sporting magazine "Skok", the Ohrid Swimming Marathon was reestablished. The route is north from St. Naum at the southern end of Lake Ohrid where the boundary of Former Yugoslav Republic of Macedonia (FYROM) ends to the town harbor of Ohrid, approximately 30 kilometers. Since 1998 the swim has consistently been a venue for the FINA

World Cup Series.[532] A glance over the history of this swim reveals times when the political situation overwhelms the athletic spirit; hopefully, this swim will be able to continue into the future.

In 2006 the #1 ranked men's swimmer was Petar Stoychev of Bulgaria and the #1 ranked woman's swimmer was Britta Kamrau-Corestein of Germany.[533] Edith van Dijk had announced her retirement in 2005.

Figure 22 In the Atlantic City professional marathon swim, they still escort the swimmers the old-fashioned way: row boats.

Figure 23 Petar Stoychev of Bulgaria and Race Director Mike Giegerich.

Figure 24 Edith van Dijk and Natalia Pankina (l to r).

Chapter 8 Staged swims

A staged swim is where a swimmer will attempt to swim a long distance over a series of days taking breaks from swimming by leaving the water. If the distance is down a river and the flow is tidal, their routine is to swim for six hours when the flow favors their progress then get out and rest for six when the flow opposes them. Hudson River swims have generally been of this nature. There are several unique characteristics that make the Hudson River a great swim. The Hudson River is tidal all the way up to Troy, just beyond Albany. This means that the river will flow in both directions. For a southbound swimmer the tidal flow combines with the natural river flow giving a tremendous boost to their swimming speed. There are sections of the river where the current flow is greater than 3 knots. One knot of current accounts for 33 yards per minute added to a swimmers speed. Thus a swimmer can break a minute for the 100 yards without taking a stroke. The swimmer "body surfs" the tidal wave thus creating as much as an eight-hour window of favorable current before the tide switches. This puts a distance of approximately 40 nautical miles[534] in one swim within reach: 3 knots from a top swimmer plus the average current push (.707*3=2.1 knots) times 8 hours equals 40.8 nautical miles. Since the distance under consideration is well short of 160 miles, you are looking at about 4 swims broken up with rest periods. Since not all portions of the river run this fast swims normally take about a week and a bit longer if only daylight swims are employed. With the clean up of the river, the waters are enjoyable and a pleasure to swim in. The river is quite wide in sections and the channel is well marked. No one has ever swum from New York City north to Albany further than the entrance to the Harlem River as the flood current is not as strong. Northbound swim in the Hudson are normally associated with clockwise circumswims around Manhattan. The tidal flow is skewed the further north you go shortening the amount of time available to swim with the current (conversely, lengthening the time available to swim south).

The first "swim" down the Hudson River was by Captain Paul Boyton in his lifesaving suit in April of 1887. Boyton first spoke about doing the Hudson River in December of 1878 right after his return from Europe.[535] He didn't start at Albany because the river was clogged with ice above Hudson, NY. He finished in 6 days and 10½ hours and no record seemed to have been kept of the accumulative time for all the stages. Description of him in his suit using a double bladed paddle traveling feet first made it sound like he was basically wearing a kayak. While Boyton may not have swum the river he could draw a crowd. At the finish, the docks were described as "…black with people…men stood on rooftops."[536] Boyton's "swims" and other assorted adventures are collected in two tables in the Appendix.

The first swimmer was Steve Brodie, who attempted the swim in June of 1888 having given up high diving for long distance swimming. He was not having a good time of it and was quite exhausted by Newburg. While saying that he wants no more of it, he nonetheless jumped in to save a drowning person (to no avail).[537] He was trying to beat Boyton's time down the Hudson.[538] This is the same Steve Brodie who jumped from the Brooklyn Bridge. He did manage to achieve his goal, arriving at the Battery on June 30, 1888. The time for the swim was 6 days and one hour from a point 30 miles longer than Boyton's swim because Brodie started at Albany leaving from the Albany Yacht Club docks.[539] When he finished his one arm that was brothering him in Newburg was now quite lame but he did win $300 upon the completion of his trip.[540]

In September of 1897, John Hooper, a long distance swimmer from England swam from Troy, just south of Albany, to the Battery beginning on Wednesday, September 1, 1897. When he first started the swim, he'd swim for twenty hours at a time meaning he attempted to swim through the opposing tide. By the time he reached Peekskill his strategy had changed to taking twelve hours off to recover. He lost over 30 pounds on the swim. The motivation for the swim was a $500 wager and a medal. He finished on Saturday, September 12, 1897 at Pier 1, North River taking 12 days.[541]

Millie Gade Corson, in August of 1921 completed the swim in a time of 63 hours 35 minutes. At this time, the swim was changed to record the accumulated time in the water as opposed to the elapsed time from the start of the first stage. By doing this, swimmers can avoid swimming during the middle of the night and give themselves more rest between swims. Mildred was remembered as the first mother to complete the English Channel to distinguish her from Gertrude Ederle.[542] She was actually over in England at the time Gertrude completed the channel. If Mildred had completed the channel first, she probably would never have tried a swim down the Hudson. At the end of September of the same year she would swim around Manhattan. Mildred was doing an awful lot of swims to attract attention including challenging Gertrude to swims.[543]

Lottie Schoemmell, swimming in 1926, bested that record by six hours completing the 150-mile swim in 57:11.[544] She swam all the way to Pier A at the Battery finishing on October 20 having begun the swim on Sunday, October 10, 1926 just as the ebb began from the Albany Yacht Club. She would take breaks for lunch, exiting the water for two hours. It doesn't appear that her support crew noticed that she missed two hours of excellent ebb current while she lunched. October was a late date to begin the swim and the journey was plagued with cold rainy weather.

The next year, two swimmers appeared who desired to better the record set by Ms. Schoemmell. They were the Zitenfield twins, Bernice and Phylis, age 13. They began their quest on June 19, 1927, from the Albany Yacht Club accompanied by their manager, George Manes and a party of friends aboard a luxurious 60-foot escort yacht. At the completion of the swim, they had covered the distance, all the way to Pier A of the Battery, in 52:30.[545] They weren't tired at all after swimming for nearly 11 days. There was one break where a seaplane flew them to their grade school graduation. They were entered in the Lake George marathon swim in July and then they were scheduled to attempt the

English Channel in August of 1927. It was not long after the twins set the record that George Creegan, age 26, of Paterson, New Jersey, set out to better the record. He did it, completing the trip from Albany to Pier A of the Battery in 50:06. This is the current record. He began his swim on October 16, 1927 and finished on October 28, 1927.[546] He used the English over-arm stroke having grown up in Belfast, Ireland. The International Professional Swimmers' Association authenticated the swim and the record.

Charles Zibleman, better known as Charles Zimmy, completed in 1937, a single swim down the Hudson River that is unlike other staged swims. Between ebb tides when the swimmer can take advantage of the current, he would rest near shore, out of the current, never leaving the water. He completed 145 miles of the Hudson River swim in 147 hours on August 29, 1937, having begun the swim at 6:10am on August 23, 1937.[547] Charles had an advantage over ordinary marathon swimmers in that he was legless. While this could be considered a disadvantage on land, in the water this attribute allowed him additional buoyancy, so much so that he could sleep while floating. The entire swim was one continuous immersion. He lost 26 pounds during the swim. This advantage was not without its detraction because several times while sleeping, he was carried back toward Albany. He had to swim past the town of Saugerties twice. He would rest a few yards from shore where the current was less or in coves. His total distance is a bit shorter than other Hudson River swims because his goal was only to swim underneath the George Washington Bridge. His eventual finishing point was just south of the bridge at Ninety-eighth Street. It was reported that at the start, he dove off a dock. The current was starting a flood tide but that far inland, the flood current lasts only for 3 hours and is a fraction of the speed of the ebb current. This allows swimmers at the beginning of the swim to maximize their time in the water; Zimmy covered twenty miles the first day.

At the completion of the Hudson River swim, he announced that his "…next big swim will be from Key West to Havana."[548] It seems that he had a wife and family living in

Florida at the time and he desired to be near them. Comments about this proposed Cuba swim were solicited from Lottie Schoemmell, living then at Miami Beach, an alumnus of the Hudson River swim. She immediately recognized the need for a net to protect the swimmer from fish and the difficulty of positioning the net around a swimmer during a swim.[549] She did not realize that the Gulf Stream would prevent a swim in this direction from being successful.

Gene Texeira of Westport, Massachusetts, completed the swim in 1952 in a time of 55:30 in preparation for an English Channel crossing.[550] He was accompanied by a small rowboat. He finished the swim at the Hudson River Day Line pier at 42nd Street, New York City. The stroke he used was the crawl stroke with a trudgeon kick. He swam during the day and rested at night. This schedule caused him to spend nearly two weeks on the trip having started on July 3rd and finishing on July 16th.

Skip Storch, a marathon swimmer from Monsey, New York, became the eleventh person to complete a Hudson River swim in 1988, in 54:50.[551] He began his swim at Port Albany, New York, and finished at the Statue of Liberty Island. He used a double arm-stroke trudgeon, breathing on both sides. Dr. Jane Katz helped him develop this stroke to increase his endurance and lessen lactic acid build-up in his muscles. During long swim periods, he would switch off to the breaststroke for a while to catch his breath. Skip would swim in six hours stretches breaking when the current went into flood. He stated when he finished the swim that he proved the "river is swim-able".[552] This was one of three swims that either began or ended at the Statue of Liberty swum by Skip Storch.

In an unusual swim, a dog swam down the Hudson River to New York City from Albany completing the swim on September 25, 1928. The German Shepard dog named *Lucky* was 3 years old and was owned by a German baker, John Schweighart of the Bronx. The total time for the dog to swim to 86th street was 44:52. This bettered the known best time for a human by 5 hours, held by George Creegan at the time. It sounds impossible that a dog could out swim a human but the dog utilized an unrecognized aspect of the tidal current flow. The dog would only swim 2 hours at a stretch thus putting the animal in the peak current flow. The elapsed time was thereby minimized compared to a human who normally swims from the beginning of ebb until the last of ebb. The average speed of the river current over 6 hours works out to 70.7% of the maximum current. The dog utilized 100% of the maximum current flow. The normal Hudson River swim takes a week or so but due to the reduced time in the water, the animal took nearly 3 weeks.[553] A human swimmer utilizing the same swim strategy could approach a time of less than 40 hours.

In 2005, Skip Storch, now age 48, utilized this strategy and an exceptional fast tidal flow to revolutionize stage swimming. From August 15 to August 25 on a window of fast tides, he completed 20 two-hour swim stages to set a new record for the Hudson River swim of 41:30.[554] He dropped his own time for the Hudson River by 13 hours and twenty minutes when he completed his second lap down the Hudson. He did not get ahead of Lucky's time until the final two stages when he delivered two swims of exceptional merit. The last stage from Spuyten Duyvil to the Battery, a distance of 11.25 nautical miles, he complete in 2:55 while swimming at speeds in excess of 4 nautical miles an hour with the current assistance.[555] The actual distance swum was 123.65 nautical miles; equivalent to 142.3 statute miles or 229 kilometers. His average speed was 2.98 knots. Part of the swim strategy was to have Skip start the swim just before peak current, watch the GPS then pull him when the swim speed dropped below 3 knots. This led to some stages being slightly longer than 2 hours and others less. This effort by Skip validated the earlier NY Times report for Lucky whose average speed was 2.90 knots.

Other staged swims

In 1915, Wendel Green, an American resident of the Panama Canal Zone completed a swim of the Panama Canal. He swam only on Sundays due to his work requirements and over a total of six days managed to swim 45 miles of the course.[556] He advised the next swimmer, Richard Halliburton, to start on the Atlantic side. Richard was not a distance swimmer; in fact, he hadn't swam at all in three years prior to his attempt in 1928 but was every bit the adventurous romantic that a swim of this proportions requires. His account of this swim in his book, *New Worlds to Conquer* is quite good and the Panama Canal swim was not his only quest he recounts. He didn't keep track of the time but rather the days; it took him eight days to manage the swim from Colon to Panama City, a distance of 50 miles. Aside from the locks, the alligators, and the barracuda, it's really a fairly easy training swim, at least according to Richard Halliburton.[557]

While it may not sound like the most repeatable swim in the world, there have been two other persons that have duplicated the feat. From the records available to the researcher, it is not always mentioned whether or not the swimmer swam through the locks. I would assume that after the one occasion, the authorities put a stop to this practice. In late June of 1950, Charles J. McGinn, a cadet at West Point, completed 45 miles of the Panama Canal in 36 hours of swimming over 5 ½ days.[558] In the fall of 1966, Mihir Sen of Calcutta, India, attempted a non-stop swim through the Panama Canal. After 15 hours of continuous swimming, cramps put an end to this dream but he did complete the distance in 32:45.[559] There was no mention of how many days it took but from the press information, the swim was to start on October 29. The swim was reported over on November 1st, so it looks like it took about 3 days to finish the swim. Mr. Sen was the first Indian to swim the English Channel in 1958. He did very well on this swim and applied himself wholeheartedly to the task.

The summer of 1988 saw the completion of a series of grueling swims across the Great Lakes by Vicki Keith, age 27, a swimming instructor from Kingston, Ontario, Canada.[560] She started her journey by crossing the Eastern part of Lake Erie, swimming 16 miles in 10:24 over July 1-2nd. She then swam 47 miles across Lake Huron in 46:55 over July 17-19th. Following that swim, she swam 45 mile down Lake Michigan in 52:45 over July 26-28th. She then completed a distance of 20 miles across

Lake Superior on August 15th in 17:00. She finished this marathon by swimming 28 miles across Lake Ontario on August 30-31, 1988, in a time of 23:33. The total distance swam across all five Great Lakes was 156 miles in 150:39 swimming a combination of butterfly and freestyle. The swims in this distance each stand on their own and it is only by virtue of their sequence, accumulated length, and proximity to each other that this could be considered a staged swim. The two swims of distances greater than 40 miles have not been bested to date. The distance Vicki swam was four miles short of the 32-mile course[561] across Lake Ontario set by Marilyn Bell in 1954 in a time of 20:55, the first person to swim across that lake.[562] Vicki set an endurance record of 129:45 for swimming in a pool in 1986. In April of 1987, she did a double-crossing of Lake Ontario, an estimated 102 miles.[563]

Tammy van Wisse of Australia completed a mammoth staged swim down the Murray River in Australia. As part of her preparation, she researched all the known staged swims down the Hudson River; but these were like tiny warm-up swims compared with the Murray River swim. It took her 106 days, to complete 2438 kilometer or 1515 statue miles starting on November 5, 2000 and finishing on February 18, 2001.[564] Noticing a reference to this being an environmental swim, it's possible that Skip Storch had some influence in lending a theme to the swim. In completing the swim, she went farther than Graham Middleton who in 1991 swam 2394 km (1487.5 miles) in 138 day. Tammy knocked that portion of the swim off in 104 days and then swam Lake Alexandrina to finish at SIR Richard peninsula. She started at Corryong, Victoria. In this remarkable swim, Tammy met and marveled thousands of well-wishers as she continued her journey down this long, long river. Her other accomplishments include being the first person to swim the Bass Straits from Victoria to Tasmania in February of 1996 in a time of 17:46. In March of 1999, she set the record for the fastest time across the Cook Strait, New Zealand in 6:49.[565]

Later in the same year, Tom Gallagher wearing a full length body suit, swam around Long Island, NY, in stages. He began on May 18, 2001 and finished June 19, 2001. He swam clockwise around the island beginning and finishing at Bellport, Long Island. The recorded distance is 302 miles.[566]

In 2004, Lewis Gordon Pugh, age 34, of England swam the length of the Sognefjord, Norway, a distance of 204 kilometers or nearly 127 Statue miles, to Eidsvik from the entrance in about 3 weeks time.[567] The difficulty of this swim is the temperature of the water, 6°C, and the salinity in fjords is very low giving less buoyancy to the swimmer. When swimmers rest, they can quite easily tread water, or float on their backs for a few minutes. In a fjord, the salinity approaches that of pools making floatation more difficult.

Ali Shadlou of Iran complete a long staged swim that started in August of 2005. He swam across the Caspian Sea, 616 kilometers in 245 hours. He started from the westernmost point of the sea at Astara on August 1st and finished on September 23rd 2005 at the easternmost location, Bandar Torkaman. The one photo of him swimming shows him wearing a wet suit; the average speed of the swim is a respectable 2.5 kilometers an hour. He is a member of the Iran Red Crescent Society's Mountain Rescue and Relief Team. He also holds a beach lifeguard certificate. There was no information about how he was supported during the swim.[568]

Figure 25 Moon light reflecting over the Mediterranean Sea. If a long swim is planned to coincide with a full moon, visibility is improved at night.

Chapter 8   Early Manhattan swims

One of the world's premiere swimming events is the Manhattan marathon. The attraction of swimming around one of the world greatest cities in a day is the reason. In military terms, if you can surround your enemy, the victory is yours; politicians often speak about getting their arms around the problem and by this they mean to come to terms with what it is they behold; and a circle has a metaphysical meaning of closure. The Manhattan marathon is all this and more. It's not easy, it's dangerous, and at the same time it's liberating. The challenge in the swim is more than the physical and mental preparation for the swim or the endurance required in finishing the swim, there's the technical challenge of synchronizing three different rivers so that you can finish.

Figure 26 View of an approaching barge. From the wheelhouse of the tug behind pushing this barge, can you imagine how much of a blind spot in the front of the barge there is? He's not going to see a swimmer or a kayak. It's up to you to move out of the way.

Figure 27 Barge safely passed by the foresight of the swimmer's support crew in setting a clear and safe course.

Background information

The waters around Manhattan consist of three rivers, the Hudson River, the Harlem River and the East River. These rivers support a tremendous amount of traffic: ferry boats, passenger liners, sightseeing boats, tug boats pushing barges, recreational boats, sailing boats, dinner cruise boats, and boats just transiting the area to somewhere else. The harbor has a diurnal tide flow meaning that the waters generally experience two high tides and two low tides every day. The assumed direction for water flow as the tide is dropping is out to sea, called an ebb tide. When the waters stop flowing this is called the stand of the tide and it lasts for only a few minutes before the water switches direction and begins flowing back in the opposite direction. This is the rising tide called the flood. It takes about an hour for the tide effect to travel up the Hudson River via the Verrazano Narrows to reach Manhattan. Because of this, the stand of the tide does not coincide with the switching of currents. In order to be sure which way the water is flowing and exactly when it is switching, an observer would have to be in a stationary position, such as ashore, and toss a floatable object into the water (and not subject to wind),[569] then observe which direction it is moving in. The water right along the shore does not move as fast as the water further away from shore. An observer on a boat has a more difficult time because the boat is moving due to the current and the wind. Unless the boat is at anchor, you can't tell for sure what the current is doing. If you are in a boat, you can come alongside an object that is stationary, such as a lobster trap buoy, a channel buoy, or a bridge abutment. Look at the extent of the wake created as the waters pass this point. If there is no wake, the current is at a minimum.

If you cannot personally observe the current flow, the National Oceanographic Atmospheric Administration (NOAA) provides prediction tables that are quite accurate. Pick up a table of currents from New York Nautical, a marine supply store in lower Manhattan. Software is available for tide prediction and most navigational software includes this feature. Tide tables provided at your local fishing store are derived from the government tables and could be assumed to be accurate except for their tendency to not reference their data source. The thing to bear in mind with tables is that they allow for astronomical effects but not atmospheric effects. Tides are a result of the gravitational effect of the sun and the moon. The atmospheric effects are air pressure and wind. If an atmospheric low is positioned over New York, it will cause additional waters to rush into the harbor. Depending on the length of time the low is over or in the New York area, the water rises 12" for every inch of mercury below normal. As soon as the low moves off, the water will be trapped in the harbor until the next ebb tide. At that time the water has six hours to leave and it starts rushing out the harbor entrance. When it comes time for the flood to begin, the ebb may have such a momentum built up that the flood current doesn't begin on time. Little effects like this happen all the time around New York and for that matter, elsewhere in the world.

When a nor'easter is blowing, after about 3 days vast amounts of water will have been blown from the Long Island Sound into the East River. Flooding occurs along the East side under these conditions because of the extraordinary high tides. The tide effect still occurs while the atmospheric effect is taking place. The destructive damage caused by hurricanes when they come ashore is increased during high tides.

From home, you can find out what the current is doing by visiting PORTS® (Physical Oceanographic Real-Time System), an Internet web site that features nearly instantaneous readings of actual wind and water conditions in New York Harbor maintained by National Oceanographic and Atmospheric Administration (NOAA) of the National Ocean Service (NOS). There is a site for the Narrows and it provides a 36 hours history that compares the actual tides to the predicted tides. You can access this extensive site at http://tidesandcurrents.noaa.gov/index.shtml.

Figure 28 Jamie Tout swimming up the Harlem River on a high tide. The current is flowing north with the swimmers at this point of the marathon swim.

Of these rivers the Hudson is the longest as 13 miles of its length border Manhattan's West Side. Because of the length, the Hudson River is the defacto criteria for judging the effect current would have on a swim. The Harlem, while long doesn't have the velocity and the East River is so fast that the time spent in the river becomes minimal. What is the effect that current speed has on a swim? Say you are choosing between doing a swim on one day when the Hudson River ebb current is 2 knots and another day when the current is 2.1 knots. The tenth of a knot difference amounts to 3.3 yards lead every minute that the swimmer is in the faster current over the slower current. Three yards is a huge difference in a 100-yard swimming race. But this is 3.3 yard every minute for over 4 hours. That can accumulate into some 790 yards by the end of the Hudson River. Take the swimmer's time for a 1000 yards and that becomes the difference in finishing times for every tenth of a knot difference in the Hudson River. Only if the Hudson River currents were the same would you look at the difference between the East River flood velocities to decide which day would give you a faster swim.

Figure 29 For fast swimmers, the Hudson River goes slack about the time the swimmers pass the George Washington Bridge.

How far around Manhattan is it? When I first began working with the swimmers a variety of distances were being mentioned. As a way to resolve this basic issue, I purchased a set of charts for Manhattan and laid out a course. Measuring the distances by dividers and then summing the segments to reach the total revealed that Manhattan is 50,200 yards around by water. That distance is equivalent to 45.9 kilometers, 28½ statue miles, or 24¾ nautical miles. The expression for the distance most commonly used is 28½ miles. Establishing the distance was important for the computer modeling developed later.

If there were no currents around Manhattan and assuming a good swimmer capable of 1¾ knot, Manhattan would take a little over 14 hours. If the swim takes longer than that, the swimmer did not take advantage of the currents, went on a slow day, and most likely missed a tide change.

In the early years of Manhattan marathon swimming, things weren't quite this sophisticated. A swimmer would secure a rowing dory with crew of adequate strength and then set off. Once the swim was established, it took marathon swimmers a dozen years to figure out how to swim around Manhattan in less than a half a day (12 hours) and that's a story in itself. We'll begin with how the swim was established.

The first successful circumswim

In 1915, on Sunday, August 15, Robert W. Dowling Jr., age 18, the son of a hotel owner, began swimming from the Battery north on the Hudson River toward Harlem with the intentions of swimming around Manhattan.[570] Up to this point, swims begun at the Battery went up the East River turning at Hell Gate to enter the Harlem River and stopping at one of the boathouses along the Harlem River shore. The swimmer would have completed half of a swim around Manhattan. Until Robert Dowling, no one thought of making it all the way around. There was a good reason for this: the Harlem River didn't go all the way around Manhattan. Spuyten Duyvil Creek and the Harlem River were dredged, widen and connected from a waterworks project starting in 1888 leading to the opening of the Harlem River Shipping Canal in 1895.[571] Robert swam all the way to Spuyten Duyvil and then gave up as the Harlem[572] was ebbing and he was making no progress against the current. He turned and swam back to 79th Street downstream in the Hudson River where he finished this attempt. The partial return trip occurred most likely on the ebb current, which started around 4pm. The distance covered in this swim was 20 miles.

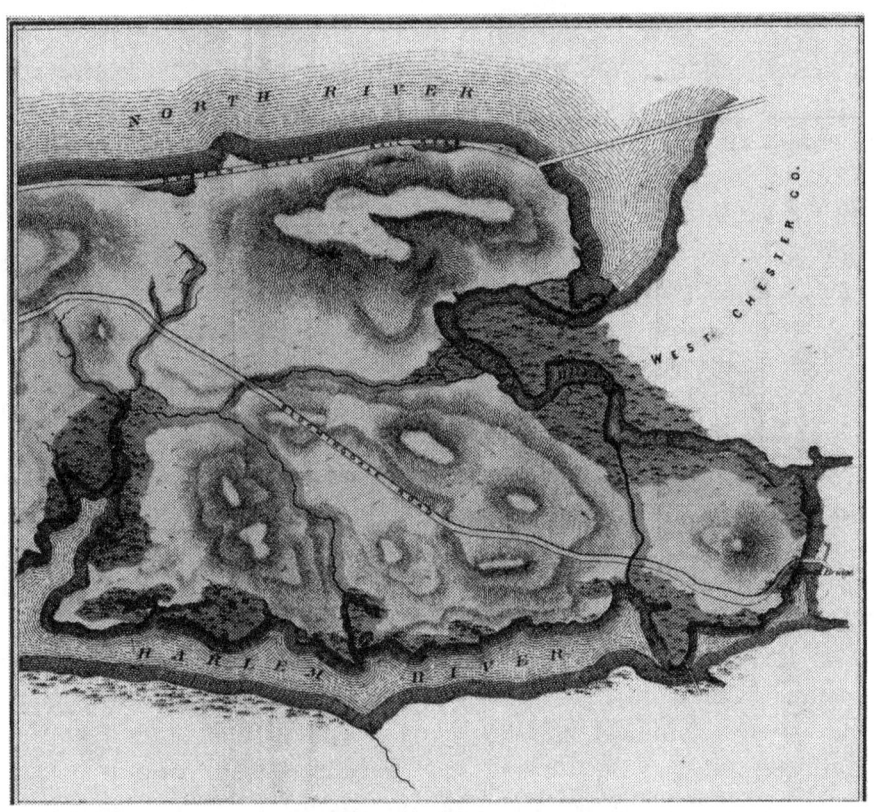

Figure 30 Harlem & Spuyten Duyvil River in 1855.[573]

Let's take a look at what the flood current was doing that day. It's not recorded what time he began his swim but the flood in the Hudson began at 9am at the Battery and the flood continued until about 4pm up at Spuyten Duyvil. The ebb current in the Harlem began at 1:30pm and continued for another six hour before it would switch and flow south on a flood current. He missed the flood current, which would have taken him south along the Harlem and wound up battling with the ebb current for an hour as it gained strength. He most likely arrived there after 2 pm when the current out of the Harlem would be strong enough to delay his transit. Regardless of that, the swim up the Hudson River in 5 hours, 9am to 2pm is remarkable because the maximum flood current that day was rated at 1.9 knots, slow by modern standards as we've learned to pick days when the current is faster. His average speed over this presumed time period given that the distance from the Battery to Spuyten Duyvil is 13 miles would be 2.6 knots. Allowing for the average current push for that day and tide, 1.3 knot, this makes Dowling's maximum average speed 1.3 knots or he could do about 43 yards a minute; he maintained a 1650 pace of about 38 minutes per mile. Robert Dowling was a slow swimmer by today's standards. Observing the swim was his father, Robert E Dowling, a Mr. T. H. Howland a swimming instructor and trainer, and a Mr. Walsh of the A. A. U.,[574] this sounds very much like the normal crew that attends to a swimmer: family, a coach and an impartial observer.

    The idea occurred to him or someone on his team after his failed attempt to go the other direction. If swimmers can make it up from the Battery up the East River and then to the NYAC club dock half way up the Harlem River, it would make sense to tackle the Hudson River after completing the part of the swim that was well known. The New York Tribune reported in its morning edition on September 5th that Robert Dowling would attempt again the swim around Manhattan using a course that started at the Battery going up the East River, then through the Harlem River and finally back down the Hudson River.[575] When the paper reported the results of the successful swim the next day, they included the starting point as Spuyten Duyvil, which was slightly different than what they had announced the day before. The paper also reported this swim as being the first ever to go around Manhattan. The swimmer's team decided to tackle the Hudson River first rather than last.

    The weather on September 5th, 1915, was not particularly difficult and Robert swam using a trudgeon crawl stroke, alternating with the side and breaststroke. The report included all the times that he made going around Manhattan. An affidavit was to be presented to the AAU with a claim for the record. There were eight witnesses to the swim including Lawrence McGuire, George Rolando, Albert and Charles Berryman, Alexander Mahon, Samuel White, Robert E. Dowling (the father) and the coach T. H.

Howland.[576]   The New York Times also reported that on September 5th, 1915, Robert Dowling became the first person to swim around Manhattan.[577]

For this swim, Robert started where he was stopped in his first attempt, at the railroad bridge across Spuyten Duyvil. He started at the beginning of the ebb in the Hudson. The Hudson River was completed in 4 ½ hours, the East River took 5 ¼ hours and the Harlem took 4 hours, total time: 13:45. The reason the Hudson was quicker that day than his first attempt is not due to the maximum current which that day was 1.6 knots but due to the fact that the current in the Hudson River southbound is easier to find. Considering the currents for that day, I estimate that he maintained a 36-minute per mile pace. The East River took longer than what swimmers are used to today because he arrived before the river had switched to a flood current. Additionally, the current takes time to build up to speed. Dowling didn't quit at this juncture because he was at a familiar location and knew the current was due to change and he had committed to a complete circuit of Manhattan. When he reached the Harlem, he found himself again swimming in an opposing current and he had now been swimming for nearly 10 hours. Knowing he was just a short swim away from finishing, Robert kept plugging away at the Harlem River just as the Manhattan marathon swimmers do today as they wait for the tide change around East 96th street.

Since Dowling's successful swim was late in the season for swimmers, no one attempted to duplicate his swim that year. The next person to swim around Manhattan was Amelia Gade at age 22 on September 26, 1921. She started at West 98th Street on an ebb tide swimming counterclockwise around the island. Her time is recorded as 15:57. She was a swimming instructor for the YWCA and became better known under her married name of Mrs. Cleminton Corson.[578]   In the same year, she swam down the Hudson River establishing herself as a marathon swimmer of note in New York. The Channel Swimming Association knows her as Mille Carde Corson. She swam the English Channel a few weeks after Gertrude Ederle with a slightly slower time in 1926.

Whenever you have two swimmers of like abilities, jealousies can be a factor that leads them to attempt swims of increasing difficulties to prove they are the better swimmer. Or one of them is tempted to challenge the other swimmer to a match race. Mrs. Corson swam the Channel but weeks after Miss Ederle; one would be tempted to ask if she had trained for this attempt and Gertrude simply beat her to the punch. In any case, on Mrs. Corson's behalf, a promoter offered in late summer of 1926 to put up $25,000 for the two of them to race around Manhattan.[579] Gertrude Ederle declined the offer. One could only wonder what gall Mrs. Corson had to even think of challenging a gold medal winner at the Olympics not to mention holder of 29 World and National records.

Charlotte Schoemmell swam around Manhattan on September 9, 1926 in a time of 14:21. She started at West 240th Street near Spuyten Duyvil and finished by swimming though an adverse tide in the Harlem River. This time slightly edged out Amelia Gade's time for the woman's record. Interest in swimming around Manhattan continued for several years, even to the extent of creating an annual marathon swim. This was during the first Golden Era of marathon swimming that started when Gertrude Ederle took up marathon swimming and ended with the Great Depression.

Onto the scene in 1927 appeared Byron Summers, age 25, who solved the problem of swimming around Manhattan in a reasonable period of time. Having beaten the time of George Young for the Catalina record the previous April, he had come east to ply his craft. Consulting with William Erickson, they picked a date of September 18, 1927, which might have had more to do with personnel schedules than picking the best current. The "Flying Fish" as Byron was called started at East 125th and the Harlem River, swimming north. His time of 8:56 established a new record that even today is a respectable time.[580] His course and the currents he encountered are the same swimmers experience today as their swims are but duplicates of his. He entered the Harlem River at the pier that stands there today on the start of an ebb current, presumably at approximately 4:30am. He entered the Hudson River from the Harlem and swam south on the Hudson ebb, which for that day was only a 1.9-knot current. Reaching the East River at the Battery, it was just starting to flood, he swam north to Hell Gate on a 3.3 knot current, turning left into the Harlem River and swimming the last mile against an opposing current of about 1.3 knots much as the swimmers in the annual marathon competition presently experience. The purpose of this swim was to establish a new record, receive some press and serve as a prelude to a planned prize money marathon in 1928. He could have gone faster if he had chosen a date with faster currents but at this point in the swim's development, they were still experimenting with the starting location. On this point, they were met with resounding success. This swim generated a story on the front page of the New York Times.

Summers' success generated an immediate response from a local NYAC swimmer, William Sadlo, Jr., much as was seen in the history of the English Channel. William attempted many times to swim around Manhattan using a similar course as Byron but he did not have the assistance of William Erickson, Byron Summers' navigator. His first attempt on September 25, 1927, on essentially the same current that Bryon Summers had, was successful. He completed the swim in 9:28 but didn't set a record.[581] He tried again on October 12th that had a phenomenal current in the Hudson River of 2.7 knots but that attempt ended in failure as he failed to make the tide change at the Battery. This information tells me that he started too late in the Harlem River.

The swim the following year promoted by the International Professional Swimmers' Association was held on June 17, 1928. There were no finishers as none of the three contestants went farther than Grant's Tomb.[582] One of the contestants was William Sadlo and the other two were Hershel Martin of Kansas City and Gustave Beu of New York. I suspect that the swimmers all got cold as it was early in the swimming season and the water temperature could have been as low as 65 degrees Fahrenheit. The currents that day were perfect for a 10am start in the Harlem with the Hudson running at a brisk 2.3 knots.

The 1928 swim was rescheduled for July 1, 1928, and the winner was William Sadlo, Jr., in a time of 9:08 but the competition had dwindled to two swimmers. There were complications during the swim, the other swimmer, Hershel Martin, decided to drop out of the race while in the Hudson and his rowing dory got hung up in the piers while removing the swimmer, dumping the three men escorting the swimmer into the water with the swimmer. A launch rescued all four. During the swim a dory set a record for rowing around Manhattan of 5 hours.[583]

The next year, 1929, two amateur swimmers set out on the same day, July 22nd, to break the male and the female record. Mingie Del Orto and Lillian Garrick, age 17. The tide timing was provided by N. H. McPhee. Mingie didn't make the tide change at the Battery but Lillian, by swimming down the Jersey side of the Hudson, was able to make the turn into the East River. This technique set a pattern in the Manhattan swim for slow swimmers that didn't change until the modern era. She finished in a time of 11:26, not particularly fast but she finished.

The following year, 1930, on July 27th, two swimmers from Florida came north to try their luck swimming around Manhattan in another contest sponsored by the International Professional Swimming Association. The race had 24 swimmers. Starting just after noon, Sam Shields, age 24, and Anne Priller Benoit, age 21, were the winners of this swim, his time was 8:35 and hers was 9:01. Both were records. The current that day in the Hudson was 2.3 knots. William Sadlo swam in this event, coming in second, besting Byron Summers time. Since it was a professional contest, the winning swimmer received a prize of $500.[584] The starting point was East 89th street where the East River and the Harlem River meet. The Health commissioner sent a policeman to the start of the swim to warn the swimmers of the health risks of swimming in the rivers. One swimmer swam without an escort boat and upon coming to the junction of the Harlem and Hudson Rivers, did not know which way to swim and sought directions from a passing canoe. Another local swimmer entered in this event was Clarence Ross who did not finish. For three years, the swim was a professional event. The onset of the Depression of 1930 dried up the money for the professional swim around Manhattan.

The next recorded successful swim around Manhattan wasn't until 29 years later. There was one abortive attempt on October 5th of 1958 by Jason Zerganos, age 48, from Greece.[585] He was aided in his swim by an impromptu visit by Gertrude Ederle who heard of the swim while it was underway over the radio. He eventually was pulled from the waters after 23 hours of swimming. I could not imagine the reason this swimmer couldn't make it around the island in all that time. It casts doubt on his claim to have swum the English Channel four times.[586] It turns out that his swims were professional swims, which are not recorded by the Channel Swimming Association. Within a year he wound up as a fatality when trying to swim the Irish Sea North Channel.[587]

Swimming around Manhattan fell out of favor during these years. There are a variety of reasons for this. One was the poor press that the last swim received. It's not that the press didn't report on the swim, just that with Zerganos' failure no one was inspired to repeat the effort. There was the fact that the memory of the public is uninformed and of short duration.[588] Additionally, the New York City Health Department determined the waters around New York were unhealthy. They had sent a policeman to warn the swimmers of the dangers for the 1930 marathon. The complaints received by the boat captains about the swimmers and the health concerns caused the City of New York to clamp down on swims in the waters around Manhattan. The rivers were truly dirty for when the marathon resumed in 1983; you could not see the swimmers arms (or any part of their body) once it entered the water and became submerged. In 1968, the Coast Guard stopped a swim by John Logan of Hoboken across the Hudson.[589] In the article, the police stated the conditions under which a swim might be allowed to proceed: one, the swimmer had to notify the police and two; the swimmer had to be accompanied by a rowboat.[590] In 1974, two swimmers were arrested and charged with endangering life and disorderly conduct.[591] The swimmers were Don O'Hara and Peter Lloyd who swam across the Hudson River in the middle of the night successfully, with Mr. Lloyd making a round trip. This legal action put a damper on swimming around Manhattan. Mr. Lloyd who claimed to have swum the English Channel[592] found the waters so repulsive that he reverted to the breaststroke the entire way. Even after the resumption of the marathon in 1982, during a solo attempt by Julie Ridge, we received the obligatory visit by the police advising us of the dangers of swimming in the water. Because of this history, the organizers for the Manhattan Marathon swim complete numerous applications for permission to swim and coordinate with the various civilian agencies in charge of New York waters. There is a disclaimer in the swim application advising the swimmers to see a doctor before undertaking the swim. The joke among swimmers was it wasn't a medical doctor that you were supposed to see. Swimmers always laughed gleefully at that one-liner. I've heard it used more than once at banquets. The waters have since been cleaned up tremendously.

Pretenders

Gus Sundstrom, an early swimming coach at the New York Athletic Club[593] is credited in his obituary as being the first man to swim around Manhattan Island. He was very instrumental in developing the American crawl stroke but like most myths, the story grows out of a smaller truth, sometimes called a half-truth. It turns out that his longest swim was from the Battery to High Bridge. The destination was near the location of the New York Athletic Clubs marine center located at 150th Street on the Harlem River.[594] There are two swims that are the basis for his claim of swimming around Manhattan. The first swim was on July 26, 1885, when he swam from Macomb Dam Bridge to the Battery at age 23 using the sidestroke.[595] This was the first reputed swim through Hell Gate. This swim took 3:38 finishing in the water opposite Hamilton Ferry. The second swim went along the same course in the opposite direction. It started from a ferryboat; Gus jumped from the Hamilton ferry when it was opposite Governors

Island en route to the City after leaving its slip at Hamilton Avenue in Brooklyn on July 28th, 1886.[596] Two unusual occurrences happened during this swim. One, he had covered his body with porpoise oil causing him to look like, "a mahogany Hercules in nineteenth century swimming drawers." But the mixture bled and Gus retreated to his support boat and spent 17 minutes rubbing his eyes. The second occurrence was even stranger; a policeman upon seeing Gus swimming in the Harlem River secured a dinghy and rowed out to ascertain that he was wearing tights!

These accounts of his longest swims are substantiated by reports published in the New York Times on the occasions of their occurrence. Also, in a correction published on September 22, 1926 after an article published on a swimmer completing a swim around Manhattan, the New York Times went over the known history of the Manhattan swim as it stood at that time.[597] This correction substantiates the information as it is presented in this history. The correction does not mention Gus Sundstrom among those that had swam around Manhattan up to that time.

Another claim to being the first swimmer appeared in United States Master Swimming Newsletter No. 4, November 1986. On page three, it was reported that US Long Distance Swimming presented a special award to Clarence Ross of Jersey Masters. It was claimed that when he was 16 he became the first person to swim around Manhattan Island. The claims further extended his prowess to include the claim of being the oldest person to complete the swim. Somehow, this incredulous myth morphed into his being the winner of the first competitive race around Manhattan as claimed in the summary of his swimming resume at the International Swimming Hall of Fame where he is an honoree.[598] This report is ludicrous and false. Again the claim grows out of a half-truth but in this case the swim that is his basis for the claim wasn't even around Manhattan. That would be part of the reason for the vagueness of the claim and its changeability.

In 1927, Clarence was at the end of a long and illustrious amateur career having won the National AAU long-distance swimming championship three times. He had decided to give up his amateur status to enter a professional meet with a cash prize of $50,000.[599] This article included a list of all his achievements up to that time. Nothing was mentioned about Manhattan in this article. The first known competitive race around Manhattan took place in early summer of 1928. He was not listed as a competitor. However, on September 8, 1928, he did beat Byron Summers in a 3-mile swim in Canada.[600] It was a professional race. Byron at the time held the record for around the Manhattan swim. In 1930, he participated in the 3rd professional swim around Manhattan. While he was in the lead at various times during the race around Manhattan, he was pulled in the East River because of a cramp.[601] He's a DNF, did not finish. This is the closest he got to swimming around Manhattan and as far as I know, he's never completed a swim around Manhattan. Adding confusion to reports is another swimmer of the same era by the name of Norman Ross from Chicago and at various times in the news reports the names were confused.

In 1921, the New York Times reported that in September of 1916, Ida Elionsky swam around Manhattan in 11:35. Little else in the article was said about her, the course she took, or the exact day. Her time beat the time of Robert Dowling but the starting place and date wasn't given.[602] Her father was known as a stunt swimmer and would often shackle himself and swim for distance.[603] Ida had previously swum from Yonkers to the Battery, the Battery to Staten Island, and New Rochelle to Sands Point, Long Island.[604] Ida herself did ten miles shackled from the Battery to the Narrows just before Roberts Dowling's successful Manhattan "circumswim".[605] In August of 1916, Ida performed a stunt where she swam with her brother strapped to her back, another event pioneered by her father, Harry. There was an accident with one of the support boats ramming into a barge but other than that, there was little else to distinguish this swim. Neither the New York Time nor the New York Tribune carried any record of her swimming around Manhattan in 1916. Since the only report of her doing so was in a short historical recall published by the New York Times in 1921, it could be possible that they were in error regarding the validity of the swim and the reporter mixed up the stunt swim for a circumswim of Manhattan.

Reporter error in their background information is still common. Al Cohn of Newsday reported in 1982 that a swimmer named Steve Ross, age 25, of Niagara, New York, broke Diana Nyad's record time in 1975 with a 7:45 in the same year.[606] Again, this was a background report on the history of the Manhattan swim that has no substantive basis. For one, Diana's swim was in October and all the subsequent tides (except for the very next day) were slower until November when it was too cold to swim.

In 2004, the Press Telegram of Long Beach reported that Greta Andersen did a double of the Molokai Straits in 1961. It turned out that there was an old report that Greta did a double in the clipping file on Greta Andersen at the Press Telegram. The reporter, who wrote the story, Bob Keissler, made a simple error and when questioned by me, he checked his sources and confirmed the erroneous report. Newspapers do make mistakes.

Figure 31 A swimmer passing by the United Nations.

Chapter 10   Modern Manhattan

A brewery broke the twenty-nine year hiatus from open-water marathon swims around Manhattan Island; Schaefer Brewing Company decided to sponsor a swim to celebrate the 350th anniversary of the Dutch exploration of the Hudson River in 1959. In order to get permission for the swim, a bill was passed in the New York City Council permitting the swim. Since the company had a considerable budget for this celebration, they sought a swimmer with some credible star qualities. This they found in the person of Diane Struble, a mother of three, who the year before had swum Lake George, a distance of 32 miles in 35+ hours.[607]   On their behalf, Diane Struble, now age 26, swam around Manhattan on August 15, 1959. The time for her swim is recorded as 11:21.[608] To successfully complete the swim in a normal time, she would have had to of left the Battery by 5:00 am; she left at 3:31am. The current that day was a respectable 2.2 knots. She even attempted a second lap[609] but city officials had two lifeguards pull her out.[610]   At the finish, Robert Dowling, handsomely attired in a business suit, met her and presented her with a bouquet of flowers.[611] This swim laid the groundwork for the resumption of swimming around Manhattan and served as a model for the relocation of the start for the Manhattan marathon in the 1980's.

The enthusiasm for swimming around Manhattan begins with a young lady whose efforts were chronicled in the local press. In order to appreciate her efforts, you must first know that the borough of Manhattan had written off swimming as a sport and prohibited swimming. Young men growing up in Manhattan would pursue the sport by diving off a dock in lower Manhattan then swim with the incoming flood tide to various beaches along the upper Manhattan shore. The boys would board subways to ride back downtown. One swimmer told a tale of a friend going under a barge never to surface again.[612] The NY Times reported an actual account of a similar incident in 1929.[613] When the city closed off the final beach with the construction of the FDR drive along the East River this ended the impromptu nature of swimming.[614] Even today, swimmers cannot just jump into the waters around Manhattan and go swimming without garnering a response from the Harbor police unit. To the ordinary passerby, a swimmer looks like a person committing suicide; more than once, I've seen a helicopter unit overhead searching the waters after a swimmer had passed by. To swim in the waters of Manhattan, you must first apply for a permit from the City through the Parks Department to access the water from one of their parks (most of the public access to the water is via Parks Department controlled land) and file a marine parade application from the Coast Guard.

It was on October 6, 1975, some sixteen years after Diana Struble, that Diana Nyad began her successful swim around Manhattan. It was the second attempt. She had tried unsuccessfully 11 days earlier.[615] Her time of 7:57 set a record.[616] She became the first person to swim Manhattan in under 8 hours. With the publicity of this event followed up by the Cuba attempt in 1978, everybody became aware of the commercial possibilities associated with the Manhattan swim. Diana started at the Fire Departments pier at East 89th Street and used Ed Lininger as her tide consultant. He had her swim down the Jersey side of Manhattan when in the Hudson River. The current that day was a ferocious 2.7 knots. The reason she failed in her first attempt was the current. On September 25th the Hudson River was only 1.8 knots and she started swimming 45 minutes before she had to. Thus when she got to the East River at the Battery, she wound up fighting the ebb tide which exhausted her. Ed adjusted her start time for the second attempt to ten minutes before the start of high tide at Hell Gate. Ed was using the tide table, as they are the easiest to obtain. It's knowledge of the current flow that makes the difference between swims. In her October swim, not having to swim as long, having a ferocious tide push her down the Hudson, and treading water off the Battery waiting for a tide change, saved Diana's strength for the East River portion of the swim. The successful swim generated a front-page notice with a single column photo in the lower right hand corner by the New York

Times. The following year Diana attempted a swim across Long Island Sound but failed on July 30 when she cramped up due to a weight training program.[617] She went on to attempt other swims mentioned in this book.

The era then submerged with an occasional swimmer attempting the swim. George Kauffmann, Tom Hetzel[618] and a few other open-water swimmers were Manhattan enthusiasts. George Kauffmann began swimming around Manhattan annually in 1977 and kept this effort up until he "retired" from the Manhattan Island Swimming Association. Another swimmer, Ben Huggard of Long Island, had completed 2 previous trips with another scheduled in 1982 then he began swimming annually with the Manhattan Island Swimming Association. The key to the swim was local knowledge.

Upon this scene entered a superstar, Drury Gallagher, whose adoption of this swim changed marathon swimming. Tom Hetzel, a childhood friend of Drury's from Rockaway, Queens, convinced Drury that a swim around Manhattan would be a source of consolation over the death of his oldest son. Sometimes, it takes the exertion of swimming in a new and different environment, perhaps even dangerous to take a swimmer's mind off a personal crisis. Swimming places you in the here and now quite literally: take the next stroke; take another breath rhythmically repeated until exhaustion. After Drury Gallagher Jr. died, this was just what Drury needed. He made a memorial swim around Manhattan on July 19, 1982, to honor his son and establishing a new record, 7:14. Notice of this swim appeared in a local paper.[619] Upon reading of his swim in the local paper, I contacted Drury to offer assistance should he attempt another swim. Drury's reply was, "Come on down next month, we're having a marathon." My involvement with the Manhattan marathon began at this point.

On September 14, 1982, the first modern era Manhattan marathon swim competition was held.[620] The inaugural swim had eleven swimmers who left from the Asphalt Green[621] dock at East 89th Street swimming north to the entrance of the Harlem River. The eventual winner was David Horning of San Francisco. During his swim, he and Todd Bryant kept pace with each other until Todd left the water just south of the George Washington Bridge complaining of the effects of the exhaust from the escort boat. There was never a more different style between two swimmers. Both were sub-18 minutes per mile swimmers. Todd was at one time the captain of the Harvard swim team and was as trim and tapered a swimmer, as you would ever see. His stroke was perfection as he carved his way through the water. Dave Horning on the other hand was built like a bear, a Golden Bear as he swam for Berkeley in college. He had massive arms and seemed to just swing them in a circle and squeeze the water. Stroke for stroke these two magnificent swimmers swam up the Harlem, at times disappearing into the murky mists that enveloped the city that morning. The reason the swimmers disappeared into the mist was the boat would occasionally die and the swimmers just kept stroking. It stuck me that since I was the only one on board the escort boat, I was the sole spectator to a fantastic swim race. There was only the occasional pedestrian along the Harlem River shore.

After Todd Bryant retired from the swim, Dave Horning swam on and when I caught up with him next, he was swimming against the tide in the East River ebb south of the Brooklyn Bridge near the heliport. As soon as I saw his predicament, I knew that he had come around the Battery too soon and to find a better current, he only needed to delay his swim at the start. This intuitive assessment of the swim was confirmed upon inspection of the current charts for Manhattan and eventually by a computer program I wrote. There is an hour and a half overlap between the end of ebb in the Hudson River and the beginning of the flood in the East River. Swimmers only need to time their swim to reach the Battery on the tail end of the Hudson River ebb current to enter the East River as the flood current is picking up speed. This is the secret to swimming around Manhattan in less than seven hours. To do it accurately and take the guesswork out of the swim, one needs to use a computer.

Computer model

Between September of 1982 and August of 1983, I developed a computer program to model times for swimming around Manhattan as part of my undergraduate degree program at Empire State College. The program would allow swimmers to pick an optimum starting time to minimize their transit around the island. The program, first written in BASIC, would calculate the speed of the current at any time in any of the rivers and add that to the swimmers speed to compute the time necessary to swim around Manhattan. With this information, the time a swimmer would pass various locations around Manhattan Island could be projected and the exact time of transit for the Battery would be known as well as the total elapsed time. The only variables that needed to be entered were the currents for the day, the swimmer's speed and the starting time. Of these three variables, the only one that was truly variable once the swimmer and the date were set was the time of the start. By running a series of analysis of different start times, the optimum start time to minimize the swim by varying the start could be determined. The beauty of this non-linear program is that it correctly estimates the current so that the projections are never very far off from the swimmers actual position. Swim optimization by computer simulation became a tool marathon swimmers could use in planning their swims.

The test of the program accuracy and usefulness was to compare the program projections against the times of an actual swimmer. The swimmer selected to participate was Paul Asmuth, from San Jose, California. Paul, at the time, was the reigning World Professional Marathon Swimmer. On August 7, 1983, Paul began his swim at 10:00 am. On board the escort boat was Drury Gallagher and Tim Johnson. Tom Golden was the escort pilot in his lobster boat. Paul Asmuth was such a powerful swimmer that three quarters of the way into the swim, by the ferry terminals at the Battery, his kick was splashing into the escort boat to the extent that support crew had to shield the papers they were recording the times and stroke count for the swim upon. Paul set a record that day of 6:48.

Paul Asmuth is the first person to swim around Manhattan Island in under 7 hours. This coincidentally was very close to the predicted time for a 20 minute per mile pace of 6:50, which Paul Asmuth had inquired about before the start of the swim. Paul's vocation is an accountant and since he handles numbers all the time, he was quite impressed.

Figure 32 Tim Johnson, Paul Asmuth, Drury Gallagher (l to r).

During the swim, as Paul would swim by various landmarks and pass under bridges, the times were recorded and compared to the projection at 13 locations around Manhattan.[622] At one point, the program was off by as much as 20 minutes in the Hudson River. Later, when comparing the program to the swimmers time, an error was discovered where the current variable referenced the Harlem River current speed instead of the Hudson River current speed. Paul Asmuth, by being such a consistent swimmer, provided the information needed to debug the program. Even with the error, the program projections were not far off, within two minutes of the actual time. Other than this error, the program's biggest deviation from the swimmer's time was in the East River around the Williamsburg Bridge where the swimmer's times lagged behind the computer projection. It made the swimmer look like he was slowing down. This error turned out to be more related to the course taken by the swimmers than computational. It would take 10 years to discover the secret to swimming around the Battery and up the East River past Corlears Hook without dropping 20 minutes to the computer projections in this section of the swim. This solution made swims around Manhattan in less than six hours possible. The original program was written in Hewlett Packard BASIC for a Hewlett Packard Model 85 computer, a 16K machine with a printed tape output and a full keyboard. The analysis consisted of plotting the points on a graph and looking for the lowest point on the curve. The very first run revealed that swims around Manhattan could be accomplished in 5½ hours. The current record at the time the program was developed stood at 7:14.

There was still a lot of work to be done even with the debugging by Asmuth; for one, the computer model needed to be tested for accuracy over a range of swimming speeds. It would be necessary to collect information from a variety of swims to test the computer projections. The 2nd annual Manhattan Island Marathon Swim provided this information. A ham radio club was enlisted to assist with data collection and reporting. It soon became apparent that the swim officials were overwhelmed with data during the course of the swim and later swims merely report the swimmers as they past 3 key locations: the Battery, Spuyten Duyvil, and 79th Street Boat Basin in the Hudson River.[623] This information confirmed the variation at Williamsburg Bridge but the program proved success in tracking and predicting swimmers finishes. Depending upon the swimmers consistency and swim course, deviations of 5 minutes or less could be determined. This allowed the swimmer to say they averaged 20, or 23.5 minutes per mile around Manhattan. One feature of the computer program would subtract out the current and reveal the swimmer's pace.

187

Plotting the swimmer's paces revealed interesting facts about initial speed of swimmers in relationship to the constant pace they'd normally hold during a swim. Fast swimmers drop 2 to 3 minutes per mile; say from 17 or 18 minutes per mile pace at the start to 20 or 21 minutes per mile for the rest of the race. Average swimmers showed more consistency at the start but tailed off near the end depending on their training. Slow swimmers had large variations in their pace and as a rule their pace started slow and got slower. For top swimmers, the program would show a correlation between the predicted times and actual time of 99.97%. What is developed is the pace information based on this computer simulation and the swimmer's time. The pace information is then used when those swimmers want to set a personal best. For any swimmer that is interested in seeing if they could break seven or six hours on a good tide, they would first swim around Manhattan, record their times passing the computer locations, then do a projection using their pace and that particular day's current. What has not been done is compare a swimmer's pool times to their actual race times around Manhattan. A computer pace time can be developed from the checkpoint times or just the finishing time but the accuracy is slightly diminished.

The chart shown in Table 1 is the computer projection for August 7, 1983. The x-axis is the delay after ebb begins at Hell Gate used to determine the start. The y-axis is the finishing time. The curves are the various plots for finishes based on the swimmer speed in 1650-pace time. They represent a family of curves. Observation of this family of curves reveal that the faster one swims, the more choices one has of a starting time to achieve the fastest transit of Manhattan. For example, the 30 minutes per 1650 swimmer has 20 minutes to set off on their swim and they will achieve approximately the same minimum finishing time. The fast swimmers have around 45 minutes to adjust their starting time and still achieve approximately the same minimum finishing time (which is significantly faster than the slower swimmers).

Table 1

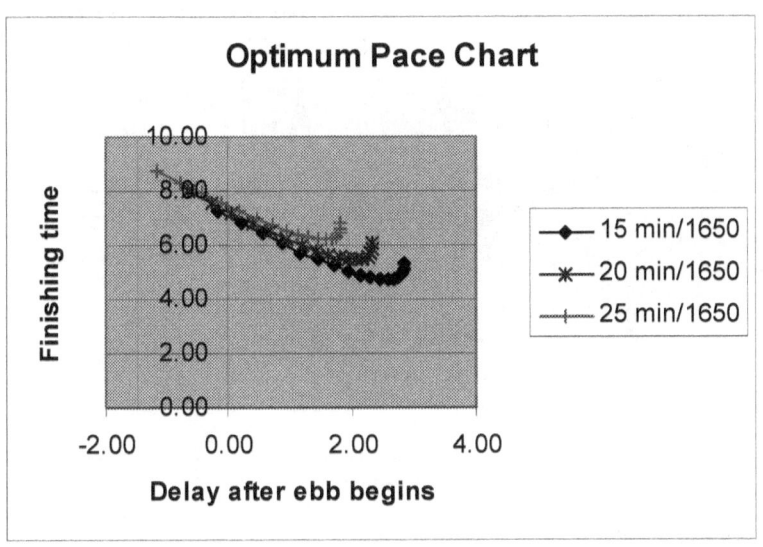

The largest curve, which I plotted alone in an Excel spreadsheet for 16 minutes per 1650, has a formula that is seen in Table 2. I used this curve to derive the formula for the curves as it had the most data points. Within the limits of the Excel's embedded statistical program, the formula reproduces the computer program data points fairly well. The data points from the computer program are Series 1 and the formula's plots are labeled Series 2. They pretty much overlay on top of one another. The x value in the formula is the delay used measured in hours from ebb begins, the y value is the finishing time in hours.

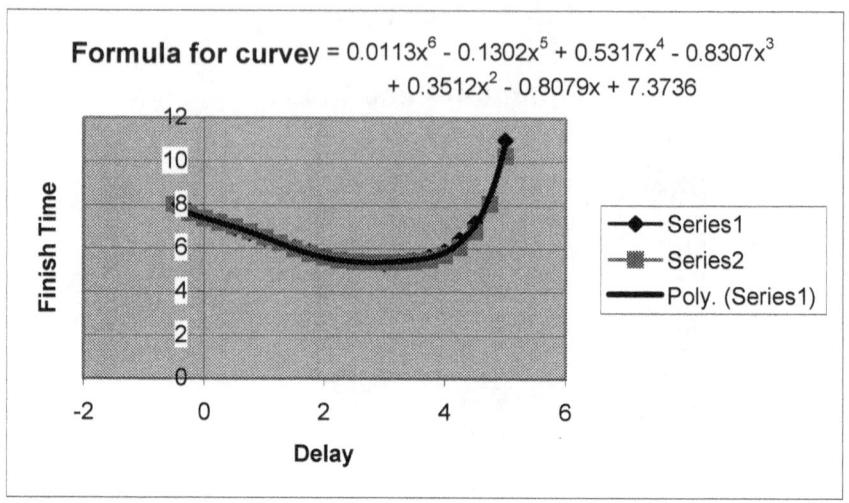

Table 2

Here is the formula:

$$Y = .0113x^6 - .1302x^5 + .5317x^4 - .8307x^3 + .3512x^2 - .8079x + 7.3736$$

This formula is not as important as the straight line joining all the minimum point of the family of curves. That formula is:

$$Y = .1518x + 3.112$$

Where the Y is the finishing time in hours and the X is the 1650 pace. This information is useless you know the optimum starting time delay. That formula is:

$$Y = -.135x + 4.795$$

Where the Y is the delay in hours and the X is the swimmer's 1650 pace.

With this information, on that date, provided you knew when ebb began at Hell Gate; you could start a swim and turn in your best time for Manhattan. Of course knowing the information is useless unless you are swimming a consistent pace. If your pace varies, you start to slip back in time. So, as a precaution for a swimmer falling off the pace, I start swimmers at the beginning of the bottom of the curve. They will still achieve approximately the best time at their pace but should they fall off by 5 minutes per

1650, the swimmers will achieve the best time for the slower pace as that is within the slower pace minimum time window. One note of caution: these formulas are accurate for August 7, 1983. The behavior of the curves on other dates stays the same but the data varies with the current.

While these formulas are unique for this venue, principles observed are applicable to all swims affected by tide: once the day and swimmer are set, the main variable that affects the finishing time is setting the swim start. The swim start decides where in the current tide cycle the swimmer is inserted and this time varies for every swimmer based on their swimming pace.

The swim by Paul Azmuth revealed some practical aspects of swimming around Manhattan. Paul began his swim on a high tide and we just step off the cement abutment onto the boat. At the finish, it was low tide and we had to climb onto the boat's cabin top to climb back onto land. This effect wasn't noticed during the 1982 race because we started from a floating dock at Asphalt Green at West 89th Street. When we lost access to that facility because a swimmer attempted to go swimming without permission creating a police incident, an alternate means of egress was necessary.

Figure 33 Julie Ridge shown exiting the water in 1986. When the swim moved to the Battery, the tide conditions were the same and the ladder became part of the swim. Swimmers swim on a falling tide all the way around Manhattan.

In pursuit of the record

After the swim by Paul Asmuth substantiated the importance of the computer program, Drury and I began planning to break the record. Before the start of Paul Asmuth's swim, he had asked why we didn't try a faster current. He sensed intuitively that the current was one of the keys to the Manhattan swim. My answer to him was that the program was untried and until it was proven, it was a gamble. I had already picked the date for the next record swim; it was September 7, 1983. I then began lobbying for a men and woman's record being set on the same day. Drury was a bit hesitant so I enlisted the aid of Jane Katz. She immediately suggested Sally Friedman who had just completed the Manhattan marathon.

Figure 34 Drury Gallagher with Sally Friedman at the awards Luncheon held at the Water Club after the 1983 MIMS.

I pulled Sally's swim times for that swim and analyzed her times. She was a very steady swimmer. I compared her and Drury's printouts and saw that Drury would catch and pass her; so we could give her a head start. Armed with this information, Jane and I convinced Drury to share the spotlight and the event was set. Sally Friedman had just finished 8th in the 2nd annual Manhattan Island Marathon Swim on July 24, 1983. She had a bouncy stroke that made her look like she was dribbling a basketball when she swam. Tommy Golden was slated to be the escort for Drury and Drury's personal boat was the support for Sally. She had Suzanne Rague as her coach for the trip along with Jane Katz. Sally was to set off first and then Drury 30 minutes later. Drury was supposed to catch and pass Sally in the Hudson River. What I didn't know was Drury tended to tire after four hours of swimming. His pace would drop off by about 2 minutes per mile. When the Williamsburg Bridge in the East River came and went with Sally Friedman still ahead of us, I called ahead to Sally's boat and asked what they were feeding her. Drury got only so close then stopped closing the distance. Sally finished first in 7:01, forty minutes faster than the current woman's record held by Karen Hartley of Massachusetts, and Drury did 6:43 breaking the record again. He was quite happy.

The simple answer to how the swimmers were able to break the record lay in picking a fast tide then starting late at East 96th Street. This reduction of the swim program to these two principles essentially worked well enough for the next record to be established. Joseph Coplan, another Vice-President of the Manhattan Island Swimming Association, utilized this approach to make an attempt on the woman's record. He arranged for Diddo Clark, age 32, of Washington, D. C., to swim on October 7, 1983.[624] Diddo managed to do a 6:52 making her the first woman to swim under 7 hours around Manhattan. At this point we had 3 swimmers who had swum around Manhattan in under 7 hours.

The organization began scheduling swims to break the record and inviting swimmers of considerable skills to make these attempts. Next was Shelley Taylor who broke both the men and women's record and established the overall record for the fastest time around Manhattan. She brought the record down to 6:12 minutes on October 15, 1985. The current that day in the Hudson River had a maximum speed of 2.6 knots. Joe Coplan arranged her swim but did not take advantage of the swimming program to calculate her times. The strategy merely copied the delayed start of 2 hours used for Drury Gallagher's swim and found out the times for the tides at Hell Gate. Assisting in the swim that day aboard the escort boat was Ed Lininger.

Drury Gallagher and I watched from the shore at East 96th Street as Ed brought Shelly Taylor in the boat out to start from the rundown pier attached to Mill Rock just off the Manhattan coastline. They circled around the water at the start looking at the current then dropped Shelley in the water just south of the pier. At the swim start, she crossed in front of the pier. At the finish, she would cross the same point. We had a short discussion of whether or not to allow a swim to qualify as a circumswim if the swimmer never leaves or returns to the Manhattan shoreline. Since we knew the English Channel and FINA Long Distance Swimming requires a swimmer to leave from and return to land; this was a serious consideration. But their requirements were for a point-to-point swim. Circular swim were not defined. The Manhattan swim was merely a route that begins and ended at the same place. Seeing that Manhattan was within the center of the route, one could not help but reason that the swim would count. When Shelly turned in such a spectacular time, we were not going to disallow her swim on a technicality and she essentially redefined the Manhattan swim start (at least for record attempts).

There were two attempts by a local swimmer, Karen Farnsworth, to best Shelly Taylor's time but neither was successful. The best Karen was able to manage was to tie the record which was a marvelous achievement because by this time, Shelly Taylor had gone on to become the premier open water swimmer of Australia and a top competitor in the professional circuit.

One of Karen's notable accomplishments in marathon swimming was surviving being run over by a motorboat. In one of Karen's attempts on the record, the Hudson River was so rough that Karen would pop out of one wave and her stroke would be grabbing thin air as the wave trough passed under her. The swells were easily 5 to 6 feet for the whole length of the Hudson River. I've rarely seen more determination in a swimmer. She looked like a porpoise swimming and diving through surf. But it was earlier in the swim that an accident occurred that made her swim down the Hudson look like a walk in the park.

Figure 35 Waving your arms randomly signals other boaters that you require attention, not that a swimmer is in the water.

Karen had just started the swim and was only approaching the Triboro Bridge when her escort boat developed transmission trouble. Karen continued swimming as the boat owner lifted the bench seat covering the engine. When she was about 100 yards away, the support crew noticed a speedboat traveling down the Harlem and they began waving their arms to alert the boat that a swimmer was in the water. None of the crew was aware that the Coast Guard recommends waving your hand to alert other boaters of an emergency; waving your arms is a maritime distress signal. The boat changed course to see what assistance was needed putting Karen right in its path. Karen's position in the water was hidden from the boat's operator view by the sun's reflection upon the water. The crew and I watched in stunned silence as Karen disappeared underneath the boat's bow. I mentally began to prepare myself to pick up body parts. Our mouths dropped open in shocked surprise and relief when we saw her in the boat's wake shaking her fist at the offending boater. If ever I saw a New York moment, this was it. Evidently, the vee-shaped hull of the approaching boat pushed Karen out of the way of the props. The hull was designed to push debris out of the way of the props and I can certainly testify to its success. Then Karen turned to continue the swim.

When the offending boat came alongside the disabled escort boat to offer assistance; Karen's coach, Foster DeJesus, and I commandeered the speedboat so she could finish the swim under escort. I've never seen anyone sober up faster in my life than the two boaters aboard the offending escort boat when we told them what had just occurred. After the incident in the Harlem River and then a heroic swim down the roughest water I've ever seen in the Hudson River, Karen was behind the record pace. As we came upon Roosevelt Island, Karen abandoned the swim. Even with an unsuccessful swim or one that didn't accomplish its stated goal of breaking the record, information is learned about conditions that will eventually contribute toward establishing a new record. In subsequent record swims, it was what we did that was different that made those swims successful.

After Karen Farnsworth a swimmer from Nebraska attempted to break the swim record. Kris Rutford competed a number of times in the Manhattan Marathon swim, even winning the marathon in 1991. He was well known in the long distance swimming community. Arrangements were made for him to make an attempt on the record on August 29, 1992, when the ebb current in the Hudson River was rated at 2.7 knots. I used Kris's previous swim records to extract an accurate model of his swimming capabilities. Using this information, a start time was developed and the date was set. Kris Rutford set out on the swim on a sunny day from the pier off of Mill Rock. Kris Rutford was such a consistent swimmer that he zeroed out 9 of the 13 checkpoints associated with the swim. His swim down the Hudson was so close to the projections that I advised the coach to slow him down a bit so he wouldn't get ahead of the current. The coach took one stroke off his pace.

When we hit the Manhattan Bridge, we were once again behind the computer projection by 10-15 minutes. This lag caused me such consternation that I launched into an analysis immediately while aboard the boat, neglecting to watch the route. The pilot did not hug the shore as we rounded Corlears Hook and we drifted wide of our normal route under the Williamsburg Bridge. Passing under the bridge on the Brooklyn side, we were 15 minutes behind and any hope of beating the record had evaporated or so it seemed.

When we passed by the red buoy # R22 set in the channel for a range marker, just north of the Williamsburg Bridge, I noticed that the current was ripping. I had never passed this wide under the Williamsburg Bridge and had never seen this much current. It seemed too good to be true. I didn't have a check-off point for this buoy so I ran the program and checked for the time when we were to cross 23rd Street: we were making up time. I told the pilot to stay with the current. The current was taking us straight across the rocks at the bottom of Roosevelt Island, north of U Thant Island.[625] Kris's escort boat had a shallow draft so we stayed with the current and the swimmer. We wound up along the western shoreline of Roosevelt Island as we went under the bridge at 79th Street missing the large upwelling right underneath the bridge. Gradually we crossed over to the Manhattan side and dodging left at the last moment as we approached Mill Rock, Kris set a new record of 5:54, the first person to break 6 hours for swimming around Manhattan. The promise of my initial look at the swim was holding up. I couldn't have been happier. Kris was pretty happy, too.

Shelley Taylor was on the phone within days demanding the opportunity to respond to Kris's swim. Via a conference call with Morty Berger, we promised her the opportunity to defend her record the next year. She wanted to come out immediately to try but I reasoned with her that the current that carried Kris to his record had passed and the next time it would come back was the following year. There was no point in trying and failing. The date we set for her attempt that put her in the best current and fit her schedule was July 14, 1995. The current that day in the Hudson would be rated at 2.7 knots for the morning ebb, the same as Kris had.

We left at 2:40 in the morning, swimming the entire Harlem River in the dark. We reached Spuyten Duyvil at 4:25am, completing the Harlem River in 2 hours 5 minutes; this was a particularly fast transit as the marathon times are usually 3 hours or more spent in the Harlem River. This day saw another fast time down the Hudson River. Shelly reached the fire boathouse at the Battery by 6:57am thus finishing 13 miles of swimming in 2 hours and 32 minutes. She averaged over 5 knots down the Hudson. At the Battery, she got hung up for about 3 minutes by the Staten Island ferry's 7am departure. While she was rested treading water and consuming liquids, I told her when she starts she would be at the exact same place in the water as Kris was on his record swim and at the same time. The difference would be in the final leg of the swim. That was about all I had to do to motivate her. According to my schedule I had prepared ahead of time, Shelly started out doing 18 minutes per mile pace or better. See Table 1. She really turned it on in the final stretch, taking seven minutes off Kris's record. Shelly finished in 5:45.

Record of Shelly Taylor's times and pace 7/14/95

Location	Elapsed time	Real time	Pace
Start	0	2:40	
Triboro Bridge	0:24	3:04	18
Yankee Stadium	0:48	3:29	18.5
Spuyten Duyvil	1:45	4:25	19
GW Bridge	2:10	4:50	19.5
79th Boat Basin	2:56	5:38	20
Intrepid	3:15	5:55	20.25
WTC wall	4:01	6:41	21
Batt. Fire Boat hse	4:16	6:57	21
Brooklyn Bridge	4:40	7:20	21.5
Williamsburg Bridge	4:54	7:35	21.75
Roosevelt Island tip	5:24	8:05	20.7
Mill Rock	5:45	8:25	20.4

This record wouldn't have been possible without all the swims that had taken place before. Two record attempts by Karen Farnsworth, where in one of them she actually tied the old record of 6:12, were learning experiences that had to happen in order for Kris's break through. Additionally, it helped to have the same support crew each time as the mistakes and disappointment, while hard to accept, were assimilated. This book is my attempt to pass along that knowledge I've learned so that the next era of long distance swimmers can benefit, achieve their goals, and reach even greater heights.

The following year, on August 1, 1996, Marcia Cleveland, age 32, of Connecticut swam around Manhattan in 5:58 becoming only the third person to break 6 hours swimming around Manhattan and the fastest American woman around Manhattan. This is a very elite group of swimmers. This swim established the 2.7-knot tide as "the swimmer's tide" for setting records around Manhattan. I asked Marcia what she remembered about this swim. She thought that she would be scared swimming in the dark, then she said, "…but it was magnificent-a wonderful view of the city. I remember just *flying* at the start, up the Harlem River, and I also remember *flying* up the 'East River during the last hour. I was really wiped out afterwards. As we rounded the Battery, the Staten Island ferry pilot waited for us. As I swam by all the commuters on the boat cheered. At the time, I didn't realize how amazing this swim had been; it took some reflection to see what a superb effort I put in and what an accomplishment it is."[626]

Secrets of the Manhattan swim

Not every swim was a record swim. There were many swims by swimmers just looking to put their names in the record books. I participated in a relay that set a record at the time from the Battery: August 12, 1990 of 8:38 on a slow tide. At the time, not many swims started from the Battery. This record has been exceeded many times once the swim start changed to the Battery. The other participants that day included Bill and Donna Hill, Karen Farnsworth, Matt Wood and Matt Nance. Part of the reason for knowing your swimming history is to recognize the opportunity for establishing a record. We also wanted to familiarize the two Matts with the swim as they had signed up to compete in the upcoming Manhattan marathon in an attempt to break the dominance of the swim by women swimmers. The secret of a swim may be that you completed the swim if no one else has every done it. Subsequent swimmers can try to figure out how to better your time.

Figure 36 All these swimmers have swung wide going under the Williamsburg Bridge.

One secret of the Manhattan swim was revealed when Ben Huggard and George Kauffmann by coincidence swam around Manhattan together. Ben Huggard was on a five-day marathon swim raising money for food shelters in Manhattan in mid-September, 1985. We were experimenting with the Battery start. As we passed by East 89th Street, the normal starting location of the marathon, I noticed George Kauffmann beginning a swim with

Ed Lininger on board coordinating that swim. While I thought Ed Lininger was from the old school, George was quite comfortable working with him. I'd called on the VHF marine radio to discuss their swim but I wasn't sure Ed knew how to work a VHF radio or if they had even turned it on. I simply watched their swim from a very convenient platform. The swimmers went up the Harlem River, stroke for stroke, and neither swimmer gaining even a 5-yard lead on the other.

Figure 37 Swimmer is proceeding up the Harlem River with a Circle Line overtaking. Note the swimmer is on the left side of the channel closest to Manhattan.

When we entered the Hudson River, Ed took his swimmer wide and went over to the New Jersey side of the Hudson River, the old route around Manhattan. My swimmer stayed close to Manhattan as we normally passed under the left portion of the George Washington Bridge, never venturing farther than a third of the way out. We crossed underneath the GW Bridge first.

Figure 38 Jamie Tout passing my Grants Tomb (left) and Riverside Church (right) in the Hudson River. He is far enough off shore to safely pass the sewerage treatment plant ahead.

Then as we approached 79th street boat basin, the other swimmer was so far behind, he was hard to pick out along the Jersey shore. By 42nd street, he had caught up with us. By 34th street he had pulled so far ahead that we could barely see him ahead of us. Eventually, we lost sight of them as we ploughed down the Manhattan side of the river. When we got to the Battery, it was apparent what Ed Lininger was up to. He was trying to get his swimmer out of the Hudson River current and into the East River current. But they had been swept so fast down the Hudson that in the mere act of swimming across to the Manhattan side, they were in danger of drifting below Governors Island. Our swim was beginning and ending at the Battery while Ed's swimmer still had to swim the East River. All together, George Kauffmann was about 400 yards ahead of us. His mammoth lead had evaporated.

Figure 39 View of the USS Intrepid Air & Sea Museum at 42nd Street.

I learned a lot from Ed Lininger that day and I've freely shared it with a number of swimmers. Because the Hudson River below 42nd Street bends slightly eastward, the current along the outside of the curve close to New Jersey runs faster. If a swimmer is in this current, they can build up a lead over swimmers on the inside of the curve. Ed Lininger's timing of when to move the swimmer to the Manhattan side was off. With a slow swimmer, you should start moving them toward Manhattan so that they hit the World Trade Center wall before Battery Park. With a faster swimmer, you can delay the transition longer thus taking more advantage of the current. With another swimmer, Paul Lewandowski, a few days later, I tried the Jersey side. We were amazed to see the difference in the current. When it came time to transition, and this was a pure guess, at about 34th street we changed Paul's course and put him on a track for the World Trade Center. It seemed forever before he could break out of the current along the Jersey shore and make some progress to the World Trade. The current was just ripping along the Jersey side. He finally did break free of the current and we wound up at the northernmost corner of the World Trade Center cement wall exactly where I wanted the swimmer at this point in the swim.

It was because of local knowledge such as this that swimmers, when they are behind in the Manhattan race, will edge toward New Jersey. This creates a problem for the marathon race because along the Jersey shore is a marked ship's channel. Tugs and barges transiting the North River, as the Hudson is known, are to be found there and the Coast Guard has, over time, established a policy for swimmers to stay close to the Manhattan shore when swimming around Manhattan.

Figure 40 This tug and barge is making for the North River ship's channel along the Jersey shore south of the George Washington Bridge. This barge is one of the reasons the Coast Guard wants swimmers close to the Manhattan shoreline.

Swim stoppers are portions of the river that will stop your swimmer from making any progress. For years this was the tide change in the Hudson River. Swimmers would start up at Hell Gate, swim up the Harlem then down the Hudson and get stopped right at the corner of the Battery wall where it turns about 45 degrees leading down to the East River. This last portion of the wall presents a special problem for slow swimmers, as it is still the shoreline for the Hudson River. The wall presents a face to the flood current directing the water into the narrower portion of the river. After Governors Island, the Hudson is quite wide but when Manhattan comes along, the river becomes narrower. The water picks up speed at this point. If a swimmer is north of this position, and the current is flooding, they will not be able to transit to the next leg of their swim. They are literally trying to swim into a vortex of waters rushing north.

There was one swimmer, Helen Laurer, who was attempting to swim butterfly around the Island during a marathon. She was caught by the tide change while in the middle of the facing wall; she only needed about another hundred yards when the current flow turns east to go up the East River. I had her swim right next to the wall, within inches, keeping her entire stoke as narrow as possible and she was able to find enough still water to make progress and reach the East River waters. She then changed back over to butterfly once past this point. When she finally came into the finish up at 96th street, she looked more like a soggy butterfly sloshing through the water. Later, at a celebratory party in her apartment she thanked me for helping her. It was then that I realized that fast swimmers have one set of problems and slow swimmers have a different set of problems. Both sets of problems are interesting and require knowledge and thought to solve. It's easy to be entertained when you look at the swim from a navigational point of view.

One summer when I was assisting Chris Green on one of his Windermere swims in England, I had the opportunity to observe a senior swimmer near the end of the swim when he became stuck in a current flow. This was a lake swim with no wind and this swimmer was swimming but not moving. When we investigated, I observed that his swim position was nearly vertical in the water, he had no kick and his legs were just dangling below his torso. From the flotsam that was visible by torch, we could observe a tiny current flow opposing his progress. He was stuck in a micro-current that was quite possibly a thermal generated flow as the sun had set earlier. It took the swimmer nearly ten minutes to break free. The solution when you are trapped in a current is to move laterally to a spot where the current doesn't flow as fast. When you are on a support boat, if the background reference points are not changing, your swimmer is stuck in a current. The clue when swimming along shore is for the nearer objects to move faster than objects farther way.

Figure 41 This location is just past the Battery and you will begin to notice the buildings passing by faster and faster. By now you should be hooked up with your support crew.

The transition between the East River and Hell Gate is particularly interesting on marathon day because the swimmers get to the Harlem River so fast the tide hasn't changed yet. As swimmers are coming north in the East River, the Harlem River is flowing south and at Hell Gate, the two current flows mix. A good portion of the flow bends around Wards Island and joins the East River as it flow out to Long Island north of Mill Rock.[627] West of Mill Rock, portions of the East River flow north into the Harlem River as the two currents interlace, much as fingers when your hands are folded together. Slivers of currents are found right next to each other flowing in opposite directions but at reduced speeds compared to the major flows. The currents flowing south eventually join up with the East River below the surface. As you get nearer the wall, there is less current action and one strategy is to swim over to the old starting location for the swim at East 96th street.[628]

Figure 42 View of Hell Gate dead ahead; FDR drive to the left, not seen is Roosevelt Island off to the right. Keep to the left at this juncture to enter the Harlem River.

The fastest route to the footbridge is to stay in the East River current, right by the edge, in the roughest part until the last minute. Swimmers should bear down on the day marker at the southernmost tip of Mill Rock then break free of the current turning left and slip into a finger of current rushing up the western side of Mill Rock clearing the pier at Mill Rock then follow the rip, staying in it until it peters out northwest of Mill Rock. If you cross over the rip, you are in current turning left (from the Harlem River) to go out to Long Island Sound. You want to pass Mill Rock on your right side. I've heard of swimmers who missed the turn and went the long way around Mill Rock. When the rip dies out, set your course for the left bridge support of the footbridge. The Harlem River current predominates in this area and you just have to slug it out from this point on until the current changes. Your crew can assist you at this point by letting you know how long you have until the current changes.

Figure 43 Fishing pier at 106th Street and the Harlem River. This is a great spot for spectator to view the swimmers and say hello.

Figure 44 Swimmers tend to bunch up at the entrance to the Harlem River as they wait for the tide change. This is a good time to feed.

Once you get beyond the footbridge and the current slows, this is the time to take a feed as your competitors are not going anywhere fast. If you stop swimming you could drift back somewhat so get over by the wall where the current isn't flowing as fast. Refrain from testing for the bottom as swimmers have cut their feet on broken bottles when they did find the bottom.

Figure 45 Approaching Circle Line boat in the Harlem River. The swim's rearguard will alert swimmers by VHF radio of its approach.

On marathon day, Coast Guard regulations for the swim require you to stay left in the Harlem River and marathon rules are set up to enforce this. The Circle Line boats have become accustomed on Marathon Day to transit the Harlem River taking the many bridge openings on the right hand side of the channels.

Figure 46 Swimmer and Circle Line safely share bridge channel.

One year the swim occurred on a particular high tide. When a Circle Line boats approached a swimmer, all the passengers went over to one side of the boat to see the swimmer. This caused the boat to heel slightly. The boat struck the under side of the bridge as a result of the passenger weight shift.

The course I described through Hell Gate takes advantage of the strongest current for the longest time. The area south of the footbridge is a mixing of the two currents: one northbound and one southbound. If a swimmer exits the East River right after Gracie Mansion, the waters are not flowing as fast because an eddy develops that is reinforced by water exiting the Harlem River. When the finishing line was at East 89th Street, swimmers would turn and swim for the finishing line as soon as they could see it. This would find them crossing current flows obliquely that were either flowing north or flowing south. I once saw a swimmer on this course overtaken, quite easily by a swimmer from behind who stayed in the current until Mill Rock then at the pier on Mill Rock, turned and swam for the finishing line directly across the current flow. His speed was unopposed by current and it was a quick finish. There is a similar effect at the finishing line for the Battery.

In 2000, two Australian swimmers came to Manhattan prepared to do battle: John van Wisse, a 27 year old swim coach and Bronwen Whitehead, a 21 year old college student.

Figure 47 John & Bronwen at the pre-race briefing.

I was invited to help out on John van Wisse's boat and his sister Tammy was on board. I was able to take advantage of an eddy unknown to the Australian coaches at the finish to allow John van Wisse to win the race. In fact, during the swim, I had promised Tammy that if John was within striking distance of the leader at the finish, he'd finish in first. In some of the wild currents as we started up the East River under the Manhattan Bridge, I noticed John just seemed to thrive in the rough water. He seemed to come alive, jumping out of waves like he was a kid at the beach. He was catching faster swimmers and passing them easily in the rough water. The technique for taking advantage of the current flow at Hell Gate described above, the Australian coaches aboard Whitehead's boat learned by watching John jump to a considerable lead over what he already had developed. Once we were north of the footbridge, she began to catch us. Since the Harlem River was still flooding, the further north John swam, the stronger the current he opposed.

Figure 48 John van Wisse and his kayaker, Richard Clifford, in the Harlem River. John's rough water stroke causes the splash in front of his head.

I sent him over near the water's edge where the opposing current wasn't as fast. We held Bronwen off until their coaches noticed John's advantage and sent her over by the edge. When I saw her move to the wall, I realized they were learning all my tricks. Their swimmer eventually passed van Wisse in the quiet water of the Harlem River. When the current switched, I moved my swimmer out into the current and so did they as they kept checking behind them. By Spuyten Duyvil, they were ahead of us and around the corner; they didn't see me send John under the railroad bridge and along the shore to avoid the chop and current mix as the Harlem River exited into the Hudson River.

Figure 49 John van Wisse taking the short cut under the Spuyten Duyvil Railroad Bridge. Tim Johnson is seen in the support boat in the foreground with the cap on.

At this point, John had cut her lead in half and nearly pulled even. We were close enough to see the displeasure on the faces of her coaches. She continued to pull away in the calm waters of the Hudson as the swimmers swam underneath the George Washington Bridge. I sent John in close to the shore to tap into the fill current after the bridge support where the river widens. John was starting to look exhausted and tired. Around this time, the current goes slack for the lead swimmers in the marathon.

When we were off 79th Street boat basin, Bronwen was just approaching the first of the ship terminals and docks. She was approximately a mile if not more ahead of us. At this time the prevailing winds filled in and a sea state developed of about 2 to 3 feet swells. It was a typical late-afternoon Hudson River chop. All of a sudden, John started to close on the leader; he came alive in the rough water. By 23rd street, John was about 500 yards behind her. At the start of the World Trade Center wall, he was about 200 yards behind her. He kept closing until the turn along the WTC wall where he was about 3 body lengths behind.

Figure 50 John right after passing Bronwen behind the clock tower on the Fire Boat House seen on the right in the photo. John is on the left.

As we approached the finish, I instructed Richard Clifford, John's kayaker, to keep him away from the wall and further out in the current than Bronwen. The kayaker was keeping him about two yards further offshore than she. When she swam into the eddy found just at the end of the WTC wall just before the Fire Boat house, John grabbed the lead in two strokes.

Figure 51 Closer look at the contest in the final 200 yards of the 2000 MIMS. From this angle, John is on the right on track for the finish while Bronwen has swung wide losing more ground.

It looked like an old water polo trick of one swimmer grabbing the others foot but it was a difference in courses of about 4 feet. She had swum into dead water and John had stayed clear of it. When the two coaches that were assisting Whitehead saw this, they turned and looked straight at me with their mouths open. I shrugged my shoulders and smiled. It was the final trick. I could have overtaken her from a greater distance by staying even wider at the finish; keeping in the current flow of the Hudson River then cutting left to swim across the weak East River current directly to the finishing line but this trick wasn't needed. Tammy van Wisse was thrilled and gave me a hug before she jumped in to swim off to the finish to join her brother.

Figure 52 Here the swimmers are in the final 50 yards of the swim. The swimmers are the white splashes near the kayaks.

They are the only brother and sister swimmers that have ever won Manhattan. I had never seen such a come-from-behind win in this race and without John's efforts all my knowledge was useless. He won that race due to his extraordinary efforts when behind and his special talent of swimming in rough water and Bronwen Whitehead should be credited with an extraordinary swim as well.

Figure 53 John and Bronwen at the finish, final 10 yards. In the upper left is Tammy van Wisse about to jump in to join her brother on shore.

Figure 54 Drury Gallagher and John van Wisse discuss the swim.

Figure 55 John and Tammy van Wisse with Commissioner Henry Stern.

Figure 56 MIF committee members Commissioner Henry Stern (left) and Paul Lewandowski (right) with John van Wisse.

Of course, the biggest secret of the Manhattan swim was how to negotiate Corlears Hook under the Williamsburg Bridge. For years I thought that the eddy was smaller than it was. You can see debris collect along the Manhattan wall as the East River bends north just before the Williamsburg Bridge; the debris defines the slack water, but its effects stretch much further out into the current. It was only because of the accidental drift wide during Kris Rutford's swim that the river yielded up its final secret.

In making an attempt on the record, you need to use every bit of knowledge about the rivers. The competition is for solo swimmers and utilizes the fastest tide available to swim around Manhattan. Assuming you have swimming a world-class marathon swimmer, the results of that swim are dependant on the tides. The record has been pushed so low that only the very fastest swimmers on the very fastest tides would have any chance of lowering the record. The tidal current must be 2.6 knots or better in the Hudson River to even come close to matching the present record, which was set on a 2.7-knot tide. These tides come in a group every 20 years.

Doubles

In the English Channel, when someone does a double that means they swam to France and back. They are allowed a fifteen-minute break on shore between laps. In the Manhattan swim, it means they kept swimming until they completed two laps. On July 10, 1979, George Kauffmann attempted a double around Manhattan but was unable to complete it, calling off the swim when half way through.[629] On August 28, 1980, Tom Hetzel, age 44, from Corpus Christi, Texas, who was contemplating a double around Manhattan, cut the swim off after one lap.[630] Then in 1983 Julie Ridge completed a double with her nemesis Ben Huggard doing a double in 1984.[631] Stacy Chanin, age 24, cast these feats, which take some 17 hours, in a shadow in late August of 1984 when she completed a triple around Manhattan in 33 ½ hours.[632] A double is 53 nautical miles and a triple is 79.5 nautical miles or 91.5 Statue miles. A triple is just ten nautical miles short of the distance between Cuba and the United States. Tommy Golden served as the escort boat of choice for these swims. After the swim, we got together and he told me that was the last triple he'd ever work and he'd never work with Stacy Chanin again. What few people realize is that Tom Golden would position his boat right next to the swimmer almost as if it was a kayak. He would be there for the entire swim looking the swimmer in the eye every time they'd turn to take a breath. It was very tiring and he was on his feet the entire time. He would not even take a bathroom break for an entire swim (a normal one lap swim).[633]

Fortunately, the rush to get in the record books for this event slowed down and the organization didn't book any more multiple-lap swims. When Stacy first expressed an interest in doing the triple, I worked with her identifying the best set of currents to do the swim on. Over the course of my working with her, I noticed that she was doing a tremendous amount work publicizing her swim so I suggested she hire a manager. I told her that when swimmers take their focus off the swim, the swim suffers. She needed to get someone to do the million and one things that need to be addressed during a big swim. The first thing the manager did was fire me. I got a chuckle out of that and I hope you do too.

There is another swim around Manhattan that doubles the distance without doing a double that has never been done. A swimmer could start at the Tappan Zee Bridge located on the Hudson River 12 nautical miles north of Manhattan at Tarrytown. The swimmer could start on an ebb tide and make the tide change at the Battery some 25 nautical miles distance and then complete a normal marathon swim around Manhattan of 26½ nautical for a swim distance in excess of 50 nautical miles completely tidal assisted. I once accompanied Manny Sanguilly, the great Cuban breaststroker, on one of his Bridge-to-Bridge swims that he does to raise money for an Asthma Foundation. He started at the Tappan Zee Bridge and swam to the George Washington Bridge in about 4 hours. As we approached the finish, I noted the current speed was still up and asked Manny if he wanted to make the Battery? Manny had focused on the bridge aspect of the swim and declined but with very little effort, he could have swum all the way to the Battery that day. Swim Across America sponsors an annual relay swim from the Tappan Zee Bridge to Chelsea Piers, a distance of over 20 miles that takes advantage of the tremendous ebb current that occurs in the Hudson River.

The reverse swim

Ever since Robert Dowling, swimmers have wondered if they could possibly swim the other way around the Island. Robert's first attempt on swimming around Manhattan began by swimming north from Battery Park in the Hudson River and was stopped at Spuyten Duyvil where the currents opposed him. There are actually 3 places to start a reverse swim. The three corners around Manhattan are at the Battery, Spuyten Duyvil and Hell Gate. Theoretically, if you start from the Battery, and swim north on the Hudson then south on the Harlem, you have four hours and 45 minutes to complete this distance. It's really impossible to do. You wind up waiting out a tide change at Spuyten Duyvil than swimming south on the Harlem and East River in six hours, a much more do-able swim because of the greater current speeds in the East River. It is possible to start at Hell Gate, swim south on the East River, if timed right, you'd only have an hour and one half to wait for the tide change at the Battery then the Hudson swim, another tide change wait at Spuyten Duyvil before finishing at Hell Gate. This would be the alternate route if the swimmer couldn't complete the Harlem and East River in one go.

On June 12, 1987, Chris Green from England, then age 37, planned to attempt this swim. His plan was to swim north on a very strong tide, the Hudson that day was rated at 2.4 knots, race down the Harlem River before it switch and enter into the East River on it's ebb tide for the short trip back to the Battery. He began the swim at 5:31pm about an hour before the current would begin flood tide. His progress was minimal until around 6:15 when the current slacken enough to allow him to begin to inch forward. The tide changed at 6:38 and it was of minimal use leaving early on this swim. He didn't make the first checkpoint, the corner of the World Trade Center wall until 7pm. The current was minimal and appeared non-existent. We had taken the reverse course that is usually traveled when southbound. He passed the Intrepid at 42nd street at 8:18pm with still no current evident. He passed 79th Street boat basin at 8:45, Grant's Tomb at 9:13 then stopped at the George Washington Bridge at about 9:45pm having swam for 4¼ hours. The main reaction to the swim at this point was where was the current that we normally see roaring at this time? He had only a little over an hour and a quarter to get to Spuyten Duyvil and then swim the entire length of the Harlem before 11pm when the current would switch on him. It seemed prudent to stop the swim at this time. This swim and another one planned for Montauk were tune-ups for a Bimini to Florida swim. The Montauk swim never happened and the Bimini swim turned into a swim from Marathon Keyes to the Gulf Stream, a distance of about 30 miles.

The next person to try this swim was Kris Rutford. Kris by this time was the holder for the fastest swim around Manhattan and this swim was just to complete his swimming resume. We elected to do this swim at the same time as the 13th Annual Marathon Swim scheduled for Aug 20, 1994 only swimming in the other direction. We would pass all the other swimmers going the other way. We began the swim at 5:15am. The Hudson was finishing its ebb and we lost ground speed as we moved out into the current; but Kris was such a power swimmer we were able to make headway. By 6am we were making 1.4 knots northbound and we hit the WTC wall by 6:11am. By 7:45am we were at 42nd Street and cruising along at 2.6 knots. By the time we made the GW Bridge at 9:12am, we hit 3.9 knots. At 9:52, Kris turned at Spuyten Duyvil and he left the Hudson River, the last reading was 3.0 knots. This was some consternation at the Spuyten Duyvil transit as the railroad bridge was closed and Kris had to go under the trestles by himself without a boat escort. The escort boat, *Miss Rissy* captained by Scott Woody picked him up on the opposite side about 30 minutes later. We made it nearly halfway down the Harlem River before the tide switched. Kris was stopped by the current underneath High Bridge just south of the Roberto Clemente apartment complex that borders the Harlem River from noon until 1:30pm. The bridge abutments caused the river to narrow just a bit and this vortex was fast enough to stop him. There was some graffiti painted on the side of the cement, an M inside a square where Kris held his own against this current. After the current relaxed, Kris continued the swim down to the East River but was discourage to learn he had lost the window to finish the swim in one swoop. The East River had switched to flood and this current Kris could not hold his own against, he's been swept out to Long Island. We elected to hold out to wait for the tide change at East 79th Street but after an hour or so of swimming circles, he called it quits.

When Kris returned the following year, we had a number of discussions of how best to tackle the swim. This time we decided to hole up at the top of the Harlem River rather than exhaust Kris swimming against the tide as he did last year. There is only one spot possible to hide from the current in the Harlem River and that is at a cove where the Columbia University boathouse is located.

This is across from the big **C** painted on the rocks on the north side of the river. Kris would have to swim circles until the tide changed then complete the rest of the swim on a single tide. The date we pick for the swim was August 12, 1995. He completed the swim in 17:48. Kris started at 8:28 from Gangway 5 at the Battery. He was at Spuyten Duyvil at 12:45 where he waited until 8pm for the tide change. He reached footbridge at 10:55, and finished at 2:17am the next day.

Figure 57 Kris Rutford swam across Lake McConaughy, the largest lake in Nebraska, before attempting Manhattan.

Even in this protected cove at the top of Manhattan, we were getting current reading of 1.3 knots as we were waiting in an eddy. We observed that the water turned warmer when the ebb tide began and the wait for the current switch was exhausting for Kris, mentally. When the switch came, he had to finish the Harlem and East River all on one tide. For Kris, this was an easy task, finishing this portion of the swim in about 6½ hours. He is the only person to have swum Manhattan both ways.

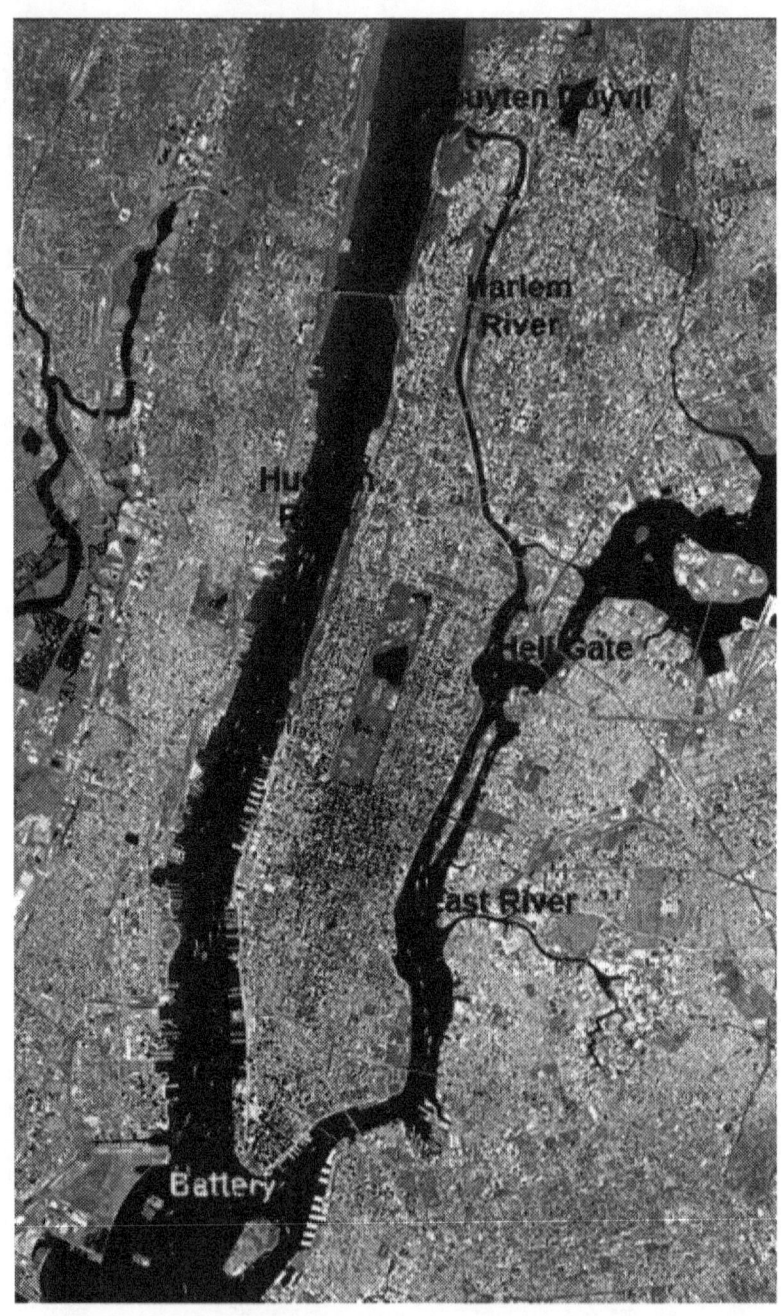

Figure 58 Manhattan locations of interest. Notice the boats?

Chapter 11 The Manhattan Island Marathon Swim history

What follows is a list of swimmers and their times recorded for their swim around Manhattan in the Annual Manhattan Island Marathon Swim. Because every year the swim is held on different days and each day the tide varies you can not draw any conclusion from the times listed that one swimmer is faster than another unless they were swimming in the same race. Even if the race were held on the same day every year, this would still be the case. The reason is the tides changes in each of the three rivers twice everyday. In a sense, this is what makes the swim interesting. With the advent of computer simulation, we have been able to predict ahead of time the finish but even then we have surprises. One year, Shelly Taylor when confronted with an opposing tide in the Harlem kept swimming hard and was all the way up to Yankee Stadium when the tide switched. Normally, the tide switches when the swimmers are around the Triboro Bridge. This placed her several miles ahead of the field and she turned in a very fast time for a slow tide. On a faster tide, even if she had swam the same, she'd been held back around the Triboro Bridge until the tide switched then with a faster tidal assist, she might even have turned in the same time.

The first swim held in modern times was on September 14, 1982. Fourteen contestants were entered and the race started at the Fire Boat House dock on East 90th Street just north of Gracie Mansion. The winner was David Horning, age 34, of California in a time of 7:25. The first woman finisher was Karen Hartley, age 25, from Massachusetts in a time of 7:41 setting a new woman's record. There were 12 competitors, ten men and two women, who started with 7 finishers.[634] The swimmers dove in off the floating dock attached to what is now known as Asphalt Green. The race developed into a competition between USC alumnus Dave Horning and Harvard alumnus Todd Bryant. They paced off each other through the Harlem River in an early morning fog going stroke for stroke. Just south of the George Washington Bridge, Todd Bryant retired from the race. Both swimmers were working off the same escort boat because there was a shortage of boats available to escort the swimmers. Their boat was a speedboat and it was unable to idle at a speed slow enough to stay with the swimmers so it circled them as they swam. This problem afflicts a number of escort boats and the association has learned to advise new escort boats to practice using a drag such as a bucket tied off the stern so the engine idles at a speed it can handle but the boat doesn't go faster than the swimmer. For slow swimmers, sometimes two drags are needed. Because a solo swimmer on an individual attempt started at the Asphalt Green location and permission were not secured, the Association lost the use of the facilities after this year.

Figure 59 Drury Gallagher shown giving Diddo Clark an award at the Water Club. Diddo at one time held the woman's record for the Around Manhattan Swim.

The second annual swim was held on July 24, 1983. The winner was Harold Johnson, age 34, of California in a time of 8:15. The first woman swimmer was Julie Billingsley, age 24, from Washington, DC, finishing in a time of 8:33. There were 28 competitors with 21 finishers. The start was in the water off a cement extension outside the railing along the East River at East 96th Street in upper Manhattan. With care, there was room to tie up all the escort boats along the sea wall. This location remained the same for the annual swim for a number of years. Until the Association moved the start and stopping location for their record swim to the pier on Mill Rock, it was the start location for all swims. This year was the first year that ham radio operators were put on every escort boat to handle back up communications with the swim.

Figure 60 Here Richard Marks introduces the word "circumswim" to the swimming world on July 25, 1983, at the 1983 Awards Luncheon at the Water Club in Manhattan. Seen are Drury Gallagher, Richard Marks, Joe Coplan, and Tim Johnson (l to r).

The third annual swim was held on August 5, 1984. The winner was Paul Asmuth, age 27, of California in a time of 7:37. The first female finisher was Shelley Taylor, age 23, of Arkansas in a time of 7:52. Two of the dominant open water swimmers of the 80's and 90's were in this race with Paul coming out on top.

This race also featured a swimmer that was 73 years of age, Dr. Adrian Kanaar. Unbeknownst to the Association, Dr. Kanaar was also a recent recipient of quadruple bypass surgery. He finished in a time of 9:30. This revealed a principle of the swim: the difference between fast swimmers and slow swimmers is equalized by the timing of the start of the swim with the fast swimmers swimming on a slower current than the slower swimmers. Paul Asmuth can swim 20-minute miles so at a speed of 3 knots, Paul could swim the 28.5 miles around Manhattan in a little over 8 hours. So the current only assisted Paul enough to cut his time by about a half hour. Dr. Kanaar finished the same distance in 9:30 giving him an effect speed of 2.8 knots. His pool speed is around 1.5 knot maximum which means it should have taken him around 20 hours to cover the distance. The current cut Kanaar time in half by doubling his speed. When the start moved in 1986 to the Battery from East 96th Street, the start time changed. By starting the swim at the Battery in the middle of the East River flood tide, both groups of swimmers benefit from the fast East River current running up to Hell Gate.

Due to boat breakdowns, swimmers were occasionally left to swim around Manhattan on their own. It became a principle of supply and demand that if you had 3 extra boats the night before a race, you'd only have enough for each swimmer the day of the race due to breakdowns meaning that if a boat died during the race (a high probability) a swimmer would have to quit the race. This is a continuing problem that the Association addresses every year, as the Coast Guard and good sense does not allow swimmers to be unescorted.

This race included Linda McGill, age 38, from Australia who had a unique approach to eliminating chafing from the myriad of problems faced by marathon swimmers. Rather than apply a coating of petroleum jelly, she would just swim topless. This approach had an unusual side effect in that it kept the boat crew quite interested in the swimmer as well as alert.

The fourth annual swim was held on July 28, 1985. The winner was Shelley Taylor, 24, from Australia in a time of 7:44.

The first male finisher was Courtney Roberts, age 23, from Ohio in a time of 7:52. There were 27 competitors. This year was the first year that the Coast Guard Auxiliary began assisting the swim by providing boats and coordinating this aspect of the swim. Gus Savaros was the contact person for the Auxilary and his home Flotilla was out Barren Island by Floyd Bennett Field. It was a great relief to find one person who could coordinate everything.[635]

As part of the permitting process, the Coast Guard wanted to know the windows or range of time that swimmers would be passing by specific points around the Island. This was an attempt by the Coast Guard to assist other marine traffic by advising them in their Notice to Mariners and in their Marine Safety bulletins announced on the day of the swim where mariners could expect to find swimmers in the water during the day of the event. Since this was our first year with this new procedure, I listed the times using the fastest swimmer would go by a point from the computer program and the latest time that the slowest swimmer would pass by. Unfortunately, I was only using for my slowest swimmer a 45 minute per mile pace or 1.3 knots. It turned out, in this years swim, we had a swimmer who was slower than that: Benn Kramer from Canada was pulled out of the water and handcuffed by the Coast Guard for attempting to swim past the Battery after the agreed to time window for swimmers had passed. The next year I added a half hour to all the windows, just in case.

The fifth annual swim was held on July 20, 1986. The winner was Richard McElwee, age 25, a swim coach from Pennsylvania in a time of 7:53. The first woman finisher was Patricia Hines, age 29, a professional athlete from California in a time of 8:18. There were 23 competitors. This year saw an extraordinary amount of jellyfish in the waters. At the awards luncheon the next day at The Water Club, Chris Green told a humorous story about his first Manhattan swim. His escort boat didn't show up at the start so we had sent him off promising to send his gear and support crew along after him. The escort boat never showed up. He spoke about how he handled this by going up to nearby escort boats and begging food and drink off them.

The venue for the luncheon was the Water Club[636] at East 23rd Street on the East River, which had large picture windows that looked out over the East River. It was hard not to stare out the window at that fantastic river during the luncheon. His punch line was "...look, here comes my boat now..." in his British accent, pointing out the window as everyone just broke up laughing.

The sixth annual swim was on August 9, 1987. The winner was Shelly Taylor, age 26, from Australia in a time of 7:25. The first male finisher was Gary Antonick in a time of 7:45. There were 41 starters. The race began and finished at Battery Park. The reason for the change was when the swimmers started at East 96th Street, by the time they reached the Battery, the swimmers were spread out over a parade about 3 to 4 miles long. Each swimmer has to be individually cleared to swim across the ferry channels at the end of the Manhattan. Some got held up waiting for ferries to dock and some didn't. Some swimmers did not pay attention to the boat coordinating this crossing. Plus it tied up 3 extra boats for coordination. This year was also the first year that the Power Squadron began assisting the Association with providing boats. One of the main contact persons was Tom Biglin. The reason for the change was the price the Auxiliary charged swimmers for boats had become excessive.

The seventh annual Manhattan Marathon swim was held on August 27, 1988. The winner was Shelley Taylor-Smith, age 27, from Australia in a time of 7:27. The first male finisher was Jim Barber, age 28 from Indiana in a time of 7:45. One of the finishers that year was Cody Brammer, age 12. She became the youngest person to swim around Manhattan. She was also the last minor to compete the swim as the Association decided to discourage parents from entering their children in this event. She had an article about her swim published in Scholastics Magazine, a widely read children magazine that is distributed in schools throughout the United States.[637]

The eighth annual Manhattan Marathon swim was held on August 19, 1989. The winner was Shelley Taylor-Smith, age 28, from Australia in a time of 7:32. This was her fourth win. The first male finisher was Jim Barber, age 29, from Indiana in a time of 7:45. This finish was practically a repeat of the previous year in nearly the same times. There were 52 contestants. One finisher, Taranath Shenoy, age 29, of India had listed in his swimming resume the Palk Straits. This is the 20 miles distance between the tip of India and the island of Ceylon. Interesting, if there is a current in these straits, then this would be the English Channel of India. Shenoy is a deaf mute and partially blind. He finished in a time of 8:29. This was the last year the Power Squadron was able to support the swim officially due to a change in the structure of Master Swimming's insurance policy.

Figure 61 Shelley Taylor shown relaxing after her 1st place finish with the winning time still showing on the official clock for the 1989 MIMS. Julie Ridge is seen with her back to the camera.

The ninth annual Manhattan Marathon swim was held on August 19, 1990. The winner was Suzy Maroney, age 15, of Australia in a time of 7:00. In second place was Matt Nance, age 24, from Manhattan in a time of 7:05. There were 43 contestants. Matt, a spirited competitor was egged on by a number of compatriots at the New York Athletic Club to end the female domination of the Manhattan swim. He might have won but his twelve-week regimen of 4000 yards was hardly adequate compared to Susie Maroney's 6½-hour daily regimen of swimming dating from her fourth place finish the previous year.

The tenth annual Manhattan Marathon swim was held on August 10, 1991. The winner was Jim Barber, age 31, from Indiana in a time of 7:06. The first woman to finish was Marcia Cleveland, age 27, from NY City in a time of 7:29. In this swim, a cruise line ship backed out into the channel cutting off the race for a few swimmers. It was the last year that the US Merchant Marine Academy participated in the swim. In the swim this year was the oldest swimmer to complete the swim, Dextor Woodford at age 77.

The eleventh annual Manhattan Marathon swim was held on August 29, 1992. The winner was John Darauche, age 28, from La Jolla, California, in a time of 8:30. The first female finisher was Patricia Robinson, age 50, of New York City in a time of 8:33. This year saw the smallest field entered. The marathon race was a bit overshadowed by the record swim set earlier in the day by Kris Rutford.

The twelfth annual Manhattan Marathon swim was held on August 21, 1993. The winner was Kris Rutford, age 32, from Nebraska in a time of 7:26. The first female finisher was Marcella MacDonald from Connecticut in a time of 7:38. Ten swimmers competed. This was the race that was featured on the front page of the New York Times. It was the first year that Morty Berger organized and ran the event.

The thirteen annual Manhattan Marathon swim was held August 20, 1994. The winner was Suzy Maroney, age 19, of Australia in a time of 7:08. The first male finisher was Igor deSouza, age 30, of Brazil in a time of 7:19. Nineteen swimmers competed.

The fourteenth annual Manhattan Marathon swim was held on August 13, 1995. The winner was Gail Rice, age 39, from Florida in a time of 8:01. The first man to finish was Aaron Drake, age 31, from Nebraska in a time of 8:33. There were 18 individual swimmers and four six-person relay teams competing. In second place was Marcia Cleveland, age 31, from Connecticut in a time of 8:03. Marcia later took over the organization for the Manhattan marathon swim and wrote a book, *Dover Solo*, about her swimming the English Channel and how to train for a channel swim.

Figure 62 Gail Rice of Florida stroking pass the Columbia C, she's at the half-way point.

The fifteenth annual Manhattan Marathon swim was held on August 3, 1996. The winner was John Gatti, age 29, from New Jersey in a time of 7:16. The first woman finisher was Gail Rice, age 40, of Florida in a time of 7:27.

Figure 63 Gail Rice, lunch is served!

The sixteenth annual Manhattan Marathon swim was held on July 20, 1997. The winner was Tammy van Wisse, age 28, from Australia in a time of 7:16. The first male finisher was John Quartemain, age 34, from England just 3 minutes behind Tammy van Wisse in a time of 7:19. There were 17 individual competitors and five relay teams.

The seventeenth annual Manhattan Marathon swim was held July 11, 1998. The winner was Shelley Taylor-Smith, age 36, from Australia in a time of 7:18. The first man to finish was Jay Benner, age 33, a swim coach from Tacoma, Washington in a time of 7:19. There were 21 competitors. Coming from a half mile behind, Shelley passed two lead swimmers. This was Shelley's seventh win and after the race she "retired". She holds 15 world-swimming titles and is the author of a book, *Dangerous When Wet*.

The eighteenth annual Manhattan Marathon swim was held on July 11, 1999. The winner was Tobie Smith, age 25, from New York in a time of 6:32. The first male finisher was Rob Copeland in a time of 6:53.

Figure 64 Winners of the 1999 MIMS under direction of Morty Berger, MIF president, Rob Copeland, Tobie Smith, and Drury Gallagher (l to r).

There were 30 competitors. This swim featured a showdown between two female Australian swimmers well known to Manhattan marathon circles: Tammy van Wisse and Suzy Maroney. Tammy finished second in the race in a time of 6:51 and Susie finished 8th in a time of 7:16. Additionally Shelley Taylor-Smith was on the water, not competing but assisting blind swimmer James Pittar from Australia who came in 22nd in a time of 7:54. Tobie Smith is not unknown in swimming circles as she was the 25-kilometer world champion. This swim was not held on an especially fast tide, the Hudson ebb that day was only 2.3 knots. This is approximately the same tide that Paul Asmuth swam in when he broke 7 hours the first time in 1983. On that basis, Tobie beat Paul Asmuth's time and she started from the Battery.

Figure 65 Tobie Smith looks really happy after setting the record for the fastest MIMS time ever of 6: 32.

The nineteenth annual Manhattan Marathon swim was held on June 17, 2000. The winner was John van Wisse, age 27, from Australia in a time of 7:53:48. The first woman to finish was Bronwen Whitehead, age 21, from Australia with a time of 7:53:51. The time difference was the closest finish in the history of the Manhattan marathon swim. There were 35 swimmers and two relay teams with 29 swimmers finishing.

Figure 66 John van Wisse winner of the 2000 MIMS and his sister Tammy van Wisse winner of the 1997 MIMS with the Gallagher Cup.

The twentieth annual Manhattan Marathon swim was held on June 23, 2001. The declared winner was Igor de Souza, age 37, from Brazil in a time of 8:02 in a disputed finish. The 1st place finisher was Morgan Filler, age 25, of Seattle in an adjusted time of 8:05. The race was interrupted five times by lightning storms. The race also featured a Millennium Relay Team of all the top female MIMS winners of the past races: Shelley Taylor-Smith, Tammy van Wisse, Tobie Smith, Gail Rice, Karen Burton, and Regan Schreiber, who was swimming for Marcia Cleveland, the Race Director that day. Karen Burton was swimming in recognition of her outstanding Catalina Channel swim. This dream relay finished first in a time of 7:43. It amazes me when a solo swimmer can be competitive with a relay: Morgan Filler finished only 7 minutes behind the relay before her time was adjusted.

The twenty-first annual Manhattan Marathon swim was held on June 23, 2002. The winner was Emily Watts, age 34, an elementary school teacher from Maryland in a time of 7:46. The first male finisher was Ron Collins, age 40, of Florida in a time of 8:00. There were 13 individual swimmers and 7 relay teams. The swim start was moved to South Cove just above the Battery due to construction of a ferry terminal to handle the passengers from the New York to New Jersey PATH riders when the subway stop at the World Trade Center was destroyed in 9/11. Several swimmers and relay teams swam in memory of lost loved ones and fellow swimmers from that attack.

The twenty-second annual Manhattan Marathon swim in 2003 was cancelled due to a spike in the fecal coliform count that day because it had rained overnight.

The twenty-third annual Manhattan Marathon swim was held on July 3, 2004. The winner was Chris Derks, age 34, from Texas in a time of 7:16. The first female finisher was Rendy Opdycke, age 20, from California in a time of 7:30. Emily Watts, the 2002-year's winner placed third in a time of 7:33. All together, 94 people participated in the swim: 22 individual swimmers along with 14 relay teams of various numbers of members. Chris Derks is a consistent winner in the Tampa Bay swim.

The twenty-fourth annual Manhattan Marathon swim scheduled for July 9, 2005, was cancelled due to unsanitary water conditions from storm water runoff related to remnants from Hurricane Cindy in a scenario similar to the 2003 race. An unofficial and unsanctioned swim was held instead for those swimmers who did not pull out when this development was announced. The lead swimmer, Jacques Tuset, age 41 from France, was in the Hudson River when the National Weather Service predicted severe weather as imminent.[638] Unlike the swim in 2001 that had no less than 4 restarts, one cancellation stopped the swim. No winner was declared because not all the swimmers started at the same time.[639] The start from South Cove at Battery Park City was conducted in several waves with the strongest swimmers going first to battle the opposing Hudson River current as they swim toward the Battery for their first leg of the swim up the East River.

The listing on the next page is a summary of the record for the fastest time around Manhattan in the modern era. The record represents the efforts of a number of swimmers, their coaches, the pilots, and the swimming organization in the late 20th century (1983-present), the second golden age of swimming.

Manhattan Island Solo Record Holders

Drury Gallagher, age 43, from Manhasset, NY, on July 19, 1982 in a time of 7:14.[640] He swam on a 2.1-knot tide. He established a new record and a new organization, the Manhattan Island Swimming Association (MISA) to commemorate the death of his son, Drury Gallagher, Jr.

Paul Asmuth, age 26, from San Jose, California, on August 8, 1983 in a time of 6:48. He swam on a 2.3-knot tide. Paul was the first swimmer under 7 hours and he proved the validity of the computer simulation for the swim.

Drury Gallagher, age 44, from Manhasset, NY, on September 7, 1983 in a time of 6:41. He swam on a 2.5-knot tide. This swim proved that an older, slower swimmer could beat a younger, faster swimmer if the swimmer uses the tides to their advantage.

Shelley Taylor, age 24, from Australia, on October 15, 1985 in a time of 6:12. She swam on a 2.6-knot tide. Shelley went on a 2 hours delay from slack ebb begin at Hell Gate. Karen Farnsworth of Manhattan tied this time a few years later.

Kris Rutford, age 32, from Nebraska, on August 29, 1992 in a time of 5:54. He swam on a 2.6-knot tide. Kris was the first person to swim around Manhattan in under 6 hours.

Shelley Taylor, age 33, from Australia on July 14, 1995 in a time of 5:45. She swam on a 2.7-knot tide. This swim is covered in detail at the end of the *In Pursuit of the Record* section of this book.

The Manhattan Island Marathon Swim organization

Drury Gallagher, Jr., was the oldest son of five children of Drury and Cathy Gallagher of Manhasset, NY. He died February 13, 1981, in an accident at a boarding school. The shock of his death found Drury and his family dealing with the loss. Friends reached out to help and Drury found a special bond with an old friend Tom Hetzel. Drury and Tom had grown up together on Rockaway Beach swimming for hours together in the surf. They talked a lot and a lot of the talk was about swimming. Tom had gone on to coaching English Channel swimmers while Drury had stayed with Master swimming and excelled. As part of the grieving process, Tom had asked Drury to come along on one of Tom's swims around Manhattan in the summer of 1981. Drury agreed and on the day of the swim, after sitting on the boat for an hour in a hot July sun, Drury jumped into the water to cool off a bit. He swam circles around Tom and after what he thought was a ½ hour, he got back into the boat to discover it was more like 3-4 hours he had been swimming. Drury loved the water and the feel of swimming in the river; it was an amazing therapy for him. Later in the swim, Dr. John Powers, another friend of Drury's asked him to go back in the water to help encourage Tom along. Drury finished the swim. It was at the end of this swim that Tom Hetzel said to Drury, "You have to do the swim and break the record". Drury's reply was a smile and a polite, "No". He had no desire to do it. Tom talked to Drury over the long winter of 1981-1982 about the swim until one day Drury said he'd do it. He'd do the swim and attempt to break the record if they set the swim up like the English Channel Association and hold a swim every year as a memorial. Tommy agreed and set about organizing the swim.

Drury recognized that this activity was a way to commemorate the death of his son and by setting up an organization; a trophy could be awarded every year in his memory. Drury and Tom did the initial commemorate swim on July 19, 1982, with Drury, age 43, setting off 3 hours after Tommy, age 46, started. Doctor John Powers calculated the tides. They were going to do a tortoise and hare swim where Gallagher was the hare that had to catch and pass Tom Hetzel, the tortoise. As Drury was passing by the Fire Boathouse at the Battery, one of his dearest friends, Jimmy McCarthy who was with the Fire Department and stationed at this location swam out to meet Drury and then swam along with him for a bit. They had swum together at Brooklyn Prep where Jimmy qualified as an All-American swimmer. Drury stopped and they talked for a brief time, long enough for Jimmy to say, "Drury, what are you doing in my pool?" A brief time later, Gallagher caught up with Hetzel around the Williamsburg Bridge. They talked for another brief moment then Tommy said, "Take it home, go for the record". Drury did just that setting a new record for an around the island swim of 7:14.[641] That night, Drury along with about 40 to 50 family and friends went out to celebrate at the Manhattan Plaza. By 10pm everyone was tired but Drury said he was wide-awake and on an adrenalin high.[642]

One of the persons at this celebration was Jane Katz, Ed. D. She had helped Diana Nyad train for her attempt around Manhattan by allowing her to swim 8 hours at a time in the pool at the Bronx Community College where Jane worked. Jane would even drop in and swim laps with Diana. She encouraged Drury's idea of doing the swim every year as a memorial for his son and volunteered to help. Just this past year she taught one of Doc Councilman's granddaughters, Leslie Morris, advanced swimming at John Jay College and got her to participate in a local meet. The author once spent a day with Jane Katz and went with her to so many pools where she conducted water aerobics or just plain old workouts that he finally had to say, "No more, just get me when you're done. I'll be in the sauna."

The first marathon swim competition occurred on September 14, 1982. It went off with the barest of essentials and support boats. Drury and Tom were busy getting the word out to round up some competitors on short notice and some of the accoutrements that we come to expect from the Manhattan swim hadn't started. I became involved when I called Drury to congratulate him on record-breaking swim. I told him that if I had known he was going to swim around Manhattan, I would have loved to come watch the swim. He thanked me then asked if I would like to come down and help out with the first competition...next Tuesday. I took a day off from work, showing up bright and early for the start at the Asphalt Green dock. There was Drury quite busy and a bunch of half-naked swimmers and with their handlers. I had no idea what was going on. Before long, Drury handed me the keys to his boat and said, "Take 'em around Manhattan." Well, to be truthful, I had never gone around Manhattan before in my life. I was vaguely familiar with the route. Fortunately, the swimmers knew where the Harlem River began and I just followed them. I had the two lead swimmers and it was the most fascinating race I had ever seen in my life. I had never seen anyone swim this fast nor this long. I was hooked.

Following the first marathon Drury called a meeting at the New York Athletic Club for a few of his friends and persons he knew who would be interested in helping out next year. I was fortunate enough to be invited to this meeting. It was mind boggling to find so many nicely dressed swimmers sitting around a conference table planning for the 2nd annual event. Just having the meeting at the NYAC was impressive, as the conference room was wall-to-wall wood paneling, a gigantic conference table, and we had a waiter just handling the room. Several of the swimmers had swum the English Channel, another was a writer; but everyone brought their enthusiasm for the swim. I recall going up to Julie Ridge at the end of the meeting, gently squeezing her biceps and remarking, "You swam the English Channel with these?" I was amazed because Dave Horning, who I had just watched win the first Manhattan Marathon swim, had biceps the size of a small tree trunk.

Not amazed was the New York City Police Department. In an official letter in May of 1984, they denied a request for assistance for the 1984 Marathon Swim.[643] Their decision was based on research of past events that revealed numerous potential safety hazards as well as considerable potential for interference with private and commercial marine traffic. They were advising the NYC Parks Department of their misgivings. Fortunately, the

Parks Department in response to a Special Event Permit request filed by me earlier had already issued a permit on April 23rd, 1984, for DeKovats Park at East 96th Street.[644] In this location the boats could tie up along the bulkhead wall as the start occurred at high tide. The Parks Commissioner, Henry Stern, was a swimmer and he endorsed the swim and threw the weight of his department behind the swim. Still we had to get the Coast Guard permission to hold the swim. I filed the Coast Guard permit on March 30th, 1984.

Shortly after the Police Department nixed our swim I received a letter from the Coast Guard that asked for further explanations with the same date as the Police Department letter. I wrote back welcoming their suggestions to place additional boats at the Battery and one at Circle Line Piers to coordinate the passage of swimmers so as not to interfere with the movements of the ferries and other commercial traffic. I addressed their 2nd concern should the swim go past 6pm and referring to the tides and twilight, I arranged for a cutoff of 6pm in the Hudson River and 7:15pm in the East River. The permit arrived June 15th, 1984 with Special Local Regulations and we had a patrol commander assigned.[645] The day of the event, the coordinator is required to check in with the Coast Guard operations center, Group New York. I knew the Police Department had not taken this laying down and had pressed the Coast Guard to cancel the swim because when I called in the day of the race to check in, the Officer-in-Charge had to check with the Captain of the Port who passed it up to the Admiral. Unfortunately, I didn't get the name of the Admiral but his comments passed to me were, "Let them swim."

Figure 67 MISA committee members Julius Carallo, Tim Johnson, Jane Katz, and Dale Petranech at the Water Club in 1983.

The Manhattan Island Swimming Association organization came into existence with some really dedicated individuals. Some of the original members at that meeting besides me included Ben Huggard, Joseph Coplan, Thomas J. Hetzel, Julie Ridge, Paul Lewandowski, Richard Ellis, Jane Katz, Ed. D., and John Powers. Drury asked various members to participate as officers depending on their time availability. By the late 80's the committee members had grown to include Victor Aguirre, James Armstrong, Herbert Barthels, Thomas Biglin, Mike Brophy, Rosemarie and Phil Butti, Julius Carallo, Parks Commissioner William Astro, D. J. Carey III, Lenny Clover, James Counsilman, Buck Dawson, Donna de Varona, Bob Duenkel, Chris Green, Kim Hansen, T. J. Healy, Kim Heinlein, William and Donna Hill, Daniel Honig, David Horning, John Hudzik, William Jaffee, George Kauffmann, Steve Keller, Leo Kohl, Wendy Koltun, Edward Lininger, Richard Lynch, Judy Meyer, Susan Peterson-Lubow, Dale Petranech, Kenneth Rooney, R. J. Recame, Ambrose Salmini, Manuel Sanguily, George Sau,

Gus Savaros, Fran Schnarr, Barry Schwartz, Jacqueline Shea, Arthur C. Smith, Parks Commissioner Henry J. Stern, Al and Ann Wellander, Bruce Wigo, and Scott and Irene Woody as committee members or officers over the years.

Figure 68 MISA committee members Drury Gallagher and Joe Coplan (deceased) at the Water Club 1983.

This was not by any means a complete listing of all the committee members and over the years members would join the organization, contribute as much as they could and then leave when they were unable to participate, their interest changed or they just needed a break. For every swimmer in the water, there were as many as 5 to 6 people working behind the scenes to make the swims come off successfully and twice that number on race day.

The first few years saw Drury sponsoring the swim by raffling off a Cadillac, selling tickets to friends. Fran Schnarr was the Association Treasurer for a number of years. She had been involved for years before as crew on Shelley Taylor's boat. Since this was her hometown swim she knew how and when to pitch in. I also knew Fran outside of swimming because we shared a common bond of working for the same conglomerate, New York

Telephone. At the 1991 marathon swim, near the end of the swim I happen upon Fran and she told me she wasn't feeling too good. We spoke and I told her to go home and rest up, the committee was a team and we'd get her job done. Fran was so relieved to hear this; her face lit up in a smile, dropped her papers into my hands and took off for home. I was glad to help out a fellow committee member with their chores. She never recovered. To the end she was a dedicated committee member. She was honored in 1998 as an International Marathon Hall of Fame Certificate of Merit Honoree.

Figure 69 Looking back at the memory of swimmers and swims past.

The Manhattan Island Swimming Association was very proud of its relationship with the New York Athletic Club. To this day, one of the volunteers, Paul Lewandowski, is a NYAC member as is Drury Gallagher, Richard Ellis, and the Hill's, Bill and Donna. The initial meetings were held at the NYAC. Many of the initial sponsors were from relationships Drury Gallagher had developed at the NYAC. Drury was taught to swim by Joe Ruddy, a NYAC member from the turn of the 19th Century, star water polo player, and member of the International Swimming Hall of Fame who swam with Charlie Daniels and every other great swimmer of that era. Much of the legitimacy of the swim derived from the fact that Drury Gallagher of the NYAC was promoting the swim.

Just as the NYAC can be proud of its contribution to the improvements of the crawl stroke, it can be proud of its role in the incubation of the Manhattan Island Swimming Association. The club's original founders who were committed to the growth and development of amateur sports would be proud that this work still continues today as evidenced by the emergence of the Manhattan Island Marathon Swim and its continued endeavor. The ideals for amateur sport are present today in the Manhattan Island Marathon Swim. The swimmers swim for a trophy, a t-shirt, and the honor of saying they swam Manhattan. No one is paid to swim or given appearance money. Marathon swimming as revealed in this history is still an amateur sport, one that anyone can participate in around the globe.

Bill and Donna Hill were instrumental in having the swim adopt the use of the Downtown Athletic Club as the marathon race headquarters when we moved the swim start to the Battery. The DAC, the acronym the Downtown Athletic Club is known by, was only a few blocks from the swim start. It turned out the Hills belonged to more than one athletic club and Donna was one of the first women admitted to the NYAC. The DAC is well known at the location of the Heisman Trophy.[646] You have to walk past it in the lobby to get to the elevators to the rooms where the swimmers and race officials stayed.

Depending on the time you could volunteer, everyone had a job working toward the success of the swim. At some point in one of our early meetings Drury asked who could handle the permitting process with the Coast Guard. I volunteered to be the liaison and began some of my key work with the organization detailed above. Satisfying the Coast Guard was important and my background in marine transportation didn't hurt because I knew how to talk to them. Drury's and my name was on the permit, we knew to listen on our designated channel for the Patrol Commander to call us. Every year, the Coast Guard would call us and either I would respond or I'd hand the mike to Drury.

When a Staten Island ferryboat captain called the Coast Guard on channel 22 one year complaining about a swimmer crossing his bow preventing him from leaving the terminal, I was right there on the horn to offer my observations to Group New York: we had called the ferry twice on two different marine channels, he hadn't responded and as we approached the ferry, no one was observed in the forward wheelhouse. It was beautiful, no inquiry.

On another occasion, I was aboard Tommy Golden's lobster boat, *Risky Business*, escorting Chris Green, a slow swimmer down the Hudson River and as we approached some boat off 34th Street the Coast Guard called us on the VHF. They asked us what our intentions were. I responded, "Maintain present course and speed." Tommy Golden and I looked at each other, and I said, "I don't know where that came from." Tommy was impressed. Twenty years earlier at the US Merchant Marine Academy where I had studied as a member of the class of 1968, we talked like that all the time. Neither Tommy nor I had any ideas what was going on until we noticed a fireworks barge anchored in mid-river. Then we knew that a Local Notice to Mariners had been filed closing the river to traffic around the barge. We were approaching the vicinity near the time the river closing was about to begin. We squeaked by right under the time limit. If I hadn't of spoken so "nautically" they'd of told us to break off the swim and move off as they didn't want anyone sneaking in and anchoring too close to watch the fireworks.

Figure 70 Gail Rice in a tight race in the Harlem with Tommy Golden's boat Risky Business in the background. Tommy was a Port Washington resident. I'd often catch a ride with him on his boat to or from the swims.

I began learning everything there was to about organizing and running a volunteer swimming organization. At times, member would get into arguments, becoming angry at each other. Drury was a skillful master at resolving these issues. Drury liked to do things first class. He wanted a quality swim that would showcase the world's best swimmers.

One year, simply because I had never done it before, I volunteered to handle the arrangements for the awards dinner which involved selecting a location, obtaining prices, and menu choices. Many of us were involved in Master swimming either as competitive swimmers or within the club structure of Master swimming. Mostly, we worked hard and enjoyed seeing that the individual swims for the swimmers were as trouble free as possible. By providing the boats, making all the arrangements for permits, providing officials and safety personnel, answering phones, processing applications, publicizing the swim, getting the swim listed in various swim calendars, keeping records, dealing with the insurance and sanctioning issues, the marathon swimmers themselves could concentrate on the task before them of training and focusing on their swim. The day of the swim involved the greatest number of volunteers: the officials, the ham radio operators, the boat operators, the committee members who handled the timing, the press, the announcing, the setting up of the start, the swimmers check in, the doctors and chiropractors and masseurs and many other tasks that happened in the background to make the swim go off with or without hitches. There are three high points on the day of the swim: when the swimmers leave, when the swimmers finish, and after the awards dinner. We all breathed a sigh of relief before beginning again preparing and improving the organization for the next year.

One problem area of the swim was going around the Battery. Every year we had the same problem of coordinating the swimmers as they go around. Every year we'd have boats that don't call in, so we assigned patrol boats to help coordinate this very difficult task of sending a swimmer by the ferry slips so that he doesn't interfere with the ferry traffic. The ferries leaving are pretty easy to spot. If the forward wheelhouse of the ferry is unoccupied, the ferry isn't going to be leaving anytime soon. If there was personnel in the wheelhouse, you could call them to find out if they were going to leave immediately if you had a swimmer approaching. If they were, you'd hold them up. Ferries arriving from Staten Island were a little more difficult and dangerous. They wouldn't stop and wouldn't deviate from their course. More than one swimmer had a near miss. The correct way to time it is to watch their route in from the Hudson River, they make two turns: one, a right turn out of the Hudson to run east into the East River, and two, a left turn to make their final approach. A properly stationed patrol boat can allow a swimmer to proceed if the approaching ferry hasn't made the right turn into the East River and hold the swimmer if the ferry has made the turn. A swimmer waiting can resume the swim once the ferry has made the left turn and is headed for the slip. By the time the swimmer gets there the ferry has gone past.

In September of 1985, swimmer Ben Huggard was on a weeklong swimming event raising money for local food banks, swimming around Manhattan once a day for a week or attempting to. By this time, my research had uncovered Diane Struble's swim around Manhattan in 1975. She started at the Battery for her swim. I had never heard of it. In order for Ben to make all the swims during the week, by moving the start on the days late in the week to the Battery, he could do the swims and make fund raising events in the evening. The change of venue from East 96th street was fraught with problems because we didn't know the problems with putting the East River portion of the swim at the start of the race instead of at the end. Ben became the guinea pig. I took a guess that if Ben left at the peak of the current flow, he'd make it up to Hell Gate before it changed three hours later. We had no experience with a swimmer in the peak of the current of the East River. Ben made the tide change at Hell Gate with 15 minutes to spare. He then continued to swim around Manhattan and this was the time that George Kauffmann and he swam up the Harlem together. The next day, the escort boat was 15 minutes late. Ben looked at me and I shrugged my shoulders saying, "You had the tide beat by 15 minutes yesterday, so you should just squeak by today." This is when we learned that the tide is not linear in the East River. The 15-minute delay meant Ben got stopped just north of the 59th Street Bridge. He needed at least another 15 minutes of current to get to Gracie Mansions and Mill Rock at Hell Gate and into the Harlem River. The 15-minute delay at the start ate up the 15-minute cushion from the day before and another 15 minutes besides. The East River swim is a non-linear function of the starting time.

The decision to use Ben Huggard as our guinea pig to experiment with the East River in full flood had its plusses and minuses. On one of those swims he got into trouble. He started off by not swimming that far out into the river, swimming just off the end of the piers at South Street Seaport being the showman so a lot of pedestrians could observe him. As a consequence of that he swam quite near to the bridge footing along the Manhattan side of the Manhattan Bridge. The Manhattan Bridge is the second bridge as you go up the East River, after the Brooklyn Bridge and immediately after South Street Seaport. The river was running so fast that Ben was making straight for the pilings for the next pier a few hundred yards up stream that sticks further out into the river than the bridge footing was placed. We called and signaled for Ben to pull further out into the river and he tried. His speed swimming laterally in the current didn't overcome the current drift and he slammed right into the pilings, turning at the last second to catch and hold onto one of the outside piles.

Figure 71 Here is the East River looking east toward Brooklyn. The Brooklyn Bridge is in the center and Manhattan Bridge is to the left.

This was an instance where an attractive feature turns into a downside. Ben could not push himself off the pier and swim around. The current was running so fast that he was pinned to the piling. To try to swim underneath the pier was sure death. This was a life and death situation. Panic broke out on the escort boat. We decide that to get him off the pier we would station the boat upstream and throw him a rope that we could use to pull him off and maneuver him clear of the pier. As the boat took up position near Ben pointing into the current, the boat crew prepared the rope. We threw him the line, Ben grabbed it and as the boat pulled forward he released his hold from the pier and began being pulled through the water. Not five feet off the pier the rope broke. Ben turn and once again slammed into the pier at full current speed which that day exceeded 4 knots. There is a reason you go into the local marine store and purchase a new line every year. The boat we were on was not a Power Squadron or Auxiliary Coast Guard boat. We prepared another line made up of the docking lines, these were much heavier and we extricated Benson from his predicament.

Figure 72 In this photo, both swimmers are too close to the Manhattan Bridge and are being directed away from shore to clear the next pier at the end of Rutgers Slip only 200 yards upstream.

Every year, the marathon positions a kayak at the foot of the Manhattan Bridge to warn swimmers away. Jokingly, we say we named the pier after Ben. That wasn't the first pier Benson had named after him. He slammed into the railroad bridge at Spuyten Duyvil once. This wasn't quite as dangerous because the pilings are widely space and there were no cables hanging in the water. Part of the problem was Ben would swim and not look up every once in a while or switch over to breaststroke when he needed to maneuver. He rolled off this piling and floated free, coming out the other side. This incident was more the fault of his support crew, of which I was a member, failing to alert him of the impending obstacle. What's obvious to the people on the boat is not necessarily something the swimmer is even thinking about.

Figure 73 Spuyten Duyvil Bridge in the open position. Notice the smaller openings off to the left on the approach to the swing bridge.

Another situation where we've had close calls is along the lower Hudson River. One competitor was swimming too close to the end of the piers. At full ebb, the current tends to fill in behind the piers. The swimmer was drifting about 20 feet toward shore immediately after every pier. Then he'd have to swim across the current to clear the next pier. This exciting swimming went on from after 42nd Street until the World Trade Center bulkhead wall. Even that he barely missed.

Figure 74 Start of the World Trade Center bulkhead wall, a timing location for swim projections. Notice the small crowd that has gathered. This is a good viewing location for the swim.

At that location you can see the force of the current piling up the water a half foot higher than the rest of the water like it was the bow wake of a boat. The swim was exciting because avoiding sure death takes some skill and bravado. It would be a trying time for the loved ones because once trapped underneath a pier, the Harbor Patrol will wait for ebb to extract the body of the drowned swimmer.

Figure 75 Swimmer pass by the 79th Street boat basin in the Hudson River; also, called the North River. This is the ½ point for the Hudson River.

I was along escorting Ben Huggard around Manhattan on one of his solo swims and his times varied considerably from my computer projects. He was swimming rather slowly. So slowly, I jumped into the Hudson by the passenger piers to get a feel for his pace. A leisurely sidestroke allowed me to keep up with him. As I was enjoying the swim, a passenger liner started to pull out of its slip. We heard the long blast followed by three short blasts on the ship horn. Since I wasn't on board to coordinate this, the pilot tried to sneak us by. Fortunately, the ship's officer stationed on the stern saw us and called for reverse engines. Ben and I bobbled about like we were corks in that prop wake. It was like being in a Jacuzzi on steroids. That was too close a call and I'm sure some salty language was used to describe the situation aboard the passenger liner.

Figure 76 When this happens...try and tuck your swimmer into a slip between piers, you just can't stop swimming because the current will carry you right into the ship. Celebrity Cruise Line's Zenith backing out into the Hudson River. Sound signal given when backing: 3 short and one long blast.

Between the piers are slips. If a swimmer is tucked way inside, the water remains fairly slack. This is a good location to hold up a swimmer if an ocean liner pulls out in the middle of a swim and your swimmer is upstream from the obstruction; otherwise, the swimmer has to turn around and swim in place until the ship finishes its maneuvering. Just remember when exiting the location and going back into the current, the water will tend to drag you downstream before you clear the end of the piers. It works best to exit the pier area closer to the backside of the upstream pier than wind up swimming for your life. I've seen swimmers carried sideways toward the piers while they are exiting the slips. Give yourself some wiggle room. Do not attempt to swim around the ship. It's the better decision to take a line from your escort boat than cause a marine incident that could impact the swim's permit.

Figure 77 View of the old Battery starting location. After 9/11, the start moved around the corner to North Cove in the Hudson as additional ferries now occupy this stretch of bulkhead. The East River begins here and you pick up speed as you move off to the right in this photo.

The immediate result of all our experiments paid off in 1986 when Ben Huggard, as President of the organization, moved the swim start to Battery Park. The visibility of the swim improved immensely.

Figure 78 Spectators along the rail at the Battery. This was the start and finish location from 1986-2001. A ladder used to exit the water is seen to the right in between the dolphins with volunteers standing on it. Once I counted 13 video cameras along the wall.

We no longer had to pay for 3 patrol boats just to sit at the Battery. The swimmers would cross the ferry slips together and all we had to do was watch for the approaching Staten Island ferry and use the same rules for a swimmer to go or not to go: if a ferry was approaching, the swim had to start before the ferry made its turn into the East River. If the ferry had turned out of the Hudson River, the starter had to hold the swimmers until it made the left turn for the ferry slips. This turns out to be a slightly difficult problem. For one, you had to get all the swimmers into the water. They get cold if they have to tread water. You had to have an official count because the Coast Guard asks if all swimmers are out of the water at the end of the swim. Both counts have to match or the Coast Guard starts a search operation. Once all the swimmers are in, you double-check the location of the ferry. They are only running one ferry on the weekends; so if the ferry is in the slip, you know exactly when it will depart. You allow the swimmers twelve minutes to cross the ferry terminal slip from the starting time at the Battery. You still have to keep the start within a 15-minute window of the optimum starting time, the middle of the flood current in the East River, which changes every day.

Figure 79 Close up of the Battery ferry terminals. The Staten Island terminals are to the left in the photo and are the more active terminals.

The marathon swim was very fortunate to have the assistance and participation by volunteer ham radio operators. The particular group we worked with is the ARC Emergency Communications Service (ARCECS) who are active with the Queens Chapter of the American Red Cross of Greater New York.[647] The group formed in 1964 as the result of an American Red Cross of Greater New York youth initiative. Their president, George Sau, WB2ZTH, and I, N2FAC, knew each other from our work at New York Telephone. I mentioned to him the particular problems we were having and in 1991, over a dozen hams participated in the swim event.

One component of the story of ham radio and swimming would be the evolution of the technology. The main reason ham radio was involved was to provide radio coverage from one end of Manhattan to the other so that the swim director could talk to the first boat and the last boat. In the Hudson River, swimmers spread out so far apart that VHF marine radio wasn't able to reach the swim director. Using repeaters, this became possible. This meant putting a ham radio operator on every boat. For the first swim or two, hams went with each boat and communications fed to the 65' motor yacht *Ellis Island* owned by Richard Ellis via VHF and ham radio. The *Ellis Island* served as the swim's command center during the early years of the swim.

Figure 80 I wouldn't be a bit surprised to discover a ham radio operator was stationed on this converted lightship anchored one year in the Hudson River. The splash in the water is a swimmer who is too far off course.

When the race entered the Hudson River, one of our communication links, marine VHF, was cut due to its point-to-point, line-of-sight range where the back of the field couldn't talk to the front of the field. The boat operators who depended on their VHF had to learn to talk to the hams. Then we realized that we needed to feed the press, who were on-shore, information while the swim was underway.

The next biggest jump in technology was when Automatic Position Reporting System (APRS) became available.[648] Hams equipped with GPS receivers can broadcast their position to packet radio repeaters and similarly equipped hams can download the information automatically to see on a PDA the real-time display of their position. This technological jump was pioneered by Bob Bruninga, WB4APR, which allows packet radio to track real-time events. APRS concentrates on the graphic display of station and object locations and movements. Hams began experimenting with this system as early as 1994. APRS became generally available in 1997. ARCECS was using this software at the 2000 marathon swim and my mouth dropped open when I was shown the display with all the hams' positions. All they needed was a chart overlaid on the device and they would have something very, very useful. By the time of this publication, I'm sure it's out there.

Communications becomes the key to running a successful swim. Not everything happens as planned but if the swim director can be contacted, informed of the situation, a means of dealing with the situations can be developed on the fly. The story of ham radio's involvement with marathon swimming is the role of communications in a mobile environment and the humans who made it happen. When the communication systems links are working, you'll sometimes hear a message being passed on one link and then the same information on the other link. Sometime in the 1990's mobile phones became generally available but I can remember the days when we were loaned 3 mobile phone units by NYNEX. This created a third communication link. Managing the links is key to a successful information flow that will assist the swim and doesn't overload it.

One year a swimmer's bag was misplaced. For 15 minutes, both links, ham and VHF, were tracking down the location of the bag on the various escort boats. That was all the communication that got through at that time. I remember one year when everything on an open cockpit boat died due to a rainstorm, the coach got seasick, and the ham was the only link to the event plus he was feeding the swimmer. He was standing up soaking wet holding his equipment in front of him on a tiny little boat and he looked like the ham equivalent of the "...the Timex that took a licking but kept ticking".

Eventually, all organizations get stale. The original group changes its composition and issues, even side issue take up much of the organization's energy. This is true of any organization. Personality conflicts emerge and dominate to the extent that the work of the committee is impaired. I can remember one time when some local swimmers joined the committee and wanted to make the swim more swimmer-friendly, (i.e.: less expensive). This ruffled some feathers and people resigned from the committee and others were forced out.

Figure 81 Tim Johnson, Harold Washington (then Mayor of Chicago), and Ben Huggard on a swim to help raise money for food banks in Chicago in 1985. Publicity associated with the swim help raise $300,000.

For a while, Ben Huggard ran the organization as President from 1986 to 1988. Then he moved to Virginia and would come up to New York for meetings. This began to wear on him so he took a step back. Drury asked Julie Ridge to run the organization as President in 1988. This worked for a while but the swim began having more problems and demands made on it than it was able to handle. It could simply be said that swimmers and groups internal and external to the organization wanted to use the swim for their own purposes.

Figure 82 Julie Ridge before one of her competitive swims in the early days when the race start was at East 96th Street. In the background is the Triboro Bridge over the East River, the footbridge is off to the left, and her dad with his back to the camera.

A sanction for a swim is suppose to provide blanket insurance coverage for an event. Insurance coverage by Master Swimming caused a problem in the Manhattan marathon in 1990. The US Power Squadron that was assisting in the Manhattan swim wished to be named additional insured and due to mishaps in other events not as well organized as the Manhattan swim, the insurance carrier refused to cover escort boats of a horse power greater then fifty.[649] This failure to take responsibility by USMS for an event that they had previously sanctioned flew in face of their other rules that required the local organizers to seek Coast Guard permission for the swim. One of the requirements of the Coast Guard permit was for an escort boat of sufficient size to remove a swimmer from the path of an ocean liner as well as provide for the pilot, the crew, the coach, an official observer, a ham radio operator, and anyone else the swimmer might desire to host aboard their escort boat. The permit the Coast Guard issued specifically forbids the use of inflatable boats in the swim. One could not satisfy the Coast Guard and meet the power limit of the USMS insurance policy and provide for safe swims; at least in New York Harbor. The US Power Squadron officially pulled out of the swim when we could not provide them an insurance statement with UP Power Squadron as named insured for the event.[650] All their training, command structure, experience, equipment and support was gone because of the diminutive vision of the US Master Swimming executive board that consisted of Carol Zaleski, Bernard Favaro, Red Siegrist, Audrey Birklid, Lee Jamieson, Ray Essick, and John Peterson. When I wrote requesting changes and suggesting their setting training standards for the escort craft personnel, their comments back to me were, "…to get out of the boat insurance business…(let) the boat owners get (their) own insurance…New York is the only one requesting this." Evidently, their concept of open-water swimming consists of events held in sheltered water supervised by kayaks and maybe one boat with a "big" 25 horsepower outboard. It's all they could handle. Neither Captain Webb nor Gertrude Ederle could get a sanction from US Master swimming for their Channel swims because their official escort boat might ask to be named insured on the insurance coverage.

    Boat availability became a big issue. Up until this point of the swim organization, I made most of the arrangement for the boaters. Scott Woody, one of the boaters, took over organizing the boat volunteers in 1990. This meant that the Association was back to securing boats in a haphazard manner from boaters that were not liability aware or concerned with liability coverage. If the

Association allowed the swim to take place without the sanction, the swim organizers were without coverage. Morty Berger eventually solved the insurance problem when he took over the reigns of the organization.

One of the organizations that assisted the Manhattan Marathon swim grow was the US Merchant Marine Academy. I had become acquainted with the swim coach at the Academy, Susan Peterson, at a Master's swim meet in Hicksville. From that chance meeting, within a year, freshman members of the King Point swim team began participating as swimmers in the marathon with upperclassmen coordinating their support. The volunteerism from the Academy to help out the swim was wonderful to see. MISA Committee member Susan Peterson accompanied some of her women swimmers to a Manhattan club prior to the swim one year and met her husband Stuart Lubow because of the swim. He began showing up and while not actually being a committee member, helped bring Dollar Dry Dock on board as a major sponsor.

A current buzzword in education is service learning; the students at King Point took it to heart and dove right in. Over the years that the US Merchant Marine Academy participated, the following swim team members swam around Manhattan, some more than once: Matt Arcy, David Blackledge, Paul Bowdich, Jeffery Callender, Mishelle Determan, William Dornacher, William Duffield, Daniel Foos, Aubrey Gabriel, Rhonda and Ronaldo Hart, Nathan Hodges, William Johnson, Richard Landerman, Krista Magnifico, Mark Miller, Kevin Morgan, James Penny, Webster Pfingsten, Kimberly Redmann, Chad Rice, Vince Riggio, Hans Rittinger, Brett Salkeld, James Shine, Ashley Smith, Eric Swanson, Alex Venetior, Jana Voracek, William Willard, Lars Wogen, and Kelli Wynne. The Merchant Marine Academy pulled out of the swim in 1992. We lost a tremendous amount of volunteer workers and support boats when that happened.

Figure 83 Who says you can't have fun on a swim? (l to r) Skip Storch, Jim Johnson, Jane Katz, Stuart Lubow, Sue Peterson-Lubow and some unidentified midshipmen aboard the US Merchant Marine Academy vessel the *Mariner*.

Manhattan Island Foundation

Drury Gallagher turned over the organization and rights to the Manhattan Island Marathon Swim to the Manhattan Island Foundation after the 1992 swim.[651] Morty Berger who completed the swim in 1991 wanted to help the swim survive. His background in business was key in his developing a business plan for the swim. He put a team together of Robert Makatura and Caroline Jaenisch; together they formed an action plan to renew swimmer, sponsor, volunteer and media interest in the race. Right away they built a board of Directors consisting of: Steve Chestler, Marcia Cleveland, Kim Heinlein, Richard Infield, Patrice Gallagher, and Martin McMahon. They were backed up by a Board of Advisors consisting of: John J. McDowell III, Glenn

Hintze, Timothy Johnson, Stephen Keller, Alan Labate, John Liona, Paul Lewandowski, Marcy MacDonald, Tom Neff, Arvind Sanger, Felicia Stoler, Andrew Warren, and Bo Walker. They divided the work up into committees: boats and kayaks, volunteers, public relations, marketing, fund raising, applications and training tips, pre-race coordination, home page, rules, coordinators, and others. A few of the members were from the old MISA organization but most of the committee members were new.

Figure 84 Marcia Cleveland, Kris Rutford, Morty Berger at the 2000 Pre-Race briefing. Notice the MIF image to the left of Annette Kellerman.

It was a fun, exciting time. I realized that I had to begin training people to replace me so for the next few years I'd take along a MIF member during the race and show them the ropes. Other MISA volunteers helped out on race day and in recruiting the boat members, especially Scott Woody. The energy and enthusiasm made it possible to continue helping out as the swim grew. It was important to remember that if mistakes were made, who's to say that the old organization wouldn't have made the same mistakes? It's a firm belief of mine that if you don't make mistakes, you'll never learn and grow.

In their first year, 1993, the Foundation received coverage of the swim with a photo in the New York Times on their front page above the fold! This was the second time in 65 years that the swim was so featured.[652] They brought on two new sponsors and a record number of volunteers. Their work to bring credibility back to the race paid off. The Foundation decided to raise money for community outreach programs like swimming classes for disadvantaged children in New York City: the Learn to Swim program of the Parks Department.[653] MIF established their website at www.nycswim.org.

One outstanding publicity coup was to have the Discovery channel film the 1993 race for a one-hour documentary called *The Big Swim*. This film did a very good job of documenting the race and I am seen discussing the race at the end of the film. In a superb effort at improving the race, volunteers and swimmers were sent questionnaires after the swim to comment on what they liked about the swim and what they thought could be improved. Nowadays, this would be called part of a constant improvement system and reflects good management. They dealt with the sanction problem by not having the swim sanctioned. In very simple terms, Master swimming brought nothing to the swim. MIF established and maintained swim standards that are recognized on the same level as the English Channel. The insurance was purchased on an event basis.

Figure 85 Morty Berger and Paul Lewandowski assist a swimmer at the finish of the 2001 MIMS.

One of the big differences between the old organization and the Manhattan Island Foundation is the new organization is a not-for-profit 501c3 corporation. This means that individuals and corporations can make donations to the swim. One aspect of the organization that Morty Berger wants to emphasize is the ownership of the swim by the volunteers. Certain aspects have changed over time. For one, the ham radio group, which once was essential, has now been replaced by cellular technology. Originally, kayaks were supplied only if the swimmer happened to know a kayaker and could convince them to come along. They worked out so well that now it's an essential feature of the race. Steve Keller was instrumental in bringing this aspect of the race along but even this needed fine-tuning. Kayak coordinators have included Richard Clifford, John Dowdell, Ralph Diaz, Brian Maxey, Jim Bixler, Michael Madkin, and Nancy Brous who bring paddlers with their kayaks from all over the metropolitan area to support the swim. One location in the swim where kayaks are essential is at Spuyten Duyvil. Occasionally, the swing bridge will close to allow a train to pass and stay closed because in a half hour, another train is going to use the bridge. The escort boats can't go by the obstruction but the swimmers with their kayak support can: they swim and paddle right underneath the bridge. MIF now puts extra boats and kayaks up at Spuyten Duyvil to handle these situations.

Richard Clifford is a kayaker who has been on as many 10 swims around Manhattan. I first met him on Arthur Coleman's record attempt in 1993 when Arthur managed a personal best of 6:19. This was a night start and my education of the role kayaks have in open-water swimming started that night. Kayaks are transported using powerboats to the start for solo swims while for the Manhattan marathon, they put in normally at the starting locations when the tide is high. At the finish, the tide is low and kayaks are either paddled or shuttled by powerboat to a floating dock back up the Hudson River to pull out. Kayaks do most of the feeding and communication with the swimmer. They are right down there at the swimmer's level. The crew will find it very easy to spot their swimmer when a kayak is helping with escort duty. They handle most of the feedings, which eliminates having the swimmer come over to the boat.

The resume of Richard Clifford, kayaker, includes: Jay Derks in 1995 to a 3rd place finish; Marcia Cleveland on her sub-six hour swim in 1996; Tammy van Wisse in 1997 and 1999, John van Wisse in 2000; the Millennium Relay in 2001; Randy Opdyke in 2004; travel to assist Tammy van Wisse cross the Loch Ness, Fort Meyers Beach to assist Randy Opdyke in her 25K National Championship swim, and with a number of other swims for good causes. Like all the kayakers, they give of their time and more effort than most of us to contribute to a successful swim. What follows are some guidelines that kayak coordinators for Manhattan and other swims have contributed to include in this history of swimming.

Kayak swim support is an integral part of open-water swimming. They have an advantage over boats in that they can get closer to the swimmer and exercise control over the swimmers route by slight modification to their own course. Kayaks have an advantage over swimmers in that they are continuously looking ahead and known where to go and have a visual height advantage of 2½ feet over 6 inches. Kayaks offer an advantage to swimmers in the marine environment because they can be seen much easier by other boaters than the swimmers. Swimmers, from a distance, look little different than flotsam to boaters especially if they are doing the breaststroke. They have a better efficiency in the water than the swimmer, which makes them more valuable as the swim progresses.

The role of the kayak changes as the swims lengthen. In short swim with many participants, kayaks herd the swimmers and will occasionally execute a water rescue. In longer swims, a kayak will provide more swimmer support, such as individual escort duty that may include feeding, providing feedback and offering encouragement as needed. The swimmer looks at the kayak when breathing and maintains a comfortable distance alongside. As the kayak changes course, the swimmer will move with the kayaker. Don't expect instantaneous responses. Some swimmers will stop to ask questions if they don't know what you are doing or ignore you.

It helps to set up a method to communicate non-verbally. You can work out a set of hand signals to tell the swimmer you are leaving them to go over to the boat. A swimmer will continue on course until you return. The swimmer can communicate by hand signals with their kayaker, slapping the water, or using leg kicks to send messages. Normally, they are letting you know they want to feed; you may have to go alongside the escort boat for supplies, leaving them. The swimmer may want to know if they need to swim faster, how far the competition is behind them, or how much farther to go. If it gets more complicated than that, the swimmer will want to talk to their coach on the boat. By hand signals, swimmers can setup the verbal communication ahead of time so that the time spent talking is minimized. Coaches have always had the advantage of one-way communications with chalkboards held over the side of the boat.

Kayakers have saved lives by assisting swimmers to safety. Swim support requires much more maneuvering than paddling. It is a team effort whether one-on-one or a swim en-mass. Kayaks identify the injured swimmers and the exhausted swimmer early and pull them out of the swim for care. It's important to carry spare floatation for swimmers such as noodles, RFDs, and Type II PFDs. Having a throw bag is essential in some situations to tow a swimmer. If that occurs, be prepared for the paddle of your life because of the drag caused by a swimmer caught in a current. Have a sound device for signaling the escort boat, alerting a swimmer to a danger or the errant watercraft entering the swim course. Keep in mind that some swimmers wear earplugs to keep water out of their ears, which makes verbal communication with them difficult, as they won't respond at normal audio levels. A whistle hung about your neck is the easiest to store and handiest to reach. Marine VHF is essential for communications at times and keeps the kayaker apprised of the overall event progress. Another problem is goggles that may have fogged up limiting the visual response of the swimmers. This problem most often occurs right after the start and swimmer will want to switch to a spare pair out of their swim bag on the escort boat.

Even the strongest and faster swimmers can benefit from the close up support of a kayak to guide them to turns and avoid piers or sea walls. If you think a swimmer is going to come too close to a pier or seawall, change their course early. If you are changing their course later, it'll be a more drastic course change and they might bang into your kayak with their hand. If you do, they are not disqualified as long as they don't hang on. If a swimmer is distressed, have them hold on at the bow of your kayak so capsizing is lessened.

Swim organizers are now announcing that if a kayak gets in the swimmers way, there's a reason and the swimmer should stop and obtain instructions. For instance, in the Manhattan swim, at the end of the race at North Cove, the marina has a narrow entrance. Unless the swimmer hits it dead on, they risk being driven up against the seawall fenders along the southern entrance wall. A kayaker will normally be stationed there to help fend swimmers off or give immediate aid. The safe approach to the end of the swim by the swimmer is to edge over close to the seawall before they reach the entrance, then turn quickly into the calm waters of North Cove.

The reason a kayaker participates is to make the event and/or charity that the swim supports a success. The first kayaker used in the Manhattan swim was with Linda McGill in 1984, she brought a kayaker who used a SOT, sit-on-top kayak to help escort her. The kayaker paddled all the way around Manhattan and got no credit. He did have the satisfaction of knowing that he helped make Linda's swim a success.

In the Manhattan marathon swim overseen by Marcia Cleveland and Richard Clifford in 2001, nature conspired to create considerable turmoil. During the event, a thunderstorm passed over the New York City area and lightning was seen and heard. In a safety procedure similar to swimming pools, the swimmers were asked to leave the water by someone who did not identify themselves on the VHF radio. The lead swimmer at the time was Morgan Filler. The dispute was regarding whether or not the lead swimmer, Morgan Filler, at the time of the first swim interruption left the water as required or if an Emergency Management trained personnel aboard her escort boat over-ruled whoever called for the swimmers to leave the water. Morgan was penalized 15 minutes allowing Igor to place first. This was decided at a meeting not open to the race official on Morgan's boat. This race highlighted the failure of the communication system to put the swim director in charge of all the swimmers. It also revealed a lack of understanding of marathon swimming rules regarding long distance races. Once a swimmer gets in a boat, the swim is over. Boats adrift in a current cannot hold their position.

This episode also revealed the lack of understanding by the swim organizers of ordinary marine VHF radio operation, which was symptomatic of a lack of a marine background with individuals in charge of running the swim. Fortunately, no one was injured: it was just egos that got bruised. However, when the Power Squadron and Auxiliary Coast Guard were involved with the swim, you could count on marine issues being handled in a trained professional manner. It behooves any swim organization to insure that persons in charge of a swim have some recognition of the Rules of the Road that govern marine events as well as basic seamanship. Both the Power Squadron and the Auxiliary Coast Guard give classes in boating that would suffice to train any swim organizer in these basics.

Additionally, the dispute revealed different ideas about lightning. Since lightning can be a factor in swims, the issues that appeared in the Manhattan Island Marathon Swim are worthy of consideration by any swim organizations holding an open-water swim. At the time the first race abandonment was called, Morgan Fuller was underneath the Triboro Bridge and in the lead. At this location, she had what in effect amounted to a 300-foot high lightning rod. Lightning strikes go to the closest ground source. She was in absolutely no danger whatsoever. The rest of the field was either being escorted by cabin cruiser boats or smaller open cockpit boats like Boston Whalers. Cabin cruisers have built into their structures grounding cables to conduct lightning through a boat where it then dissipates into the water. A swimmer next to a boat so grounded is in no danger from a lightning strike but you don't want them right next to the boat. About twenty feet away should be perfect because you need the charge to dissipate. Small open boats are not normally equipped with lightning rods. The swimmer at about 6" about the water level is safer than their support crew standing up in the escort boat. This is a situation akin to a public swimming pool. The swimmers in the pool are perfectly safe in the water because surrounding the pool are these chrome lifeguard towers. It's just that the lifeguards have to get off the "default" lightning rod and can no longer perform their function that requires the swimmers to leave the water.

Figure 86 Small boats like this Boston Whaler have no built in lightning protection. The people standing up in the boat become the default lightning rods.

Around Manhattan, if the swimmers are in the East River or the Harlem, near a bridge or shore, they are in no danger. Watch the Empire State Building and you'll see it absorbing nearly every strike. The entire Manhattan underground water supply system acts as a ground conducting the current potential from the tall buildings. In the Hudson River, if you are in the middle, over a mile from the George Washington Bridge, and in an open boat, it's time to think about seeking shelter. If your swimmer is near shore in the Hudson River or swimming off the end of the piers, the height of shoreline buildings, structures, and trees will provide adequate shelter. A storm blowing west to east across Manhattan means the storm will have discharged last over New Jersey and will be looking at New York City for its next strike. The circumstances described for a shoreline are not the same as those found around Manhattan.

Figure 87 This swimmer is approaching the entrance to North Cove.

One of the successes of MIF is the changing of the start venue to South Cove around the corner from the Battery in the Hudson River. Morty decided in November of 2001 to move the swim start location because the Battery location we had been using as our start was now dedicated to a ferry service for commuters to NJ due to the disruption of normal PATH train service from the terrorist attack on September 11th, 2001. Since one of the swim stop points is that corner of the World Trade Center wall it needed to be tested. In May of 2002 Morty tested the start with 5 swimmers of different speeds. He checked with me as to what the normal start would be on one particular Saturday and then had swimmers start at South Cove and swim around the corner to the Battery. He was able to prove the validity of the start and get his fudge factor to add into the timing for the East River. This location does make it a little bit harder to check the ferry status but by the time the swimmers reach the ferry terminals, their escort boats are alongside. They are still bunched fairly closely at this point. The swim has started at this location ever since.

The Manhattan Island Foundation has expanded to include a number of other events that puts people in the waters around Manhattan. The organization as an acronym is pronounced *miff*.

Their experience now that they are approaching the 25th year anniversary of the modern swim is that the event is no longer an Everest, a freak show with swimmers beating their chests. It's now a way of life where swimmers come in every year to swim and/or help out in any way they can.[654] The swimmers and volunteers are team players. Kris Rutford and David Blanke do the swim and then help with the clean up or the organization prior to the swim. It's a group that hugs each other and asks what they can do. Especially gratifying is to see Manhattan alumnus set up successful swims elsewhere or working as volunteers in a local community swim. It takes a tremendous effort to make a complete circumnavigation of Manhattan whether swimming, paddling, or motoring and when the swim is over, the paddles put away, the boat stowed for winter, individuals will pause to ask themselves, what's next? Just like athletes, the next goal will incorporate the successes and lessons of the past. Visit their web site: www.swimnyc.org for more up to date information. Because of MIF, more swims are held in the Hudson River than anywhere else in the world. Over the summer of 2005, they incorporated an entirely new swim: Around Governors Island Swim. It wasn't completely around and the distance was only 2 miles but it was a first. Mike Rossner, age 40, from Manhattan, New York, won the initial event in a time of 34 minutes 15 seconds.

Figure 88 The loneliness of the lead swimmer...

Figure 89 Finish line at South Cove in 2002.

Chapter 12   Cuba

If there ever was a swim that attracts swimmers looking for immortality, it is the swim from Cuba across the Straits of Florida. The swim has never successfully been completed. The difficulties are the distance: 90 miles between the nearest points of land between the two countries, the Gulf Stream current you have to swim across, the dangers imposed by the presence of sharks and jellyfish, and the political hostility that has existed between the two neighbors.

The first instance of reference to this swim is from Zimmy.[655] After he complete the Hudson River swim, he declared his next swim would be to attempt the Florida Straits. Some time in 1950, a team of Cuban swimmers[656] attempted to cross the Florida Straits. They nearly made it until their shark cage fell apart. The first solo attempt was by Diana Nyad in 1978. She made a gallant effort and it attracted considerable press and attention because of the hostile political relationship in existence at the time between Cuba and the United States. The coordinator of the escort boats, Richard Dumoulin (who I met in Hemingway Marina, Havana, during Skip's Storch's 1993 attempt) commented that when the swim came to an end, there was considerable wailing by friends and supporters of the swimmer. Her cage was propelled by four outboards motors. As Diana neared the US coast, she was down to one motor. When a wave broke over the motors, the last engine failed, causing the swim to be called off after 41:47. Diana did not have the best weather window for attempting the swim as the Cuban authorities wanted to delay the swim to August and the swimmer's contingent with limited availability started the swim rather than return. She started in Bihid Banka along the north coast of Cuba, west of Havana to make allowance for the current. This was not a particularly good location to start the swim because she had to swim out to the Gulf Stream unnecessarily lengthening the swim. The distance the current carries you is free mileage and once you are in the current off Havana, the closest point to the

United States, the distance you have to cross stays the same as the current follows the curve of the Florida Keys.

After Diana Nyad, Walter Poenisch from Illinois attempted the swim but used swimming aids not allowed in ordinary distance swims. He finished around Marathon Key, halfway up the Keys. The next attempt was by Skip Storch of Spring Valley, New York, on June 2, 1993 who managed 33 miles.[657] His press coverage attracted the attention of an Australian swimmer, Suzy Maroney, who at that time was just beginning to claim a share of the world marathon stage.

The attempt in 1993 by Skip Storch began three years earlier in 1990. When Skip and I got together at the conclusion of his Liberty Swim to discuss the future, I asked Skip if he was ready for the "the big one". Skip's ears picked up immediately and wanted to know what swim it was and I told him it was swimming from Cuba to Florida. I then gave him a quick history lesson and outlined my ideas for tackling the crossing. Skip said very little, asking a few questions and committed to nothing. Skip is an organizational genius and once he got the last leg of his Liberty swim out of the way, he devoted two years of his life to pulling this off. His greatest challenge was in obtaining permission to enter Cuba for the swim. He named his swim the "Coral Relief Peace Swim" thus combining two concerns of two countries: the Floridians concerns about the coral reef surrounding the Florida Keys and the Cuban peace propaganda vehicle.

The experiences of helping to organize this swim and the subsequence drama in Cuba revealed more about the politics of the era than swimming. Once all the permissions were secured and the swim set, Skip and the entire swim team were invited to the Cuban Mission to the United Nations for a reception. It was held in Manhattan at their residence, 315 Lexington Avenue, in early 1993. I'd been by this building a number of times and never really noticed anything particular about it but this time the security seemed visible. We were in a large reception room on the first floor off on the right. The personalities were being introduced to various members of the Cuban delegation. Noel Blackman, from

Wesley Hills, New York, the Event Director, was having a swell time and handling most of the introductions. I met Dr. Jay Hyman from Delray Beach Florida whose purposes with the swim eluded me. While in Cuba, it was explained to me that he had once hosted Fidel about his yacht in Cuba. As I walked around nodding and smiling to people, sampling the wonderful spread of food, a thought occurred to me: what with the fall of the Berlin Wall on November 9 1989, this group of people was one of the last remaining communists in the world. They were the true believers, unique, and they were all jammed into this one room. I noticed three young men come in late and greeted them. I asked them who they were and they proudly announced they were the Young Communists Workers. I commented to them that at their age I too was politically active as a member of the John Birch Society for its shock value.[658] Their eyes and mouths dropped open and they then asked what was I now? I told them I was a Democrat. They seemed relieved. I got a good chuckle out of that.

I wondered just how much Skip had to compromise to arrange this swim and got an earful when we were in Cuba. The Cubans held a press conference with Skip at Hemingway Marina. The place was packed with journalists and a lot of other people. Truthfully, there was nothing any more virulent anti-American than the usual political discourse during the campaign of 2004 and none of it was coming from Skip. However, Noel Blackman and Dr. Hyman dropped any pretense of being loyal Americans and led the choir. It became painfully obvious that in order to get permission from Cuba to do the swim, Skip had to allow these individuals control over the swim's message.

Noel Blackman revealed the extent of his involvement with the Cubans during a conversation we had concerning the starting location of the swim. Within a few days of our arrival in Havana, he laid it all out when he approached me and told me I either agree to the swim starting at Hemingway Marina or he "would have me escorted out of Cuba by the military." I couldn't believe an American was threatening me with being thrown off the island. It turned out, Fidel Castro wouldn't come down to the swim start in downtown Havana (the point closest to Florida) but he would come to Hemingway Marina because it was in a controlled environment. This whole swim for Noel was a vehicle to manipulate Castro. Hyman and Noel wanted to be seen as the friends of Castro and the Cuban people. I've no idea what motivated these individuals but I can assure you it had nothing to do with swimming. The swim was merely the vehicle by which their political agenda was being carried along.

I got a chance to see the Cuban people in a tour conducted during our stay there. We visited the National Cathedral. Prostitutes populated the entrance and the interior was devoid of any religious symbols. The Cuban National Cathedral which I know at one time in the past was filled with pomp, circumstance and ceremony had become a hallow, empty tomb. I saw a tour guide down an aisle and I wonder what she could possibly be talking about, there was no religion practiced there. For a person who valued religious freedom, this scene was devastating. Fibber and I took a cab back and stopped in the poorer section of Havana. That was refreshing. I thought we would be mobbed because we were Americans but these people seemed to have enough to deal with getting through their daily lives. We passed by, noticed but undisturbed among them. Daily we could see people going to work, all-be-it by walking, bike, motor scooter, bus, motorcycle with sidecar, dilapidated 1950-era American vehicle, or Russian Lada sedans. Their issues were the commute, their jobs, and their families. Everyone seemed pretty much to be like everyone else in any large city. Except for the large number of military, shopping and the daily needs of life filled their days. As Fibber and I worked in the marina to get Skip's cage ready for sea, the workers there seemed just like union workers everywhere only with a longer lunch hour. In the meetings held with the various groups that were supporting the swim, such as GeoCuba, there was always a military person in the meeting. Whatever was decided was run by them for the final decision.

There was one episode that bears mentioning. The captains, their wives, and the crews of the escort boats took a tour of Havana conducted by the Cubans that included the zoo. One wife was especially upset when they came back because of the condition of the animals at the zoo. She said they showed sign of malnourishment and looked as if they were being starved. She was very upset. I listened to her as she told me what she had seen and tried to visualize the problem. It was then that it occurred to me that we hadn't seen any overweight Cubans either. This was an island with a serious problem and there was really only one man responsible for that problem, Fidel Castro.

There weren't many boats in Hemingway marina although a sailing regatta had just been held and a number of French were there. The morning after we arrived, a group of US fishing boats left to return to the United States, they had been there for a shark-fishing tournament. As we moved along the coast looking at spots to set up the swim start, I noticed the local competition for the shark contest; individuals with a fishing line, a hook, and an inner tube were doing all the fishing. The Mariel Harbor boatlift of 125,000 Cubans that occurred in 1980 had taken every single vessel that could float out of Cuba. All that was left to go to sea on were State owned vessels or military, thus the preponderance of inner tube fishermen. We visited Cojimar, where Hemingway kept his fishing boat. There is a Hemingway statue in the town square. The people loved him and call him Papa to this day. He's like a saint to the Cuban people. While the harbor was a nice hurricane hole, the swimmer would have to swim out about one-eighth of a mile to meet the cage. Plus, the pier he'd have to step out on didn't look all that substantial. The best place for the swim start was right off the wall along the Avenue de Maceo from Central Havana. This location would allow for the biggest crowd to see the start. A slight bit of an advantage can be obtained by starting the swim east of the Castillo de los Tres Reyes del Morro, the old fortress guarding the Havana Harbor entrance but except for Cojimar, we didn't have time to scout out any other start locations.

Figure 90 Skip smiling during a break on his swim.

While Skips swim did not last that long, the cage performed perfectly. I remember most vividly during the early evening about a half an hour of bioluminescence as Skip swam through some plankton that glowed with a green fluorescence whenever they come into contact with oxygen. The turbulence cause by the mesh of the cage passing through the water created the bioluminescence along with Skip's stroke and kick. As the night got darker, the scene became more and more beautiful until he passed out of the location. It was as if Skip was being sprinkled by fairy dust and it left a green glow in a little trail swirling behind him. It was spectacular to watch. It made the swim seem mystical. While Skip was swimming he made good progress but Havana seemed to take an extraordinary amount of time to disappear over the horizon. We made the Gulf Stream and started our eastward drift as he swam north. Unfortunately, Skip took breaks that were too long. There was very little wind but even that slight amount was blowing the cage back in a southern direction. By the early afternoon, I had to tell Skip that he'd have to work harder.

Overnight, he had gotten cold and put on an additional wet suit. In the end, we made about 33 miles. Skip was exhausted. As an assessment of the swim, I suggested that the next swim be a team effort (a relay) so we can have a better idea of what is involved in this swim. We'd have a better idea of the time needed to swim the distance and the route that the current would let us take. But even this effort may be duplication as Walter Poenisch already has come ashore after crossing the Gulf Stream at Little Duck Key.

It seems that not just the American public was watching the swim but thousands of Cubans were too. In 1994, there was a raft exodus from Cuba that gradually escalated until on August 5, 1994 there was a riot in Central Havana after which Fidel allowed people to leave unmolested.[659] The exodus was estimated at over 30,000 people. Rafts made out of inner tubes, polypropylene, wood, and metal crossed the Straits. Some, we can assume died coming across the Straits because their poorly crafted vessel broke up and dumped them into the waters, others were imprisoned upon their return to Cuba after being picked up by the US Coast Guard. It created a crisis and the US immigration policy was changed to allow for 20,000 immigrants to the US annually from Cuba. Skip didn't cause the exodus; but his example the previous year must have lead many a Cuban to believe they could paddle better than Skip could swim. There was a payment made in human toil by those many thousands that was not foreseeable by Skip or anyone connected with the swim. Having been to Cuba and seen the conditions the people were being held in, one certainly can understand what would motivate them to undertake this journey so ill-prepared. In 1996, it was not with any sort of self-importance that I told Suzy Maroney support crew that they couldn't fake the swim because they would have thousands of people following them if they made it look too easy. They looked at me strangely. Of course, they couldn't understand why I couldn't spend any money in the country either.[660]

There is a lesson to be learned from the swim from Cuba. In 1831, a slave named Tice Davids was fleeing his captivity and upon reaching the Ohio River, swam across to Ripley, Ohio. The river is approximately 600 yards wide at that point. Tice was hard pressed by his master who could not swim and had to wait to obtain a boat to cross the river. Tice could easily be observed fleeing into the woods surrounding the town of Ripley, as the distance was not great. Upon reaching shore, the Kentuckian could not find his slave and went into Ripley asking for information. No one had seen the fleeing slave. When the townspeople asked what he thought might have become of his slave, he responded by saying, "the nigger must have gone off on an underground road" which the residences of Ripley found quite amusing. The story was repeated often enough that when the Underground Railroad was formed, the name was already in place.[661]

One might wonder what role swimming plays in society? Truly here is one slave who desired to be free and found the ability to swim played a crucial role in achieving this desire. The story of the Underground Railroad is placed here in the text so that by juxtaposition one can easily see that the role the Ohio River played in times past is now 90 miles wide and swimming still plays a crucial role for those people who desire freedom. It would be thoughtful should an open-water swimming contest across the Ohio River be held in celebration of freedom for enslaved people all over the world. Swimmers who escaped would attend to commemorate their journey. In keeping with the ideal of commemorating the journey, an event for rafts or other conveyances could be part of the program.

Chapter 13   Bogus swims

In writing a history of swimming, one becomes aware of the placement of swimming entries in indexes of newspapers. Swimming comes after Suicides and before Swindles. It could be said that marathon swims, in a queer way, are the same; some border on suicides and others border on swindles. This chapter is about swims that come closer to swindles than suicides. These are swims that don't really qualify as a swim due to certain aspects of the swim that would disqualify the person in a normal open-water competitive swimming event. Hanging onto a boat, obtaining assistance from a propulsion source other than ordinary current or an enhancement of their strokes beyond what would be legal in a pool swim would be definite disqualification from consideration as a swim. Capt. Boyton's transit of the English Channel is definitely not a swim but he never held it out to be thought of as a swim. It was solely a demonstration of his lifesaving suit. In later years, he and Captain Webb went head to head in swimming competitions where Boyton wore his suit and used his paddle. Swimmers who appear to be swimming but are in actuality taking advantage of some artificial condition gives them an unfair advantage over other swimmers. If you are born with size 14 feet, you'll have a tremendous kick but a swimmer with smaller feet who trained better could still win. Swim fins, hand paddles, and buoyancy aids will improve your swimming ability beyond what you were naturally born with and would put the swim in a different category from a swim. The essences of the rules are to allow another swimmer the possibility of duplicating the feat and because of natural ability, training, or expertise to perhaps better the effort of a previous swimmer.

Some pseudo swims actually make swims possible in the sense that Captain Paul Boyton's demonstration of his lifesaving apparel in the Channel motivated Captain Webb to swim the channel. Then again, Diana Nyad's failed swim across the Florida Straits motivated Walter Poenisch, a baker from Grove City, Ohio, to complete a swim from Cuba to the United States in 1978.

Walter was not a real swimmer for he used swim fins, a snorkel, a cage, and two exits from the water for a total of seven minutes to receive medical treatment for jellyfish stings. He traveled 128.8 miles in 34:15 from Havana to Little Duck Key, Florida.[662] Publicity received by Skip Storch for the same swim caught the eye of Australian swimmer Susan Maroney who launched an attempt to swim the Straits. She claimed to have completed the swim in May of 1997. She then went on to make several other swims to Cuba of increasing length. None of them were unassisted swims. Shortly after Suzy swam from Cuba in 1997, Outside Magazine published an article about athletes who claim to walked, run, climb, or visit various distances and places but are a bit short on verification.[663] The list includes Rosie Ruiz, Ben Johnson, Richard Byrd, Frederick Cook, Robert Peary, Ffyona Campbell, Sebastian Cabot, Louis Hennepen, Thomas Dryer, Tomo Cesen, Donald Crowhurst, and Louis Anderson. These men and women were explorers, climbers, and extreme athletes. In the article the author talks of the deception, the rationalization, the anger, and the guilt and what it does to the athlete. The article covered the denunciation, the arguing, the taking of sides, and the debate about the truth. Humorously, the author includes the press anger when they are denied "one of the rituals of modern sport: the public stoning". Hopefully, this chapter will help put into context what I am calling the bogus swim and we'll explore ways to deal with them.

Sanctions

Swims need to have sanctions to have any legitimacy. What is a sanction? A sanction is issued by a swimming organization to an individual who is organizing an event. The event could be a swimming meet or a long distance swim attempt. Either way, the swimming organization has set up rules that are adhered to in the conduct of the event. The main swim sanction body is FINA, Federation Internationale De Natation, founded in 1908, which is made up of 189 affiliated federations.[664] In the United States, one affiliated federation member is US Master Swimming. Within USMS is the Long Distance National

Committee, which controls long-distance swimming events and governs with the Local Master Swim Committees (LMSC). Their definition of a long distance swimming event is a swimming event of any distance conducted in an open body of water. Their rules allow for solo swims. If the event is sanctioned by USMS it receives a sanction number issued by the Local Master Swim Committee, the swimmer must be a member of Master swimming, and sign a release. The organizer contacts the LMSC and finds out the one person in the organization that issues the sanctions. You call or notify them that you wish to apply for a sanction. They send you a form upon which you describe your event and send it back with a check covering the fee required by the LSMC to issue a sanction. The form is eventually returned to you with a sanctioning number. The form lists the main points that need to be observed by the organizers to fulfill the requirements of the sanction. At the end of the event, the results are reported to the sanctioning body. Incidental to the sanctioning is blanket coverage of the event officials by an insurance policy.

Some events are sanctioned and others are not. Sanctions are the means by which recognized swim standards are applied to a swim.[665] Even a swim that is not sanctioned can observe these standards. They are listed in the rules for Long Distance swimming and a swimmer can not pick and choose which rules they'll observe or not. For instance, Master Swimming Long Distance Rule 303.2.4 B specifically prohibits drafting off escort boats. A cage can be construed as an extension of the escort boat whether it is towed or attached to the escort boat.

The essence of the problem—doing good

What would motivate a good swimmer to "cheat"? For one, they don't believe they are cheating; they are using a swimming aid for what to them appears to be a good cause: the setting of a record or being the first. It's when they claim to have swum from point to point and not credit the assistance received, that they discredit themselves. I bring up the example of Captain Paul Boyton whose transit of the English Channel was not a swim and was never claimed to be a swim in the press. His example inspired a swimmer to make the same attempt. Years later, the Channel Swimming Association came into being to verify who has attempted and completed a swim as well as clarify what is meant by swimming and what is not. Quite simply, their rules have stuck ever since. The swim begins and ends on shore (if the swimmer leaves the water; the swim is over), no assistance (no mechanized contraptions for propulsion such as fins); it's you and the bathing suit, no floatation (the swimmer can't hang on and the bathing costume must have neutral buoyancy), with the allowance for goggles, a cap, and some grease. Over the years, long distance swimming committees have prohibited drafting. The most famous example of drafting is a record speed achieved by a bicyclist, Charles Murphy, in Freeport, NY, in 1899 of over 60 mph trailing a locomotive inside a specially designed open hood[666] on a wood track laid between the rails that was as flat and level as a billiard table.[667] After this ride he became known as *mile-a-minute Murphy*.[668]

From the pages of history is presented the following story of an early example of a swimmer who stretched the truth. On Friday morning, August 13, 1897, a professional lifesaver, David Dalton, began a swim from Coney Island to the Sandy Hook Lightship, a distance of 14 miles offshore. He was accompanied by a rowboat with two men from Massachusetts, one of whom was described as a sporting man; the other was staying at Judge Peter Ravenhall's summer residence. The swim began some time after 8:30 in the morning due to the tardy arrival of one of the men. The swimmer got out in front of the rowboat right away and even when observed by glasses as the day wore on, the rowboat lagged behind. David was about 45 years old and had been working at Judge Peter Ravenhall's pier since the beginning of the summer. The swim out to the lightship was one that David had been talking up all summer. He was an Englishman and the one thing he was proudest of was swimming the English Channel. He had medals for saving lives, diplomas and certificates attesting to many difficult aquatic feats. He was well liked so when night fell and they had not returned, fear had gripped the community. They left the lights on the pier all night and panned searchlights about. Dalton's plan had been to let the ebb tide take him out and on the ensuing tide, make the lightship with little effort. The lightship was to telegraph his arrival. No telegraph came. As the news went to press on Friday night for the August 14th edition, no word had been heard from the men.[669]

The next day, it was reported that David Dalton had swam in, panting and exhausted with tales of a 30-hour struggle. The story of his amazing survival included heart-rending tales of gigantic waves, weather and waves so bad that he had been swept far past the lightship at the harbor entrance. But he endured and to let everyone know how badly the swim went he mentioned that the escort boat had capsized at one point during the swim requiring it to be righted and bailed out. It was a remarkable, heroic tale. The people of Coney Island were relieved to know he survived and that their concerns were without grounds. Yet by the afternoon, suspicion began to grow that they had been duped, that their cheers at his returned were "...extorted by false pretenses". Captain Dalton wasn't sleepy after his long battle with the immense waves and his escort boat caused more suspicion when it was returned to the rental dock. Someone looked inside the rowboat and found four of the six ham sandwiches packed the day before in the boat and they were not soggy. The press coverage was quite blunt about this discover, "...while the endurance of a Coney Island sandwich is known to all men, it was argued that no sandwich had ever been known to climb back in a boat and dry itself after it had been the victim of an upset."[670]

This Coney Island swim was a complete sham but his claim to having swum the Channel was based upon disputed facts. [671] Dalton left from France aboard a boat and entered the water outside the harbor at some point. Needless to say, the first swim of the English Channel after Captain Webb that was successful wasn't until 1911. These subtleties of marathon swimming escaped the notice of the press, as evidently, that news hadn't reached Coney Island yet. Two years later, David Dalton, also known as Davis Dalton, wrote a book, *How to Swim*.[672] By 1899 he was Chief Inspector of the United States Volunteer Life Saving Corp. He was credited with saving hundreds of lives.[673] These accomplishments and his disputed swims give us some insight into an aspect of swimming still present today.

Unfortunately, Dalton wasn't alone in exaggerating. In fact, it wasn't unusual at all for persons to claim this status of having swum the English Channel. In Washington, D. C., the Countess Walburga von Isacescu, from Austria, was successful in parlaying this accomplishment into considerable publicity in 1900 by claiming to be the first woman to swim the channel.[674] In 1927, Dr. Dorothy Logan swam half the channel then pulled a Rosie Ruiz just to prove that you could fake the swim.[675] Can you imagine trying to pull that off in this day and age? It really isn't that hard, I watched Suzy Maroney appear on a late night talk show after her "successful" swim from Cuba to Florida.

The "Liberty Swim" was a three year, 400 mile swim by Skip Storch featuring three marathon swims either starting or finishing at the Statue of Liberty: the Hudson River swim to the Statue, the Long Island Sound Swim down the length of Long Island starting at Watch Hill, Rhode Island, to the Statue, and the Atlantic City swim from the Statue to Atlantic City, New Jersey.[676] The common basis of these swims was the environment. As swims, the last two of the three legs fell a bit short of their goals. The first swim in this trio of swims was covered in the chapter on staged swims. I joined the support team as Swim Director for the next two swims. The second swim to Atlantic City was completed on July 23, 1989 over a one-week period.[677] In the initial swim from the Statue of Liberty, July 17, 1989, Skip stopped two miles short of coming ashore at Sandy Hook, NJ optioning to pick up the swim the next day.[678] Skip swam practically the entire Battery to Sandy Hook course in less than 5 hours during his swim but because he didn't come ashore, no record was set or claimed.

Due to an appearance schedule, he started the next day at a point further south from where he left off. Skip on one occasion started a swim just out of view of the spectators ashore and then swam up to them. As Swim Director, I was appalled that Skip wasn't swimming the complete distance. In a private discussion with Skip he told me his focus was creating an awareness of the environment and not swimming per se. New Jersey had just come out of a disastrous summer season due to trash floating up to the shore.[679] While the scientists argued over the source of the pollution, Skip was making a much-needed point, which I could support. Over all, he swam approximately 85 miles of the New Jersey coast, a distance equivalent to all the open public swimming areas between New York and Atlantic City.

The third swim of the trio, down the Long Island Sound was an ambitious project and the initial stage on July 16, 1990, featured a swim from Watch Hill, Rhode Island to New London of which Skip finished about 7 miles short of the 22 mile course.[680] The next day he picked up the swim starting in The Race, a narrow opening at the end of the Long Island Sound where the waters run just as fast as Hell Gate. Skip is the first person to swim this stretch of water but it's hard to define the particular course since he began and ended the swim at random locations. Of the three legs of the Liberty Swim, I was aboard for two of them. I can't speak for the Hudson River swim but the staged swims I observed were not necessarily contiguous: meaning he did not begin the next day where he left off the previous day. The swim total for this swim was nearly 100 miles.[681]

The issues with the swim were left for the swimmer to explain. The local newspaper, the Stamford Advocate, featured the swim on the front page with a picture of Skip swimming, Jane was coaching and I was operating the support boat. The accompanying article was all about the environment and the health of the Long Island Sound marine environment. Skip was delivering his part of the bargain that the environmental groups had sought: giving them an opportunity to sound off on their pet cause. It took this swim to help focus the media on this particular issue and Skip was more than happy to oblige.

Figure 91 Skip Storch swimming with Jane Katz and Tim Johnson outside Stamford Harbor, Conneticut, on an environmental swim.

The final day, everyone was onboard; the supporters were going to stick it out to the finish. It was over the entire length of the East River. He began at the foot of the Throgsneck Bridge on July 21, 1990 as ebb tide began, swimming past LaGuardia Airport, right through Hell Gate, down the East River and past the Battery to finish at the Statue of Liberty. The swim this day could stand on it own as a significant swim. The water was so rough going through Hell Gate that Jane Katz was knocked off her seat to the deck of the escort boat. Skip completed this swim at the Statue of Liberty in 5:30.[682] Because a sanction was obtained, no assistance was received, he didn't wear a wet suit, the swim was from point to point; this swim was a legitimate swim that could stand on its own. This could be the only swim that ever went the entire length of the East River.

In 1996, I was involved with the attempt by Suzy Maroney to swim from Cuba to Florida across the Florida Straits. Since this swim didn't achieve its goal, falling about 15 miles short of Florida before she was pulled from the water, a drafting advantage gained by using their cage was of no consequence. It was during the following year on her 2nd attempt, May 12, 1997, when she claimed to have successfully swum from Cuba in 24½ hours that I have some objections to her claim of swimming the distance.[683] In the news footage seen in the United States, Suzy can be seen swimming in the cage and directly in front of her is the spillover from the front of the cage. It's a huge waterfall. That is the source of the draft. The water directly behind the spillover is still water. Any kayaker knows the tendency of the water at the foot of a waterfall to move toward the edge of the entering water. It's a neat technique for drafting but not for an open-water marathon swim of any credibility. This drafting allowed Suzy Maroney to maintain a speed of 3.67 knots.[684] This is an incredible rate to maintain for any distance much less 90 nautical miles especially since the current is across the swimmer's path and not behind the swimmer pushing the swimmer along. There is no current assistance of any sort on a course between Havana and Key West but to this point we will return later. To make the speed more comprehensible to swimmers, Suzy did 110 repeat 1650's at a pace of 13 minutes and 18 seconds each, considerably faster than the world record for *one* 1500-meter swim.[685] If she were swimming around Manhattan or any other current assisted river swim, speeds this fast would be understandable as the current is behind the swimmer.

Memories of Suzy Maroney

Suzy Maroney's mother first wrote me on August 1, 1994, after Skip Storch's swim. Suzy it seems could think of nothing else but Cuba after reading Charles Sprawson's article about Skip Storch's swim published in the Sunday Magazine of the Sunday Telegraph. Suzy's mother had written Charles to ask whom should she consult about attempting such a swim. It was nice to know that my efforts to make Skip's swim count for something were beginning to pay off. Suzy, I first met on August 18, 1990, at the Downtown Athletic Club in New York when the swimmers were being introduced to the press for the 1990 Manhattan Marathon swim. She had just completed her English Channel swim and I asked if she knew the course she followed crossing it. At the time,

I was interested in the courses swimmers were taking across the channel as I was just starting to figure that swim out. Suzy had with her the navigation chart that plotted her positions as she crossed the channel. We opened it up and looked at it. It was the typical arcing curve that swimmers take when crossing the channel. I knew right away that the slack tide was in the middle of the swim just from the shape of the curve. While Suzy talked of Cuba, I thought of the Channel.

My relationship with the Maroney family began on a friendly note and continued that way until I left their team in Cuba. The family's point man was the mother, Pauline. I arranged for an introduction to Skip Storch, as they were anxious to know from a swimmer what his perspective on the swim was. In talking with Skip, they got much more because he had put his swim together from scratch and could advise them on all phases of the swim. The next big issue was the cage. I put them in touch with Fibber McGee for construction of a cage but they first wanted to try their own design. I was to advise them on navigation, marine issues such as boats, and secure a sanction for them. In other ways, I became a personal trainer by encouraging Suzy during the long years involved in the planning of the swim. I had suggested to Skip that he do a 24-hour swim in preparation for the Cuba swim and he relayed this advice to Suzy. Unlike Skip who took a nap during the night; Suzy set a world record for distance in her training swim of 50.5 nautical miles (93.6 kilometers).[686]

Pauline Maroney kept up a serious letter campaign to keep me advised of their preparations. At one point, the financial need became so pressing that I suggested they postpone the swim until 1996. They sent me a letter thanking me for this advice. After Suzy's 24 hour swim, I sat down and wrote her a letter talking about what it would be like in the cage after 24 hours in one year's time and having another 24 hours or less to go. Pauline wrote back thanking me for such an inspirational letter and said that Suzy keeps it under her pillow. This was sweet and I've reread the letter I sent; it was good but after everything was said and done with this swim, I wonder whether or not the Maroney's were using their daughter.

When the Maroney's had difficulty finding a boat they could afford, I suggested they look for a boat in the Keys just before the swim for a more sympathetic boat owner or in Cuba. Both approaches worked. On the Key West side we used *Fatal Attraction*. From the Cuban side, the Maroney's hired *Arcadian III* owned and operated by a French Canadian named Jerry. This boat was a decent workboat and probably would have been all right except for one thing: the pilot knew nothing about swimmers and the navigational challenge they entail on any swim in a current. In discussing the swim with him, he stated that he would take Suzy right up to Key West simply by putting her cage on his starboard side of the vessel. I asked him if he thought the Gulf Stream ran at a different speed on the starboard side of his boat as opposed to the port side. He had absolutely no concept of the limited speed of the swimmer, the difficulty of attaching a cage alongside, the effect the backwash of his bow wake would have on the swimmer, the effect of oceans waves reflecting off the side of his boat back into the cage, the affect diesel fumes have on swimmers, or the drift that would affect the swim. Their entire approach ignored advice and lessons that were learned over the years by previous swimmers and their crews at great expense. I consider the entire Maroney team from the mother on down as selfish in wanting to be able to walk out on the deck, look over the side at Suzy swimming, and yell "encouragements" at her.

The ideal marathon swim using a cage

The best place for a swimmer is away from the boat. By towing a swimmer in a cage behind the boat and using radio communications, the boat can match speeds with the swimmer. The swimmer, with a "spot" painted onto the bottom of the cage, can position themselves within the cage to avoid crashing into the sides. Ocean waves only pass by a swimmer once, not twice when the wave reflects off the side of the boat creating turbulence in the cage from the wash. The swimmer is more one with the swim not seeing the boat and directed by his orientation within the cage. The design by Fibber with the pontoons allowed the cage to lift up with the wave as the swimmer is.

Figure 92 Skip's cage being towed by the escort boat *Toucan Express*.

If the cage begins to surf down steep waves, a rudder assembly can correct for broaching and the cage handler can attach drags to slow the cage if it accelerates. The support team can watch the swimmer from chairs fixed to the pontoons. They can walk back and forth along the pontoon and even to the other side if needed on easily attached catwalks. Over the cage is a canvas awning affording the swimmer the luxury of shade, as the sun over the ocean is the same sun on a desert. To the top of that can be affixed signs for advertisements and publicity as required. The swimmer is away from the diesel fume and the distractions aboard a boat. The focus for the swimmer has to be on the swim and not the issues related to the support of the swim. Once the escort vessel matches speed with the swimmer, the boat is out of the equation. On the swim, the skipper doesn't need to learn how to match speeds; he should have already noted the engine RPM of the swimmer from practice swims when the swimmer reaches their pace. The swimmer, conversely will have trained with the vessel and know how long it takes to get the cage up to speed and how long it takes to slow down. The swimmer adjusts their swim starts to synchronize with the inertia of the cage. A VHF radio maintains contact between the cage and the escort boat for starts and stops.

During swim breaks, crews can be changed or by having a dinghy on a long rope, the dinghy can be dropped back to the cage for visits by press, spectators, and crew changes while the swim is underway. While it was not possible on earlier swims, with present day technology, an inexpensive video camera can be used for live views of the cage with audio so the escort boat's bridge team can have a visual picture to accompany radio instructions from the crew.

Figure 93 A view from the side of the escort boat and the swim cage being towed far astern of any diesel fumes. By dropping back from the escort boat a dinghy on a line, crews can be exchanged without stopping.

Cage construction

When Chris Green visited with me in 1987, we were planning a swim from Cuba. When I informed him about the difficulty of getting permission to swim between the two countries, he eventually changed the route to the swim along the Florida Keys similar to a disputed cage swim Ben Huggard did to Bimini. We even used the same starting point Benson Huggard used: Sombrero Key. This location is about 10 miles offshore of Marathon Key and has a fixed light beacon tower structure on it. A swimmer can actually stand in water less than waist high and begin their swim. Occasionally, on exceptionally low tides this Key is above water. It is a location where there are lots of scuba divers and as we brought the cage closer, we became as curious a spectacle as the fishes on the reef the divers were observing. We actually got Chris's cage stuck in the sand as we maneuvered the cage close to the start. In hindsight, we could have left the cage in deeper water and just let Chris swim out to it.

Chris had first used a cage on his Gibraltar Strait swim in 1986.[687] The dimensions of the cage were 18' by 6'. He said it was like swimming in a washing machine. Chris wanted to make some improvements on that design for the Florida swim, mainly increasing the length to have inside dimensions of 24' by 6'6". We needed someone to build a cage in Florida and Chris flew over to Florida during the swim preparation phase to locate a welder and some sponsors. He found a welder named Fibber McGee who came highly recommended by all the boat owners Chris contacted in Boca Raton for his 1988 cage swim. Fibber was a gem of a welder because he also understood the vessel aspect of the cage. For floatation, we use polypropylene pipes sealed at both ends, a technique which dated from Chris's first swim.

One problem we had was moving the cage from shore to Sombrero Key. The cage when ready for a swim is submerged and the floatation is positioned along the edges to keep the cage afloat. We could use the same floatation to hold the cage completely above the water when we were transporting it. By having the dual locations for floatation, the cage could be moved much more rapid than when it was submerged. The floatation was fairly easily relocated once the cage was in position. When the cage arrived at Sombrero Key we removed the floatation from under the cage and put it along the top of the cage, about a foot down. Even so, the cage floated with about 6" of freeboard. This eventually caused Chris to terminate his swim as a jellyfish come into the cage at the top of a swell. Near the end of the swim the sea state had risen to over a foot, and water was coming over the top of the cage. After the swim, Chris and I discussed the problem and we realized the depth of the cage needed to be increased so that the freeboard could be raised. Chris then went off and designed a new cage with a bow and had it tested at the Hydrostatic Department at Liverpool University. Chris even worked on designing baffles for keeping Portuguese man-of-war tentacles out of the cage. At this point, Chris had run out of money and the new cage he had commissioned was sold to Skip Storch.

Figure 94 Swim cage designed by Fibber McGee of McGee Welding in Boca Raton based on Chris Green's original design. Not seen is the swim door at the rear.

Before Skip went to Cuba, Fibber made a tremendous contribution to cage construction. He added pontoons to the cage. The pontoons were adjustable by means of clamps to be positioned anywhere along the side of the cage. That change would allow the cage to be transported over the water at boat speed trailing the cage behind with the pontoons in the lowered position. It immensely improves this phase of the swim logistics. Once the cage arrives at the swim start location, the pontoons can be raised thus dropping the cage between the pontoons preparing the cage for the swim. The pontoons also made it possible for observers to be stationed on the cage during the swim. Fibber attached a battery case and now the cage could be rigged with running lights for navigational purposes. He even attached a chair at one end. The swim cage is normally sunk at the end of the swim. The reason is once the cage has been submerged in salt water, it begins to rust away. The swim cage could be used for a second swim, if it occurs within a reasonable period of time. Basically, you have to drain all the water out of the tubing and flush the metal with fresh water. Sinking the cage is not ecologically disastrous, as they become instant fish habitats.

On Chris Green's swim, when he retired from the swim after about 8 hours of swimming, since his design used inflatable tubes to support the cage in the water, Jerry Leach, one of the support crewmembers, pulled out a small caliber firearm and began shooting out the tubes. The cage sank before he could shoot holes in all the tubes. Mortally wounded, the cage sank. As it was sinking, I was visualizing the cage sinking to a certain depth where the floatation would equalize out at several hundred feet down. The cage was in the Gulf Stream, which meant it would continue the journey across the Atlantic underwater. Since it was made of metal, submarines could acoustically ping the cage. I'm just hoping we didn't cause an alert in some submarine command for an unidentified submerged object.

Figure 95 The swim cage from the front. The pontoons can be removed and reattached at the base to transport the cage to the swim start location by water or removed to meet maximum road width requirements when towed.

The cages are called shark cages but their primary purpose is to keep jellyfish away from the swimmer at night. Jellyfish rise to the surface at night. It would become an impossible task to have an escort boat using searchlights to look for jellyfish and direct the swimmer around them. Why are the cages called shark cages? Well, you can be the judge: what's more heroic, fighting off sharks to compete a swim or threading, nay tiptoeing your way through jellyfish?

Chris's design had added a wedge shaped front end to the cage, which improved its appearance, but its main purpose was to allow the swimmer to attach shields to keep the jellyfish out of the cage. The wedge as opposed to a cage with a blunt end would tend to push jellyfish aside as a swimmer comes upon them; a flat fronted cage would find a jellyfish trapped up against the cage and eventually its parts would break off and enter the cage to sting the swimmer. The idea is to keep as many jellies out of the way of the swimmer as possible.

Another improvement that was made in the first swim was to increase the size of the cage. In reviewing the video made of the Chris Green's swim, Chris was seen entering the cage by climbing over the edge of the cage, this was a violation of the no holding on rule and we designed into the cage a swing door at the rear of the cage. During Skip Storch's swim, I observed Skip bouncing up and down off the floor of the cage and after thinking about it, I made a trip back to the cage to tell him, since I was the person reporting the results of the swim to the sanctioning organization, he couldn't bounce off the floor of the cage. The swimmer is in a cage but the cage has to be transparent. It couldn't be used to any advantage by the swimmer over a swimmer not in a cage, except for its stated purpose. By the time Suzy Maroney had her cage built, Fibber, in consultation with me, decided to increase the depth to give an 8' draft. We further increased the size of the cage by expanding the width out to 8 feet; we kept the flat front behind the wedge to improve the strength of the cage. We decided to keep the length at 24 feet. This length was adequate for stopping the cage at the same time as the swimmer; you don't want the cage banging into them at full boat speed. Its best if the swimmer signals they want to stop; then slows their swimming down to match the cage's forward motion as it slows down. Thus the swimmer and the cage slow to a stop together.

How do you know you have a good cage? The cage should not give a swimmer in a cage an advantage over a swimmer not in a cage. The cage should be transparent. If you put a fine enough mesh over the front of the cage, the larger jellyfish are kept out of the cage. You then need to test the cage for its water flow efficiency. As the swimmer swims, he should be encountering water that is as undisturbed as a swimmer without a cage. The best and easiest way to test for this effect is to drop something that can float in the cage and at the same time drop a similar object outside the cage. These objects become markers of a stationary point in the water and relative to these two points; the flow of water through a cage can be measured. A ping-pong ball would float but could be affected by wind so you need something that floats but is submerged to a large extent. A piece of wood could be used but an orange is a perfect test specimen because they float and they're round making them omni-directional. The two test oranges are then watched to see if both make it to the rear of the cage at the same time while the cage is being pulled through the water. If they do, the water in the cage is effectively flowing unimpeded through the cage.

To determine the draft that is present in a cage, time how long it takes both markers to reach the back of the cage. Divide the time for the marker in the cage by the time for the marker not in the cage and convert it to a percentage. Suppose an orange dropped inside the cage takes 25 seconds to the back of the cage. Assume also that the orange dropped outside the cage at the same time takes 20 seconds. Then 25/20 is 1.25 leaving one to evaluate the cage efficiency at 125%. Or put another way, the swimmer in that cage has a 25% speed advantage over the swimmer in open water. On Skip Storch's swim, we had the test video taped and the markers arrived at the back of the cage at practically the same instance. It was so close we repeated the test several times to confirm our observations. It was that hard to distinguish any delay between the water flow in the cage and the water flow outside the cage. Skip's cage had 100% efficiency and 0% draft.

The source of the drafting

When the Maroney support team, which included her brother, was setting up the cage in Cuba, I saw them install a large Plexiglas insert on the front flat section of the cage. I asked them what that was for and they claimed it was to keep the jellyfish out. I told them they couldn't have that there and I told them the reason: that it prevented water flow through the cage. As an alternative, I suggested they use a fine mesh or netting as we had on the Skip Storch swim. I was off the swim within 24 hours on a trumped up excuse that I was costing them too much.[688] Since I was no longer associated officially with the swim, I mentioned my concerns to the video crew taping the event. I explained to them the simple method of testing for drafting described in the previous section. Afterward, in speaking with the video crew, they mentioned that they had surreptitiously tested the cage while the swim was underway. I was told that the marker stayed in the front of cage for ½ an hour before it reached the back of the cage. Suzy Maroney was swimming in still water as she was being pulled along at 3.67 knots.[689] She could have gone even faster but the turbulence was too much for her to stay in the slipstream. Her team had tested her ability to stay in the cage's sweet spot. This I saw with my own eyes during a test run prior to her swim in 1996 and my leaving. In the video that was produced for this swim, *Suzy is A Fish*, Suzy can be seen swimming outside of her cage because she was sick from the motion of the wave inside her cage. After a while when she felt better, she went back into the cage. On the audio track, her brother can be heard telling her while she is eating inside the cage (and not swimming but treading water) that she is going as fast as she was when she was outside the cage swimming.

Let's take a look at the numbers. Suzy's own pace unassisted for distance swims was set in a pool when she broke the record for a 24-hour swim. On April 23, 1995, at Sydney's Carss Park Olympic Pool, Suzy Maroney swam 50.5 nautical miles (93.6 kilometers) in 24 hours surpassing the previous record of 50.2 nautical miles (96 kilometers) in 24 hours set by Melissa Cunningham of Australia.[690] Suzy held a 1650 pace of 23 minutes and 12 seconds.[691] It's an admirable feat and I applaud her swim; she was going 2.06 knots through still water[692]. Suzy's 1650 pace for the 1997 Florida Straits swim is 13 minutes and 18 seconds.[693] What this means is Suzy Maroney found an ocean current that dropped her pool speed by 10 minutes. The ocean current would have to push her 704 yards every 13 minutes on an average because using her pool speed she would have swum 946 yards in the 13 minutes at the pace she was keeping on this swim.[694] The current would have made up the missing distance. The nautical value for this current speed is 1.6 knots.[695] There is no known current running at 1.6 knots from Havana to Key West where she landed.[696] The only known current in this vicinity of the world is the Gulf Stream and it runs west to east, not south to north. When asked about this problem in 1996 at the home of Julius Koenig in Oyster Bay, all the Maroney team would state is that their pilot, Jerry, found a current.[697] The only current he found that took her from Havana to Key West was the draft in her cage. Now, if Suzy had worked with the Gulf Stream current, she would have landed up around Marathon Key[698], the swim would have taken well over 24 hours, and we would have seen some phenomenal speeds for a swimmer sans drafting, but she didn't. When you add the pool speed to the speed the drafting gave her, you get 3.66 knots, just the speed needed to complete a 90 nautical mile swim in 24 ½ hours.

Figure 96 Downtown Havana from where Susie Maroney started her swim. Not seen is a source (such as a river) for the alleged 1.6-knot current the Maroney's claimed their pilot found.

The fact that the general public recognized the swim as legitimate highlights a need to regulate cage swims. Swim sanctioning is a function of FINA member organizations. The Long Distance swim committee leaves it to the sanctioning body of the various countries to regulate the swim claims of swimmers. A world record attempt is always going to push the boundaries of what is an acceptable swim and what is not. In the Florida Straits swim, there is a tiny bit of a loophole. The swim is between two different sanctioning bodies. Under normal conditions, the sanctioning body of the country the swimmer leaves from is the controlling body. They issue a sanction and provide the officials that would observe the swim and then report the success or failure of the swim. When I was sanctioning the Montauk race, the New York Swim committee had raised the price on their sanctions. I got a sanction from New England Master instead. They offered a better price. The loophole in the Florida Straits is that Cuba's sanctioning committee was supplanted by the political agenda of Fidel Castro. You would think that the sun doesn't rise or set with his approval.[699] For a swim of this magnitude to happen, he has to be involved. He becomes the sanctioning body. In a casual conversation, the head of the Cuban Olympic committee told me that it was a good thing that Manny Sanguily didn't come. Manny had been involved in the early stages of the swim advising Suzy concerning nutrition. They had a problem with him. Manny had at one time swum for the Cuban National team and they remembered him.

When I worked with Skip Storch and Suzy Maroney, I met with the Cuban oceanographers at Geo-Cuba for consultation. They are a fine group of dedicated individuals who are understandably proud of their body of work and knowledge of the Gulf Stream in this section of the world. I consulted with them and recognized a tinge of melancholy when they told me they couldn't go the whole way with us to the end of the swim. With Skip Storch's swim, their research vessel accompanied us for the initial portion of the swim. As we approached the limits of their territorial waters, they broke off and by radio we thanked them for their assistance. Upon my return with Suzy Maroney in 1996, I met with them again and the first thing they wanted to know was what happened on the Skip Storch swim.

After Suzy's unsuccessful swim in 1996, the Maroney team was desperate to get the swim sanctioned. I had secured a sanction from the Florida Master's committee for the 1996 swim arguing that the Cuban sanction body was defunct. I was, also, the official observer for that swim. After disposing of me, there was no one to serve as the official observer. The Maroney's sought out Tom Hetzel who was along on the swim for an on-camera interview. In the video *Suzy Is A Fish* Tom Hetzel with strict qualifications, gave them that sense of purpose that sanctioned swims enjoy. In no way was his endorsement a sanction, which implies legitimacy. Since that time, I've no idea who has been sanctioning Suzy's subsequent swims or if they even bothered. Besides the Cuba to Florida swim on May 12, 1997, she claims a swim from Isla Mujeres, Mexico, to Cuba on June 1, 1998, for a distance of 107 nautical miles in a time of 38:33,[700] and another from Montego Bay, Jamaica to Marea del Portillo Beach, Cuba on Sept 14, 1999, for a distance of 102.6 nautical miles in 36 hours.[701]

Figure 97 Cage position for Suzy's last two swims.

The Mexico to Cuba 1650 pace dropped to 17 minutes and 36 second and in the Jamaica to Cuba swim the 1650 pace picked up slightly to 17 minutes and 9 seconds in hurricane stirred waters. There is the obvious unexplained difference between the pace maintained in the first of the three Cuba swims and the later two. In the press releases for the later swims, the swim cage is shown attached to the stern of the escort vessel, an obvious indication that Suzy's support team is now attempting to alleviate the turbulence seen in her Florida Strait swim and drafting directly off the escort boat now appears to be an issue.[702] In the swim from Mexico, Suzy has to swim east across a strong northern flowing current. In the swim from Jamaica, Suzy has no current that has coalesced into a stream with the strength like that seen on the western channel between Cuba and Mexico or between Cuba and Florida.[703] Yet, she maintains in both these swims essentially the same speed.

In a BBC report and on CNN/Sport Illustrated web site on the swim it was mentioned that the swim cage was designed and donated by Fidel Castro.[704] One can only wonder how many Cubans (besides Castro) are dreaming of departing by what I affectionately called in 1996, the *Cuban Water Taxi*, or any other means available for the United States? Suzy can leave and come back to Cuba as often as she desires and even be treated to a meal in Revolution Palace with her friend and benefactor, Fidel Castro.[705]

More assisted swims

Following Captain Webb's death, William Kendall of Boston swam the Rapids of Niagara in 1886 using a cork lifesaving vest for a $1000 stake.[706] His comment upon finishing was that he'd never do it again. In 1901, Carlisle Graham made his first swim down the Niagara on September 9.[707] As if to prove Kendall wrong, he made a second swim on August 31, 1902.[708] It was not what it seems for Graham wore a life preserver around his waist and another item called a neck float. Even with this assistance, his life was still endangered when the current threatened to throw him upon a large boulder. He floated all the way down to Lewiston. He was making plans to repeat the stunt again combined with a staged swim all the way down the river to Youngstown, Toronto, through Lake Ontario, past the rapids of the St. Lawrence River, finally finishing in Montreal some 300 miles distance over 30 days.[709] While we are on the subject of Niagara River swims, by the 1930's it was fairly commonplace for swimmers to cross the Niagara River below the falls around the vicinity of the Maid of the Mist boat landing, a ten minute swim.[710]

Louis Lourmais, of France, began to make a name for him as a swimmer of cold-water rivers. In December of 1958, he began a planned 500-mile swim down the Fraser River in British Columbia, Canada, to prove that the Fraser was "not too cold for skin swimming." On the third day of the swim, he had covered 52 miles alternating swimming with climbing over ice floes, but here he was pulled from the river with his rubber suit frozen, his face bleeding and frozen.[711] There was no record of his having completed the swim nor do I believe he proved his point. In March of 1960, Louis changed locations and waited for the spring thaw to swim 600 miles down the Rhine covering the distance between Schaffhausen, Switzerland to Rotterdam, the Netherlands.[712] A frogman outfit that allowed him to brave the rather cold waters of the Rhine aided his swim.

An early cage swim was by Jim Woods of Orlando in 1964 from N. Bimini[713] to Florida, 60 miles in 27.5 hours.[714] He came ashore at a location about 10 miles north of Palm Beach.[715] He swam across the same Gulf current as Suzy and wound up drifting north by 73 nautical miles. Bimini is slightly less than 50 nautical miles off Florida. His speed through the water across the current was 1.8 knots. The average current speed was 2.6 knots. His speed over the ground averaged 3.1 knots.

In 1968 there was a 25-mile Bering Sea swim. On July 22, 1968, two New Jersey men wearing cold-water swimming gear swam from Wales, Alaska, to Little Diomede Island, a distance of 25 miles. Ben Schlossberg and Stephen Friedland, both age 27, completed this swim in 18 hours starting in the evening on July 21, 1968.[716]

In an epic semi-swim that seemed to have no point, Guy Delage, age 43, swam across part of the Atlantic Ocean in 1995 from Cape Verde Island to Barbados wearing an immersion suit and flippers.[717] His support consisted of a raft that he would pull behind him when he swam and could climb aboard to rest at night. The trip took 55 days. He kept some records of his actual mileage that he swum, 1259 miles.[718] The trip covered 2,335 miles so he drifted aboard his escort raft more than he swam.[719] It turns out that the swimmer was deeply in debt and hired out for the swim with Sector OceaNates based on his reputation as a daredevil.[720] As if to underscore the pointlessness of a staged Atlantic Ocean swim, another Frenchman, Ben LeComte swam back the following year leaving from Cape Cod on July 16th and arriving in Quiberon, along the Brittany coastline of France 73 days later with a side trip to the Azores for rest and relaxation lasting a week.[721] The distance between the two points is 3,716 miles. The press reports that he swam for six hours a day. Using a generous speed of 2 knot for the swimmer speed, he swam an estimated 876 miles, a quarter of the distance.[722] He used an escort boat sans cage opting instead for 25-foot electromagnetic field called a protective ocean device to protect him from sharks. The protection claims are somewhat dubious for if a shark can feel the field at 25 feet, what would the swimmer feel at a lesser distance?[723] Dropping a radio antenna in the water and then turning the device on creates an electromagnetic field. I hope he didn't pay too much for this protection. And what protected him from the jellyfish? Most sharks are kept away from a boat by running the engine and props. The acoustical vibrations are all a shark needs to sense the presence of a boat, which would mask that of a swimmer alongside. A boat does not in and of itself attract sharks. The videos of sharks swarming or alongside a boat are due to the chumming of the water.

In August of 2000 Zhang Jian, age 36, a physical education instructor at the Beijing Sports Academy, swam using a wet suit across the Hohai Straits. This body of water is the large inlet north of the Yellow Sea. The distance at the start was 109 kilometers. He began on August 8 from the southern tip of Liaodong peninsula. He finished August 10th after 50:22 hours of swimming at East Beach of Penglai shore, Shandong province, having swum 123.58 kilometers due to currents, a typhoon, and around small islands.[724]

About the same time Tammy van Wisse was swimming the River Murray, Martin Strel from Slovenia swam down the Danube 3004 kilometers[725] or 1622 nautical miles in 58 days.[726] This unbelievable time amounts to about 28 nautical miles a day. In 2002, he swam the entire Mississippi River, 3885 km or 2098 nautical miles, in 68 days to give an average speed of 31 miles a day. These were not his only swims. In 2003, he swam the Yangtze, 6300 km or some portion of it in 40 days. To do the numbers, that's 85 miles a day, pretty unbelievable. Current speed in a river is a function of the channel width and the gradient, difference in height between the two measuring point and time. Allowing six hours a day for rest and recovery, the swimmer would have to average 4.7 knots to complete the swim. The Martin's claims exceed the minds capacity to imagine. Finally, the swimmer appears in photos in his web site with a complete neoprene suit with fins. In 2006 he added the Amazon River to his list of rivers he claims to have swum.

Another long swim that stretched from June 4, 2002 to July 1, 2003 was Christopher Swain's jaunt down the Columbia River. All tolled, he swam 1243 miles in 165 days of swimming. This was not attempted in consecutive day as it took over a year to complete the swim. The focus for this swim was not so much the swimming of the river but environmental concerns.[727] He utilizes a wet suit and swim fins in his swim. In 2004, he tackled the Hudson River including its upper reaches covering 315 miles.[728] You don't need to be a young man to engage in an environmental swim. In 2004, Paul Ellis, age 61, completed a 35-mile swim assisted by wet suit and fins from Cozumel Island to Cancun, Mexico.[729] For $35,000, Paul was able to publicize his concern for the coral reefs at his favorite dive locations. If you've wondered what it costs to finance a swim, Paul Ellis's $1000 a mile swim is pretty close to normal when everything is factored in.

The latest fashion has found cold water swimming fashionable. Not even swims from land masses but just in the vicinity of a pole, the closer to the pole the better. Not only do these swims not make any sense, they are not even swims. They are nothing more than immersions. It would be less expensive to simply launch off the shore of Iceland but then there'd be no press in that. The minimum requirement for a swim is that it is reproducible. In other words, another swimmer on another day can come along and duplicate the swim; possibly even set a record for the swim in the time honor sense of minimizing the elapse time between points. Swimming is not about how low the temperature was or how far north/south the swim took place but about proceeding through the water from one point to another (not GPS coordinates which are accurate at best to 10 yards) without assistance and for curiosity, we record the time to compare swimmers to one another.

In 2006, Paul Timmons swam across the Delaware Bay entrance, 11.4 miles in 7:14 wearing a wet suit. He left from from Cape May, NJ, and swam south to Cape Henlopen, Delaware.[730]

If wet suits are okay then the Distance King and the Stamina Stud for 2006 is David Meca, age 31, swam what amount to over 3 English Channels transits when beginning on Wednesday, January 3 and finishing on Thursday, January 4th, in 2006, he swam from the Spanish mainland leaving from the Alicante beach resort of Javea at 9:30am and arriving at the Mediterranean Island of Ibiza located 110 kilometer due east of Spain's Valencia coast at 11:27 where he was taken to the hospital for hypothermia despite the neoprene suit he was wearing. His time was 25:57. He averaged 4.2 kilometers an hours which was just behind Deke Zimmerman's time in a tidal-assisted 70 kilometer swim. He even pulled a Christopher Columbus landing at a smaller island Ses Bledes at hour 22 of the swim then setting off for the Port of San Antonio. During one point of the swim, the ship's motor gave out but not Dave. When the vomiting became severe, a doctor on board gave him an injection which allowed him to continue. Ibiza is a member of the Balearic Islands. He swam half way to Mallorca, one of the other idyllic islands for vacationing Europeans.[731] This is a huge swim by a well-known swimmer but why do the swim in January which would force you to wear a wet suit?

Six swimmers from Sydney's Balmoral Beach Club swam 60 kilometers across crocodile infested Lake Argyle in Western Australia's Kimberley region. For a good portion of the swim they utilized a cage modeled off the designs for the Florida Straits swim. They described their experience as being in a spin cycle of a washing machine. The swim extended over two days beginning June 24, 2006.[732]

Some swims are naturals and others make you wonder why they didn't just take up hiking. Mimi Hughes made an "environmental swim" 1770 miles down the Danube River in 2006 beginning in Germany on May 7th and finishing at the Black Sea on August 4th. What is remarkable about the swim is that she managed to get the 10 countries the river flows through to allow her permission to swim through their country.[733] This was a full body suit swim and it retraced Paul Boyton steps 150 years later.

Swimsuits

Normally, swimsuits don't cause too much of an uproar. The suit either meets the established standards or it doesn't. Use of a non-regulation suit puts the swim in a different category and subjects the user to disqualification. This is an argument that dates back to the original argument about what constitutes a swim which was the impetus for the Channel Swimming Association. The same problems keeps resurfacing. Earlier in the book we mentioned when a record swim by Charlie Daniels was disqualified and he had to swim the race over in a regulation suit. And we find the same issue surfacing again in an open-water swim in South Africa in 2005 with a different result for different reasons.[734] FINA has approved full-body suits for pool events and FINA Open Water rules incorporate changes from those events. In the particular event the swimmer, Christof Wandratsch, wore a suit that was sleeveless and came down over his thighs. This was different than the normal swimsuit that officials are accustomed to seeing; in fact, it was quite similar to a triathlete suit. After the swim which established a record, he was disqualified upon receipt of an objection by Gordon Pugh, an observer, that the suit didn't meet the open-water standards used in South Africa which were modeled on the rules of the Channel Swimming Association. A test performed on the suit established that the suit didn't float and it was made of Lycra or similar material. The disqualification was rescinded. During times of change and innovation, old standards are hard to give up and at times it seems there is no reason to. Gordon Pugh is known for cold water swims and it is for good reason he objects to any addition fabric covering the body. It makes his efforts seem in vain. The question that the open-water community has to ask itself is should it accept carte-blanche dictates from FINA pool swimmers?

Another swimmer, Jim Dreyer, ignited a press fire-storm when he claimed to have swum across all five of the Great Lakes in 2006. He used a wet suit[735] and the Canadian Long Distance Swimming Association was having none of it. Jim then offered the reason that he was using triathlon rules in his swims. There is no question that Jim can throw his arms out in front of himself time and again to make it across a lake but the question is if he uses a wet suit, why doesn't he use a fairing on a recumbent bicycle when he is doing a triathlon event? The reason is the competition is suppose be about the humans au natural (except that required for modesty) and not the suit.

Water quality

Skip Storch's background and education is in the environment; he once worked as an investigator for the Interstate Sanitation Commission, an agency that monitors water quality in the Hudson River for New York, New Jersey and Connecticut. The environment was the basis for his focus of his swims. He called himself an "environmental swimmer" and in organizing his swims he meets with environmental groups, community groups and government getting them "...to work together toward the common goal of the environment".[736] He was very successful in his effort to raise consciousness about the quality of the water.

Fecal coliform is a bacterium that originates in the feces of warm-blooded animals including people, dogs, marine mammals, and shore birds. The fecal count is an indicator of sewage contamination. Feces are a transport mechanism for hepatitis A, bacterial meningitis, encephalitis, and E. coli. These are all diseases you don't want to contract. The smaller the numbers for the fecal count the better; you don't totally eliminate the problem, you just lessen the chances. Fecal counts above 200 per 100 milliliters *may* pose health risks for recreational activities. Total coliform bacteria are naturally occurring and originate from decaying plant materials. They are not as dangerous. The recommended ratio of Fecal to Total is suggested to be less than 1 to 10. If the Total coliform count exceeds 1000 per 100 milliliters, it becomes a concern.[737]

In the last leg of Skip Storch's Liberty Swim, the final stage was down the East River in 1990. On the day of the swim, the water purification plant for NY City on Wards Island lost power and shut down, in effect, opening the overflow directly into the East River. Millions of gallons of raw sewerage were being dumped directly into the water, the very water Skip was swimming in. While the swim was underway, radio stations were calling the support boat asking for comments. I took one of the calls and was asked, "What did it look like?" After pausing to inspect the river for offensive objects, I replied, "No perceptible difference, it looks just the same as any other day on the East River," to the astonishment of the radio commentator. Skip was not so lucky. After the swim his suit was coated with feces turning it black; it had acted as a filter as the water flowed through it. It was a memorable sight as we pulled away from the pier of Skip being mobbed by the press in lower Manhattan covered in the feculent marine environment from which he had just emerged.

I remember going with another swimmer to a New York City swimming pool located in the Hunter Point neighborhood after it was closed. Closed in New York can mean one thing to one person and something else to another. We were able to walk in through an open door and go swimming after the crowd had left.[738] In one corner of the pool had gathered floating debris, food, and other garbage and it made the pool look disgusting. At the time, I noticed it and thought how authentic the pool was to train for a swim in the East River. I just swam around the spot where the breeze had blown the items.

A Japanese film crew arrived in the early eighties with a rather odd request. They wanted to photograph a swimmer swimming around Manhattan with a full head of hair then after swimming through some flotsam, be photographed swimming with a shaved head. Well, the Manhattan swim committee was so well versed with the movement of the debris line around Manhattan; we could tell them when and where to go out to find it. I gave them one piece of advice, that if the swimmer cut himself while shaving his head, he was not to go back into the water. On high tide, debris is lifted off the shoreline and it begins as a group to float off shore if the wind is blowing right. The debris then follows the falling tide in a random manner as the current draws the debris along. Swimmers would come upon these lines and by following their escort boats through them, they could avoid collisions. Paul Asmuth crossed a debris line on his record swim in 1983 and he just turned over and backstroked through the debris. For the Statue of Liberty dedication in 1986, the Corps of Engineers dedicated a special boat to sweep the waters around New York to clean up floating debris. It has made a great deal of difference to swimmers not to mention boaters.

There is hardly a swim that in some way is not conscious of the water quality. In the early days of the Manhattan swim, swimmers would exit the water with a tan line *and* a scum line. You could tell the difference because one was red and the other was dark in color. Swimmers really needed a bath when they exited the swim. Some days were better than others. When the North River Wastewater Treatment plant opened the preliminary treat in 1986, the water quality improved immensely. It was the first time that raw sewage was not discharged by the City into the Hudson River.[739] In 1991, secondary treatment began and you could at last see your arm pass underneath your body when swimming. There was a gradual improvement and a constant war against floating garbage.[740] In 1995, the New York Times announced the harbor was cleaner.[741] By 2000, the State of New York was promoting swimming in the Hudson River and was seeking locations for bathing beaches.[742]

In 2003 and 2005, the Manhattan marathon was cancelled because of water quality issues. What happened? The day before the swim, a heavy rain drenched Manhattan and washed the streets clean but the drainage for the gutters leads to open discharges in the harbor. Water quality sees a spike in fecal count after a rain since the residences may be conscious about curbing their dogs but perhaps not about bagging it. In previous years, high fecal counts were considered but ignored. In 2000, the Key West swim was cancelled for water quality issues. This may be hard to understand for swimmers accustomed to swimming in Boston and New York harbors, but sewage plant discharge due to rainwater overflow includes both the excess rainwater and any effluent. It obviously is more easily detectable in clean, clear water than murky waters.

While muddy or dirty waters are celebrated in song,[743] swimmers are just as enthusiastic about the water when it is just mud and not effluent. They really hate the inconvenience when water quality causes cancellations. It's a resourceful organization that has a contingency plan as backup when faced with a swim cancellation.

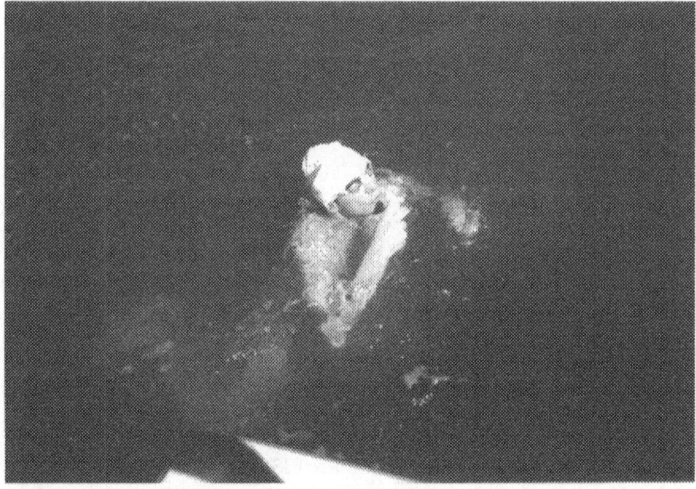

Figure 98 Proof that the water quality in New York has improved is this photo of Jamie Tout of Texas. Just visible in the photo is his legs about 4 feet below the surface. At one time swimmers could not see their own hands pass below them when swimming.

What is it that swim organizers have to consider when they include the water quality in their plans? For one, if the health department closes the local beaches, after one tide, enough new water should have flushed any problem water out. If not, the swim could be abbreviated so as to take advantage of the water that is cleanest. If there is a point source for the pollution, the swim can miss that section of the water, swimmers boarding their boats to be dropped back in after passing by the suspected location. This alteration of the swim has to be a factor because once the swimmers leave the water, the swim is no longer continuous and it becomes a staged swim. If any portion of a swim is not swum, then it no longer is a swim between principle points but staged with arbitrary resting locations. For this reason, swims are often cancelled or postponed.

It behooves organizations in their planning for contingencies to have alternate locations for a substitute venue if cancellation dates don't work. Was this not what was learned in the 1874 contest between J. B. Johnson and Alexander Trautz? Isn't this the reason for knowing your history: to incorporate the mistakes and successes in the past in your planning for the future. Rumor has it that a group of swimmers at the 2003 Manhattan marathon went and held their own swim elsewhere and the same thing happened in the Keys. With the start of the Manhattan marathon at the Battery and now South Cove, if for any reason the start cannot take place on time, an abbreviated swim can begin at the old starting location of East 96th Street. The race would have 3 hours to move the starter, the swimmers, and the boats to this location. From that location the swim can start at slack water or even as much as an hour after ebb begins.

Finally, in discussions after the Maroney failed bid in 1996 with Jack Gohegan, the legal counsel for Master Swimming, said that if he had known a sanction was issued for the Maroney swim, he would have pulled it. The public is not always sophisticated enough to distinguish between a legitimate swim and a bogus swim. The public trust in the press is strained when swims are erroneously labeled swims when they are not. When surveying the environmental swimmers who came after him, Skip Storch has suggested that swimming needs a category for assisted swims. When one looks at the variety and range of swims that occur with assistance, it appears that there are different levels of assistance. The Channel Swimming Association[744] has recognized the desire of people to cross the channel by any means necessary or available and has established the Channel Crossing Association.[745] I think the swim community needs to learn from this example. On some swims, I was the swim director and the observer and would send in the report. There really needs to be an observer independent from the swimmer's support team to verify swims.

Figure 99 Support boat should always have an assigned person to keep their eyes on the swimmer...so, who's watching the swimmer?

Figure 100 Moon jellies tend to group together. Your crew should be able to guide you around them. More annoying than dangerous.[746]

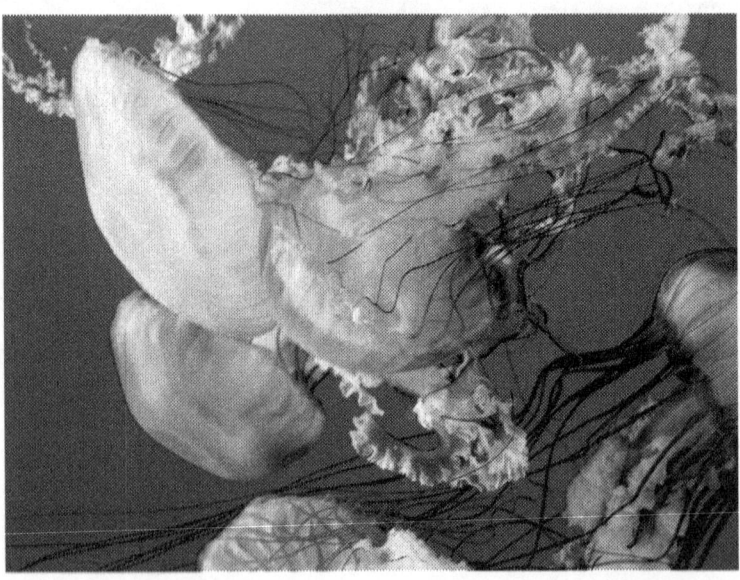

Figure 101 Sea Nettles, Lion's Mane, and Portugese Man-of-War look similar and can be dangerous. Time to retreat to the safety of the boat.[747]

Chapter 14   English Channel information

The best place to begin your swim of the English Channel is by referencing the web site of the Channel Swimming Association.[748] This organization was formed in 1927 to regulate and authenticate swims across the Dover Straits. They provide a great deal of information for swimmers regarding the best way to make the swim safely and observe all the regulations. By registering with the organization you obtain the Association's Handbook which contains a history, a list of successful swims, and the rules. The association has some general rules concerning the organization of the swim. They provide an observer who is neutral and unconnected to the swim organizers. The pilot must be a licensed commercial pilot, he retains the over-riding authority to terminate a swim, and the pilot must be registered with the association. The escort boat must meet certain minimum safety standards that incorporated means for the possible rescue of the swimmer from the water. Based upon the report from the observer and the pilot, the association validates and records swims. They have several basic rules that formulate the basis for determining if a swim is valid. These are: the swim must start and finishes at the natural shore, the swimmer receives no help and must not be touched by anyone, the swimmer may wear one standard cap and bathing suit, goggles, nose-clip, ear plugs, grease, and a light-stick at night.

   A proper look at the challenge facing a swimmer when tackling the Channel begins by purchasing a chart (seen on the next page) from the Admiralty.[749] Most prominent on the chart are the shorelines of England and France. The next most prominent feature is the traffic zones with the separation area marked in purple. Seen, as a slice of blue in the southbound lane, is The Varne, which swimmers may pass over where the water can appear disturbed. To the north and off the chart is Goodwin Sands, a shifting area of sandbanks caused by the discharge of the Thames. These are the lower and upper limits of a swimmers course if it is to be a successful swim.

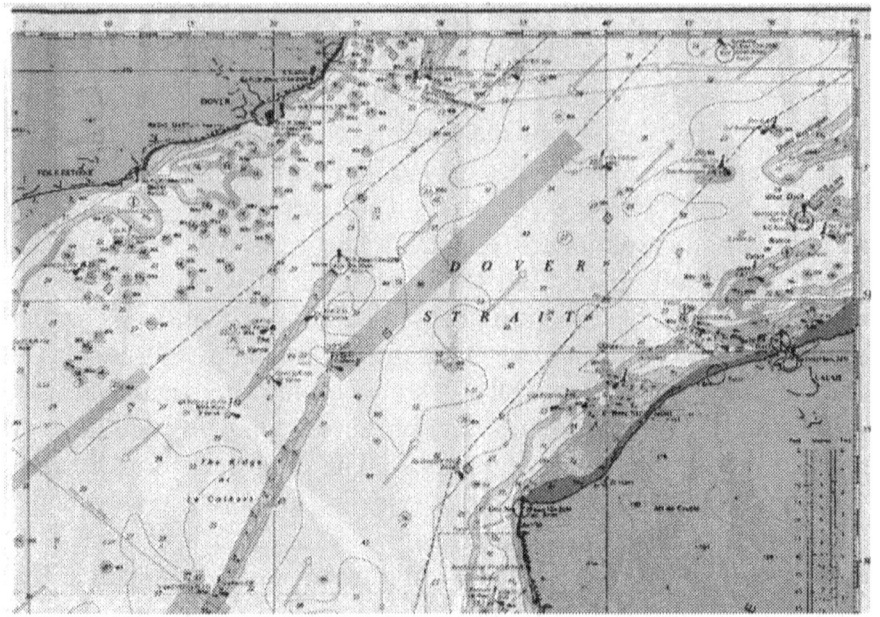

Figure 102 Chart SC1892 of Dover Strait.

Swimmers that are carried farther haven't the speed to make the distance in one tide change. Gap Gris-Nez is seen surrounded by rocks and to the north by a very shallow sandbank that stretches northeast for nearly two miles. The present day scheme for a successful swim has the swimmer waiting for a neap tide, the weaker of a set of tides.[750] The swimmer sets off in the middle of a flood tide (current flows northeast) then when the swimmer is half way across the ebb current (current flows southwest) begins and set the swimmer down onto the shore of France around the village of Wissant. The slack water in the swim occurs in the middle of the swim or a little over 4 hours after the swim starts.[751] The escort boat anchors off shore in safe water and the escort boat's launch takes the swimmer the last mile or so.

English pilots calculate swim starts based on the times of high tides at Dover. Chart SC1892 has in its upper left hand corner a conversion table from tides to currents. The values are averages at tidal stations located at various positions on the chart[752] for two very specific tides called spring and neap tides. The spring tide is the fast waters that swimmers prefer going around Manhattan. The neap tides are the slow waters preferred by swimmers crossing the channel. In the first case, faster waters propel swimmers around Manhattan more rapidly and in the latter case, the slower waters deviates the swimmer less allowing the swimmer to cover less distance in the crossing and apparently swimming less. The speed of the current is based on the range of the tide. The greater the range of the tide the faster the current flows.

There is a basic difference between the channel swim and swimming around Manhattan: there are no programs for the channel that can forecast your swim ahead of time. In researching the tides for the channel I was able to write a program that would forecast channel swims and it's based on the same principles I use in the Manhattan swim: knowledge of the current, knowledge of the swimmers speed and course and knowledge of the time of start. The English do not track their swims based on current speed but rather the height of the tide. This information is practically useless for computational needs. The Hydrographic Office in Taunton, UK, provides a Tidal Stream Atlas for Dover Straits that has a Computation of Rates conversion graphic that allows the user to take that difference between the two tides encompassing a swim and converts it to a tidal stream rate in knots. These streams are related to the Tidal Streams locations A through V found on the Admiralty Chart SC1892.

The English Admiralty doesn't publish the currents directly as the United States Oceanographic Administration does but they do publish an Admiralty Tidal Stream Atlas, NP233. From this publication you can determine the current flow using a graphical method. A formula for the calculation of the approximate maximum flow of the current for a specific range between any two tides for any tidal station can be derived. That formula is: (range-3.2)/(2.8/(Spring rate-Neap rate))+Neap rate=maximum current speed. With this value, you can enter the formula for the calculation of current speed at any time found in the Appendix discussing the computation of current speed at any time. One difficulty is in placing the exact start of the tide known as the stand of the tide given the time of high or low tide from the daily tables. In a study conducted by the author, he was able to verify the ebb current quite accurately[753] but not the flood tide. It was in reviewing the discrepancy that another unique aspect of the currents in Dover Straits became apparent. The tidal cycles are asymmetrical. The period for the ebb is different significantly from the period for the flood by approximately a half an hour. It was by adjusting the period of the sine wave that a correlation between the simulation of the current in a computer and the test floatation devices could be made.

A further complication of the determination of the current speed arose when the Admiralty decided to only publish an average speed of the current for the two tides in a day. This last aspect might simplify the life of a captain in a vessel capable of twenty knots transiting the Straits but it immensely complicated the life of a swimmer whose top speed is barely equal to that of the water they desire to swim across. Software was available that breaks out the tidal information in the diurnal norm from Nobeltec using their Tides & Current software package provided you paid for the additional disk covering British Admiralty, Region #1. However, when the author upgraded his software in 2002, he was informed that they were no longer providing support for this region. There is another way to derive the information from historical sources. Tides cycles repeat over a 19-year Metonic cycle also known as the National Tidal Datum Epoch. The solution to this problem is not simple and may even require the use of an astronomer to ascertain the exact length of the cycle and a seller of antique books, as you'll need some old tide tables. I don't want to make this problem seem overly complicated but good questions will elicit good answers if care is take to be thorough.

Returning for a moment to the asymmetrical aspect of the tidal currents, the flood tide lasts longer than the ebb. Is it any wonder that most of the early records were set when the swimmer swam from France to England? Even Gerald Forsberg in his book *Modern Marathon Swimming* noticed the advantage and reasoned that the current direction aided the swim.[754] There were two factors at work in this course that a swimmer swimming from England to France does not have: one, they are farther across when the current switches and two; they can see the destination (the White Cliffs). All a swimmer would have to do is start the swim on the coast of France at the beginning of a flood tide and swim west while the current carries the swimmer north. If the swimmer is fast enough, they will be approaching the coast of England just as the current dies and in a slack current, make the dash to shore. This concept is applicable in either direction. The concept is simply this, let the swimmer cover the longitudes (the east-west distance) between the landmasses and the current will take care of the latitudes (the north-south distance). The devil is in the details.

The software application would make an estimate of the time it would require a swimmer leaving Shakespeare Beach just south of the port of Dover to cover the ten and one-half nautical miles of longitude while the current is carrying the swimmer south fourteen and one-half nautical miles. This means that the current is doing 3/5 of the work of swimming from Dover to Cape Gris-Nez making the English Channel quite similar to the Manhattan swim in terms of time and current push. The entire problem breaks down into one of vector addition. The swimmers vector is variable meaning that swimmers speed can be adjusted (slower than a maximum) and the direction is totally variable. The current vector is less adjustable in that the direction is set but the speed can be adjusted by picking the right day and time to leave on thereby adjusting the current speed. The estimate of the current speed and direction is complicated by slight variations at various points along the course. However, these variations are well known and by mathematical reduction, a single vector representing all the current vectors along the path can be derived based on that day's tidal difference. Once this is known, the swimmer's speed and direction can be adjusted so that the swimmer arrives at France just as the current dies out. The author has developed a spreadsheet similar in nature to his Manhattan spreadsheet for calculation of an English Channel swim where the current speed can be varied and the swimmer's speed and direction can be varied.

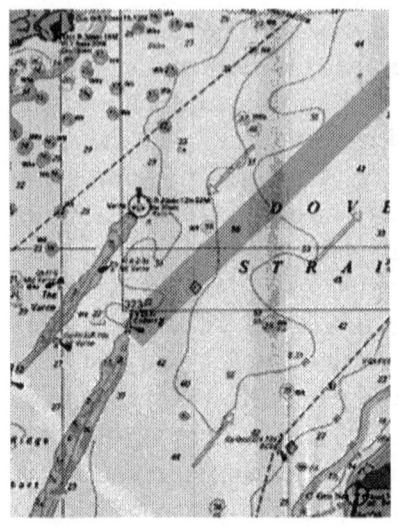

Figure 103 Section of the English Channel for visualization of swim and current vectors.

In software simulations, swims of six and one-half hour appear achievable. If the Channel swim is anything similar to the Manhattan swim, immediate results will happen (new records) but it will take ten years of attempts to smooth out the computational results with the actual results. The initial phase would involve a series of test swims over portions of the channel to see if the computational results are dependable before attempting a complete swim. Once the swim software is debugged, swimmers can be assured that if they deliver a solid swim, their finishing time will be predictable to within 5 minutes as it is in the Manhattan swim. Without involving a swimmer, a SkiDoo can make the crossing provided it doesn't exceed a swimmers rate in still water and it holds a constant heading across the channel. This is also a method for testing out any swim course in any location.

Another way of viewing this approach to a vectored crossing is to take a picture frame view. Suppose you had a picture frame that was 11 inches across and 17 inches long. Using chart SC1892 you could frame out the channel crossing with the English coast in the upper left-hand corner and the France coast in the lower right-hand corner. The ebb current flows from the upper right to the lower left. If a swimmer was to swim due east from Dover, they would be nearly facing the current head on and their over the ground speed would drop considerably. The swimmer would be facing east but their course would reveal a course that would point toward France. This swimmer would never make it across the longitudinal distance of the Channel in the time that the current flows south, approximately 6 hours. However, if the swimmer were to turn and swim toward France, their speed toward France increases because they are not fighting the current as much but their speed across the longitudinal distance is less than the maximum possible, and they are also aiding the current flowing south. This swimmer would be south of Cape Gris-Nez before the current finishes flowing south and would have to turn to swim east to get in.

Picking the correct heading when the destination is in sight is fairly easy. When you are off shore, or in fog or at night, finding the right heading in the English Channel has been a problem that has plagued swimmers since the beginning. I have derived a formula for calculation of the optimum course heading using as the inputs the swimmer's speed, the current speed and direction. This formula is discussed in the Appendix for those interested. With the required information given, there can only be one optimum heading for the swimmer. The computer spreadsheet program figures it out and all that remains is for the swimmer to hold that particular course and they should show up in France within five minutes of the predicted time. Naturally, the swimmer is following the boat so the heading is for the benefit of the pilot. On a big swim, the theory can be checked out prior to the actual swim provided there is money in the swim budget for such luxuries. There is one other trick that I haven't revealed and that is how do you keep the swimmer on course when there are dynamic conditions in the field causing changes to the computer's assumptions? It is my hope that in a future edition of this text that this information will be laid out for all to know. In the meantime, doesn't one hold close to their vest their cards until the stakes are high enough for them to be laid down?

In order to check the simulation of a computer program you have to measure the current flow. In my preparation for my plans of becoming an English Channel pilot, I undertook an oceanographic survey of the current flow of the Dover Straits. This can be difficult if you don't have a boat. In the late spring of 2000, I traveled to Dover for the expressed purpose of finding an appropriate boat to use as an escort vessel. While there, I attended a Rotary club meeting at Broadstairs; a bit up the coastline from Dover but the meeting location was at the Charles Dickens restaurant. The allure of making a meeting and having dinner at the Charles Dickens restaurant was too much for an aficionado of all things Dickens. One of my delights while in Dover is to have breakfast in the Charles Dickens Square in downtown Dover.

    I attended the Broadstairs Rotary Club meeting and to my surprise it was the installation dinner for their new president. Five clubs were in attendance so that there was an overflow room filled with gentlemen all in proper dress. I chose to attend in attire typical of Americans on vacation and they in their generosity chose to sit me at the head table as a guest of honor. Darn but what they didn't quote Dickens at the meeting. After a toast to the Queen, dinner was served and I had the opportunity to meet many of the distinguished guests. As we talked I inquired of boating, everyone referred me to Roger Barwick whom I eventually found. Roger had spent a number of years in Philadelphia as controller of a multi-national business. He was quite inclined to go sailing the next day having just brought his boat around from the Solvent single-handed. I was impressed.

    We met the next day at the Dover marina aboard his 30' sailing boat the *Zander*. We dressed for the weather as a small craft warning advisory was heard on the VHF; as a precaution we put one reef in the sail. I took the helm, which was a tiller as Roger cleared us with Dover Coast Guard to move out of harbor. The wind was out of the north so we sailed off on a port tack close-hauled to the wind. We waited out the arrival of a hovercraft before our departure from the harbor. We were headed to a destination 3 miles offshore to drop a current marker in the water. Then by taking GPS reading every five minutes, I would have a valid current vector. It was important in the selection of the marker that it not be susceptible to the wind yet it had to be visible above the water. I choose to use an orange; they float right at the top of the water and present as low a profile to the wind as imaginable.

The water was in an ebb as we headed out Dover entrance and it was so strong that, even pointed as we were toward the northeast, we were sailing due east. We were making no way toward the north. The wind was quite strong hitting 39 knots and the waves were up to a respectable 16 feet. To keep the boat on a straight course, I worked the tiller as though it were an oar; sailing up one side of a wave and down the back on different points of sail as the wind changed direction in the troughs. Undeterred, we sailed on until we were off shore in the vicinity of Tidal Stream mark J as seen on chart SC1892. Dropping our marker, we made passes tracking the orange for twenty minutes when I said enough.

Roger and I thought that it would be prudent to put another reef in the sail for the trip back. The wind hadn't abated and the seas were still significant. Roger went forward to prepare the sail. We headed up into the wind, motoring slowly to hold our heading. It was a new sail and was a bit stiff. As Roger attempted to pull the sail down, it jammed. He stepped back to the rail to take a look up the mast to see what the trouble was. He was standing on the port side by the shrouds. As he looked up, the boat rolled to starboard lifting him into the air and with the momentum from lifting his head up and stepping back, he did a perfect back flip off the boat into the water. Needless to say, he stepped back about a foot further away from the shroud than he should have as his hands failed to connect with anything to stop the fall. By the time I exclaimed, "oh, my God!" and gathered myself up to look over the side, there was Roger but a yard off the port quarter swimming for the boat. Roger is a diver and as such quite comfortable in the water. I threw him a line and he scrambled aboard the stern swim platform. He lost his wallet, watch, and spectacles. When he recovered, Roger went back up and finished the reefing and we made for Dover. I think the part that was most shocking to me was as Roger was standing on the deck, dripping wet he said something about it being the second time that year that he had gone overboard! As we made the safety of the harbor and were glad to have made the adventure as short as it was; but I couldn't help notice another sailboat was leaving the harbor obviously aware of the sea state conditions but oblivious and fully prepared to handle them. I found the boaters and sailor of the North Sea serious sailors indeed. It was the information collected on this difficult day that my spreadsheet program matched up perfectly. I was delighted.

Precautionary aspects of Channel swimming

An aspect of open water swims not often thought about by swimmers is the regulatory aspect. A swim by virtual of its immersion in water becomes a marine event. Observing the regulations governing marine events is crucial to the continuation of any swim. All waterways have some maritime jurisdiction that controls the waters from who can fish there to the type of vessels that can travel over them, to what type of buoys can be placed where, to who can legally captain a vessel, and what agency that is in charge of enforcement of the regulations. For the English Channel, the jurisdiction is shared between the British and the French Coast Guard. The British Coast Guard is not opposed to having swimmers make the attempt provided that they realize they are not the only marine traffic that is in the channel. Rules have been established that escort boats are required to observe. The French no longer permit swimmers to initiate a swim from their shores. They will permit a swim to continue provided there is no danger to commercial traffic. Swimmers have to realize that their swim is insignificant compared to the ecological and financial exposure that their swim might cause should a marine accident occur because a swimmer would not stop their swim and yield a right-of-way. This is the main reason that the French no longer permit swims to originate from their shores.

The author has stood on the cliffs of Dover, observed channel traffic, and marveled at the skill with which the Channel pilots thread swimmers through the traffic. On a typical day, 10 vessels transiting the channel can be seen just in the southbound traffic lanes and a like number in the northbound traffic lanes. The swimmer is attempting to swim across all this traffic at a speed that does not exceed 3 knots or approximately 100 feet a minute for a fast swimmer. The marine traffic is most likely proceeding at 20 knots or approximately 2000 feet a minute. A modern containership can be 200 feet wide. It would take the average swimmer (swimming 66 feet per minute) about 3 minutes to cross the width of one of these ships. The ship has traveled over a mile in that time. This is far too close for comfort and crossings decisions have to be made with the vessels farther off. This places considerable weight on the experience and judgment of the escort vessel.

Swimming the channel is not without other dangers.[755] Fausta Moreno, age 41 of Mexico, died during the 1999 season from medical conditions pre-existing that were acerbated by the swim.[756] When approaching the French coast on August 12, 2001 an escort vessel lost sight of a Swiss swimmer, Ueli Staub, and reported him as lost.[757] The swimmer's body was eventually recovered drowned. While this sport is not as brutal as mountain climbing has become, it's not without its dangers. Even a short swim can be dangerous: in 1897 a swimmer, Denis Sullivan, age 29, was presumed drowned trying to cross the East River at night for a $2 bet.[758]

While the hazards of the water are bad enough, those of the bureaucracy can be equally as daunting. The Channel Swimming Association has suffered a schism. As with all human organizations, personalities and money were a factor in this development. The CSA is an association who has helped channel swimmers for years and years. Some problems had developed with their Secretary, Michael Oram, and he was forced out. Michael Oram and swimmer, Alison Streeter, decided to thumb their noses at the organization and formed the Channel Swimming and Piloting Federation in 2000, presumably to lower the costs for swimmers. The CSA attempted to deal with the realities of the situation by allowing any swimmer being escorted by CS&PF pilot to register with the CSA as long as a CSA observer observed the swim. The cost involved is minimal and expected. CS&PF has refused to allow CSA observers on their boats and presumably provide their own independent observer. By CSA rules, that swim is not recognized. You don't get on the same list as Captain Webb.

Presently, both organizations are functioning and successful. The question you need to address is which one to book your swim with. Personalities are great for starting organizations or initiating a movement but organizations are what deal with the day-to-day realities and long-term survival. Clara Barton was instrumental in starting the American Red Cross and expanding their role into disaster services beyond just wartime medical care,[759] but she was forced out of leadership of the Red Cross over bookkeeping issues of expenses. This was a contentious period for the Red Cross that played out in the press.[760] Her work was not diminished because of the brouhaha and her role has been idealized over the decades. The fulfillment of the mission of the Red Cross was carried out. It won't have helped if she had started a separate organization.

The lesson that swimming needs to learn is that swimming is not about one individual but traditions and standards. Bicycling will tell you that an individual rarely wins a long race but the pelotron is the real muscle. Swimming history is littered with long forgotten swims that weren't supported by an organization. This book is about them. The ones that aren't forgotten are the ones that were adopted and supported by an organization. FINA is swimming official organization to protect and remember pool swims. I have already mentioned the confusion that existed in the United States about the fastest world record around the 1900's. There is a reason for this confusion; FINA hadn't been brought into existence yet. There was no one place to go for a source for information.

The British are great for standing on tradition and there is the 70-year history of the CSA. In 2000, I showed up at the docks of Dover looking to get certified as a Channel pilot. I have all the documentation to run boats across the channel for hire. With my swimming contacts in New York, it would have been very easy for me to set up my own shop and start running swimmers across the channel. I didn't. I applied to be a pilot with the CSA. When I didn't get approved, I was disappointed but I accepted their decisions and knew that if I followed their recommendations for approval, I'd eventually get listed as a CSA pilot. During the process, I was impressed with their emphasis on safety for the swimmer. I can't say with the same certainty the CS&PF has as rigorous a standard. The Swiss swimmer that the escort boat lost sight of in 2001 and drowned had a CS&PF pilot on his first escort.

Finally, in 2001, the CSA at its General Meeting rejected handling of assisted swims but approved the creation of a Channel Crossing Association to work in close association with CSA but independently. This organization is for swimmers with wet suits, fins, and various craft desiring to cross the Channel.

Eventually, I would hope that some people swallow their pride and resolve this problem because it's not good for swimming to have two organizations offering the same service. Manhattan has had several disgruntled swimmers but has not had to suffer the fate of a schism: two competing organizations. It's always better if people can settle their differences. If that doesn't happen, I would hope that a commission would be appointed with swimming interest at heart and a decision rendered. I had the opportunity to participate in a ceremony when the City of Dover dedicated a new park with a historical time line in 2001. Right there with the Romans invading, the building of the lighthouse, the bombardment during World War II, was the marker for the formation of the Channel Swimming Association. That was impressive to me because history matters. You either deal with history or you are destined to repeat it.

Channel training, Montauk

One of the requirements of swimming the channel is the completion of a significant training swim. This swim is best suited for training if the water temperature is comparable to expected English Channel temperatures, traditionally between 65° and 68° Fahrenheit. The distance doesn't have to be the same length but a swim of approximately 8 hours duration is a good precursor for predicting success in the Channel. One swim located off Montauk,

Long Island, satisfies those requirements easily and has other similarities to the English Channel swim. Swimming from Montauk to Watch Hill, Rhode Island, across Block Island Sound, one encounters crosscurrents of similar strengths. The course crosses the currents at a similar angle to the channel crossing and the swim is exposed to the Atlantic to the south so open ocean swells creating wave action similar to the channel can be expected. Plus, you are swimming to a point of land calling for navigational skills on the part of the support crew not unlike that needed for the channel. Finally, the current turns against the swimmer at the end causing the swimmer's progress to slow as they stroke their way to land. The swimmer goes through a tide change just like the channel and has to develop coping skills. The swimmer is out of sight of land, just like in the channel, and must depend on their crew for guidance. The swim stresses the swimmer as well as the crew. The best part is that the swim is shorter than the channel, being only 13 nautical miles in length and if the swimmer wants to delay their cold-water training, the swim can be scheduled for the warmer months of July and August.

The first person to attempt the swim was Sally Friedman of Manhattan, New York. I had heard that Sally was training for the channel and I rang her up and asked her if she'd like to do this swim that I was developing for channel training. Without hesitation, she agreed to swim the distance. Since this was an inaugural swim, I decided to have the swim video taped for possible TV viewing. I contacted Ambrose Salamini of Salamini Films who helped me out and I became a film producer. On Thursday, July 26, 1990, she completed the swim in 8:57.[761] She left from a sandy beach near the lighthouse on Montauk Point at 12:30am and began swimming south due to an error on the part of her pilot, Loretta DeRose, who was Sally's gracious host in Montauk at Snug Harbor Motel. She didn't go south very far or long as the 3.1 knot current was flowing north and she gradually made her way out toward Great Eastern Rock. Upon correcting the course, Sally took off leaving Great Rips at 12:50 am to leave Swagwong Reef abeam by 1:30pm.

Sally began the swim approximately 3 hours after flood began at The Race, she could have started as early as 2 hours after flood begins at the Race. This late a start took full advantage of a flood current sweeping her northwest toward Cerberus Shoal, marking the halfway point. By swimming due east at the start of the swim for about a half a mile, a swimmer is able to take advantage of a strong current inside of Great Eastern Rock to get up to Cerberus Shoal. By the time the current goes slack, a swimmer should be at the latitude[762] of Cerberus Shoal so they can position themselves out of the ebb current headed in the reverse direction. After swimming for a while in the lee of Fisher's Island, the swimmer's final task is to swim across an ebb current that is sweeping around the north end of Fishers Island and running down the southern shore line of Rhode Island.

When the current went slack around 4pm, Sally turned north eventually entering the ebb current that swept her eastward threatening to take her past Watch Hill Point. Here she fought the current making very slow progress as night fell. In the darkness, ahead we could see breakers offshore due to a reef southwest of the point. In consultation with Jane Katz, we decided to end the swim at a buoy, R2, about 50 yards off Watch Hill Point without having Sally swim into shore. This swim took 8:57 to complete. Had she gone to shore, the time would have been slightly longer. The author had neglected to scout out the finish not realizing the finish would be in the dark. Since this was a training swim, Sally's task was complete and the decision not to risk a landing among rocks, jeopardizing her attempt at the Channel only two weeks hence, was well founded.

That swim was not to be as her husband and coach, Paul Carter, died in an accident on the day they were to leave for England. I sold the right to the video to Sally about a year later as this was the only video she had of her and Jack together. This swim is recalled in Sally's book, *Swimming the Channel*. I found Sally to be totally fearless in tackling this swim. Many swimmers that I approached to do the swim only replied to me with one word, "sharks". Sure enough, around the corner from Loretta's motel is where the largest shark ever caught[763] was landed and they have a plastic replica in place to commemorate that event.

MOMS

The Montauk Marathon Swim occurred on September 24, 1994, as part of the Long Island Fall Festival held that year. Weather wise it was a tight schedule for a swim. No sooner had one low-pressure system blown through the Northeast than another followed two days later. When I originally planned the swim a year prior, I never would have imagined the difficulties thrown up by Mother Nature. The water temperature held through September in the mid-60 range and at race day the ocean temperature was 66° dropping to 64° off of Rhode Island. On Friday, the day before the race, 12' waves were observed south of Jones Beach Inlet, small craft warnings were announced on the official NOAA weather station yet the forecast called for 4 foot swells that Saturday. Ed Trainor, one of the skippers for the Connecticut swimmers, had called me after talking with the Montauk Coast Guard station where it was blowing 35 knots. I told him to sit tight, I'd consider a postponement but I wanted to look at the situation first hand. Sure enough, at Montauk Point by the time I arrived at 3PM on Friday, September 23, 1994, occasional white caps were to be seen south of the point and none at all to the north. The swim was on.

But where were the swimmers? Very few had checked into Snug Harbor, the designated hotel and combination boat marina. Gradually, as swimmers and their boaters checked in, the swim began to take on some dimensions. Finally, Marty McMahon and some of his fellow COAST swimmers arrived complaining about traffic all the way from Connecticut. Once Marty was briefed on the status of the swim, calls went out to alert the remaining swimmers in Connecticut to meet their boats at 5am to journey across the Long Island Sound to Montauk by boat for the swim start. I understand that some swimmers arrived home to simply drive to the boat, who needs sleep when you can swim? I began to marvel at similarities of this swim to the English Channel swim where I'm told you get a call in the middle of the night to show up the next morning: come prepared to swim.

The flood tide began that morning at 7am, and I reasoned that even though I preferred an 8 o'clock start, I could live with a 9 o'clock start considering what a later start could do to a swimmer nearing the midpoint of this swim. The earlier the start, the closer to Rhode Island the swimmer would be when the ebb begins, and then you would have about an hour of gradually increasing tide before the swimmer would have to deal with the full force of an opposing tide. Since the swimmers on the Montauk side wanted as much of the favorable tide as possible, I agreed to a split start, sending Marty on one boat out to meet the rest of the Connecticut swimmers whom were still 7 miles away (1 hour). Since for Sally Friedman's swim, the rocky shore was too difficult at the end of the island, the swim start was moved to Turtle Cove, about a ½ mile west of the Montauk lighthouse along the southern shore of Long Island. This is a sandy beach making for an easier start but a slightly longer swim.

When I got to the starting location, I could see the first heat's escort boats just about reaching position to drop the swimmers off in the water. They were to swim in to shore, receive an official start and thereby begin the swim. I advised the surf fishermen who where fishing that people were coming ashore and they stopped fishing to watch. There were also about 50 surfers in the water but mostly further west of our location. I wondered what the surfer must have thought as they walked past the signs directing spectators to the "Swim start, Montauk to Watch Hill". The surfers were all dressed in wetsuits and carried floatation devices (their boards). The surf was so rough that Tina lost her swim cap and goggles coming ashore. The first heat went off about 8:40 as I recall, consisting of Jim Barber, age 34, from Indiana, Tina Piantidosi, age 26, from San Francisco, California, and Nasin Arafet, age 30, from New Jersey were the solo swimmers and Dan Gustafson, age 22, from Connecticut as the first swimmer for the McMahon family relay. Members of the relay were Lisa McMahon, Patrick McMahon, Denise McMahon,

Brenda Baron, and Marcia Chambers. Just 7 minutes later the 2nd relay went off which consisted of Ira Wolfe, the team captain, age 57, from New Jersey; Chris Gebhandt, age 21, from New Jersey; John Pier Jr., age 24, from Connecticut; and Carlos Lloreda, age 40, from New York who was the first swimmer. Finally, Ed Trainor's boat pulled into view. They had left at 5 am from Watch Hill that morning. Still, it took quite some time for Marty McMahon age 31, from Connecticut who was swimming solo and Jeffrey Lindner, age 21, from Maryland, to swim into shore for the start. Jeff was on the Collette family relay, which included Alan Collette, Jeanine Colette, Curtis Colette, John McNulty, and Shannon Sullivan. They started officially one hour behind the first heat. Evidently, Marty missed his relay boat with his family on it and hooked up with the Colette family relay team.

As Marty and Jeff swam back out into the surf after the start, their escort boat started motoring away from them. I called Ed on the VHF radio and gave him reports spotting the swimmers in relationship to where he was. The current that morning was taking the swimmers east toward an offshore shoal where the waves were breaking. It was important that the escort boat come alongside and directs them away from this turbulence. As I watched the two swimmers, mere dots by this time, and the approaching boat, one of the dots disappeared and then reappeared about 30 yards away on the other side of the surf line. This was to cause havoc for Marty during the rest of his swim. In hindsight, kayaks would have been very helpful at the start.

Then my official watch reset itself. Fortunately, I had asked everyone to maintain a separate watch on each boat and to observe when I dropped my hand for the start plus I broadcast the countdown over the VHF radio as well. As I walked back to my vehicle to drive back to the marina to catch my boat, from the parking lot for Montauk Point Light, I could see all of the swimmer's boats in a line headed north from the point. It was a beautiful sight. I got aboard a spare relief boat, which only became available because it had showed up an hour late from Watch Hill, and we proceeded to catch up with the swim. Some swimmers were on a direct line for Watch Hill and others were letting the current take them west as I had suggested and as had happen during Sally Friedman's swim. The swim was beginning to spread out. Being in the lee of the South Fork on Long Island, the ocean settled down into gentle 3-foot swells with a long time period and by the end of the race was as smooth as a lake.

After pausing at each swimmer's boat and seeing that everyone was busy about their business, I sent my boat on ahead to Watch Hill because the skipper's wife was seasick and they were going to help with the shore reception. They dropped me on Jim Barber's boat. He was perhaps four, five miles from Watch Hill and comfortably in the lead when he withdrew from competition. He had taken a wave at the start and swallowed quite a bit of water and he was understandably ill. From the description by Jim and his skipper, the wave that sunk his swim was in the same location as the one that later took Marty McMahon on his underwater ride. On their way back to Montauk, I was dropped aboard Tina's boat.

Art Coleman had originally booked himself as a competitor for this swim but following his Manhattan Island marathon sub 7-hour swim only two weeks earlier, he understandably had not recovered sufficiently to justify participation. He volunteered to help coach Tina across. And coach he did, coming fully prepared with charts, extra boats, cheering squad, an understanding of the swim gleaned from continual questioning of me and my knowledge of the swim gathered from Sally Friedman's swim four years earlier. We both bemoaned the withdrawal of Jim Barber from the race because it eliminated the possibility of comparison of race strategy. Barber was drifting with the current up toward Fisher's Island and Tina was making a beeline across. Another race, another day and perhaps the answer to the question of which is better will be found.

In the meantime, Tina was cranking out 80+ strokes a minute as we churned our way northward. Then we observed ourselves being overtaken by Marty's escort boat, which had finally located him. We learned that Marty had withdrawn from the swim. I computed Tina's ground speed from the Loran, 1.6

knots. She was losing too much to the current, but in Sally's swim her ground speed had dropped as low as 1 knot. More time went by as we drew near to Watch Hill and when we were only a mile from the point, I ventured a guess that Tina was going to break 8 hours. She could do a mile in a half an hour easily. The swimmer Nasim in his escort boat drew alongside to watch, he had pulled out after 7 hours of struggling with the waters. Watch Hill loomed right there in front of us and yet we were being swept eastward rather rapidly. Soon, East Beach, a sandy beach just east of Watch Hill Point, came into view, ahead we could see the calmer waters on the leeward side of the point from the ebb, and 8 hours rolled past. Tina swam and swam and swam until finally it was too shallow for the boat to safely continue. The escort boat dropped anchor and Tina swam on through the breakers; upon standing up the clock was stopped at 8:28.

While we waited for Tina to return, she had gone ashore to take a shower, we saw the Wolfe relay team finished in 9:17. They swam in from out of the east to East Beach having been swept eastward while holding a course due north. They looked happy. As we motored back to Montauk, we caught sight of the McMahon relay. They were but a mile from land and finished in a time of 9:45. We didn't see the Colette relay but spoke with their escort boat as they were navigating around Napatree Point to go into Watch Hill harbor.

A planned second swim marathon was advertised but never held because I had just retired from the phone company and was beginning a second career, which took up a lot of my time. The swim was not successful financially and that in combination with a lack of time was the reason the second swim didn't occur. In 1996, I graduated from New York Institute of Technology with a Masters degree in Electrical Engineering and moved to Massachusetts further complicating a resumption of this swim.

GEMS

In October of 2005, I began looking at establishing a memorial swim in honor of Gertrude Ederle. There was no question in my mind that it had to be the Sandy Hook swim; anything less daunting wouldn't do justice to the memory of Gertrude Ederle. The Battery to Sandy Hook swim was her first choice as a practice swim for the Channel, it was local, and it was in the media capital of the world. My first task was to find a swimmer capable and worthy of undertaking a swim that would forever tie them to Gertrude Ederle. They would literally be swimming in Gertrude Ederle's wake. With an initial swim on the books, an annual competition could then be undertaken. I even trademarked the name of the swim: Gertrude Ederle Memorial Swim and established a website: www.trudyswim.org.

I contacted Tammy van Wisse of Australia. Ever since I accompanied Skip Storch in his record setting 10-day swim down the Hudson, she had become my hero what with her 106-day swim down the Murray River, her Discovery Channel swim across Gippsland Lake, her swims of Bass Straits and Cook Strait, and her Manhattan Island Marathon swim win. She was highly credentialed. The question was could I talk her into doing this swim? After an exchange of emails she agreed to take the project to her sponsor, Melaleuca, who gave their approval on May 1, 2006. Tammy had begun to put her team together: I, Richard Clifford the kayaker, and Bea Hartigan of USA Swimming out of Connecticut. Everyone contributed to the swim in the run up to the event. Tammy got her sponsor locked in, Richard got the escort boats contact, Bea Hartigan secured the sanction from USA Swimming when the US Master Swimmer sanction hit a snag, and I secured permission from the US Coast Guard for the swim to take place. Tammy had her training going forward in Australia with Chris McHattie, her fiancé whom she met during her Loch Ness swim. He would also handle the helm on the escort boat during the swim. During the actual swim, her personal trainer was Nancy

Schnarr who was the daughter of Fran Schnarr, the trainer for Shelley Taylor when she swam in the United States.

In what was probably the highlight of the swim, the sponsor in the person of Antonio Lima, the public relations account manager of The Summit Group Communications representing Melaleuca arranged for a private dinner with 15 members of the Ederle family, Gertrude's nieces and nephews, and Tammy prior to the swim. None of them were alive when Gertrude established herself in sport history. They all either came along on the swim or met Tammy at the finish. During the actual swim, Steve Ederle, a Fort Schuyler graduate and licensed Master Mariner and I plotted Tammy's swim together and discussed strategy when we reached Romer Shoal. When Mary Worth, the family spokesperson, arranged to have Gertrude's older sister, Margaret, brought to the awards presentation at the finish, I knew how much this event meant to the family and was proud to have played a part of this moment in marathon swim history.

It was a beautiful day for a swim, Friday, July 21, 2006, that that got off on schedule with pomp and ceremony. I had drawn up a spreadsheet with projected times which showed Tammy finishing in 4:58. Tammy hit the first mark, the turn down Buttermilk Channel at the northern corner of Governors Island, 2 minute behind my estimate. After a fast trip down an empty channel we turned south at Red Hook, Brooklyn, to run through Bay Ridge Flats off Gowanus Bay. This location due to the change of current could be a giant eddy and slow Tammy down. It took an hour to cross this section to reach the Bay Ridge Pier where the shore effect picked up Tammy's speed to 3½ knots. Behind us we could see storm clouds gathering but they passed north of us crossing mid-Manhattan that morning. The next two miles to the Verrazano Narrows Bridge were completed in thirty minutes meaning Tammy's speed had picked up to four knots. She was only four minutes behind my schedule. As we passed south of the VZ Bridge near the eastern bridge support, the morning haze had not burnt off and the next mark was difficult to pick out. As we progressed along it became apparent that I had picked out the wrong mark and redirected Chris in the escort boat back toward the red side of Ambrose channel. Three minutes later, with some urgency, I had to again call Chris and instruct him to turn Tammy to swim perpendicular to the channel as a containership coming out of the fog was bearing down on us. Tammy made the safety of the edge of the channel with about a minute to spare. The water up until then had been quite calm so the 4 foot boat wake was singularly impressive. The Coast Guard escort at this point came alongside and requested that we stay out of the channel.

Tammy swim progressed fine down the red side of the channel as we ticked off the buoys. Her speed was slowly dropping when we reach the bend in Ambrose channel for Romer Shoal at Red Buoy #10. There was boat traffic in the channel so instead of crossing immediately, we send Tammy down to the next red buoy where she crossed the channel in ten minutes to the green side reaching green buoy # 7 at 11:07 am. Tammy completed the swim from the VZ Bridge to R#10 in 1¼ hours, a distance of 4½ nautical miles. The current was dropping because her over-the-ground speed had slowed to 3.6 knots from 4 knots. But the next 1.4 nautical miles took 21 minutes increasing her speed to 4.6 knots. This was caused by what physics calls the Venturi or nozzle effect. All the water gushing out of NY harbor hits Romer Shoal and turns left causes the water in Ambrose Channel at this point to speed up because of the narrower dimension that the water has to pass through. This same effect occurred around the VZ Bridge which speeded up the water when we hit Bay Ridge. There is for all intends and purposes, a huge water slide for swimmers existing on the north side of Romer Shoal during ebb tides.

Romer Shoal is also the boundary between two different water domains. North of Romer is controlled by the Hudson River; south of Romer is water that flows into and out of Raritan Bay. These waters are not synchronized because the flood filling Raritan Bay starts an hour earlier than the ebb ends coming out of the Hudson giving a swimmer just 5 hours of favorable current. In the swim strategy underpinning the swim, based on my earlier experiences with Skip Storch in these waters, to avoid swimming directly into opposing waters, the swimmer stays in the Hudson water flow until they can turn and swim across the northbound water thus keeping their forward speed to close the last 2½ miles to Sandy Hook shore. We held Tammy for six additional minutes in the favorable waters before turning her to swim south across the incoming waters. Except that the maximum current that day was below two knots, meaning she could swim over any opposing current, we would have held her for a longer time in the Hudson River flow. The plans were originally to turn her at buoy #3A well past Romer Shoal. The final 2½ miles took an hour and 21 minutes. Her over-the-ground speed dropped to just under two knots. The elapsed time was officially: 5:06:47.5 breaking the 81 year-old record by two hours and four minutes. The distance swum was approximately 15 nautical miles, far short of the 22 mile distance for the swim claimed by the originator of this course: Charles Dobrowski. The difference could be accountable to the fact that Dobrowski most likely counted the distance he meandered in his swim as part of the course.

On the return trip, the weather which had cooperated all morning turned ugly and a terrific downpour occurred dropping visibility to less than 25 feet and drenched the victorious team. On a bright note, Tammy and her fiancé, Chris McHattie, were married on the lawn at Larchmont Yacht Club in Larchmont, NY, on Sunday, July 30, 2006 before their return to Australia. Tammy has announced her retirement from marathon swimming.

The swim by Tammy was just the tease to inspire marathon swimmer to participate in the GEMS scheduled for October 21, 2006. The distance for this race is 17½ statute miles. I was not able to develop a cohesive group of local swimmers to organize this swim and for a while it looked like the race would be cancelled. Morty Berger of the Manhattan Island Foundation stepped in at the recommendation of Earl Sandvik, the boat coordinator for Tammy's swim, and volunteered to pick up the swim as a tribute to Gertrude Ederle pioneer work in women's sports and because she was a local New York resident. Once that was arranged, Morty's team handled all the details and two swimmers competed on a very rough day over the Ederle course. Winds that day were over 20 knots and increased so the conditions were very Channel-like. Both swimmers were channel veterans which contributed to their success. Nancy Steadman-Martin of Oceanport, NJ, age 52, finished in a time of 5:53 and Michelle Davidson, age 36, of Neptune City, NJ, finished in 6:27. As both swimmers crossed underneath the Verrazano Narrows Bridge, they were only few minutes behind Tammy van Wisse's pace. Once into the open waters south of the bridge, conditions worsen and slowed the swimmers considerably. Traffic at the Ambrose Channel crossing, buoy R#10, delayed the swimmers as they notched two additional red buoys before slipping safely across. The wind was out of the northwest so when they turned to swim to shore; they were swimming right into waves of 4 to 5 feet.

    A stipulation by the Gateway National Recreation Area, Sandy Hook Unit, was that swimmers are allowed on shore at North Beach (40°28'07.46" N, 73°59'48.74"W) or immediate vicinity only. This regulation is because of the protected status of the Sandy Hook shoreline. They did not want any boats including kayaks coming ashore or any boats anchoring within a ¼ mile of this sanctuary. Swimmers were to land and then swim back to their boats. The latitude and longitude should be used as a waypoint for the swimmer's escort boat to direct them to this location when they leave Ambrose Channel. A visual mark that works fairly well is the light house. Depending upon where the swimmer drifts during the swim, the lighthouse is a good location to point toward but as you come closer to shore, look for groups of bathers along shore to determine the exact location of North Beach.

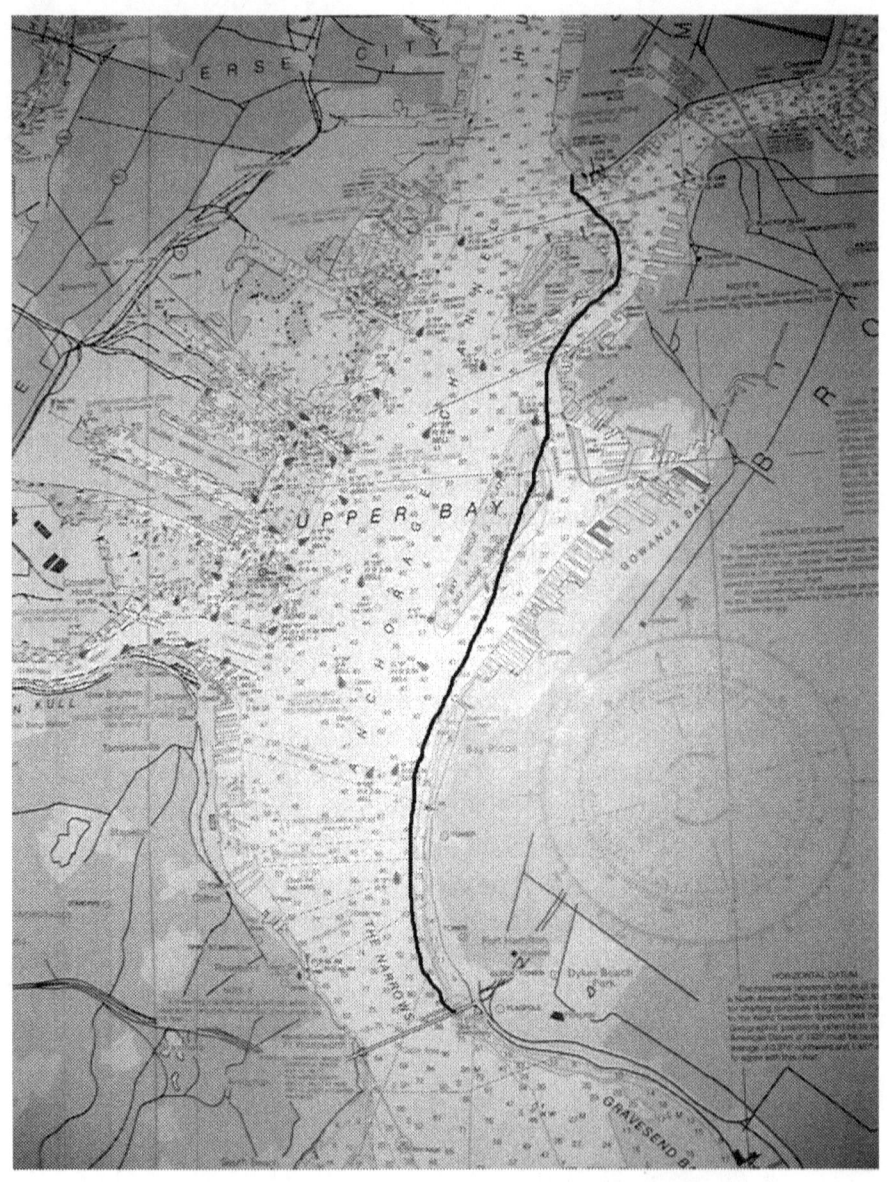

Figure 104 First half of the GEMS course from chart 12327.

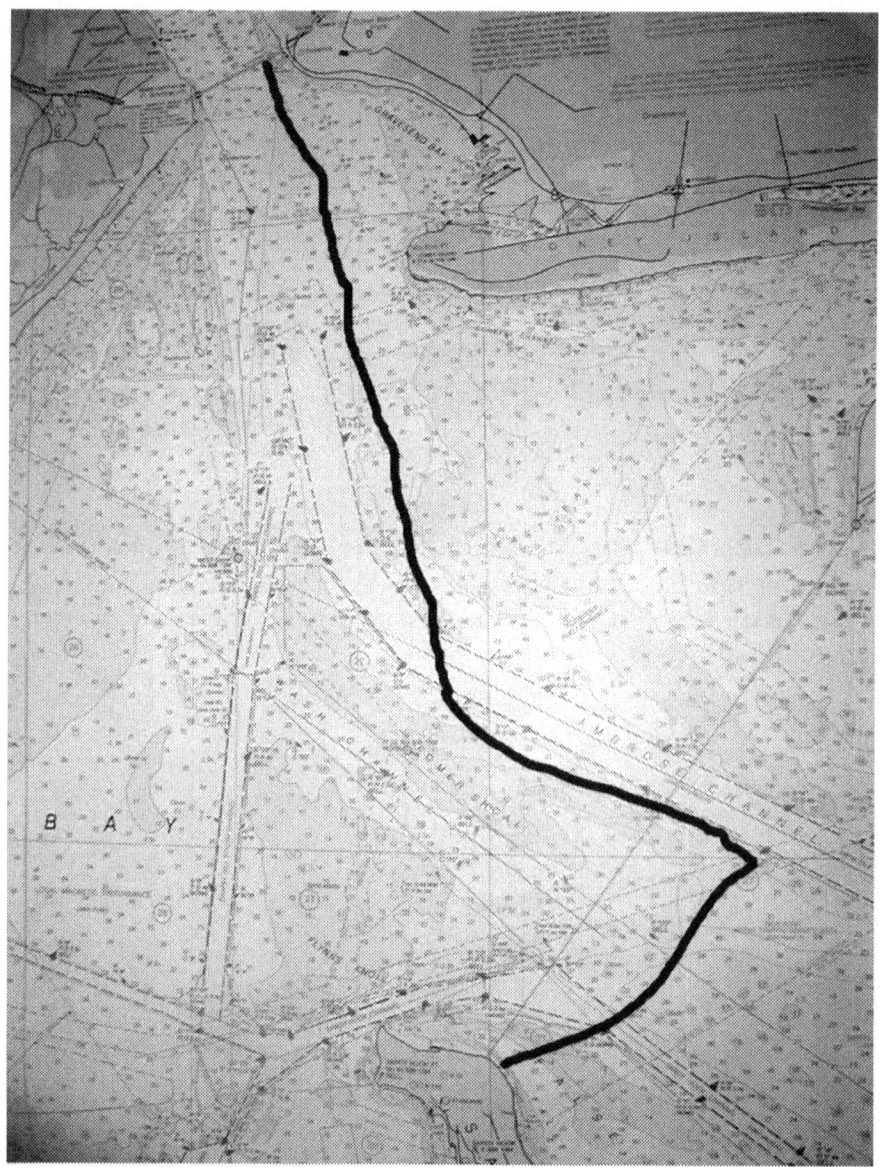

Figure 105 Second half of the GEMS course from chart 12327. In Tammy's swim, she turned before reaching buoy 3A to swim directly to the beach.

Figure 106 While passing the Statue of Liberty, Tammy ran into a boat wake. That's Bea Hartigan amidship; Nancy Schnarr at the stern quarter.

Figure 107 Tammy right now is cruising at 4 knots in the current south of the VN Bridge. Brooklyn is in the background.

Chapter 15   Organized swims

Florida swims

Ron Collins wanted to bring some attention to the Tampa Bay Open Water Challenge, a 3½-mile swim across Tampa Bay he helped establish in 1997. So with the help of Randy Nutt, the organizer of the Key West Marathon Swim, and his coach, Kelly Allen, he swam 24 miles down the length of Tampa Bay in 9:52. The following year, 14 swimmers showed up to compete over the distance. That year, 1999, was won by Chris Derks, a veteran of the Manhattan marathon in a time of 8:23. The first woman to complete the swim was Gail Rice in the 1999 race; she had eight dolphins come alongside for the last two miles. They shrieked so loudly, Gail couldn't hear the boat engine.[764] The following year on April 22, 2000, Chris Derks again won in 8:31 over 19 competitors. April 23, 2001 once again found Chris Derks winning although with his slowest time, 9:04 over a field of 21 swimmers. April 20, 2002 saw Chris Derks, now age 31, ramp it up with his best time yet, 7:41 against 14 competitors. Randy Nutt has kayaked for him in every one of his wins. Finally, on April 19, 2003, saw a new champion in Dave Parcells, age 44 of Connecticut, finish in a time of 10:24 against a field of seven swimmers. In 2004, Denis Crean, age 43, of Washington, DC, finished first out of 13 competitors in a time of 9:20. This was his first swim in a distance over 4 miles. Their web site for more information is: www.distancematters.com.

The Key West Marathon Swim is 12½ miles and features clean, clear, warm waters with very little current in a fabulous swimming location: Key West, Florida. The race is one lap around the island and it first began on July 4, 1977, when Anna Fugina-Pennella, a registered nurse, age 25, decided to swim around Key West. She started out swimming in a clockwise direction from Mallory Square in the northwest corner of Key West accompanied by friend in a rowboat. Within the first mile of the swim, she turned east and went under the Fleming Key Bridge fighting a current but when she came to Cow Key Channel along the eastern edge of Key West, she had to hold up in a cove out of the current until the tide changed. She started the swim at daybreak and finished just before sunset, taking 12:58 to make the circumswim. By the next year, she had met a boat captain, Chris Markley, who helped her time the swim better. Anna invited some friends along for the swim in 1978, finishing in 8 hours and the Key West swim had begun in earnest.

1st Place Finishers
Annual Swim Around
Key West

Year	Name	Time
1977	Anna Fugina	12:59
1978	Anna Fugina	8:00
1979	Maria Martin	6:17
1980	Chris Howe	5:35
1981	Karen MacGinnis	5:34
1982	Karen MacGinnis	4:59:45
1983	Karl Miller	6:46:29
1984	David Scofield	6:25:18
1985	David Scofield	6:01:39
1986	Paulette Maccione	6:12:28
1987	Paulette Maccione	6:47:28
1988	Rick Canaveri	5:14:00
1989	Dave Emmich	5:10:07
1990	William Black	4:28:31
1991	Ham Homan	4:36:12
Tie	Alex Ryan	4:36:12
1992	Matthew Honan	5:35:05
1993	Richard Kramer	4:22:12
1994	Gail S. Rice	4:23:19
1995	David Tyler	4:12:06
1996	Gabe Lindsey	3:43:57
1997	Mildtag Vasic	3:46:54
1998	Alex Kostich	3:45:35
1999	Gabe Lindsey	3:31:28
2000	Diane Dedek	5:46:00

2001	Bill Welzien	5:51:22
2002	Bill Welzien	5:27:20
2003	Bill Welzien	5:29:00
2004	Bill Welzien	5:35:29
2005	Tim Waid	5:22:49
2006	Marcos Diaz	3:54:31

Over the years the swim start changed just as it has in the Manhattan swim. Presently, the swim starts at the Smathers Street Beach, east of the Bertha Street Boat Ramp along the southern coast of Key West, west of the airport. The swim is still swum clockwise. Coming out of Cow Key Channel are some mud flats that force the swimmer to keep in the designated boat channel and the occasional submerge rock that you should be aware of. Randy Nutt was the race director from 1993 to 2000 and the swim grew from small numbers to over 300 one year. The application for the 2007 swim, the swim's 31th anniversary, on June 16th is found at their web site www.swimaroundkeywest.com. The current race director is Bill Welzien who has swum around Key West over 24 times. He has been known to rip Portugese Man-of-War jellyfish from his chest and keep on swimming. A safety precaution is every swimmer must have a kayak or rowboat accompany them. The swim has more than one version. Lori Bosco is the contact for the other Key West swim. Her contact is aqualb@aol.com. When visiting Key West, conch soup is a source of local pride and who can forget their key lime pies?

Caribbean swims

One of the direct results of the Key West swim was the St. Croix swim in the US Virgin Islands. Elizabeth Armstrong and Bob Halk came to Key West in 1995 as part of a relay. They asked Randy Nutt to help them start a swim in St. Croix. The first year, 1996, Randy Nutt talked them through the process then joined them for the successive years. This swim is 5 miles long in the US Virgin Islands. It starts at Buck Island, two miles off the St. Croix coastline and then swings eastward along St. Croix's rocky beaches into Mermaid Beach at the foot of the Buccaneer Hotel. George Gleason won the first race in 1996 in a time of 2:27. The second year, 1997, saw 77 swimmers with a Junior division swimmer, Kieran Locke of the Blue Marlin Swim Team, posting the fastest time of 1:49, considerably faster than last year but it turns out he had lots of company. The 3rd Annual swim, 1998, saw Bill Smith of New York, NY, winning in a slow time of 1:53 but he was 8 minutes ahead of the previous winner, Kieran Locke. Then in 1999, Alex Kostich from Los Angeles began showing up and winning. He is the swim superstar, his winning times: 1999, 1:50; 2000, 1:44; 2001, 1:44; 2002, 1:36; 2003, 1:45; 2004, 1:47; 2005, 1:37; 2006, 1:43. Jim Barber from Indiana has given Alex some competition over the years. Jim was the 1991 Manhattan Marathon winner as well as the first male finisher in 1988 and 1989 behind Shelley Taylor. The next swim, the Twelfth Annual Coral Reef 5-Mile Swim, is scheduled for October 21, 2007. [765] Visit the web site for the Buccaneer Hotel in St. Croix, www.thebuccaneer.com, and click on Events.

Randy Nutt began organizing a swim in the Dutch island of Bonaire in the Netherlands Antilles after leaving the Key West swim in 2000. The Bonaire Ecoswim features a 5K swim in beautiful waters over reefs that have been protected since 1979. Their reefs start 20 yards off the beach, much like Hanauma Bay in Hawaii. The swim course leaves from Captain Don's Habitat on Bonaire, south along the coast, west across the channel separating Bonaire from Klein Bonaire, north along the Klein Bonaire coast to a turning buoy and them back via the same route to the start. A talented Dutch youngster named Vincent van Rutten, age 14, from Curacao took top honors against a very strong field in the first race held on November 30, 2001. His time was 1:13 with Evan Welting, age 27, of Loganville, Georgia, just 16 seconds behind. The top female finisher was Welting's older sister, Laureen, age 36, in 1:14.5 who is the assistant Masters coach at The Olympic Club in San Francisco. Proving that his first place was not a fluke, the next year saw the same youngster again take all comers in storm-tossed waters on December 7, 2002.

Figure 108 Bonaire swim start.

New races at different distances have been added since then. This information and recent events results are available at the web site: www.RandyNutt.com. Randy recommends that when you are on the island to check out the homemade deserts at Capriccio's Restaurant.

Randy has undertaken coordination of an older swim in the islands, The Annual Bermuda Around the Sound swim. This swim has been around for nearly twenty years. There are a variety of lengths up to 10K.

A new swim in the Caribbean area is the Power Swim first held on St. John, Virgin Island in 2004. It's a three mile swim from Maho Bay to Hawksnest Bay. This year's swim was won by Kieran Locke in a time of 1:11, two seconds ahead of 2nd place finisher, Josh Laban in the dash to the finish after a dead heat in the water.[766] More information on this swim can be found by contacting Friends of the Virgin Island National Park at 340-779-4940 or visit www.friendsvinp.org and click on news and events.

Boston Light

The Boston Light Marathon swim is the oldest in the nation having competitions dating from 1907. It is a regional event, similar to the 100 years old Boston running marathon. Over its history the swim course has varied but the one constant is Boston Light. The present swim starts in the water at the foot of the 102-foot tall Boston Light, the only manned lighthouse on the east coast, located at the southern entrance to Boston Harbor on Little Brewster Island. Swimmers on a flood tide make their way into the L Street Baths in South Boston, the home of the L Street Brownies. They swim along Nantasket Road passing a number of islands that are now called the Harbor Islands and under the Long Island Bridge. Turning left past Thompson Island, you can make a beeline for the finish. If you are fast enough, you beat the tide that slows the rest of the pack behind the winners. This swim is a perfect test if you are thinking about the English Channel. It is ideal for swimmers who would like to try an ocean swim in cold water before tackling any significant distance events. The swim benefited significantly when the quality of the water in Boston harbor was questioned in the 1988 Presidential contest between Michael Dukakis and George H. Bush. The result was a massive cleanup of the harbor that makes this one of the best swims in the country.

At one time, Jim Doty was the driving force behind this swim and he is still a familiar face at the race. John Werner is the present race director whose team consists of Fred Knight and John Langton, Jr. The swim course has changed over the decades. Originally, the swim began at the head of the Charles River to the lighthouse at the southern entrance to Boston Harbor. Swimmers would leave on an ebb tide. The course is through the harbor islands, is in protected waters, and is 10 statute miles long. Like all positives, there are some negatives: the picturesque islands that mark your course create eddies and crosscurrents that complicate the swim. In the nineteen twenties, amateur swims were first organized starting at the lighthouse and finishing at the L Street Bath house in South Boston. Present day swims follow this same course where the swimmers start on a flood tide. The swimmers meet for a pre-race dinner at a local yacht club where swim traditions are learned and swim stories are shared. The top prize for the race winner is the silver Paul Revere Liberty Bowl.

More information can be found on their web site: www.bostonlightswim.org. If you are visiting in Boston, sample the New England clam chowder for a taste of the local cuisine. My favorite seafood establishment is the *Barking Crab* on the Fort Point Channel by Rowe's Wharf.

Figure 109 A view of the Boston Lighthouse with Boston in the background.

The early history of the swim stretches back for almost a century and the first swim are lost in the haze of history. The swim is mentioned in the newspapers during the 1907 Old Home Week celebration held in September of that year. Three men were known to have competed, Samuel Richards, Alfred Brown, and Louis Jacot. Louis hung on to win seeing the other men had dropped out of the swim.[767] They swam from Charlestown to Boston Light.

On August 29th, 1909, Alois Anderle[768], age 46, of New York swam from Charlestown Bridge to Boston Light. The distance he swam is 8.3 nautical miles or 10 statute miles via the shortest route: out the mouth of the Charles River, through the inner harbor, keeping north of Lower Middle to join President Roads, south to Nantasket Road via The Narrows to the Lighthouse. Alois was originally from Austria. The contest began at 8:30 am with eight other contestants but he was the only one to finish. The time was 5:38.[769] One year Alois was disqualified because he walked across a small island called Nixes Mate.

In 1910, Rose Pitonoff, age 17, finished the swim in 6:50. The following year, 1911 the competition included four swimmers: Samuel Richards of Boston, Charles Durborow of Philadelphia, Edward Gunnerson of East Boston, and Louis Hagan of South Boston. The only one to finish was Samuel Richards, Jr. of Boston who completed the swim in 6:15 on August 6, 1911.[770] On August 20th, another 17-year old girl, Alsie Aykroyd, was the only successful swimmer out of four to complete the swim. She managed to finish in 7:12.[771] One of her competitors who dropped out was Alois Alderle, the first person to complete the swim.

The year 1912 saw Richards complete the swim to Boston Light in 5:15 and in a second swim swam to the light and back, a distance of 24 miles in 13:09.[772] Another competitor in that swim to the Light on July 14th, 1912, was John Bray. The 1914 swim saw 17 swimmers line up for the contest on Sept 6th. No one reached the light, possibly owing to a miscalculation of the tides. Jack Hurwitz was awarded first place for being in the lead at the time the swim was called off. Charles Durborow was in fourth at the time.[773]

On August 19, 1915, Henry Miren, age 18, swam from Charlestown Bridge to Boston Light in 4:54 on an ebb current. Henry picked up the fastest time having bested the 5:15 by Sam Richards done in 1912. Both were members of the L Street Swimming Club.[774] On August 14, 1921, Charles Toth won the swim in 5:37 against 4 competitors.[775] The following year, 1922, John Bray at age 60 won the event.[776] As the event developed over time, it featured a professional race and two amateur races, a men and women race that may or may not occur at the same time.

In 1925, 16 amateur swimmers started on August 16th at the Warren Street wharf in Charlestown, and two competitors actually finished the race, a first for the swim. The winner was Max Patterson, age 39, of Bridgeport, Connecticut, in a time of 7:20. The second place was by Max Freedman of Beachmont in a time of 8:30.[777] The L Street Bath sponsored this race even though the race didn't start or finish at L Street. A second contest was held on August 30th sponsored by the AAU with a race for women and a race for men. Irene Hesenius won the women's race in a time of 8:07 and Thomas Quinn won the men's race in a time of 7:02. The race went from Charlestown to Boston Light.[778] In 1927 Frances Vincent of East Boston won the woman's race.[779]

In 1928 no one finished the traditional course from Charlestown to Boston Light. The swimmer who went the furthest received first prize: Miss Grace Currier, age 16, who swam nude, taking her suit off after entering the water and replacing it before exiting.[780] In the same year, 1928, the first swim from Boston Light to the L Street Bathhouse at Carson Beach was held. Jimmy Cullen of Charlestown won swimming the trudgeon stroke in a time of 4:46.[781] The same event was held in 1929.[782] Anna Pearson won the women's race in 1929 from Charlestown to Boston Light in a time of 7:26.[783] In 1930, San Richards won the professional race from Charlestown to Boston Light in 6:10 against six competitors.[784] The year 1931 saw a disputed finish in the men's race. Bill Hanley won the race from Boston Light to Carson Beach but was disqualified at the awards ceremony because he had swum the course a week earlier in the professional race, won by Jim Cullen. The declared winner of the 1931 swim was John Mullen who finished 5 minutes behind.[785] Hanley protested, as he had not entered the earlier swim as a professional.

The next year 1932, the swim from Charlestown to Boston Light held on August 14th featured a combined professional and amateur swim. The professional swimmer, Joe Nunan, age 20, finished in 5:01 and the amateur swimmer, John Jarosh, age 24, finished in 5:05.[786] The Boston Globe erroneously declared both men as setting the professional and amateur marks with their times.

The paper seems to have forgotten that Henry Miren broke the five-hour mark in 1915. The next year saw Joe Nunan wining the annual swim to Boston Light in 5:44.[787] In 1934, Charlotte Arne, age 17, swam to Boston Light and back in 13:30 becoming the first women to complete this feat.[788] In 1936 Joe Nunan was the only finisher in the race from Boston Light followed by Johnny Mullen in 1937 who set a record of time of 3:35 from Boston Light to the L Street Baths. In 1938, Russel Doucette wins the same race in a time of 3:43 passing Johnny Mullen while doing so. Joe Nunan was a six-time winner of the event.[789]

When the swim resumed in the mid seventies after a lapse, the swim was held once a summer over the reverse course, this distance is approximately 8 nautical miles. The swimmers would start in the water in the vicinity of Boston Light and initially would swim to the Aquarium in Boston Harbor. The first year, 1976, Jim Doty, age 39, was the winner in a time of 5:39. The next year over the same course RoAnn Costin, age 24 and a former All-American swimmer from Radcliffe College, won the event in a time of 5:21.

Modern Records Boston Light Swim (incomplete)

Date	1st Place Finisher	Hometown	Time
2006	Mark Warkentin	Santa Barbara, CA	2:26
2005	Dori Miller	Somerville, MA	3:04
2004	Bill Ireland	Los Angeles, CA	3:14
2003	Will Riddell	Cambridge, MA	3:05
2002	Marcia Cleveland	Riverside, CT	2:47
2001	Fred Knight	Wayland, MA	4:59
2000	Meryem Masood	New York	3:31
1999	Tom Dugan		4:36
1998	Ireana Sombera	Orleans, MA	3:13
1977	RoAnn Costin	Cambridge, MA	5:21
1976	Jim Doty		5:39

Other New England swims

Another swim of like difficulty to the Boston Light swim was the Boston to Graves Light. The Graves is an island at the end of an archipelago, some little more than rocks that uncover at low tide, on the *northern* entrance to Boston Harbor. The distance from South Boston is 7½ nautical miles via President Roads, past Deer Island Light, through Hypocrite Channel, and finally passing Roaring Bulls to reach Graves Island. Jim Doty and others would swim on an ebb tide out to Graves then return on the flood tide. It took them a little over 11 hours to complete the swim.

The Egg Rock swim was just north of Boston. The city of Lynn looks out over Nahant Bay. About two miles offshore is a small, uninhabited island called Egg Rock that birds live on. For a period of time, a race around the island was another swim that Jim Doty organized. The distance from Lynn Beach around Egg Rock and back was very close to four miles.

One swim that will never have too many takers was successfully completed by Jim Doty on his second try was a swim around Cape Ann. He left from the northern end of the Annisquam Canal by the yacht club. The Annisquam Canal makes Cape Ann an island. He finished by swimming across Gloucester Harbor, pass Norman's Woe Rock[790] and up onto shore at Norman's Woe in a time of 12:43. The distance is around 14 nautical miles of cold, open-water, ocean swimming. With the right tide, he could have made it completely around by swimming up the canal, but that will await another day and another swimmer.

In a swim in Maine, he swam from the entrance of the Saco River, just north of Kennebunkport to Prouts Point, a distance of about 6 miles. This swim crosses the cove that defines Old Orchard Beach. He kept extending the swim as he went along because two dolphins came alongside. As long as they were with him, he kept swimming. He enjoyed immensely the thrill of this opportunity to swim with the dolphins. Incidentally, this location is less than ten miles north of Cape Porpoise, Maine.

Jim Doty didn't believe in doing the same swim twice. Another fun swim in the vicinity of Cape Ann he completed was from Marblehead to Gloucester, a distance of slightly over 9 miles with lots of interesting islands, such as, Great Misery Island. One of the islands in Salem Sound, Bakers Island, is inhabited. What he remembers about this swim was the frothy water; a storm had blown through the night before and stirred the water up.[791] He also swam out to Appledore Island in the Isles of Shoals, a group of islands 5 miles off shore from Portsmouth Harbor. Jim started this swim from Jenness Beach just south of Rye Harbor making the distance around 6 miles. One of the shorter swims he and Jack Starett did was to swim out of Rockport Harbor across Sandy Bay to the breakwater, a distance of 1½ mile. Further north, Jim swam all the major lakes in New Hampshire. This would include Lake Winnipesaukee, the largest lake in New Hampshire. The course for that swim was from Alton to Center Harbor, New Hampshire, a distance of approximately 22 miles.

Not wanting to ignore Cape Cod and vicinity, Jim Doty swam from West Chop on Martha's Vineyard to Woods Hole on the mainland, a distance of less than a mile but in waters feared by mariners because of the ferocity of the currents in the close vicinity to rocks. Jim completed a series of swims in Buzzards Bay from each of the Elizabeth Island to Pandanaram-Harbor. The names of these islands and distances are: Naushon, Pasque, Nashawena, and Cuttyhunk. All these islands are between 11 and 12 miles in distance from Pandanaram, a lovely, picturesque village on an inlet west of New Bedford. During the swim from Cuttyhunk, the seas in Buzzards Bay were serious enough that Jim enjoyed bodysurfing down the backsides. He noticed below him a huge number of lion mane jellyfish that were staying submerged due to the rough conditions on the surface; otherwise, he said his swim would have been compromised.[792]

Lake Winnipesaukee in New Hampshire was first swum in 1964 by Dr. Harry Briggs. Besides Jim Doty, Bob Weir swam the length, a distance of 22 miles, in 1994. On 1995, Julie Burnett, age 29, of Stoneham, Massachusetts became the first woman to swim the lake. She started at 3am from Downing's Marina in Alton and finished 12 hours later at Center Harbor.[793]

Further south in New England, Jim Bayles, age 52, a resident of Westport, Connecticut, has been churning out a variety of swims since the late 90's.[794] Jim swam from the Tappan Zee Bridge to Midtown Manhattan in 1997. This course is similar to the one followed by the Swim Across America organization sans the full body wetsuits permitted in their swims. In 1998 he swam from Greenwich, Connecticut, to South Street Seaport in lower Manhattan via the Long Island Sound and the East River in approximately 12 hours. His next swim was the reverse of the Battery to Sandy Hook swim whose record is held by Gertrude Ederle of 7:11. Jim swam in the opposite direction on September 20, 2000 in 9:07. He is the first person to swim the course in this direction. In 2004 he swam from Cape Cod to Nantucket Island. The start point of the swim at the southern tip of Monomoy Island was at one time connected to the mainland and he landed at the foot of the lighthouse at Great Point on Nantucket, the northern most point. His time for this swim was 5:02. His most recent swim in 2005 was from Point Judith to Block Island. Point Judith is a point of land near the western entrance to Narragansett Bay. Block Island is located east of the end of Long Island and was at one time a sought-after resort for vacationers. He is the first person to swim this course in over 20 years after the venue was abandoned by the professional swimming circuit. His time for the swim was 5:04.

Lake Champlain, a long narrow body of water that serves as the border between upstate New York and Vermont, has an 8 mile marathon swim from Willsboro, NY to Oakledge Park in Burlington, VT. The swim is a fund raiser for the Greater Burlington YMCA and is in its eight year. On August 5, 2006, thirty-seven people made the swim through white-caps and boat wakes. The winner was Lisa Neidrauer, age 33, of Toronto in a time of 3:51.[795]

British Long Distance Swimming Association

An organization dedicated to open water swimming is the British Long Distance Swimming Association. It was formed in 1960. Most swimming clubs organized to promote open water swimming among local swimmers belong to this organization. They coordinate finances, awards, recognition, a championship, and records for long distance swimming in the United Kingdom. An early objective of the BLDSA is to have the sport of long distance swimming recognized with a place in the Olympic Games. There is a regular circuit of swims on: Lake Coniston, 3¼ miles; Lake Windermere, 10½ miles; Loch Lomond, 21.6 miles; Wykeham Lakes, a small lake with races of varying distances utilizing laps; Torbay, an ocean swim of 4 miles and 8 miles (a return lap); Bala, with swims up to 6 miles (2-way); Lynn Regis, with events of varying lengths; Rivington Reservoir with events up to 4 miles; Derwentwater, a lake near Keswick with swims up to 5¼ miles; and their Champion of Champions swim held in Cotswold Water Park whose distance were multiple circuits of a one mile course of up to 5 miles. The Channel Swimming Association regularly sends a secretary's report into the BLDSA. They have a regular means for recording swims outside of normal events. The swimmer has a swim certified by an observer who would be a member of BLDSA. The observer would certify that all the open water-swimming rules were observed. This allows for a bit of independence and ingenuity on the part of swimmers to undertake unusual swims in locations where no local swim organization exists to certify a swim. Chris Green has completed a half-century (50) of Morecambe Bay and recorded them all along with his international swims. It adds a measure of confidence to report a certified swim that meets known standard. More information can be found on their web site: www.bldsa.org.uk. The history and details of these swims is contained in Gerald Forsberg book *Modern Long Distance Swimming* published in 1963.

I was the observer for Chris Green's record swim of Morecambe Bay when he broke Gerald Fosberg's long-standing record for swimming round-trip across Morecambe Bay. Gerald credits a Professor Stearne, a swimming instructor from Manchester, as the first person to cross Morecambe Bay, in 1907 in a time of 3:45.[796] Chris had just returned to swimming the Bay after being severely stung by a jellyfish on his 49th crossing. The swimmer begins in Morecambe, a town just north of Blackpool, near the wharf and swims to Grange-over-Sands. The swim is completely tidal as the entire bay except for a small channel is a mud flat that fills with water at high tide. Chris had as his pilot, a local fisherman who understood well the current flows and to whom most of the credit for the record should go. At the finish, Chris using the current swept around the new pier at Morecombe into some slack water behind the pier and made it to shore breaking the existing record by 4 minutes.

The BLDSA 49th Windermere Championship was held on September 3, 2005. Adam Harvey and Rebecca Lewis finished first and second in times of 4:06 and 4:08 over the 10.5 mile course. Lee Portingale was the 2nd male finisher in this race and Chris Green was 13th. The Champion of Champions 5 mile swim and for that matter the 3 mile and the 1 mile was won by Lee Portingale of Bristol against a large field in times of 2:01, 1:15, and 0:23. The event was held at Cotswold Water Park on June 12, 2005. Lee also swept first place in the 48th Annual Torbay Championship 8-mile swim with a time of 3:09. The Coniston Lake swims were held and the comment about the swim was that it was a "veritable steam bath" what with the water temperature at 68~ on July 16, 2005. Rebecca Lewis locked in first place for the 5.5 miles with a 1:50. The premier event, the Loch Lomond Championship, a 21.6 mile swim was held starting on July 31 and finishing on August 1, 2005 and featured a moonlight swim. Six swimmers started, five finished and the winner was Dee Llewellyn at 10 hours flat establishing a new course record.[797]

The Channel Islands

A group of 8 inhabited island that belong to the Crown yet reside closer to France is populated by about 160,000 people[798] with more marathon swimmers per capita than anywhere else in the world. One donation to the New World was the name New Jersey. The two main islands are Jersey and Guernsey. Jersey is so close to Frande that 8 people have actually swum to or from the Continent. The distance is only 14.8 miles. This past summer two swimmers vied for the title for fastest transit with Lt. Col. Tim Lawrence of the USAF Academy in a new record of 8:17. The local residences put up their own champion in the person of Ian Jones, age 34, who lowered the record to 7:47.

This course was first swum in 1966 by 16 year old Denize le Pennec in a time of 9:35 after swimming the English Channel. Denize then upped the ante by swimming around Jersey in September of 1969 in a time of 13:55. This was no small swim as it's a 41 mile journey in one go. There are tides to consider. To date 48 people have made the trip around Jersey, some more than once. The records for this marathon swim stands at 9:54 set in August of 1989 by Alison Streeter.

Swimming around Guernsey didn't begin until 1998 but is not nearly as popular as swimming around Jersey. The other island have had a few takers along with swimming between islands. The first recorded swim in this neighborhood was in 1962 when a Ruth Oldham swim from Guernsey to Jersey, 18 miles, in 15:15. There is a local long distance swimming club that organizes and maintains the records: Jersey Long Distance Swimming Club. They regularly organize relays and send members and teams overseas to compete in other well-known swimming venues.[799] I was personally present in 2006 at the International Swimming Hall of Fame dinner where Alison Streeter was being honor and the Jersey swimmers challenged the Connecticut swimmers present to a relay race across the English channel two years hence. Their web site is www.jerseyseaswims.org. The club has a unique advantage because it has its own support boat for ocean swims.

Hawaiian swims

Channel swims in warm water would seem ideal to marathon swimmers but few have traveled to Hawaii to partake of this pleasure. Except for the Auau (Maui) Channel swim, which is a popular relay swim, only a handful of swimmers have tried any of the seven channel swims with the Auau Channel being the most popular. No one has swum all seven although Linda Kaiser has completed five of them with Harry Huffaker and Carl Kawauchi having complete four.[800] Here's the list:

Channel	From	To	Miles	1st Swimmer	Year	Total
Kaiwi	Molokai	Oahu	26	Keo Nakama	1961	8
Auau	Lanai	Maui	8.8	Jim Caldwell	1970	114
Kalohi	Molokai	Lanai	9.3	Bob Justman	1978	11
Alalakeiki	Kahoolawe	Maui	7	Carl Kawauchi	1992	8
Palilolo	Maui	Molokai	8.5	Jim Caldwell	1973	16
Alenuihaha	Hawaii	Maui	30	Harry Huffaker	1970	1
Kaulakahi	Kauai	Niihau	17	Linda Kaiser	2003	4

Keo Nakama's swim from Molokai to Oahu woke up the Hawaiians to the nearly limitless possibilities of ocean swimming.[801] The story to his success comes from the failures by another swimmer. In January of 1961, Greta Anderson was toasted by Moroni Medeiros (a.k.a. Ron Maury), who ran unsuccessfully for Lt. Governor, in a "Salute to Greta Andersen" dinner and spectacular water show in the Duke Kahanamoku Lagoon at the Hawaiian Village Hotel. Greta received tremendous assistance and cooperation by all the Hawaiian swimmers who participated in the tribute: Richard Cleveland, Tom Haine, Takashi "Halo" Hirose, David and Duke Kahanamoku, Thelma Kalama, Fujiko Katsutani, Evelyn Kawamoto, Herbert Kobayashi, Ford Konno, Chic Miyamoto, Julia Murakami, Keo Nakama, Charlie Oda, George Onekea, Pete Powlison, Carlos Rivas, Bill Smith, Jr., Allan Stack and Bill Woolsey. She also received encouragement from Hawaiian swim coaches: Dad Center, Bobby Rath, Soichi Sakamoto and Yoshito Segawa at the dinner. Surfers participating were Noah Kalama, Peter Cole, Conrad Canha, George Downing, Wally Froiseth, Richard "Buffalo" Keaulana, Rabbit Kekai, Tom Kekuna, Jane Koapuiki, Joseph Koapuiki, Ethel Kukea, Turkey Love, John Lind, Nappy Napoleon, Gene Smith, and Edward Whaley. The state outrigger champions came: Bobby Beck, Doug

Carr, Timmy Guard, Henry Hollinger, Bob Moncrief, and Rick Steere with their coach, George Downing. It was a great send off and auspicious occasion for the initiation of a great swim by a great swimmer.

The first attempt on January 28, 1961 began at 6:55am leaving from Ilio Point on Molokai. After nine miles of swimming, she was locked in a struggle with a current and made no progress for 3 hours. As night fell, Greta detected the presence of four sharks as large as surfboards by the phosphorescence created by their wake, swimming below her. She yelled at her escorts but they didn't believe her. Stung by jellyfish and seasick, she eventually pulled out of the swim at 11:33pm about 4 miles short of Oahu.[802] In March, she promised another attempt using the tide information learned from the first swim and she would take seasick pills.[803] In April of 1961, using a 12' by 16' shark cage made by George Downing of Honolulu, she set off again after delaying the start two days for a storm. In hindsight, they might have been better off waiting an additional day as they encounter rough seas where she got seasick again. This was prior to the medical studies by the space program that developed newer, more effective drugs to counteract motion sickness. Still she swam for 22.5 hours and 18 miles before giving up.[804] While she felt badly at not having made the swim, her efforts were valuable lessons to those observing the swim. On September 29 of 1961, Keo Nakama completed the 26-mile swim in 15:37. While Keo swam alongside a support boat, as a precaution, a shark cage made of rebar and chicken wire was brought along. To succeed where Greta Anderson had failed who was an Olympic champion, an English Channel record holder, and the first person to do a double in the Catalina Channel was quite an accomplishment.

The Auau (Maui) Channel has been taking place for over twenty years. It occurs during the Labor Day weekend. The nine-mile race is between Lanai and Maui Islands. The race is a popular relay event and fun. Names for the teams are made up and records of who swam are not easy to find. One consistent top finisher is a relay team made up by Bob Placak, a former All-American swimmer from UCLA. In fact, he has been in 18 races as of 2003 and his teams have finished first 14 times.[805] The winning times are close to the 3-hour mark. There are lots of divisions and solo swimmers in this event are the reason the Auau Channel swim has the highest total of successful swim seen in the table above. The best information regarding Hawaiian swims can be found at www.hawaiiswim.org.

The Hawaiian Islands Channel Swim Association (HCSA) was formed in the 1980's to record and certify channel swims. Carl Kawauchi is keeping the records for the HCSA. Hawaiian channel records have not made a practice of recording the times for all of the crossings and rather than publish an incomplete list, they've decided to simply acknowledge the swim but not publish any times.[806] Carl made the 1st crossing of Kahoolawe to Maui. An interesting story about that swim is the start was changed by happenstance. His planned initial starting location of Becks Bay it turned out was loaded with sharks. This information was learned from Navy Lt. Young assigned to escort him on a tour of the island before the swim start.[807] Lieutenant Young had spent time on the island of Kahoolawe and remarked that he could see sharks in Becks Bay from the top of the 1000' cliffs surrounding the bay. Carl is quite happy he had this observant young officer assist him on his scouting out of the swim. Carl's final thought on the subject was that if the sharks could be seen from a thousand feet away, they must be big sharks.

Fish is an important staple of the Hawaiian diet. Local chiefs have taken traditional Hawaiian food and blended new delights from the different cuisines of the immigrant cultures present on Hawaii, making what is known as fusion cuisine.[808] It's hard to not enjoy a trip to the Hawaiian Islands to take a swim.

Irish Sea swims

If you are thinking about an Irish Sea swim, possible across the North Channel, contact Joe Gunn of the Irish Long Distance Swimming Association at: jgunn1135@aol.com. He will put you in contact with a local person to help coordinate your swim. The pilot that has handled most of the swim for the last twenty years is Brian Meharg. His boats, *The White Heather*, a 1926 motor yacht, and the *Purple Heather* have been sold and he is now looking for a new boat to run his tourist business.

Be forewarned that the North Channel is tough. The summer months find the red *Lions Mane* jellyfish in abundance and the temperature of the water is much colder than the Channel. The average summer temperature is 56° F at best.

The first person to swim the North Channel was Tom Blower, age 33, on July 28, 1947 in a time of 15:26. He swam from Donaghadee in County Down to Portpatrick in Scotland, a distance of 21.6 miles. He died an early death, at age 41 of a heart attack.

It was a few years before anyone repeated the swim. The second person to swim across was Kevin Murphy from Middlesex on September 11, 1970 going from Ireland to Scotland 11:21. On August 29, 1971, he made a second crossing in the same direction in a time of 14:27. For his third and final crossing, 18 years later, he chose the opposite direction, going from Scotland to Ireland in 17:17, on September 7, 1989. He was going to do a double but the weather turned against him. The decision to swim again might have been motivated by some competition as Alison Streeter had turned her attention to the North Channel in Ireland.

Before Alison began her string of swims, Ted Keenam from Enniskillen in Northern Ireland crossed from Ireland to Scotlandin 18:27 on August 11, 1973. Ted is the only person from Ireland to have made the crossing. Ted also has notched on his belt the English Channel and the Bristol Channel.

In 1988, Alison Streeter began her trips across the North Channel. The first was on August 22, 1988, crossing from Ireland to Scotland in 9:53. This is the record for a crossing and still stands today. The following year, on August 25th, 1989, she crossed from Scotland to Ireland in a time of 10:04. These times are remarkably close for being in different directions requiring a different approach to the navigation. It was after this second swim that Kevin broke out his suit and knocked off a third swim.

Allison took a few years to reply but on August 18, 1997 she crossed from Scotland to Ireland in a time of 10:02. Besides being the Queen of the Channel, we could add consistency.

Allison's first swim was followed the next day, August 23, 1988, by Margaret Kidd from Ayrshire in Scotland in a time of 15:26. In 1999, on July 27th, Paul Lewis from Dorset in England swam from Scotland to Ireland in 14:28. The next year, Stephen Price from Somerset in England swam from Scotland to Ireland in 16:56. Finally, the most recent swim was on July 31, 2004, by Colm O'Neill from Dublin, Ireland, who swam from Scotland to Ireland in 11:25.[809]

Only 8 people have actually swum the North Channel. Normally, they have from 2 to 3 attempts a year. Besides Joe Gunn you can contact William Wallace, the secretary of the Irish Long Distance Swimming Association at 20 Cherryvale Avenue, Co. Antrim BT36 7UG, Tel. (011-44) (0)289-096-3536.

The North Channel is not the only place to swim in Ireland. In a first, Ned Denison of Cork swam clockwise around Great Island in Cork Harbor along the southern coast of Ireland in 7:18. He started and finished at Cuskinny Bay in the 16 mile circumswim. In his lead up to the swim he competed in three tune-up events organized locally: the Lee River swim (1900 meters through the town of Cork under 8 stone bridges), the 8-mile InisBofin swim, and an 8-mile Lake Champlain (State side) swim. The website: www.swimireland.ie links to Open Sea Swims that have a complete listing of their swims up to a 17 kilometer swim across Upper Lough Erne for their Irish Championship.[810]

Long Island Sound

The Long Island Sound is bound on the north by the Connecticut shore. The southern shore of this estuary is Long Island from which the Sound gets its name. The Sound runs the length of Connecticut and of Long Island, nearly 160 miles. The eastern end has the Race, Fisher Island and the North Fork of Long Island as it merges into Block Island Sound. It has varying width from the western end where the East River begins right at the

Throgsneck Bridge to the eastern end at Orient Point where the ferry from New London, Connecticut, docks. A powerful current sweeps the Sound from one end to the other exiting and entering from either The Race off Orient Point or by the East River. At its widest point, the Sound is 18 nautical miles wide. As the Sound broadens, this current lessens.

The history of swimming across the Long Island Sound begins on August 12, 1915, a 13-year old girl, Alice Lord, swam across Long Island Sound from Glen Cove to Rye, a distance of 3½ nautical miles, in 3:40.[811] Another short swim across the Sound occurred in 1924. On July 23, 1924, Axel Lindstrom, a Dane employed aboard a yacht docked in Rye, swam across the Long Island Sound from Hem Inlet near Rye Beach to the New York Yacht Club landing in Glen Cove, a distance of 7 nautical miles. The trip took 3:01. At the finish, he grabbed a bit to eat then returned to Connecticut via the launch that accompanied him.[812] The earliest reference to a swim across the width was in 1921 by Walter Patterson. The course was from Lordship Beach in Bridgeport, Connecticut, to Old Field Lighthouse, Long Island, which took Walter eleven hours even on August 31, 1921.[813] There appears to be some confusion in 1924 about the record as Paul Zegger of Hartford, Connecticut, on August 10, 1924, crossed the Sound in a time of 11:44 and claim to have bested Walter Patterson record time in 1919 by 11½ minutes.[814] Walter came in third in the 1924 race. In June of 1926, Clarebelle Barrett of New Rochelle, NY, swam from Hudson Park in New Rochelle past Premium Point to the Larchmont breakwater before across the Sound to Sea Cliff, Long Island, in 10½ hours.[815] This was a tune up for a channel attempt and some point was made that the water temperature wasn't over 60 degrees. That year, 1926, the Bayville Aquatic Club sponsored a swim from Greenwich, Connecticut, to Ferry Beach, Bayville, a distance of 8 miles. They had 25 starters and Adam Lucason of Worcester Boys Club of Worcester, Massachusetts, won the race in a time that was reported as less than 6 hours.[816]

In the Thirties, the swim started at Old Field Pt., Long Island with a destination of Lordship, Connecticut. This destination dropped a mile off the previous swims to Bridgeport, as the new distance for the course is 10½ nautical miles. On August 29, 1932, this swim had some difficulties with most of the 7 participants dropping out. The official launch even dropped out because they were running low on fuel. This caused a lack of communication. When the eventual finisher Leo Januski came ashore nine hours later at Milford, Connecticut, (a few miles further east) he was hailed as being saved.[817] Rather odd that because the organizers lost track of their swimmers, then when they do show up, they were regarded as having been saved. While the current is weak at this point of the Sound, over time it still causes considerable drift for the slower swimmers. They wind up swimming longer distances than the faster swimmers. This is the opposite effect of the Manhattan swim.

The swim went into a hiatus for a few years as we next hear of the swim in 1979 where it was a fundraiser for the Muscular Dystrophy Association (Jerry Lewis) as a one-time event. That swim was successfully completed in 5 hours by Ben Siebecker and is covered elsewhere in this history. There is one exception to this hiatus, a skin diver, Ray Griffith, age 33; starting at Bridgeport swam underwater across the Sound to Port Jefferson in 1960.[818]

The history of the venue morphing into a fundraiser is interesting. It's hard to ignore a swim that can raise $2 million dollars for a worthy cause. The present day Swim Across the Sound is just that and more. The swim is across the Long Island Sound from Port Jefferson, Long Island, to Captain's Cove in Bridgeport, Connecticut. This organized swim started in 1987 as an amateur relay by personnel from St. Vincent's Medical Center and one of its cancer patients who had lost a leg to cancer. The purpose was to raise awareness of the impact that cancer can have on an individual and their families. Each year funds are raised to help cancer patients deal with real life issues. In the swim's inaugural year, only $5000 was raised and the swim was the only fund raising event. This has now been expanded to include numerous other events like dinners, lunches, and breakfasts with or without celebrities, golf tournaments, bike rides, aquathons, radiothons, and walkathons. The programs funded by the swim and its related events have reached out to over 16,000 individuals in Southern Connecticut.

After five years as an amateur swim, the event became a venue for the FINA professional circuit. In 2001, another Shelley appeared in the United States, also from Australia ready to swim the arms off of her competitors. Shelley Clark finished first in the Swim Across the Sound marathon in a time of 5:58 for a 15-mile course from Long Island to Bridgeport, Connecticut.[819] This was a stop in her tour of Canada, US, UK, Italy, and Egypt professional swims over the summer of 2001. She then spent time down in Atlanta with Australian coach Gary Toner before continuing onto the UK. In 2006, the Swim Across the Sound was held on August 6th. An amateur record was set by Jeremy Virgil, age 26, of 6:32 for the course. He described the water as tasting very salty with jellyfish, water plants and "...a hint of diesel fuel".[820] The swim is a fund raising event held for the St. Vincent Medical Center Foundation with swimmers pledging to raise $1000 each. In this year, the swim event alone raised over $275,000 for the hospital. More information about this event is available on their web site: www.swimacrossthesound.org.

Australian swims

The world's largest open-swim held regularly is across the Rottnest Channel between the mainland of Australia at Fremantle and Rottnest Island a distance of about 20 kilometer (10.8 nautical miles) and it has been a huge success. Fremantle is a small town along the shore of Western Australia near the entrance to the busy harbor of Perth, Australia. The first person to swim across the channel was Gerd von Dincklage-Schulenburg on January 24th, 1956. Swimming from North Mole, Fremantle to Natural Jetty at Rottnest, he arrived in 9:45. This swim captured the imagination of a number of swimmers and nine swimmers competed in a race across the Channel with four of them finishing. Then the swim went into a hiatus for 13 years. Leslie Cherriman, swam across the channel from Rottnest to Fremantle on April 13th, 1969. She then repeated the swim in 1970. In 1971, she swam the channel from the other direction. Then the swim went into its second hiatus. The next swim wasn't until 1983 when the swim was adopted as a right of passage by freelance open-water swimmers. Swimmers began swimming across the channel on a regular basis.

In December of 1989 the Rottnest Channel Swimming Association was initiated by John Whitehead to promote swimming of the channel. The RCSA mission is to observe and authenticate persons who swim the Rottnest Channel; promote safety; advise and encourage swimmers wanting to make an attempt as well as gathering and preserving historical data from the crossings. It took a year to get the first race organized in 1991 and ever since then the swim takes place on the third Saturday in February. It's grown from 43 swimmers that first year to over 2000 annually. The responsibility of conducting a safe swim has grown, too. The RCSA works with an Emergency Control Organization that involves the Royal Life Saving Society, Fremantle Sea Rescue, Water Police, Department of Fisheries and the Rottnest Island Authority. Annually they review their management plan and safety systems using feedback from the various partners responsible for the safety of everyone participating in this event. Just the number of kayaks is staggering. The Australians and the RCSA are to be congratulated for putting the mechanism in place to handle this large number of swimmers safely over a significant ocean swim. In 2007 the event was cancel due to deteriorating weather conditions for the first time in its 17 year history. The present record for the swim is held by Mark Saliba of 4:00.[821] There is more information at the web site: www.rottnestchannelswim.com.au.

Located in the northeast corner of Australia is a swim from Magnetic Island, one of the offshore islands that make up the coastal barrier borders, to Townsville, Queensland, Australia. The distance is 5½ miles across Cleveland Bay with the swim starting in Hawkins Point on Magnetic Island to Townsville Harbor.

Douglas Pitt was the first person to swim cross on Australia Day in 1924. He was raising money for an attempt on the Channel when less than a dozen had made that swim. Douglas was a well-known Australian distance swimmer who never achieved his goal due to an early death. He was from Torres Strait and his knowledge of the local conditions led him to design and swim in a cage. The Cleveland Bay is notorious for shark attacks with over 30 reported attacks since Townsville was founded at the time of the original swim. Two years later, Bert Gard swam across, also on Australia Day and in another cage. He completed the swim in 3:23 and claimed a record.

It was over 30 years later before these pioneering swims were undertaken again and the onerous for the resumption was a visit to Townsville by Queen Elizabeth. A member of the Royal Tour Celebration Committee, Bob May, suggested and organized the event, which was held March 14, 1954. The Queen was only in Townsville for an hour but the committee in their exuberance organized two weeks of celebratory events. Following the custom, the first three competitors also swam in cages thus establishing the Magnetic Island Swim as the only shark cage competition in the world. The first organized competition went so well that the committee elected to stay together and thus in 2004 the swim celebrated their 50th anniversary. Due to the expense of providing cages, competitors are limited in number to less than 10. The record time for the crossing stands at 1:15 by David Stanton of Townsville set in the 1990 race on May 20th. Bob James is the local contact for this swim and can be reached by email at bobjames@ozemail.com.au. The Townsville Museum and Historical Society has just published the history of this swim that is well written, concise, and packed with photos. It offers a look at Australian swimmers on their home turf that is rarely seen.

1st Place finishers—Magnetic Island to Townsville Swim

Date	Name	Hometown	Time
4/14/1954	Kauko Kaurila	Ingham	2:04
4/3/1955	Ron Morrison	Picnic Bay	2:32

4/8/1956	Noel Craig	Townsville	2:10
5/26/1957	Noel Craig	Townsville	2:09
4/20/1958	Brian Hutchings	Bondi	2:10
4/19/1959	Chris Bell	Townsville	1:54
5/1/1960	John Gibson	Brisbane	2:15
4/23/1961	John Gibson	Brisbane	1:51
5/13/1962	John Kissane	Sydney	1:53
5/19/1963	John Rigby	Brisbane	2:03
5/3/1964	John Koorey	Sydney	2:01
5/9/1965	John Koorey	Sydney	1:58
5/15/1966	Rod McLeod	Ayr	2:00
5/15/1967	John Koorey	Sydney	2:11
5/19/1968	Rod McLeod	Ayr	1:57
11/2/1969	Barry Duhne	Adelaide	1:30
6/14/1970	Craig Crozier	Townsville	1:48
5/16/1971	Craig Crozier	Townsville	1:46
1972 thru 1976	Swim not held		
6/12/1977	Erick Blechen	Townsville	1:40
6/4/1978	Laurence Reece	Southport	1:44
6/17/1979	Mark Scully	Newcastle	1:33
6/15/1980	Jonathan Catana	Cairns	1:49
1981	Swim not held		
6/13/1982	Liz Grant	Sydney	1:33
6/5/1983	Justin Lemberg	Queensland	1:20
4/22/1984	Duncan Smith	Sydney	1:22
6/2/1985	Michael McKenzie	Brisbane	1:37
6/15/1986	Steve Holland	Queensland	1:24
8/2/1987	Guy Leech	NSW	1:41
8/21/1988	Michael McKenzie	Brisbane	1:29
8/13/1989	Duncan Armstrong	Brisbane	1:22
5/20/1990	David Stanton	Townsville	1:15:42
10/13/1991	David Lachea	Palm Beach	1:28

5/10/1992	David Stanton	Townsville	1:25
5/16/1993	Melissa Cunningham	Currumbin	1:37
7/17/1994	David Bates	Currumbin	1:18
6/18/1995	Joseph Mitchell	Newcastle	1:21
6/2/1996	Grant Robinson	Gosford	1:33
7/13/1997	Josh Santacaterina	Home Hill	1:34
7/12/1998	Josh Santacaterina	Brisbane	1:51
7/18/1999	Dylan Rackley	Burleigh Beach	1:26
6/25/2000	Melissa Irwin Jessica Affleck	Brisbane Townsville	1:21 (tie)
9/23/2001	Penny Palfrey	Townsville	1:40
6/30/2002	Leigh Bool	Ipswich, Qld	1:42
7/6/2003	Liam Anderson	Townsville	1:44
8/21/2004	Lauren Ardnt		1:32
9/10/2005	Bill Hall		1:41

Like all organizations, the people involved change and for a short period during the seventies the swim went into a hiatus. It's a compliment to the community, the swim supporters, as well as the swimmers when a swim can survive as long as this swim has.

Other swims in Australia are competed over shorter distances with the average length being 2 kilometers. The contests are held year-round. Some of these swims are the 2.2-kilometre Brighton Open Water Winter Classic, the Bondi-to-Watsons-Bay swim, the Palm Beach to Whale Beach swim, Sydney's Cole Classic at Bondi, and others. When winter temperatures or wearing a wet suit doesn't appeal and the budget allows, Australians head north for warmer waters at the Cocos Islands lagoon swim, Fiji, Hawaii, Vanuatu, and the Solomons. Many of these swims are listed on a website for ocean swimmers founded by Paul Ellercamp called www.oceanswim.com.[822] Some of these smaller swim attract upwards of 4,000 swimmers.

Monte Monfore, age 45, swam 3 kilometers across the Bali Straits on May 18, 2006 in a time of 00:29:30.[823]

Mid-Atlantic swims

Brian Joseph Earley, age 21, swam across the upper portion of the Chesapeake Bay from Kent Island on the Maryland shore to Sandy Point State Park on June 13, 1982, in memory of his father, Joseph Earley who had died of diabetes complications a year earlier. The distance is about 4½ miles and a conveniently place bridge roadway marks the course. Brian began an annual event and shortly afterward, Fletcher Hanks began a swim across the entrance to the Chesapeake Bay also marked by a bridge roadway. The Chesapeake Bay Bridge Tunnel was a considerably longer swim of 13 miles. In 1993, the two swims merged with the smaller venue being chosen to host the Great Chesapeake Bay Swim. The course now leaves from Sandy Point State Park, about 5 miles northeast of Annapolis to a sandy beach south of the William Preston Land Memorial Bridge adjacent to Hemingway Restaurant on Kent Island. The swim is now a fundraiser for the Maryland Chapter of the March of Dimes and is limited to 600 swimmers. US Masters Swimming does not sanction this swim, like the Manhattan Island Marathon swim. Swimmers are allowed to wear wetsuits which give your competitors an advantage, so in this sense, the swim is strictly a fundraiser. A problem with the currents in the early 1990s is discussed in the next chapter.

The Chesapeake Bay is a large estuary about half way up the United States eastern seaboard. The Bay borders on a number of states and communities and a trip to this swim requires one to indulge in a Maryland crab dinner. More information about the swim is located at: www.bayswim.com. Chuck Nabit is the Race Director for the Chesapeake Bay swims.

Atlantic City is closely tied to its wonderful waterfront and shoreline. Before Trump, there was the beauty pageant that made the Atlantic City boardwalk the place to be for beautiful girls and swimming. Gertrude Ederle came to Atlantic City after her channel swim for vacation. The Atlantic City Beach Patrol is renowned for their lifesaving skills and rowing. This combination has lead to a number of open-water swimming events, some amateur and some professional. The first event was an amateur swim because a non-monetary wager was placed on the outcome. In June of 1907 the bathing season had opened. The lifeguards were on duty. The new style bloomer bathing suits were seen but were not in general use. Their use had been sanctioned by the authorities. A Mr. Shackelford had built a bathing deck on the end of a pier for the convenience of the bathing public that wished to avoid the surf. On June 29th, Miss Dorothy G. S. Currey of Haverford, Pennsylvania, began a swim that was bold and daring. She left from the Inlet wharf swimming out onto the ocean then down to the Heinz Pier, a distance of two miles. During the swim she rested three times on her back eventually reaching the destination. She collected the quart of ice cream that her friend had wagered. The press hailed the swim as one of the "biggest and best swims that have ever been attempted in Atlantic City." To the concerned public, it was announced that "she suffered no ill effect from her long, hard swim."[824] This last pronouncement was to allay the fear that she might have cause harm to herself by this exertion. This was a perception of women athletes commonly held in this era.

It was fourteen years before an organized swim was begun. The first Atlantic City Pageant swim was in 1922. In 1928, Ray Ruddy swam in the 6th Annual Pageant swim winning it in a time of 27 minutes 26 seconds.[825] The present day course is from States Ave. to Missouri Ave. swimming out beyond the steel pier for a total swim distance of approximately 1 mile. The winner for the 2004 competition was Ross Thomas, age 17, from Linwood, New Jersey in a time of 19 minutes 26 seconds. He was the lead swimmer in a group of 17 year old swimmers. More information is available at the Atlantic City Beach Patrol webpage: www.acbp.org. This is an amateur swim and no prize money is offered.

Following the establishment of this swim, a longer marathon swim was initiated. The Atlantic City 15 mile Ocean

Swim was held in 1927.[826] The event was won by William Erickson of the Bronx who was the only swimmer to finish the distance. His winning time was 13:36. All the other participants dropped out due to the cold water still present off shore on June 25th.[827]

The current Atlantic City marathon swim began in 1954 as an attraction for tourists on the occasion of the 100th anniversary of the city. The idea of swimming around Atlantic City, located on Absecon Island, was conceived by Jim Toomey but at the time, no one had ever swum around Atlantic City. Jim hired two lifeguards, Eddie Stetser and Eddie Solitaire, to make the attempt for $100 each and the rest is history. They swam clockwise around the island in about 14 hours. Further refinements to timing the swim so that it coincides with the currents around the island assisted in lowering the elapsed time to the current record of 6:37 held by Stephane Gomez of France set in 2001. The swim was held annually from 1954 to 1965 when it went into hiatus due to an economic downturn in the local economy. The swim was revived in 1978 when casino gambling was legalized and continues to this present day. This swim has had a on again, off again relationship with FINA as a venue for their professional races. With the establishment of the FINA Swimming Marathon World Cup Series, Atlantic City has been the default venue for the United States since 1998.[828] The complete list of finishers and more information is available on their website: www.acswim.org.

Gibraltar Strait

The first swim recognized by the Gibraltar Strait Swimming Association across the Gibraltar Strait occurred on May 4, 1928 by Mercedes Gleitze from the United Kingdom. She completed the swim in 12:50. She began the swim in Tarifa, Spain, and finished in Punta Leona on the Moroccan coast. It seems that Ms. Gleitze had maintained she had swum the English Channel but could not provide an affidavit to that effect so for this swim she had a document attesting to her swim signed by 60 witnesses. This was her fourth attempt.[829] The swim was not duplicated until twenty years later. Daniel Maciotti swam across in 1948 in a time of 9:20. Since that time there have been over 120 crossings recorded. The men's record today stands at 2:51 set on November 9, 2005, by Mateo Campos of Spain.[830]

Figure 110 Gibraltar Strait seen from space in a 3-D image. Tangiers is on the lower right. Swimmer depart on an ebb current from Gibraltar.

Gibraltar Strait is nearly 8 miles wide at the narrowest point. The reason swimmers swim a longer distance is due to the currents, up to 3 knots. This current will carry them downstream and depending on which tide they start on, that's the direction they will be pushed along the opposite shore. A flood tide is considered to fill an inlet and an ebb tide will empty it. In the case of Gibraltar, flood is seen as filling the Mediterranean Sea and ebb as emptying. Thus if a swimmer leaves on an ebb tide, they will be carried out to the Atlantic Ocean. A difficulty not mentioned is the marine traffic. Gibraltar Strait is a busy avenue of maritime commerce, just like the Channel. The ships can be traveling at 20 knots or closing at the rate of a mile every three minutes. They can't stop and their ability to turn in the Strait is restricted by the traffic channels. The swimmers have to thread their way through this traffic. This could be compared with marathon runners that have to cross from one side of a street to the other and they have to weave their way across traffic that's not going to stop. Currently swimmers are leaving from Tarifa, Spain. In the NASA photo, Spain is on the left, Africa on the right. Gibraltar is the large prominence seen at the end of the peninsula at the upper left. Tarifa is the portion of Spain that is the furthest south, in the photo, the furthest to the right into the Straits. Where you land depends upon which tide you swim on. For a complete list of all 159 successful swims (through 2006), visit the Strait of Gibraltar Swimming Association website at www.acneg.com and click on the One Way Cross List. They also have doubles and neoprene lists. They have taken to posting photos of all their swimmers for the last few years.

Cook Strait

New Zealand is a beautiful country, described as a hiking and swimming paradise. One swim found here rivals the English Channel currents and cold temperatures, Cook Strait. Sixteen statute miles of open water separates the two major islands that make up New Zealand. Less than 50 people have swum the distance since it was first crossed 53 years ago, that's an average of less than one swim a year. One cannot discount the effect of Lynne Cox's crossing in 1975 for popularizing the swim. The islands are named North Island and South Island but swims are in an east or west direction.

Two swimmers had their eyes on being the first across the Strait, Barrie Devenport and Keith Hancox. The first successful swim was in 1962 by Barrie Devenport. Both swimmers were prepared to make the attempt but Barrie's pilot made the first move. Leaving from Cape Terawhiti near Wellington, he slugged his way across taking 11:13. Not a great time but indicative of all first crossings, more determination than technical finesse that overcomes the lack of knowledge that only comes after a swim history is built. Keith answered the challenge two years later and benefited from the knowledge gain by Barrie, chopping two hours off the crossing. Ten years later, Perry Cameron, reversed the course and made the history books as the first to swim from the South Island. The fastest crossing is 5:04 from the South Island to the North Island by Denise Anderson in 1986.

One of the most influential swimmers of the strait is Philip Rush who was only 16 when he first made the crossing in 1980. Today, he is Mr. Cook Strait. He's earned it (2 solo crossing and 2 doubles) and he lives it. He's the contact point for swimmers interested in crossing the Strait. Phil has notched on his swim belt a double and a triple of the English Channel. When asked to compare the Cook Strait to the English Channel, Philip described the Cook Strait as "colder, cleaner, and clearer". He tries to make the swim swimmer friendly by running the swims from a swimmer's point of view. Swimmers are accompanied up-close by an inflatable. The main pilot for the swims is Chris McCullum. His skill as a navigator has an important role in swims because there is less shoreline to finish the swim upon than in the English Channel: 5 miles on the South Island and 2½ on the North Island. Also, if the current changes, it can sweep you back into the middle of the strait. They rarely see any large vessel traffic on their swims. The biggest problem is hypothermia. The website for the swim is www.cookstraitswim.org.nz.

Another swimmer that has her name all over the swim is Meda MacKenzie. Her resume includes the Foveaux Strait, which is the crossing from the southern tip of the South Island to Stewart Island. She's done a double of the Bristol Channel and an 18-mile circumswim of Rarotonga, an island belonging to the Cook Islands, northeast of New Zealand. Another swim in New Zealand is Lake Taupo, 26 miles across, in the center of the North Island. One should keep this swim in mind if the weather doesn't allow a Cook Strait crossing. Philip can give you the low down on this swim as he's completed a double here also.

The list of successful swims of Cook Strait

Name	Age	Sex	County	Date	Time	From-To
Devonport, Barry	27	M	NZ	20 Nov 1962	11:20	N-S
Hancox, Keith	25	M	NZ	7 Feb 1964	9:34	N-S
Cameron, Perry	30	M	NZ	12 Jan 1972	9:36	S-N
Cox, Lynne	18	F	USA	4 Feb 1975	12:07	N-S
Coutts, John	20	M	NZ	13 Feb 1977	9:25	N-S
McKenzie, Meda	15	F	NZ	03 Feb 1978	12:07	N-S
McKenzie, Meda	15	F	NZ	17 Feb 1978	11:23	S-N
Coutts, John	21	M	NZ	18 Feb 1978	6:46	S-N
Hurdley, Chris	30	M	NZ	24 Dec 1978	9:04	N-S
Christie, Alan	28	M	NZ	24 Dec 1978	9:05	N-S
Benson, Pat	22	M	NZ	24 Feb 1979	10:18	N-S
Rush, Philip	16	M	NZ	24 Feb 1980	8:56	N-S
El-Meseery, Mohammad	21	M	Egypt	24 Feb 1980	9:12	N-S
Smidt, Rhonda	17	F	NZ	10 Mar 1980	8:56	S-N
Shields, Belinda	18	F	NZ	24 Mar 1980	8:32	S-N
Wordsworth, Carolyn	17	F	NZ	08 Apr 1980	7:15	S-N
Koorey, John	37	M	Australia	01 Feb 1981	5:37	S-N
Carr, Kristine	21	F	NZ	14 Feb 1981	7:54	S-N
Quinlivan, Michael	20	M	NZ	28 Feb 1981	7:58	N-S
Horner, Elizabeth	15	F	NZ	14 Mar 1981	7:22	S-N
Horner, Elizabeth	15	F	NZ	10 May 1981	11:33	N-S
Vincent, Alan	31	M	NZ	30 Mar 1981	8:21	N-S
McLay, Sheryl	21	F	NZ	17 Jan 1982	6:59	S-N
Bisley, Karen	16	F	NZ	14 Feb 1982	6:46	S-N
Jack, Wayne	14	M	NZ	21 Feb 1982	10:02	N-S
Rush, Philip	20	M	NZ	13 Mar 1984	7:51	N-S
Rush, Philip	20	M	NZ	13 Mar 1984	8:25	S-N
Blewett, Sandra	34	F	NZ	26 Mar 1984	13:30	N-S

McKenzie, Meda	21	F	NZ	26 Mar 1984	11:27	N-S
McKenzie, Meda	21	F	NZ	26 Mar 1984	11:39	S-N
Barry, Scott	18	M	NZ	29 Mar 1985	7:51	S-N
Bisley, Karen	19	F	NZ	29 Mar 1985	11:11	N-S
Bouzaid, Donna	22	F	NZ	01 May 1985	8:15	N-S
Anderson, Denise	21	F	NZ	20 Jan 1986	5:04	S-N
Koorey, John	42	M	Australia	18 Feb 1986	6:59	N-S
Barrett,.Helen	16	F	NZ	30 Mar 1986	6:34	S-N
Greenslade, Ingrid	15	F	NZ	25 Feb 1987	7:18	N-S
Reid, Jeffrey	14	M	NZ	23 Mar 1987	7:10	S-N
Rush, Philip	23	M	NZ	23 Mar 1987	8:27	S-N
Rush, Philip	24	M	NZ	9 Feb 1988	9:05	S-N
Rush, Philip	24	M	NZ	9 Feb 1988	9:32	N-S
Davey, Richard	25	M	England	12 Feb 1988	7:17	S-N
Doig, Karena	15	F	NZ	18 Feb 1989	8:31	S-N
Williamson, Myra	19	F	NZ	5 Feb 1994	8:01	N-S
Shenov, Taranath	25	M	India	25 Mar 1996	7:46	S-N
Kane, Jo	40	F	NZ	26 Mar 1996	10:52	N-S
Repale, Romdas	16	F	India	9 Mar 1998	19:44	S-N
Pearson, Thomas	42	M	NZ	8 Feb 1999	6:50	S-N
van Wisse, Tammy	30	F	Australia	10 Mar 1999	6:49	N-S
Moss, Grainne	31	F	Ireland	6 Mar 2001	12:25	N-S
Johns, Kate	14	F	NZ	16 Mar 2001	7:06	N-S
Merrill, Yvonne	39	F	Australia	17 Mar 2001	11:05	N-S
Bula, Chowdhury C.	31	F	India	25 Mar 2003	9:04	N-S
Gray, Jeremy	21	M	NZ	11 Apr 2003	7:25	N-S
Yudovin, David	52	M	USA	16 Jan 2004	9:38	N-S
Pittar, James	34	M	Australia	5 Mar 2004	8:31	S-N
Hains, Chris	.	M	NZ	15 Mar 2004	7:24	S-N
Gatfield, John	13	M	NZ	25 Mar 2004	8:08	S-N
Raut, Aditya	11	M	India	20 Feb 2005	9:09	N-S
Sibtsen, Cara	17	F	NZ	4 Mar 2005	5:48	S-N

Hockings, Tania	17	F	NZ	4 Mar 2005	5:48	S-N
Binney, Robert	43	M	NZ	10 Feb 2006	7;11	N-S
Palfrey, Penny	43	F	Australia	5 Apr 2006	8:26	S-N

South Africa swims

South Africa has several open-water swims of interest. In 2004, Carina Bruwer, age 24, of South Africa swam around Cape Agulhas, at Africa's southern-most tip, in 2:16 on April 27.[831] A previous swim in 1994 by Gordon Pugh took over 4 hours to finish. Carina swam from east to west starting at Spookdraai Bay and finishing at Old Bay, a distance of 5 ¾ nautical miles. She had the advantage of a good current which could explain the vast difference in times between her swim and Pugh's as he swam in the other direction. This 10 kilometer swim has attracted some interest. Erica Moffett from New York dropped by to knock-off a 2:03 on April 23, 2005 swimming east bound.[832]

An 11-kilometer swim known as the Triple Cape race began in 2004[833] has the swimmers passing by three capes; the swim starts at Maclear Beach near the Cape of Good Hope, passes Cape McLear and Cape Point to finish at Buffels Bay. The swim is around the tip of the Cape Peninsula south of Cape Town where the Cape of Good Hope is located. The present record is held by Christof Wandratsch set in 2005 of 2:59.[834] A shorter version of this course was first swum in 1979 by Lynne Cox.

Another swim in South Africa is a 7.5 kilometer swim from Robben Island[835] to Bloubergstrand on the mainland known as the Vista Nova Big Swim. Robben Island is located 11 kilometers north of Cape Town and Bloubergstrand is due east of the island. Christof Wandratsch holds the record of 1:33 set on February 7, 2005 for the east-bound swim.[836] He broke the existing record by only 12 seconds. Of interest in this swim is that he wore a typical Speedo swim suit. In 2005, 39 swimmers competed and 8 relay teams. The winner for the fifth consecutive time was Steve Klugman, age 38, in a time of 2:04.[837] Steve also holds the triple record by virtual of being the only person to complete a triple swim. His time was slightly over six hours.[838]

A 10.2-kilometer swim from Robben Island to Three Anchor Bay on the shoreline of Cape Town starts at the island but swimmers travel south. Christof Wandratsch set the record of 2:11 on February 6, 2005. There was an inquiry into the type of suit that he wore for the swim and after consideration and much discussion, the disqualification was rescinded.[839]

There is also a swim around Robben Island. Carina Bruwer holds record, 3:07, for this 11 kilometer swim set on April 27, 2005.[840] This date is known as Freedom Day in South Africa.

There is an annual swim from Simon Town to Muizenberg, 10.5 kilometer distance, across False Bay called the False Bay Ironman Swimming Challenge. The 35 kilometer swim across the width of False Bay has been successfully crossed only twice: first by Annemie Landemeters of Belgium in 1989 with a time of 9:56 then in 2004 by Steve Klugman on a slightly different course in 14:15. Annemie also holds the record for the Ironman swim set in 1990 of 2:18.[841] Because of the number of great white sharks in this bay, the escort boats have taken to carrying and electronic shark repellent device called the "Shark Shield."

West Coast swims

The newest swim located on the west coast is the Pennock Island Challenge. It is at the same latitude as the Irish Sea North Channel swim. This swim was first swum on July 11, 2004, by William Shultz, age 38, a veteran of the Catalina Channel. The island is located just off Katchikan, Alaska, in the midst of the Tongass Narrows. The distance is 8 miles and the swim is timed to coincide with the tidal flow. The first annual challenge held on August 28, 2005, was won by Sean Seaver in a time of 2:36, their current record.[842] Visit their website for a map of the course and more information: www.alaskateamada.com. The "ada" in the address is for the American Diabetes Association.

An interesting development happened in San Francisco: no one swim has attracted such a following that a single organization has developed around a single event. Instead two clubs, Dolphin Club and South End Rowing Club have supported swimming, rowing, boating, running, and a variety of other sports much as athletics clubs elsewhere do. These two clubs even share the same building at Aquatic Park at the foot of Hyde Street in San Francisco. The Aquatic Park is a sheltered cove on San Francisco Bay along the southern shore by the Golden Gate Bridge. The park's eastern boundary is the Hyde Street pier and encircling the cove from Van Ness Avenue on the western boundary is the other breakwater. I must confess that I don't understand why there are two clubs instead of just one but this arrangement works. There is a club camaraderie that is intensified by an interclub rivalry that is tempered by we're-all-in-this-together attitude that makes competition and cooperation interesting. It's the difference between competing against and competing together. The Olympic Club located in downtown San Francisco, was originally a gymnastic club but has produced high-caliber swimmers. Swimmers gravitate toward these support groups and have thrived. Here is an example from The South Ender, the South End Rowing Club newsletter, of the types of activities the clubs support:

Amazon River
On Tuesday, August 19, 1997, South End Rowing Club swimmer Gary Emich swam an international version of the daily Sunriser eye-opener. Joined by Iliana Fujimori, niece of the former Peruvian President, the two intrepid aquatic adventurers jumped from the relative safety of their jungle boat into the piranha-infested Amazon River ten miles downstream from Iquitos, Peru. They swam approximately one-half mile in the silt laden and extremely murky water (visibility less than 6 inches) to the safety of the shore where they then proceeded through the rain forest on a 3-hour jungle hike. Upon their return to the boat, they found that the captain had taken advantage of the lull, fished from the cockpit and landed a dozen small piranhas. According to the natives, these lethal predators only attack if you are bleeding and wounded! Gary and Iliana corroborated this local piece of lore.

Lake Titcaca
The following week, on August 26, 1997, Gary did a solo swim in Lake Titcaca, Peru (elevation 12,500 feet above sea level) - water temperature a balmy 59 degrees. What made this swim noteworthy is that he swam around

an artificial island that is constructed entirely of the "Tortora" reed. The Uros Indians who inhabit this island not only build islands of the tortora reed (it's like walking on a waterbed quipped Gary) but they also build their houses and their boats out of the versatile plant; and they eat its delicious root. In fact, these are the same Indians who helped Thor Hyerdihl construct his famous Kon-Tiki that he sailed from South America to Polynesia. As Gary finished his swim, there was a paucity of accolades from the natives but a plethora of comments containing the words "gringo loco!"

Gary Emich is typical of the swimmers belonging to these clubs, crazy enough to enjoy traveling the world to go swimming. Sometimes you don't have to go far to have fun. He is presently working on his 3rd century mark for the Alcatraz swim having written his thoughts after the first hundred in "A Swim Criminal Looks at 100", a rather enjoyable booklet that deals with swimming with San Francisco Bay. Club members earn nicknames based on their exploits. Some of the names include L. Sharko, Bricko (aka. Bucko), Fast Eddie, Rocketman, and Reptile-Brain.[843] The clubs are quite proud of their members that have completed the English Channel swim and typically produce 3 to 4 successes (or attempts) a year. Gary shares a locker at the SERC with Dave Horning. An honorary Dolphin club member is Jack LaLanne.

Open-water swims either supported or organized by members of the three San Francisco clubs include a 3-mile Kirby Cove swim, a 6-mile Pt. Bonita swim, the cross Tomales Bay swim, the 12-mile Trans-Tahoe Relay swim, the Escape from Alcatraz swim, and a 10-mile Bay to Breakers swim. This is not a complete listing of all the swims. The Bay to Breakers swim was first swum in 1987 in concert with the Bay to Breakers run held annually in San Francisco only the swim is out the harbor under the Golden Gate Bridge to Ocean Beach. The Trans-Tahoe swim, organized by the Olympic Club, is in its 28th year. There is now a category for solo swimmers. Dan Rogers in a time of 4:37 won the solo event in 2005; the winner relay was in around 3:39. The course is from Sandy Harbor Beach, Nevada, to Skylandia Beach, Lake Forest, California.[844] Since this swim crosses a state line, I suppose I should mention that you are not allowed to bring certain fruits into California and they have a border inspection policy.[845]

Tomales Bay is a narrow inlet that is north of San Franciso along the coast. On the Pacific side is the Point Reyes National Seashore. This spit of land jutting out and upward into the Pacific Ocean along the east coast would be nothing more than a sand bar and the sheltered water, shallow and clogged with weeds requiring dredging to make the channel hospitable to boating. On the west coast the landscape consists of rolling plains that rise to drop off with a dramatic cliff at the waters edge. The water is deep and hospitable to marine life. The Bay is also considered breeding grounds for Great White sharks. The Tomales Bay swim is held several times during the year, organized by the Tomales Bay White Shark Swimmers Association and takes the short route across the bay starting at Heart's Desire Beach. Christ Blakeslee (aka. L. Sharko) while training for the English Channel in 2004 was the first to swim the length of the inlet, 15 miles, from Oak Island to Inverness in a time of 5:39. During the swim a boater came alongside to warn his crew of the reputation of Tomales Bay as a breeding ground for the Great White Shark. The prepared response didn't garner any sympathy from the concerned boater who was told, "Sharko is not planning on breeding any White Sharks today!"

Down the coast from San Francisco is a short swim with a long history, the Santa Cruz Rough Water Swim. It is now in its 31 year sponsored by the Surf Lifesavers Association. The course is a one-mile distance around the Santa Cruz pier. It is perfect for novice ocean swimmer to cut their teeth on; for the veterans there is the 10K Pier-to-Pier swim. Santa Cruz is located on the northern edge of Monterey Bay while along the southern border is the city of Monterey.[846] A 10-kilometer swim from Capitola wharf to the aforementioned Santa Cruz pier, affectionately called the Pier-to-Pier swim has been happening for about 15 years beginning in 1990. Only during one year was the swim called off. This year, the winner was 55 years old, Alan Bell, in a time of 2:38.[847] He was the previous year's winner and it's not for a lack of younger swimmers not trying. The swimmers take advantage of a countercurrent to cut their times when swimming west from

Capitola to Santa Cruz. One swimmer has gone for the homerun, crossing from Santa Cruz to Monterey, a distance of about 22 miles. That was Cindy Cleveland on Sept 17, 1980, in 15:21.[848] A relay of South End Rowing members swam the same jellyfish strewn distance on Saturday, September 29, 2001, in 12:24.[849]

Another swim south of Monterey at San Luis Obispo is the Pismo to Avila Pier to Pier Swim, 6.2 miles. The swim was cancelled in 2003 due to the death of an ocean swimmer while training on August 19th by a great white shark attack. The swim has not been resumed since.[850]

Further down the coast just north of San Diego is a swim that's in its 75th year: the 3-mile Gatorman swim from La Jolla Cove to Scripps Pier and back. This year has seen Alex Kostich score his fifth win with a time of 57 minutes 51 seconds.[851] The LaJolla Cove Swim Club, formed in 1970, hosts a number of swims and social events. They have a special relationship with Florence Chadwick by hosting an annual memorial swim in her honor. Check their webpage, www.lajollacoveswimclub.org, for more details.

Channel Island swimming

Off the coast of California lie two clusters of islands called the Channel Islands. One group located toward the south includes the well known Catalina Island and is closely tied to the mainland with a ferry service to Long Beach and a rich swimming history. The other group of islands further north is associated with Santa Barbara. The year 2006 marks a new chapter in Catalina Channel swimming history because the Santa Barbara Channel Swimming Association was established and there is no Catalina Channel. This forces the marathon swimmer to consider one of two options: go with the older more established swim or write history with the new group. We also have to be clear about which channel it is that we are crossing: San Pedro or Santa Barbara.

Historically, The Catalina Island swim doesn't have an authentic swimming origin in the sense that swimmers had been trying and failing for years to swim to or from Catalina Island with someone finally making a heroic effort and succeeding.[852] It was more of a pecuniary interest that led to the first swim and not just on the part of the swimmer. Santa Catalina Island, 20.14 miles off the California coast, was owned by Santa Catalina Island Company. William Wrigley, Jr. of the chewing gum company owned a majority share of the company and sought to increase the tourist revenues to the island. Around this time, Gertrude Ederle had gained fame for swimming across the Channel. He thought that by having her swim across during the winter months it would impress upon the public mind the ease of access to the island. So Wrigley offered Gertrude $5000 for all expenses in the venture then found he had to increase the purse. Meantime, word had leaked out of the generous offer. Soon, swimmers wanting a chance to swim besieged him. When Gertrude waxed disinterest because of theatrical obligations that would interfere with her training, he offered $25,000 to anyone who would make the attempt. Eventually, 102 swimmers would show up at the starting line on January 15th, 1927. Prior to the race, on September 10, 1926, an 8-member relay time swam the channel in 23:17. This provided the race committee with valuable information regarding conditions. George Young, age 17, of Canada was the one and only finisher in a time of 15:44 having lead most of the way across.[853] Over 120 swimmers have successfully completed the Santa Catalina swim either from the mainland to Catalina (MC) or visa versa (CM). To view the complete list of solo swims, you are asked to visit the Catalina Swimming Federation website: www.swimcatalina.org. The point man for the Catalina Channel Swimming Association is John York, 1244 Voorhees Ave., Manhattan Beach, CA 90266, and whose email is: swimcatalina@earthlink.net. One swimmer has swum around Catalina: Cindy Cleveland in August of 1979 in a time of 34:24. The distance is approximately 36 miles. In 1994, 3 relay teams organized by David S Clark duplicated the feat.[854]

    Emilio Casanueva is the founder of the Santa Barbara Channel Swimming Association. While the organization is new, swims from the islands off Santa Barbara stretch back to 1978 when Cindy Cleveland swim to one of the nearby island, Anacapa, and back to the mainland, a distance of approximately 32 miles in 12:48. This was followed in 1982 by David Yudovin swimming from Anacapa to the mainland in 8:27, a distance of 16 miles. A year later, 1983, David swam from the larger Santa Cruz Island to the mainland in 15:15, a distance of 26 miles. In 1984, Ashby Harper swam from Santa Cruz to the mainland in 16:24. The record for Anacapa to the mainland was set by Scott Zornig in 2001 at 5:19. Their first official season 2006 saw two swims from Santa Cruz. One north to Santa Barbara, 26 miles, by Paul Lewis of England in 13:16. The other was from Santa Barbara to the east toward Oxnard landing at Hollywood Beach in 10:27 by Ned Denison, a former All-American water polo goalie.[855]

Canadian swims

Open water swims in British Columbia have a swim history dating from 1955 when the Strait of Juan de Fuca was first swum. The characterization of the difficulty of that swim possibly lead to its demise as there have been no attempts after the initial rush to get in the record books. The tides and currents in this area are quite complicated, varying from diurnal (2 sets of high and low waters) to having only one tide change over a 24-hour period. The rise and fall can vary from as little as two feet to as much as 9 feet.[856] In 1967, the Strait of Georgia, which separates Vancouver Island from the mainland is a portion of the Inland Passage to Alaska, was first swum by Mike Powley in a time of 9:23. The swims leave from Neck Point just north of Departure Bay by the city of Nanaimo on Vancouver Island. The distance across to Sechelt on mainland along the Sunshine Coast north of the city of Vancouver is a little over 16 miles. This is up the Inland Passage about 25 miles from Vancouver. The course is in a northeast direction when swimming from west to east. Going the other direction requires the swimmer to make Departure Bay before the current takes them south of Gabriola Island most northern point. Intervening islands limit the locations swimmers can start and finish at in this swim. This is the widest point for the Strait of

Georgia. Vancover Island looks a little bit like Catalina Island only longer.

Successful Strait of Georgia Swims

Name	Date	Time
Mike Powley	1967	9:23
Ernie Yacob	1967	11:13
Fran Caldwell	1972	15:07
John McDermott	1978	14:10
Shane Collins	1994	10:50
Debbie Collins	1995	13:53
Shane Collins	1998	9:55

The surprise with the Strait of Georgia swim is that the first swimmer set the record. Shane Collins on his second crossing shaved almost an hour off his time but didn't quite achieve his goal of lowering the mark. The first woman to complete the swim is Fran Caldwell in 1972.[857] The Canadian Ocean Marathon Swimming Association organized the more recent swims but swims of this caliber sometimes will only see attempts once every decade or so. There is a similarity between the Irish Long Distance Swimming Association and COMSA in the frugality of the organization, the scarcity of swims, and the enthusiasm of the proponents.

For variety, Shane and Debbie created a circumswim of Bowen Island, an inhabited island that is northwest of Vancouver at the mouth of Howe Sound. The distance around is 22-miles first successfully swum in 1997 by Shane Collins in a time of 10:48. His wife, Debbie, duplicated the effort in 1998 in a time of 9:20. It's apparent that they learned a thing or two during Shane's attempt. Starting in the northeast corner of the island at the beach at Finister, Shane swam clockwise around the island. He ran into a bit of current but finished just the same. When Debbie swam, she left from the same location and swam counterclockwise turning in the better time.[858]

In 2001, Shane swam 26 miles down Howe Sound from Squamish Harbour just outside the town along the coast to Horseshoe Bay where the ferries dock at Whytecliff. He finished in a time of 9:10. The water temperature was between 56°F and 62°F during the swim. Shane and Debbie haven't slowed down or lost their enthusiasm for their hometown swims but have branched out to swim the English Channel and other significant swims.[859]

For the less adventuresome there is a 7¼-mile swim down the length of Lake Skaha also located in British Columbia. This swim started in 1983, the same year as Manhattan began. The current record holder for the Open competition (non-wetsuits) is Don Nicholson in a time of 2:40 set in 2003. The women's record set by Celia Spence is but ten minutes slower set in 2001. The swim starts in Penticton, BC, and finishes in Okanagan Falls, BC.[860] This lake is located about 20 miles north of the border with the United States. More information their swims can be found on their web: www.ultraswimcanada.com or at www.openwater.ca.

From another era, Ann Mundigel Meraw swam as a member of the World Professional Marathon Swimming Federation competing in the CNE Toronto Marathon in 1934 and 1936. Since WWII prevented her from swimming the English Channel, Mundigel completed a 14 mile swim to Howe Island from Vancouver in 7:14 losing her suit along the way. In 1958 she completed an 88.5 kilometer swim in Lake Okanagan from Kelowna to Penticton in 32:12.[861]

Swims across the Great Lakes are recorded at Brian Finlay's website: www.soloswims.com, click on Ratified Swims in Solo Swims of Ontario. Presently there are 45 successful swims across Lake Ontario, 11 swims across various parts of Lake Erie, 5 swims across Lake Huron and Georgian Bay, 1 swim across both Lake Michigan and Lake Superior.[862]

Mediterranean swims

Besides the Gibraltar swim, the Mediterranean Sea provides venues for any number of swims. Members of the San Francisco swimming community organized an 18-mile swim from

Capri to Ischia. Both these island border the entrance to Naples, Italy. A six-member relay completed this swim in the Gulf of Naples in 10:15.[863]

A commercial venture, Swim Trek,[864] offers organized fun swims around the Mediterranean. Of interest for the average ocean swimmer is the island-hopping 6-day swim through the Cyclades. The Cyclades are a group of 11 islands off Greece and everyday, the group swims from one island to the next island on their agenda. Their luggage and the non-swimming spouses accompany them in a 40' sail boat. The distances vary from one mile to five. Mixed in this tour are hikes past Mt. Zeus. Don't forget to bring your sunscreen.

Japanese swims

The swims listed here are short but represent an indication of the interest in open water swimming in Japan and the extent to which they will travel to swim.[865]

The Atami Open Water Swims are for distances of 3200m, 800m or 4x800m. These swims take place at Atami Sun Beach in Atami City, Shizuoka Pref., Japan. The same series of swim are also swum at Tateyama City in the Tateyama International Open Water Swim in Chiba Pref., Japan. Contact for both these swims is International Recreation Systems Inc., 5F Hakozaki Park Bldg., 20-3 Hakozaki-chou, Nihonbashi, Chuo-ku, Tokyo, 103-0015 Japan. The Tateyama City also features a 4km swim from Kagamigaura Shore sponsored by the Tateyama City Educational Committee on a different date than the series swims.

The Tokyo Islands Series is swum at Niijima Island, Tokyo. The Niijima Island Open Water includes 1.5km, 3km, and a 5km swim. Contact: Tokyo Islands Series Event Committee, Saison Tamagawa, 2-24-24 Tamagawa, Setagaya-Ku, Tokyo, 158-0094 Japan. Another swim held in Kinko Bay is from Sakurajima Island to Kagoshima City, Japan. The distance is 4km.

While Guam is not in Japan, 90 swimmers from Japan attended the 2.5 mile Manukai 15th Annual International Cocos Crossing, held there. The swim is from Cocos Island to Merizo pier on the southern coast of Guam. The swim was won for the 5th time by two-time Guam Olympian Dan O'Keefe, age 32. Dan was off the pace from his personal best of 0:42 finishing this year with a 0:47 barely edging out the women's division winner Tomomi Yamaguchi, age 29, from Tokyo by one second. The oldest swimmer competing was Takeshi Suzuki at age 72 who finished in 1:16 just beating the youngest swimmer Jonathan Diego, age 9, who finished in 1:19. This race according to Tomomi, a former Japan national swimmer, is well known in Japan.[866]

Saipan saw members of the Umiou Swim Club compete in the 3rd Annual Escape From Managaha Island Ocean Swim on May 28, 2005. This 3 kilometer race from the island to Saipan's Micro Beach has been held three time but this was the first time they had finishers. The winner was Tatuya Motoyama in a time of 00:37:09. Saipan also has races in Tinian and Rota.[867]

Modern records of note

The current record holder for swimming from Catalina to the mainland is Karen Burton of Monument, Colorado. Her time of 7 hrs and 43 minutes was set on the late date of November 10, 1995. The course was from Doctor's Cove to Rancho Palos Verdes, California. The previous record was held by Chad Hunderby of 8:14 set in 1994. Prior to that, the record for this direction of swim had stood at 8:33 for twenty years and was held by the queen of open water swimming, Penny Lee Dean. The two previous swimmers are former English Channel records holders. Penny Lee Dean still holds the record swimming from the mainland to Catalina in 7:16 on September 1, 1976.[868]

The most recent record holder for the English Channel is Chad Hunderby of Irvine, California, with a time of 7 hours and 17 minutes set on September 27, 1994. The time of the start was at 4:15am. This bested the time set by Penny Lee Dean of 7:40 that stood for 16 years set on July 29, 1978. This record was nearly broken in 2003 by Christof Wandratsch of Germany who swam a 7:20. Christof returned on August 1, 2005 to shave 13 minutes off the record. The new record is now 7:04.[869] The fastest double of the Channel is held by Suzy Maroney of Australia in a time of 17:14 set in 1991. Philip Rush of New Zealand set the fastest triple in a time of 28:21 set in 1987.[870]

The current record holder for the fastest transit of one complete circumswim of Manhattan is Shelley Taylor of Australia set on July 14, 1995. Her time of 5 hours 45 minutes broke the previous record of 5 hours 54 minutes held by Kris Rutford of Nebraska set on August 29, 1992.

The Guinness Book of World Records lists several records of interest to long distance marathon swimmers. Ricardo Hoffman is listed for the longest continuous swim from Corrientes to St. Elena, Argentina in 1981. The longest distance swum in a pool in 24-hours is 101.9 kilometers (63.3 Statue miles) held by Anders Forvass of Sweden. This was set on October 28-29, 1989 in a 25-meter swimming pool in Linkopling, Sweden. This speed is equivalent to 2.29 knots.[871] The woman's record is 95.675 kilometers (59.44 Statue miles) held by Kelly Driffeld of Australia. This record was set on June 28-29, 1997, in a 50-meter pool at the Mingara Leisure Center, Tumbi Umbi, NSW, Australia.[872]

The following world records will never be exceed by a swimmer during a marathons swim except when a swim is current assisted. They are good to use as a standard for comparison of pace times and as a check of conditioning if there is significant changes indicating the swimmer is slowing down which is a normal condition. The world record for the 1500 meters[873] swim in a 50-meter pool is 14 minutes 34.56 seconds set by Grant Hackett of Australia on July 29, 2001.[874] This speed is equivalent to 3.468 knots.[875] The world record for the 100-meter swim is 47.84 seconds set by Peter van den Hoogenband of the Netherlands on Sept 19, 2000.[876] This speed is equivalent to 4.06 knots.

The formula[877] that gives a world record performance in knots over any distance in meters out to 24 hours and beyond in still water is $6.036*x^{-.0843}$. Simply put the distance in for x (in meters) and the calculation will give you the expected world record speed (in knots) that is accurate to within 0.9%.[878]

The largest number of swimmers to participate in a swim was held at Sun Moon Lake, Taiwan on September 26th, 2004, when 17,305 swimmers swam 3 kilometers or 1.6 nautical miles. The Taiwan Master Swimming Association organizes the swim. Tsai Shu-Chou of the Puli Four Seasons Swimming Club and their members assist in this gigantic effort. The swim is in its 22nd year.[879]

The longest held open-water marathon swim record over a contested marathon course is by Gertrude Ederle from the Battery, NY, to Sandy Hook, NJ, 22 miles in 7:14 set on June 15, 1925. She held the record over 81 years when Tammy van Wisse swam the course on July 21, 2006 in a new record time of 5:07.

Figure 111 Christof Wandratsch of Germany.

Chapter 16 Swims, believe it or not

Probably of little consequence in the world of swimming, the accidental swimmer will inadvertently, in an attempt to save their life, complete a swim of marathon proportions. When you consider that they had not trained for the swim, they are even more remarkable. In other cases, you wonder what they were thinking.

In 1873 were three swims that came about due to unusual circumstances. In June of that year, a transport steamer *L'Orne* stopped in Melbourne, Australia, for supplies. Aboard were 500 communists being taken to a French penal colony on New Caledonia. The ship was well lit and guards abounded to prevent any prisoner from escaping. The ship was anchored in the lower harbor, about 7 miles from shore. One prisoner, named Michael Serigne leaving through a port-hole clambered aboard a collier[880] alongside and immediately covered himself with coal. The night was dark, there was no moon and it had rained. After midnight, he climbed down to the water and made his way to the back of the barge where a small boat was tied up. After pulling the boat away for a short distance, he thought he heard a disturbance aboard the transport and he swam off away from the boat. He could see lights at Sandridge and swam for them. After an hour, he could swim no more but came upon another vessel at anchor. Lashing himself to the anchor chain with his belt, he rested. After some time he resumed his swim making landfall at Sandridge and walked into Melbourne. Since Australia, a member of the British Commonwealth, did not have an extradition policy for political prisoners, he remained a free man.[881]

The second swim in 1873 was on July 20 near Detroit. A black crewman aboard the *Artic* fell off the boat when it was a full two miles from Malden. The man's name was Joe Long. He kicked off his boots and began swimming on his back toward shore. After a bit, he came across a board about a yard long that made his journey a bit easier as he now has some floatation and he could rest. There were no witnesses to his falling overboard or to the swim but Joe could provide the name of the person who picked him up at the beach and the physician who treated him with stimulant.[882]

The third swim was a swashbuckling an event as could be imagined happening in an impromptu manner. The recounting of the swim is an excerpt from Chambers's Journal[883] published by the NY Times on September 14, 1873. This account is most likely a recounting of a soldier's barracks tale, told for its entertainment value. A young English officer, unnamed so we will call him Chambers, was returning from Turkey to his regiment and had booked passage to Malta aboard the *Pera*, at anchor off Constantinople in the Bosporus. After a day ashore, he had but one coin left to hire a boat to take him out to it. A storm was coming up but he secured an old Turkish seaman to row him out. His friends urged him to wait out the storm but if he missed the vessel sailing, his career was finished. As they rowed, the seas rose and eventually the old man could row no more and the boat broached, turning them out into the waters of the Bosporus. He came up and found the going very tough in the breaking seas as his swimming had been on lakes and streams. Eventually, he came upon an anchor chain attached to a ship. He attempted to rest but found the swells prevented it and the current was pulling hard. Eventually, he released his hold and was sucked under the boat. After bouncing down along the length of the vessel, he popped up in the lee of the boat and right next to a small boat. With the last of his strength, he climbed aboard once he could time his pulling with the lifting of the swells. There he rested until it occurred to him that he needed to catch his passage. He then attempted to raise the crew aboard the large vessel to which the small boat was attached. They responded after a bit, were annoyed to find him in their rowboat and hoisted the rowboat up to the main deck by davits only after a woman speaking Greek berated them. Once there he attempted to negotiate to have them bring him to the *Pera*. They were reluctant and the coinage he had left wasn't persuading them. They suggested that he swim there, so well known was the English skill at swimming.

As the captain and the crew discussed their options, Chambers discovered the woman on aboard the vessel was Mme. Achmet, the wife of Achmet Pacha.[884] Chambers was surprised to discover this woman. All of Constantinople was looking for her: the Pacha had argued with his wife and she had run away. To facilitate her departure, she has removed some items of value from the harem and had hired this boat to carry her home; she was Greek by nationality. In a double cross, they had anchored up and began negotiations with the Pasha for her return. The arrival of the Englishman was an inconvenience. When the captain and the crew returned, the captain told the woman to go below and began to struggle with her. Chambers grabbed him and landed two blows upon the Captain before the crew fell upon him. As he lay upon the deck with swords and blades all about, in the distance was heard a voice hailing the vessel. It was the Pasha's armed men come to retrieve their possessions.

This became a matter of great concern to all on board. Ignoring Chambers, the crew hid in the shadows as the Captain went to the rail and timidly addressed the approaching galley. At this time, Chambers stood up and saw in the distance, approaching was the *Pera*, she had sailed; he saw his chances and career disappearing up in smoke when he jumped into action. He signaled Mme. Achmet to be quiet and they climbed onto the rowboat on the davits. They cut the lines allowing the boat to fall into the seas. Grabbing the oars, he began stroking for all his might as the *Pera* approached and he knew the ship wouldn't stop for him unless he made them. Lookouts on the deck saw him coming and tried to warn him off. He crashed the rowboat into the side of the *Pera* as it passed. Once again he was cast into the Bosporus. Immediately lines were thrown over and he and the lady were pulled to safety. He had caused the accident because it was the only way possible to get the *Pera* to stop. Upon his return to his regiment, the Mme. Achmet spent some time with them as she outfitted herself in European costume before going onto Paris. Chambers was rewarded with a diamond and his regiment with a silver salver. This was a most remarkable fictional account of an accidental swimmer twice thrown into the water of the Bosporus in the same night.[885]

In possibly one of the first reported shark attacks, a boy of 14 was bitten by a shark while swimming off Red Hook, Brooklyn on August 8th 1878.[886] Charles Gates had gone crabbing with a friend and he decided to take a dip. His friend frightened the shark away with a well-placed stone, thrown from the boat they were using. Pulling Charles back into the rowboat, he made for shore and eventually got him to a hospital. The surgeons were sure that the wounds were not fatal and sewed up his backside. Unfortunately, Charles made the mistake of going to a hospital prior to the adoption of the practice of sterilization and antiseptics. He died of infections a week later.[887] Dr. Joseph Lister, the father of antiseptics, had only been appointed chair of Clinical Surgery at Kings College a year earlier and his precedent setting antiseptic operation on a kneecap had only taken place the previous October 26th in London. His adoption of this practice caused considerable opposition in the medical community when it was publicized much to the misfortune of patients like Charles Gates.[888]

Before this was the episode of Brook Watson recorded in 1778 in a painting by John Singleton Copley, *Watson and the Shark*. The story of the painting, which is a verbal history that accompanied the commissioning of the painting, is from Brook who in 1749 at age 14 was swimming in Havana Harbor in Cuba. When a shark attacked him, nine sailors rowed to his aid, driving off the shark and saving a future Lord Mayor of London. The surgeon who attended to Brook amputated the leg below the knee, most likely used the anesthetic of the day, whiskey and four strong men.

Horse-drawn carts were common sights along the streets of New York City in the era that swimming began to get organized. Is it little wonder that these creatures went swimming occasionally? In November of 1885 a runaway horse got into the East River and took a swim. While aboard a ferry passing from Brooklyn to Manhattan, the horse broke loose from its harness and jumped overboard around 9:30pm. The ferry held to its route and the horse swam off. The next day, at 3:45 am, the Grand Street ferry (near the present site of the Williamsburg Bridge) saw the horse and called a policeman. With the aid of ropes and planks they rescued the animal. The animal spent about 7 hours in the river. The owner claimed the horse later that day.[889] In all, there are four recorded episodes of horses taking a swim in the East River. They all survived. The latest occurrence was in 1940.[890] Horses were appearing in diving shows as early as 1900. Prof. G. F. Hollways's show in Washington, D. C., at River View featured horses diving from a height of 50 feet into a tank head first with a depth of 12 feet.[891] In a rather unusual story, on June 4, 1905, an elephant wandered away from Luna Park on Coney Island and swam across the Narrows to New Dorp, Staten Island, a distance of some 5 miles. The animal was temporarily housed in the police horse stable until the owners showed up to claim him.[892]

In 1899, a short swim caused a tremendous amount of consternation on the part of the public but saw no resolutions to a young lad's dilemma. Harry McDonald, age 16, escaped from a juvenile lockup on Randalls Island[893] known as the House of Refuge by swimming across the Harlem River[894] on Friday, January 13, 1899. The swim, while short, was in the dead of night in the middle of winter. On his crossing, Harry nearly wound up dead himself as he swam into the path of a paddlewheel boat transiting the river. He left from Randalls Island opposite 117th Street and came ashore at 107th Street. He swam across the entrance of the Harlem River. He came to be in the lockup when his parents, unable to cope with him found him in possession of a pistol. Harry had spent 3 weeks on Randalls Island and tired of the rigors associated within the confines. He secured an extra set of clothing to dress himself with to endure the cold from the water. So sure was he of his success that part of his escape plans included overalls to cover the striped pants they wore. Harry was known as a good swimmer, most likely having learned to swim in the traditional manner off the piers of Manhattan. Upon exiting the waters, he went to his Aunt's home on East 108th Street where he obtained dry clothing and rested. His aunt summoned his mother whom had been alerted by this time by the authorities that he was presumed drowned, so sure were the authorities of the remoteness of their location. When his mother arrived, the boy pleaded not to be sent back. The mother suggested that they wait for the father; which decided the case for the boy. Before the father arrived the son has disappeared.[895] On August 8, 1899, 4 boys tried the same tactic during daylight hours with mixed success. Two wound up being plucked out of the Harlem River by a tugboat and were put in solitary confinement on bread and water while two that went through Hell Gate managed to make it to the far shore on Queens and escaped.[896] As late as 1931, boys were still escaping from Randalls Island and risking their lives swimming across the East River.[897] The House of Refuge was transplanted to Welfare Island, renamed Roosevelt Island, by 1939 in order to clear space for the Triborough Bridge.[898]

When the author worked in Astoria for the phone company he met other employees who told him of seeing individuals transiting Hells Gate in wooden wheelchairs. The unfortunate persons were thought to be escapees of the psychiatric hospital also located on Randalls Island.

On September 3, 1939, young Stephen A Kole Jr., age 6, of Chicago swam across the Hudson River a mile above the George Washington Bridge in slightly less than forty minutes. He had previously swum across the Mississippi at St. Louis on July 1, 1939. The boy's father, described as jubilant, is an athletic coach and the mother was similarly employed. There seemed to be no end of the abilities that the child was capable of performing: throw a baseball ninety feet, punt and pass a football twenty yards, chin the bar 15 times, do 60 push ups, do ten different dives from a diving board, row a boat, paddle a canoe, wrestle, box, hurdle, and sprint. He was quite chatty while swimming the breast stroke, side stroke and the crawl and was heard to say, "Dad, I've declared war on the Hudson" and "How about a beer when we get ashore?" The father's ambition was to get his son into the movies.[899] If the father only wanted to get Steven into the movies, I'm sure that a

Saturday afternoon feature wouldn't have set him back as much as this cross-country trip did.

Even the aforementioned swim by such a young swimmer, while remarkable, pales when compared with the mindset of a young adolescent boy out to make big money. Warren Baptiste, age 15, won four bets when he swam across the Hudson River on Sept 7, 1940, at Poughkeepsie, New York. At this location the river is about a half a mile wide. When the youth was reported missing, and why not, he didn't use an escort boat, police and fire rescue were called who began searching for him. He was found walking back over the Mid Hudson Bridge to collect on the money his friends put up: two 25¢ bets and two 10¢ bets.[900] Mr. Baptiste, get better friends.

During World War II, a swim that took place involved daring, courage, and stamina not to mention plain old swimming ability.[901] During the Japanese attack on the Philippines, Lieutenant Damon "Rocky" Gauss swam from Little Baguio, Bataan Peninsula to Corregidor Island in the mouth of Manila Bay. His swim began with a leap from the bridge across the Lamao River on April 9th, 1942, to escape the approaching Japanese Army with another solder.[902] After hiding by burying themselves in the mud of the river from the pursuing enemy, they worked their way to the mouth of the river on April 10 during the night. By hiding in the ocean surf they arrived at the village of Cabcaben, near the tip of Battan on April 11. Going ashore to look for the regrouped American forces, he was captured and imprisoned in a makeshift camp about 200 yards from the beach. He wasn't there long, escaping within hours. He had to kill a prison guard while making his break. The alarm raised, he dodged bullets during the pursuit and managed to pick up a piece of driftwood before launching himself into the ocean for the 3-mile swim to Corregidor.[903] Along the way, he observed an inter-island steamer aground. He swam for it and boarded it, sleeping for hours. He then launched a lifeboat and began rowing for Corregidor. The Japanese had seen him go aboard the vessel and set up a machine gun on the beach. When they saw him row out from behind the vessel, they opened fire; they managed to sink the rowboat but he escaped unharmed by diving overboard. He made the rest of the distance by swimming until sometime around sundown on April 11th. He collapsed on the beach and woke up in Malinta Tunnel having been carried there by the defenders. He was nursed back to health by a classmate from his high school in Georgia they had both attended: Millie Dalton, now a WAC nurse on Corregidor.

On May 5th, when General Jonathan Wainwright ordered the surrender of the island, Lt. Gause received permission to escape by whatever means available. He and a Filipino, Lt. Alberto Arranzaso, planned to escape by leaving from the northern edge of the island for the mainland, six miles across the bay under the cover of darkness. While scouting the beach, they found an outrigger canoe that they launched. Before long a Filipino scout joined them in the canoe, he had been swimming for shore at that point. Their canoe was shelled as the island was under continuous bombardment. It upset but they were alive. They righted the canoe and continued paddling. When dawn broke, they were only a third of the way to shore. Being sighted, they were strafed by airplane and all three went over the side. Lt. Arranzaso was wounded so Rocky and the other man bandaged him up as best they could and draped him over the canoe. They pushed the canoe ahead of them for the rest of the day. They were several hundred yards from shore as night approached but fighting a current along the shoreline that in their weaken condition they couldn't break through. They hadn't eaten in two day, they had no water for 24 hours, and now as Japanese patrol boats passed by they tried to summon assistance. Rocky thought he had lost all hope and become delirious. He sent the Filipino scout to shore to find help. As night fell, and he was alone with Lt. Arranzaso, his partner in the escape gave up the struggle and slipped under the seas. Even still, Rocky tried to rescue him. Unable to find him, Rocky turned to swim to shore and finally reached the beach where he collapsed. While passed out, a Japanese patrol stumbled upon him, kicking him in the side to ascertain his condition. His reflexes were so slow that they presumed him for dead and continued on their way.

After they left, he scrambled into the jungle where he eventually made his way to Australia to report for duty at General Douglas MacArthur's headquarter. The book his son released recently contains many more unbelievable escapades.[904]

A swimmer's desire to win is hard to measure. You can't just tell by whether or not they attend practice or by the number of medals won. Here's a story that illuminates that desire in the extreme. A week before the 1972 Olympic Games were to begin in Munich, Germany, Steve Genter of the US team suffered a collapsed lung. Doctors inserted a hollow needle into Genter's chest so that air trapped outside the lungs could be removed. This normally takes a week but Genter managed to clear the air in a day with vigorous physical therapy. After three days, the doctor removed the needle without anesthesia and sealed the wound with 13 stitches. Genter did not want anything in his body that might make him fail a drug test. He had every intention of competing. He bit the bullet and had four attendants hold him still for the surgery. He stayed 3 more days and scratched his first event. Once he left the hospital, he went to the Olympic pool for a workout with his doctors as observers. The next morning he qualified for the 200 meters freestyle. It turned out he had a bigger problem than the collapsed lung standing between him and a gold medal. He was in the lane next to Mark Spitz whom he had beaten in the U. S. championships. Mark expressed concern about his condition but Steve merely said that there was one gold medal in the race and he wanted it. If you're not 100%, you're not going to beat Mark Spitz. Steve hung on for a second place. He was a member of the 4x200 meter relay that took gold. In the 400, he placed third but was awarded second when the first place swimmer, Rick Demont, was disqualified due to an inadvertent use of a banned substance given to him by the US team doctors.[905]

Previously mentioned in the Manhattan marathon swim history were two swimmers who were arrested for swimming across the Hudson River in 1974. There is a bit more to the story than just their arrest. It seems that Donald O'Hara, an Irishman with theatrical ambitions, Peter Lloyd, a Canadian citizen recently unemployed as an advertising executive, and their friend Tom Dooley from Boston were sitting in a workingman's pub in mid-Manhattan (8th Avenue and 55th Street). Mr. O'Hara had aspirations for the theater had only realize, so far, a bit part as an idiot Irish coal miner in a production about the Molly McGuires and had a six-day run to his credit. Mr. Lloyd claimed to have swum the Channel[906] and was a graduate of the University of London with a diploma in Zoology along with an MBA. Since leaving business and working as a cab driver, he was writing a novel. Somehow, after a few beers the conversation turned to swimming. A boast once made is taken and the two men decided to swim to New Jersey that night.

All the men worked part-time as cab drivers and it was by cab that Dooley join Peter and Donald on the ride to the river even though the tavern was on 8th Avenue and the Hudson River was but a short walk. They jumped into the water off Pier 94 located at the end of 55th Street. Peter who has thought to pick up swimming trunks before leaving on this adventure and Donald who was swimming au natural began calling out to each other in the dark so they could swim using the buddy system. To their friend Tom Dooley and the cab driver, it sounded like they were in trouble so the cab driver called the police to report a double suicide. Eventually, both men made it across the Hudson River to Hoboken at the SeaTrain container piers where Donald got out of the water. Peter swam on making a round trip back to Manhattan landing near the Downtown Athletic Club in Lower Manhattan.

Donald, naked in New Jersey, managed to secure some clothing from the night watchman at the piers and bus fare from the Weehawken Police back to Manhattan.[907] In the meantime, the Coast Guard had mounted a search and the New York City Police were searching for the lost men. Peter, finished with his swim, returned by cab to the bar from lower Manhattan by 3:15 to have a celebratory drink before the bar closed at 4am and then went to his nearby apartment to sleep. He had seen helicopters about but didn't realize that they were looking for him. Donald, after arriving back at the bar when it opened at 6am and hearing the news on the radio about the missing persons, went to wake Peter and together they went to the Midtown North Precinct to turn themselves in.[908]

Perhaps the most unusual aspect of this swim was the publicity it received. The men not only had their pictures in the paper, but had three columns devoted to the story. Peter even worried that his mother might find out he was working as a cab driver, as if that would be her only worry. What was wrong with this swim? They were drunk, it was night and they had no escort boat. Nor had they scouted out where they would land, an important aspect of any swim and then of course, there are the logistics of the gear, what to do with the swim bag…but that was what their friend Tom Dooley was for. However, if swimming needs a Pamplona,[909] a symbol of the excess of middle age, under employment, recklessness, and drunkenness, this is it.

Swims gone bad(ly) might seem like an odd name but it does happen. In the second year of the Liberty-to-Liberty Triathlon, occurring on July 4th, 1984, the swim route was across the Hudson River from Battery Park to Liberty State Park. The swim portion of the triathlon was scheduled early in the morning while the Hudson was cresting at full ebb. During the briefing held on July 3rd for the athletes, I was introduced at the end of the talk from the back of the room. I pointed out that for the swimmers to make it across the river; they would have to swim toward the clock tower on the old railroad terminus building seen on the New Jersey shoreline directly west of the Battery.[910] I don't think they all paid attention to my instructions. Plus, the lead boat provided by the NY City Harbor Police went straight toward the Statue of Liberty with swimmers following it. Some broke away and began swimming toward the clock tower. Before long, the majority of swimmers were south of the Statue of Liberty and trying to swim upstream.

I had twelve support boats working that day and I called to them all to start picking the swimmers up. We had one large workboat that we used as a temporary ferry to carry the swimmers into the finish at Pier 7 of Liberty State Park behind the Statue.

The smaller boats would pick up the swimmers and then drop them off either on shore or on the workboat. I remember coming alongside of one fine athlete somewhere in the Hudson River between the BayRidge/Gowanus Flats and the Jersey Flats south of buoy R28 who was swimming beautifully as he was slowly backing out of the harbor. I almost hated to interrupt his swim but we had to complete this rescue effort and there were many more athletes needing to be picked up. Eventually, the workboat filled up with swimmers piled all over its deck and railings. I told the skipper to take the swimmers already on board into the finishing line to drop them off. Now this gentleman works in New York Harbor, that's why I hired him, and I noticed he wasn't tracking for the green C1 buoy to turn into the channel that leads to Liberty State Park. I told my skipper, "I sure hope he knows what he's doing" because the shortcut he was taking leads across a mudflat at low tide just south of Bedloe's Island, now known as Liberty Island where the Statue is located. I was thinking that maybe he knew of a path through this foul territory. Perhaps he did, but he didn't factor in the weight of the seventy odd swimmers[911] on board for he went aground. He had to off load the swimmers to float free. At this point some of the swimmer took off and finished their swim. Others who were just too tired or cold to take another stroke were just standing there waist high in the water looking at the boat as it floated free. They reminded me of penguins on an ice floe. I was overcome with a strange emotion of laughing and crying at the same time. Everyone was safely rescued.

    When we rescued what appeared to be the last swimmer, I picked up the binoculars and swept the waters south of our location. Not a swim cap to be seen. I can't emphasis enough the importance of a brightly colored swim cap. If you are in trouble, you want to be seen. I swept the area several times then looked again. I then announced on VHF the end of the rescue effort knowing that if some swimmer came ashore at a point other than Liberty State Park they would eventually make their way to the finishing line by land. In the back of my mind was the prospect of having to deal with a missing person report the next day. I affectionately call this event the largest lifesaving exercise ever conducted in New York Harbor.[912] The next year, the Coast Guard instituted a policy of obtaining a report of the count of the swimmers entering the water from the swim director. Then before releasing the support craft, the Coast Guard wanted a count of the swimmers exiting the water. The two numbers had to match. Someone on shore had to be checking off the swimmer's numbers as they arrived. Everyone had to be accounted for. They wanted a race official to certify that all the swimmers had left the water. It's a good policy.

The problem was cured in subsequent years by arranging for the swim to run north or south along the New Jersey shore using the starting and finishing locations of Liberty State Park and the railroad ferry terminal building in Jersey City. In 1991 and 1992 the Chesapeake Bay Swim, a 4.4 miles, was faced with a similar problem only they had twice to three times the number of swimmers in the water. In the 1991 swim, after the radio communications failed the Coast Guard called the swim off and directed the rescue of 720 swimmers. In 1992, 283 swimmers were picked up.[913] The problem in both cases was the simple fact that slow swimmers are simply overwhelmed by the slightest current. The maximum current on July 28th, 1992, the swimmers were told to expect was .9 knot, which it was once you got on the other side of the main channel. Leading up to the channel on the Annapolis side of the bay was 1½-knot ebb current.[914] Even for a fast swimmer, for every hour to crossing this portion, they will be carried about 1.5 miles south from their course. When this occurs during a swim, most swimmers will turn and try to recover their course slowing their forward progress lengthening the duration the current affects their swim. The swimmers were going on what is known to the English Channel veterans as a Spring tide. If the swim had started at 2pm, it would have made all the difference because the currents later in the same day were all less than ½ knot flood.

Swims that are probably the toughest to complete are those that the swimmer is not properly prepared for. I call them accidental swims because the swim takes place as the result of an accident. Once after training for months for my first mile swim at a Masters event, I cut my hand at work. I bandaged it up and went to the meet. As I sat there trying to figure out whether or not to swim, I rationalized that if because of a marine accident, I found myself in the ocean, I could possibly be injured much more seriously than this cut and I'd still have to do a swim. I did the swim and because the pool water was essentially clean water, the cut healed fine in days. In the Manhattan marathon swim of 1986 Susan Westnedge from Atlanta had cut her hand before the swim and decided to swim despite the open wound. When I came upon her at the Battery, the hand was swollen up and discolored. Without leaving the water an emergency medical technician tended to her leaving her to swim with her hand covered by a rubber glove. She finished the swim but the cut nearly finished her. She would spend a week in the hospital near death from the infection as a result of not taking the precaution of seeking immediate care for this injury. Swimmers in an accidental swim are faced with this reality with less training and little choice.

On October 23, 1993, Steve Francis, age 39, and pilot Don Urquhart, age 40, were taking a helicopter flight over the Spencer Gulf having just left from Whyalla enroute to Adelaide, Australia, when they crashed in the ocean. Both survived the crash, Don injured more than Steve. Unable to radio for help prior to crashing or put on floatation, the men had no choice but to swim for shore, approximately 6 miles away. Don had a visible gash across his forehead and was lightly dressed for the 61° water temperature. Steve kicked off his shoes and the two began swimming around 8:15am. Don struggled to keep up and began dropping behind. Don sank beneath the wave sometime around midday when his friend could no longer support him. Swimming into the evening hours, Steve came to shore and discovered a bog he had to transit in his exhausted condition. His legs were weak and he could barely stand. Shortly after 9:30pm, he was discovered and help summoned once he could convince his rescuer that he was exhausted and not drunk. It was estimated that he swam 7 miles in 7½ hours.[915]

Another example is from the Gulf war. Marine Lance Corporal Zachary Mayo, age 20, was knocked from the aircraft carrier he was aboard into the Arabian Sea a little after 2am on November 23, 1995. Surviving the 65-foot fall into the boat wake, he watched the craft disappear with no one noticing his fall or calls for help. He tried not to panic. He remembered his boot camp training of inflating his pants with air for an emergency floatation device. Pulling off the overalls he was wearing, he tied knots in the sleeves and legs and whipping them overhead, he had a pillow for a few minutes. He wouldn't be missed until morning muster then the ship would have to be searched. Small fish gathered about him until daylight biting him and he had to kick them away. As his arms grew tired from swinging the coveralls over his head, he found he could blow up the improvised floatation by exhaling into it. He also discovered a small tear in his coveralls, which he repaired by pulling up excess fabric and fastening his watch around it. This allowed his floatation to last for ten minutes. That meant only six times an hour would he have to pump up the coveralls. As daylight passed into the evening, it wasn't even discovered he was missing aboard the ship until the next morning. That night a storm broke out submerging him as waves broke over him. By the time the 24th hour had passed of his immersion, the storm had subsided. With the time in the water plus the time he was awake prior to his fall from the ship; he began falling asleep around daylight. He'd wake up when the overalls floated off dropping his face into the water. Finally, after 34 hours in the water, into the 2nd day, Zachary, in delirium, threw away his coveralls and began floating on his back sculling the water with his hands. That was when fortune smiled on him. About noon, a group of Pakistan fishermen came upon him and pulled him from the water. He slept for much of the return trip to their village, eating occasionally. His ankles wouldn't support his weight the next day. His face was seriously sunburned while his lips and tongue were black. But he was alive.[916]

One tragic occurrence that bears retelling because it reveals the nature of the beast that is the water environment around Manhattan. On June 12, 1991, the New York City Police Harbor Patrol unit was conducting a simulated helicopter rescue at the juncture of the East River and the Hudson River near the Battery. Mariners know this location as *The Spider*. The United States Coastal Pilot tells how vessels with a keel or any significant draft react to the opposing currents when transiting *The Spider*.[917] The name comes from the description of how a boat behaves when crossing *The Spider*; it's as if the vessel had sailed into a huge spider web and is trying to break free. Ships crossing through this area may experience a temporary loss of helm control. That is where the demonstration was taking place.

Kenneth Hansen of the Harbor Patrol went into the water and was not wearing a lifesaving vest. It's pretty hard to simulate a drowning person with one on. He was a good swimmer being part of their harbor patrol team and had assisted in harbor patrol operations for years. As the exercise began he was treading water when he disappeared. For an ex-lifeguard such as myself who has participated in many a drill, I would simulate a drowning person by submerging and resurfacing. Rescue swimmers are taught to approach a person underwater to control them by swinging them around and holding them from behind. A rescue swimmer has to be able to go underwater where the drowning person disappeared to pull them out. In Manhattan waters, when you submerge, disappearing is not hard to do in this era as the harbor was not cleaned up yet and visibility is nil. However, more was going on at that location than poor visibility. The East River was in full ebb and the Hudson was ebbing at the time of the demonstration. There was a sheer wall caused by the two hydraulic forces perpendicular to each other. There could be an intertwining of water but based on where the body was found, right underneath the spot he disappeared from, I'd venture a guess that the entire East River turns downward and goes underneath the Hudson River mixing there. Kenneth was sitting on the top of a waterfall. The water is still on the surface.

Skip Storch was called by the Harbor Patrol and asked if he could help them find Kenneth. Skip called me. I speculated that the East River would have carried the body into the Hudson River, which would have taken him south of the location. Nothing like that happened at all. When we discussed it later in the summer, I mentioned to Skip that he had swum right over that spot in his East River swim. When you are swimming, you are only dropping your hand two to three feet below the surface. You are not positioned vertically in the water. The water got a hold of the officer and pulled him under. Even if the Harbor Patrol had selected a location in the East River upstream from *The Spider*, the current flow would have caused them to drift down to this crease in the water; there the still water on the surface would have positioned Kenneth right on top of it. This is a frightening scenario but it can happen anywhere hydraulic forces are this massive.

The next story is a bit more cheerful. Over the summer of 2006, an Irish relay team was attempting an unheard of swim: a circumswim of Ireland! Imagine the cold, the storms, the wear and tear on a swimmer's body, the sea creatures, the coordination of logistics, the time and money required; but I'm getting ahead of myself. First the big numbers: total distance: 720 nautical miles (1333 kilometers) in 33 swim days out of 55 consecutive days. The swimmer portion of the team consisted of Nuala Moore, Annemarie Ward, her brother Ryan Ward, Tom Waters, and Ian Claxton. The marine coordinator was Derek Flanagan and his wife Kathleen. The swim was a fund raiser for the RNLI, Royal National Lifeboat Institute, so there was a built-in support group. The boat crews were members of the Sheephaven Sub Aqua Club. Derek was aboard the *Abhainn Ri* the large support boat where he directed the course and logged the daily swim start and stop locations.

Swimmers were supported up-close by two Ridged Inflatable Boats (RIBs). There was one swimmer in the water, one swimmer on one of the RIBs, two on the other RIB, and a spare swimmer back on the *Abhainn Ri*. The disadvantage to RIBs is the swimmers were out in the open all the time getting bounced around in their swim gear as they took turns swimming and there is no shelter if it was raining or spray was coming over the bow. Occasionally they would fall asleep as they waited their next turn in the water. They would be sitting in the RIBs tired, cold and hungry (it was difficult to eat between turns) for up to 12 hours a day.

The team stayed ashore each night and depending on the Port the support boats could pull into would cause the ocean commute to change daily. The daily routine was wake up at 7am, breakfast, briefing at 8:30am, cast off by 9:30am or 10am, commute to "work", swim 20 miles in relay, commute "home", find the B&B, shower, change, dinner, and then sleep. The weekends usually were off as the rescue unit was changed over with a new team each week. Down days were weather calls although the team would see some huge swells. When the RIBs had trouble staying close by or getting in and out was too difficult, the team would called it a day and have to make up the mileage the next.

Individually, everyone gave up wages for the 9 weeks of the swim. Companies sponsored most of the costs associated with the swim otherwise it would not have been possible. The down days were not factored in so that added to the personal cost. Training began 18 months earlier with practice swims in water as low as 6°C.

The swim began in Donegal on the northwest coast of Ireland at Carrickfinn Blue Flag beach. The swim took the team in a clockwise direction. They stayed about 10 miles offshore to avoid minor obstructions, current ebb and flood when crossing harbor entrances, and wave reflections when waves bounced off cliffs. It was easy in the beginning, then the physical exertion began to take it toll. Quitting was never an option. Even when the team encountered jelly fish, lion's main, on the east coast; the team just dealt with the pain as the jelly fish were impossible to avoid. Nuala Moore thought their bodies got stronger, adapted to their surroundings and that help them deal with it mentally. When the days were going poorly, it was just "today is not a good time for me!" There were good days and days where dolphins swam nearby. The team's longest swim was a 5 kilometer that Annemarie Ward tore off who was feeling in the groove with her stroke that day. The funniest moment during the swim was when the fellows put on women's swim suits. The evenings included a glass of wine, time to ourselves, and to time to recover. Overall, the team had the best fun, met the best bunch of people and found reservoirs of energy they never knew existed.[918]

Figure 112 The mike in the face and the question is, "What are your thoughts?" Are you ready for this because the press starts as soon as you get out of the water. Photo of Tom Hetzel after one of his seven Manhattan Marathon, one less than his English Channel crossings.

Appendix

Contained herein are the mathematical calculations and the formulas that have proven useful when discussing swimming in open waters. The swimmer enters a maritime world that has it own system of position reckoning and recording of distances and speeds. Swim organizers would do well to become trained in boating and nautical terms. This is the world that deals with swimmers, for you are either swimming, or standing on shore, or boating. I highly recommend the classes given by the Power Squadron, the Auxiliary Coast Guard, and other organizations that teach seamanship and boat handling. Marine Science has a long history and a terminology that is extensive; the knowledge learned in the study of marine science comes in handy at the least expected time. Marlinspike is a skill of seamanship rarely taught at liberal art colleges but quite handy if you spent any time on a boat. At most colleges, a sailing team is as close as a student can get to seamanship and an appreciation for the writing of Joseph Conrad.

Calculations

1. Conversion of knots to 1650 pace

What is meant by 1650 pace is the time in minutes the swimmer is taking to swim a mile (a swimmer's "mile" race is 1650 yards which is close to 1500 meters). All distance swimmers know their 1650 times and can easily relate to this number. They also know that their pace through the water for a distance swim greater than one mile will be less than their fastest 1650 time. A time over the ground includes the current component if there is any.

Multiply the number of knots by 2025.4 yards to determine the speed in yards per hour

Divide this value by 60 to determine the yards per minute.

Divide 1650 by the speed in yards per minute to find out how long in minutes it would take the swimmer to swim a 1650 at this speed.

Formula: $(1650)/(X\ knots*2025.4/60) = 1650\ pace$

Short cut: $48.9/X\ knots = 1650\ pace$

2. Conversion of knots to yards per minute
Multiply the number of knot by 2025.4 yard to find out the number of yards traveled in one hour. Divide this by 60 to find out how many yards per minute the person is traveling.
Yards per minute= # Knots*2025.4/60
Shortcut: Yds/min= # Knots * 33¾
Analysis: for every knot of current speed, swimmers pick up 33 yards every minute. 3-knots of current account for 100 yards added to the swimmers speed every minute provided the swimmer is swimming with the current.

3. Conversion of tidal range to current speed
Using a publication called Admiralty Tidal Stream Atlas, NP 233; you can derive from a graphical diagram a formula for the calculation of the approximate maximum flow of the current for a specific range between any two tides for any tidal station addressed by NP 233. That formula (presented without proof) is:

(range-3.2)/(2.8/(Spring rate-Neap rate))+Neap rate=max current

The range is entered in meters. Spring rate and neap rates in knots are found on chart SC1892 in the table for the various time periods. This formula was derived from information on the English Channel current and may not apply in other locales.

4. Calculation of current speed at any time
The maximum current must be known as this calculation uses the well-known sine wave curve as its model for the current speed. Not all locations are well represented by this mathematical model. Some reach a peak speed then flatten out. In these cases, a piecewise approach is recommended to calculate the swim. In still other cases, the current can be modeled if a modulating frequency is known. For Manhattan, the sine wave curve is adequate to model the current speed. The maximum current for the tidal station[919] is used as the amplitude for the sine wave (Cur_{max} in the

formula). The units used assume an hour for the time period and are expressed in knots. The period is one tidal cycle, ebb and flood (normally 12 ¾ hours) but ½ a tidal cycle can be use in a solution. The length of the cycle varies slightly daily so the actual length can be calculated from the published times of slack ($Tide_{cycle}$ in the formula). The calculation of any time is allowed by using a fraction of 180 degrees ($180*(Time/Tide_{cycle})$). The maximum current which is in knots will derive the current speed in knots as well which can be converted by formulas above to more useful information if needed. The consistency of units requires the time during the current cycle to be in hours since the start of the cycle. The cycle duration and current speed are converted to minutes for use in spreadsheet calculations. Also, some sine functions required degrees converted to radian, if this is the case include pi (π) divided by 180 to convert the degree representation.

$Cur_{max}*sin(180*(Time/Tide_{cycle}))$

Since the calculations are cumbersome, I use the following guidelines for back of the envelope calculations. The first and last hours of a current are a straight line from 0 to .707 of the maximum current. The very maximum current occurs at mid cycle but for practical calculations, the middle four hours of a cycle are assumed to be maximum speed. You have 15 minutes of essentially dead water on either side of slack except in the East River when you have 3 minutes. If the swimmer is with the current, the swimmer's speed adds to the current speed. If the swimmer has an opposing current, the current speed is subtracted from the swimmer's speed. If the calculation results in a negative number, the swimmer is drifting backwards[920]. Currents at other angles are considered in the next topic.

5. Calculation of swimmer's course heading given current speed and direction and swimmer speed (solution for optimum English Channel crossing)

Mathematically let the swimmer's course be heading θ and the current direction is ϕ. The swimmer's longitudinal speed is $\cos(\theta-90)*S_{speed} - \cos(270-\phi)*C_{speed}$. The swimmer's latitudinal speed is $\sin(\theta-90)*S_{speed} + \sin(270-\phi)*C_{speed}$. Using the well known Distance=Rate* Time, we can substitute in the longitudinal and latitudinal speed for the swimmer into two separate equations:

Distance (longitudinal) = $(\cos(\theta-90)*S_{speed} - \cos(270-\phi))*C_{speed}*$Time

And

Distance (latitudinal) = $(\sin(\theta-90)*S_{speed} + \sin(270-\phi)*C_{speed})*$Time

Since the values for the two different distances are known, let's substitute them in and solve for Time; in other words, divided the distance by the rate. Plus, since the solution for Time in both formulas is the same—in a swim that is successful the swimmer arrives in France at one particular time—we can write one equation that drops Time all together (we can go back and compute Time separately). This equations looks like this:

$10.5/(\cos(\theta-90)*S_{speed} - \cos(270-\phi))*C_{speed}) =$

$14.5/(\sin(\theta-90)*S_{speed} + \sin(270-\phi)*C_{speed})$

This formula looks complicated but there is only one unknown in it and that is: θ, the swimmer's course. The current's direction is known and the current speed (C_{speed} in knots) is known as well as the swimmer's speed (S_{speed} in knots). The only thing that is unknown is the swimmer's heading. This is what the entire problem crossing the English Channel resolves down to: what direction to head to reach France at a particular spot (in the least amount of time, otherwise it wouldn't be interesting or you could willy-nilly swim any-old-way across the channel and eventually you'll get there). Once you have the heading for the swimmer, you can return to one of the two distance formulas, substitute in the derived heading and obtain the elapsed time for the swim. The optimum heading allows the solution of the two distance formulas so that the terminal distances are reached at the same time. This time will be the minimum time possible for the specific current and swimmer. The formula assumes the swim is completed over one tide as described in the chapter on the English Channel.

6. How to determine current speed using a watch

The use of a marker is required for this determination. Two types will be considered: a small float submerged but visible and a swimmer.

Prior to timing the marker, measure a known distance (in feet) off in the current. If two points are not found, anchor a boat in the flow and use the boat length in feet for the distance. Drop the marker at the bow and record the time in seconds the float takes to drift to the stern. The boat length is divided by the seconds to determine the feet per second the current is flowing. Multiply this number by 60 to calculate the feet per minute the current is flowing. Divide by 100 to convert the current speed to knots.

$$(\text{Distance}_{\text{in feet}} / \text{time}_{\text{in seconds}}) * .6 = \text{current speed}_{\text{in knots}}$$

In order to use a swimmer to determine the current speed, the swimmer needs to covert their 1650 pace to knots using the following formula:

$$(1650/(1650\ \text{time}))/3\ 3.75 = \text{swimmer}_{\text{speed in knots}}$$

The next part of the procedure requires the swimmer to swim into the current for a short period of time, stop and note the time, then swim back to the starting location, stop and note the time. The starting location can be a boat at anchor or a buoy. Subtract the times from each other to get the time difference that the current makes and sum the times to get the total time swimming. The current speed in knots is a fraction of the swimmers speed. The formula is:

$$\text{Swimmer}_{\text{speed in knots}} * (\text{Time}_{\text{difference}} / \text{Time}_{\text{total}}) = \text{current}_{\text{speed in knots}}$$

Swimming related injuries

Swimmers spend quite a bit of their time alone with themselves in the water. Other than the occasional glance about as you swim, and the stops at the wall to rest, a swimmer has only his self to deal with. This being alone provides time for reflection. Coaches would prefer that you think about your stroke, your swim plan, visualize winning, etc. But once your competitive days are through, what then?

Swimming is about becoming comfortable in your body in the water. A workout is over when it achieves its goal. The distance you have to swim, the condition you are in, are factors that vary for everyone for the optimum workout. We can't spend forever in the pool; we have lives and obligations so the time we spend is best spent to achieve its purpose. Swim workouts for competition allow us to focus for a limited time on specific outcomes. Swimming brute distances is not swimming any more than cramming for a test is learning. Any coach that would over-train their athletes doesn't respect them. A posted yardage practice is a recommendation, not a minimum or maximum.

Swimmer's shoulder, the most common swimming injury, can be caused by overuse and is an inflammation where the tendons slide in the shoulder, specifically, the supraspinatus and biceps tendons. This is called bursitis. The pain is noticed when holding the arm extended out in a horizontal position from your side, raised even with the shoulders. The treatment: rest, gradual resumption of exercise with modification to the arm stroke. Treatment may also include medication, inject of cortisone, and physical therapy. Since complete rest leads to reduce aerobic capacity, a rest followed by slight exercise then followed by moderate exercise over a period of weeks is an alternative to continued activity with more serious consequences. If it hurts, there's a reason. Swimmers need to recognize and listen to their bodies.

There is a different pain from muscle starvation for oxygen during an anaerobic exercise and genuine musculoskeletal injury.

A survey of injuries from 1993 found shoulder pain as common as 47% in 13-14 years olds, 66% in 15-16 year olds and 73% of college swimmers.[921] These are **epidemic** proportions. While technical flaws in the stroke can stress the shoulders and lead to overuse, incident levels this high can't all be related to technical flaws in the stroke.

Water-Borne Parasites

This is not anything swimmers like to talk about but it is a subject that they and swim organization need to be cognizant about. Swimmer will occasionally emerge from the water complaining about stinging pin pricks under their suits. Within a few hours, a rash develops that is itchy. There are three different causes for this itch: that caused by cnidarian larvae, that caused by cercarial larvae, and that caused by schistosome cercaride, a free swimming parasitic flatworm found in FRESH water.

"Cnidarians are a group of marine animals that contain stinging structures known as nematocysts, and include jellyfish, corals, sea anemones, hydroids, and Portuguese Man o'War. There are more than 9000 species of this group of marine animals; however, it appears that the larval form of Linuche unqui culata, also known as a "thimble jellyfish," is responsible for outbreaks in South Florida and the Caribbean".[922] The bathing suit acts as a net for these microscopic creatures and friction or pressure from the suit can cause their nematocysts to fire. They also collect in hair. The medical journals say that the dermatitis "resolves" normally in a week. Treatment is application of over the counter 1% hydrocortisone cream and an antihistamine. Prevention is changing out of your bathing suits as soon as possible after swimming and a shower. This type of itch is called Sea Lice.

A second type of dermatitis called cercarial dermatitis is cause by trematode parasite in the second larvae stage of its lifecycle. This parasite moves from an animal to an aquatic snail and back again. For those who know their snails it's the Lymnaeidae or Physidae snail. The parasite is called sporocysts in the snail and it produces larvae called cercarial that is released into the water. It's the snail's larvae that's the problem when a swimmer is nearby. The larvae actually bornes into your skin thinking you are the host creature. It eventually dies because this particular larvae can not live in our bodies.[923] You get red spots and an itch. This rash is called Swimmer's Itch.

One difference with Sea Lice is this itch develops where the bathing suit did not cover the skin. The discomfort is slightly less than the previous pest but the treatment and prevention is exactly the same with the added precaution of don't swim with the snails.

With regards to the last source of dermatitis, this parasitic flatworm is found only in fresh water (but not necessarily clean) and the host animal for the flatworm is humans. It has the same life cycle as the parasite that lives in ducks and other wild animals that doesn't brother us. If you've been swimming in fresh water in the developing world, had a rash from exposed water that went away or wasn't noticed and you're running a fever, chills, cough, or muscle aches 1 to 2 months after the swim, see a doctor.[924]

"Swims" of Captain Paul Boyton[925]

Date	Location	Start	Finish	Time	Comment
10/21/1874	Coast of Ireland	From steamship *Queen* en route to Liverpool	Cape Clear, Ireland	9 hours	Leaped off deck and swam to shore in a storm
Oct., 1874	Dublin Bay	Unk	Unk	Unk	Demonstration swim
4/10/1875	English Channel	Dover	France	DNF	1st attempt, failed to finish
5/29/1875	English Channel	France	Dover	23:38	Completed the crossing
Oct., 1875	Rhine	Basle, Switzerland	Cologne, Germany	Unk	400 miles
Summer, 1876	Danube	Lintz	Vienna	83 hours	While "sleeping" in his suit at night he went under a water mill wheel and was injured. A citizen upon coming to his aid, fled thinking he was a sea monster.

Summer 1876	Sections of River Po, Arno, & Tiber	Unk	Unk	Unk	Greeted by 100,000 people coming into Rome
2/16/1877		Isle of Capri	Naples	Unk	Large reception upon arrival
3/16/1877	Straits of Messina	Unk	Unk	Unk	Fought off a shark and broke a rib
May 1877	Rhine	Seyssel	Lyons and Arles	60 hours	400 miles
Nov. 1877	Sommes	Amiens	Abbeville	Unk	Someone tried to shoot his foot off, thought it was a duck
Jan/Feb 1888	Tagus	Toledo	Lisbon	Unk	Met by 200,000 people in Lisbon
March, 1878	Straits of Gibraltar	Tarifa	Tangiers	Unk	
August 1878	Seine	Nogent	Paris	75 hours	

More "swims" and adventures of Capt. Boyton

Date	Location	Start	Finish	Time	Comments
Jan. 9, 1876	Mississippi River	Alton, Illinois	St. Louis, MO.	12 hours	Makes a river trip.[926]
2/24/1876	Lower Mississippi River	Bayon-Goula	New Orleans	24 hours	100 miles this time.[927]
3/16/1876	Ohio River	Louisville	Traverses the falls of Louisville.[928]		
2/7/1879	Allegheny	Oil City, PA	Pittsburgh, PA	Unk	Start of trip to New Orleans[929]
2/18/1879	Ohio	Pittsburgh	Waiting for ice flows to clear up before continuing.[930]		
2/21/1879	Ohio	Louisville, KY	Nearly run over by a paddlewheel boat. Missed Louisville and goes through rapids again.[931]		
2/27/1879	Mississippi	New Orleans	Boyton arrives in New Orleans and is cheered by thousands.[932]		
5/1879	Nantasket Beach, Boston, MA	One mile course off the beach.	Repeat laps until finished	Dispute over finish,[933] referee declares "no race"[934]	Match race against Webb[935] rematch set.[936] Never happens.
10/15/187_	Merrimac River, MA[937]	Unk	Unk	7 days	200 miles
9/1881	Peru	Webb had been hired by the Peruvian Government to improve their torpedoes. Was taken prisoner when Chile overran Lima.[938] Eventually released with British influence some time after May 20th, 1881.[939]			
19/1881	Mississippi River	St. Paul	St. Louis	Stage	Enroute to Cairo[940]

11/1/1881	Yellowstone & Missouri Rivers	Glendive, Montana	Omaha	Unk		Paddled 2500 miles in 47 days.[941]
5/7/1885	NY harbor	Plants a fake bomb under the keel of the British ship HMS Garnet.[942]				
5/20/1885	East River	Pulls unconscious man, Robert Odlum, from East River who had jumped off the Brooklyn Bridge for fame and fortune and dies in his arms.[943]				
6/29/1885	Cincinnati, Ohio	Boyton demonstrates the planting of a bomb on a ship; accidentally reveal method of fishing using dynamite.[944]				
1/24/1886	Manhattan	Fallen on hard times, Boyton holds an estate sale, to become beer salesman.[945]				
3/29/1887	Off Cape Henry	Jumps overboard off Cape Henry intending to swim ashore, storm overpowers and he hails passing ship.[946]				
April 1887	Hudson River	Albany	Battery	150 miles		Makes one last swim.[947]
4/9/1887	Manhattan	Boyton signs to appear with Barnum circus with Prof. Beckwith in tank at Madison Square Garden.[948]				
Dec. 17, 1888	Manhattan	Boyton starts an act with seals. Home near Lake Michigan with other animals.[949]				
9/30/1893	Brazil	Report Boyton captured by British attempting to blow up blockage ships off Rio de Janeiro, reported to be working for Brazilian government to break blockage.[950]				

4/20/1924	Obituary	Relates some of his exploits. In 1893 he was in London with his seals at the Earl's Court Exhibition. He returned to settle in Coney Island, developed the Capt. Boyton Boats rides, by the descriptions: a log flume water ride. He continued to travel to the West Indies and South America to collect rare birds. The cause of death was pneumonia contracted on a trip abroad. Of his three sons, Paul managed Sheephead Bay Bus Line, Joseph was Treasurer of Ringling Brothers-Barnum and Bailey Circus, and the third, Rev. Neil, was a professor at Georgetown University.[951]

Captain Paul Boyton was certainly one of the more colorful characters from the past. His invention and superb demonstration of the life-saving suit bears merit and attention even today. In an account by the 2nd mate of the vessel *Merlin* on a trip to Sicily from Malta in January of 2004, of the rescue of survivors from a shipwreck we see the disastrous results of merchant sailors not prepared to abandon ship. The *Merlin* was a ro-ro[1] ship en route in the Mediterranean when it heard a distress call from another vessel just before 1 in the morning. Both vessels were riding out a storm with winds of 55-60 knots and seas building to 23 feet. The *Merlin* has a very high freeboard (the sides of the ship), as much as 50 feet from the deck to the water line all the way around.

The vessel in distress was the *Kephi*, a 328-foot bulk carrier with a crew of 17. It was taking on water. When 16 miles away, the *Merlin* went to the rescue. This wasn't the coastline of the United States where the Coast Guard would send the appropriate rescue craft, the Greeks don't send helicopter out to sea 150 miles in storms and Malta Rescue Control Center informed the crew of the *Merlin* that they were it as far as first responders were

---

[1] a roll-on, roll-off vessel for the transportation of vehicles.

concerned. The *Merlin* was 7 miles away when the *Kephi* disappeared off the radar screen. It took the *Merlin* 2 hours to arrive at the site of the sinking from when they first responded to the call. Several lights were seen in the water from personal strobe lights attached to life vests. The *Merlin* attempted to come alongside the distressed mariners, which in the storm was incredibly difficult because of the immense sail area the sides of the *Merlin* present to the wind. One survivor they came upon was only 50 feet away but upwind of the boat. The crew was unable to throw a life ring to recover the survivor and the boat was drifting faster than the individual. When they eventually came around, the night and the sea had swallowed the survivor.

After two hours of searching they came upon nothing but empty life vests and life rings with working lights but no people. After 3 hours, they saw a flare and by 0730 they came alongside a life raft. The vessel stopped upwind of the raft and attempted to pass a line to them. In their weakened condition from not wearing survivor suits the two men took considerable time to secure the life raft with the line from the *Merlin*. The survivors now could be fetched off the raft and onto the *Merlin*. From the aft deck where the life raft was secured, 30 feet above the waterline, the probability of the survivors climbing a pilot ladder were poor so the crew threw a line rigged with a loop. The first person pulled it over himself, under his arms, and the crew hauled away. The problem was at the bulwark (the solid railing around the deck) where the man got stuck. He was slipping out of the loop pulling his clothing and life jacket off. Soon the lifejacket and the loop were off of him and two crewmen were holding onto his arms as he hung off the edge of the ship. The men pulled on his arms and a third crewman got a grip on a leg eventually wrestling him onto the deck. The second survivor while being pulled up fell out of the loop into the water and was unable to climb back into the raft. He drifted slower than the *Merlin* and he was soon upwind before another line could be passed to him. His body was later recovered by another vessel.[952]

One out of seventeen men was saved. This is not a very good record. It's been nearly 130 years since Captain Boyton demonstrate for Queen Victoria his lifesaving suit whose concern for her sailor was a message to the maritime nations at that time. Ships sink in rough seas and the equipment needed to save them needs to be made with this condition in mind. Captain Boyton jumped overboard in a storm and made it safely to shore when off Cape Clear, Ireland.[953] Through technology advancements the Boyton suit has evolved into the survival suit of today. It only needs to be provided and used.

When thousands gathered to welcome him on his arrivals often through rivers clogged with ice, what a curious sight he must have been. He surely was a man ahead of his time. Based on the account of the rescue of the survivor of the *Kephi*, he still is. The International Maritime Organization has now made it a requirement for all cargo and bulk carriers over 500 gross tons to carry one immersion suit for every person on board starting July 1, 2006.[954]

Jim Doty of New England Master Swimming invented an inflatable Safety Pack. By pulling a lanyard, a pouch, about the size of a fanny pack storage bag, would inflate into a horseshoe shaped life-saving float. Swimmers could then attach the float around them to rest when swimming. It was designed to be carried in the small of a swimmer's back so it would not interfere while swimming. A CO_2 cartridge inflated the device, which could be stowed away, and the cartridge replenished for subsequent usage. He had few sales but the Coast Guard did like the idea.[955]

Another device that would be helpful in situations where a swimmer has to be removed from the water is a *Jason's Cradle*. This is a full-body hoist that wrapped around an individual. Exhausted swimmers sometimes need assistance climbing ladders and this horizontal rescue system is designed to do just that.[956] If such a system had been available on the *Merlin* designed for its high freeboard, the second survivor might have been recovered alive.

Team Millennium

In celebration of the 20th Anniversary of the Manhattan Island Marathon Swim a relay team was made up of all women with four members former solo champions of the Manhattan swim. Five have swum the English Channel. On Marathon day, June 21, 2001, they finished in a time of 7:43 ahead of all the solo swimmers. Their kayakers for the event were Randy Nutt and Pete Muller.

Tobie Smith, Chappaqua, NY:
>1998 FINA World 25K Champion
>1994 NCAA Division I Champion, 1650 Free
>1999 Manhattan Island Marathon Swim Record Holder

Karen Burton Reeder, Colorado Springs, Colorado:
>World Record, Catalina Island to California, 1994, 7:43
>World Cup 25K Champion, 1992

Tammy van Wisse, Springvale, Victoria, Australia:
>World record across Cook Strait, New Zealand, March 1999, 6:49
>World record across Loch Ness, August 1999, 9:06
>1997 Manhattan Island Marathon Swim Winner

Regan Stacy Scheiber, Mukilteo, Washington:
>2000 Atlantic City 34K Marathon Champion
>2000 Champion Swim Across Long Island Sound & course record holder

Gail Rice, Miami Shores, Florida:
>Fastest person across the English Channel in 1999
>Swam 12 miles around Key West butterfly in 1998
>1995 Manhattan Island Marathon Swim Winner

Shelley Taylor-Smith, Manly, NSW, Australia:
>1991 World No.1 Ranked Marathon Swimmer, Men and Women
>Women's World No.1 Marathon Swimming Champion Seven Consecutive Years, 1988-1995
>1997 Women's World No.1 Ranking for 25km
>Fifteen World Records (1983-1997)
>>Atlantic City, USA; Manhattan Island, USA; Sydney Harbour, Australia; Long Island Sound Swim, USA; Lake Magog & Lake St. John, Quebec; Capri to Naples & Italian Riveria, Italy; Beaver Lake, Arkansas, USA; Rio Coronda & Hernandarias, Parana, Argentina; Womens 25km International, Japan
>Two World Championship 25km Gold Medals, 1988 & 1991
>Two World Championship 25km Team Gold Medals, 1994 & 1996
>Three Pan Pacific Championship 25km Gold Medals, 1991, 93, & 93
>Two Pan Pacific Championship 25km Team Gold Medals, 1993 & 97

Sicily to Malta Relay World Champions, 1996
Australian Women's National Swimming Champion, Nine National Titles 25km
Five Time Winner Manhattan Island Marathon Swim, 1985, 87, 88, 89, & 98
Two Time Holder of Manhattan Island Solo swim record, 1985-92, 1995-
Sydney to Wollongong swim, 1995
51 First Places in International Marathon Races, 9 outright 1st overall (Men & Women).

Figure 113 Shelley Taylor-Smith, Hon. Secretary FINA Marathon Swimming Committee-TOWSC.

Team Millennium was made up of star performers from the open-water swimming world. There was another star swimmer whose life was devoted to swimming and urban planning: Robert Moses. He was born in 1888 at the beginning of swimming competitive era in New Haven, Connecticut, and moved to New York at a young age. Undoubtedly, he was made aware of the living conditions for immigrants in the lower East side through his parent's charitable work. In 1905, at age 17, he began his college education at Yale. His swimming improved along with the rest of the swimming community and competing alongside the likes of Charlie Daniels as a member and captain of the Yale Union Swimming Association. He was also a member of the track team.

One swimming meet during his college days was particularly poignant for it was the foreshadowing of his life's work. On January 20, 1908, the opening of a new bath at Avenue A and 23rd Street was celebrated with a water carnival that included a ribbon cutting, speeches, a tilting contest, a water polo match, and swimming competition that saw two new indoor records established by Charlie Daniels before the large crowd. The president of the borough of Manhattan, John Ahearn, made an opening address to the throng. The Commissioner of Public Works and the Superintendent of Public Baths were present and to Robert Moses who was there representing Yale, these speeches and the crowd reception probably made as big an impression upon him as the records that were set. Robert won his heat, the first, in the 50 yard swim and won the semi-final heat in a time of 32 seconds. He came in 3rd in the final heat, well off the winning time. Charlie Daniels, swimming in the 2nd heat established a new record of 24.6 seconds dropping the indoor record below 25 seconds for the first time. He then scratched the rest of the 50 yards swims to save himself for the 200 yards swim where he broke Baney Karen's record of 2:15 by two seconds in the third heat. Daniels swam the finals for the 200 yards but was spent as his record was set in the last heat before the finals coming in second to the winning time of 2:22.6.[957] The cheers, the marveling, and whole atmosphere that day were unlike any other swimming meet for the public attended wholeheartedly. It must have made an impression upon Robert Moses as a young man who was known for his poetry.

Robert went on to graduate from Yale, received a Master's from Oxford, and a Ph.D. from Columbia. At Oxford, he was so highly regarded as an orator that he was the president of the Oxford Union which is a debating society. He returned to New York and became involved in politics and in 1919 under Governor Alfred Smith formulated a political system devoid of patronage as a means for reforming civil service based in part on his doctorial dissertation on the British Colonial administration. He came to represent a vision that is known as the progressive playground movement: he believed in recreation and not conservation. In 1924 he crafted legislation for *A State Park Plan for New York* which he was appointed as chairman of the commission once the legislation passed. This was the beginning of his public service which lasted 44 years where he held as many as 12 chairmanships at one time that built the parks and the roads to make them accessible to the city dwellers. He was not an engineer but he built bridges, parkways, two world fairs, housing, tunnels, zoos, civic center (Lincoln Center), stadiums, and playgrounds. When he was retired in 1968, not by choice, he left New York State with 2.5 million acres, half the acreage of all the parks in the United States, 658 more playgrounds than when he began, 416 miles of roads, many major bridges and 15 swimming complexes.

In the Thirties there was nationalistic competition with Nazi Germany in numbers of battleships, Olympics, World Fairs, and transportation. It was the later two categories Robert Moses excelled at and his leadership provides a contrast between the two world powers. He was known to work 15 hour days and yet it was a rare day that he didn't manage to go swimming. He served the public gratis.

I've driven on his road, I've swam in his pools, gone to his beaches, and attended ceremonies and shows at his stadiums and civic centers. He envisioned a megalopolis for the multitudes and millions have benefited from his creations.[958] His legacy continues today despite attempts to sully his reputation.[959]

Reference books for more detailed information:

Adam, Norbert. Schwimmania 1899/1999 (Swim Mania1899/1999). Horn, Austria:Druckerei Ferdinand Berger & Söhne, 1999.
American Red Cross, Swimming and Diving. Garden City, New York:Doubleday, 1938.
Armbuster, David. Swimming and Diving. St. Louis, CV Mosby Co., 1968.
Campbell, Gail. Swimming-Marathon. New York:Sterling Publishing Co., 1973.
Cleveland, Marcia. Dover Solo. Canada:MMJ Press, 1999.
Cox, Lynne. Swimming to Antarctica: Tales of a Long Distance Swimmer. New York:A.A. Knopf, 2004.
Fosberg, Gerald. Modern Marathon Swimming. London:Rootledge and Kegan Paul, 1963.
Friedman, Sally. Swimming the Channel: A Widow's Journey to Life. New York:Farrar Straus & Giroux, 1996.
Halliburton, Richard. New Worlds to Conquer. Indianapolis:The Bobbs-Merrill Co., 1929.
Hetzel, Thomas. Conquest of the English Channel. Corpus Christi, Texas:T. Becket Publishing Co., 1985.
Mallon, Bill and Ture Widlund. The 1896 Olympic Games. Jefferson, North Carolina:McFarland & Company, Inc., 1998.
Sprawson, Charles. Haunts of the Black Masseur: The Swimmer as Hero. NY:Pantheon, 1992.
Vickers, Betty and William Vincent. Swimming. Dubuque, Iowa:W. C. Brown Co., 1984.
Wennerberg, Conrad. Wind, Waves, and Sunburn, London:A. S. Barnes and Company, 1974.

Photo Credits
Figure

1. *The Diver's Tomb*: from the National Museum of Paestu, Italy.
2. *Children Swimming in a River* from plate 27 of Emblemata of Paolo Maccio, Spencer Collection, The New York Public Library.
3. *Wolves Swimming Across a River* from plate 44 of Emblemata of Paolo Maccio, Spencer Collection, The New York Public Library.
4. *Leander Swimming Across the Hellespont to Hero*, Carlo Cesio, San Francisco Museums of San Francisco.
5. Leander close-up. Detail of previous engraving.
6. William Percy's engraving from the library collection of the Mariner's Museum website: http://www.mariner.org/library/new/items.php.
7. London Bridge, image provide by Lake Havasu City Convention and Visitors Bureau, www.golakehavasu.com.
8. Gertrude Ederle from the public domain.
9. *A swimming bath on the Seine*, at Paris, pages 540 & 541 from Harper's Weekly, 21 June 1873. From the Fine Arts Museums of San Francisco. Artist: Simon Durand, Swiss, 1838-1896.
10. Steve Brodie from the play "On the Bowery" portraying himself. From "American Icon:Incorporating Tension in the Brooklyn Bridge" at http://xroads.virginia.edu/~MA03/pricola/bridge/peoples
11. The Brooklyn bridge and South Street Seaport in 1900, (Photo by Library of Congress, Prints and Photographs Division, Detroit Publishing Company Collection, LC-D4-90107.)

12. 1904 Olympic team photo courtesy US Olympic committee web site.
13. Annette Kellerman from Wikipedia image.
14. Chesapeake Bay: from Visible Earth, NASA website.
15. Baltic Sea: from Visible Earth, NASA website.
16. MDA charity swim courtesy of Ben Siebecker, PE.
17. Teresa Skilton from MIF photo archives.
18. Sri Lanka: from Visible Earth, NASA website.
19. Courtesy of Caprice Schaefer.
20. Courtesy of Caprice Schaefer.
21. Lake Ohrid: from www.navis.gr/space/greece/11m.htm.
22. Race photo coutesy of Atlantic City Around-the-Island Marathon Swim webpage. www.acswim.org.
23. Petar Stoychev from Atlantic City Around-the-Island Marathon Swim webpage. www.acswim.org.
24. Edith van Dijk and Katalia Pankina courtesy of www.acswim.org.
25. Photo from Flickr.com by Ruta Saulyte.
26. View of approaching tug from Manhattan Island Foundation (MIF) photo archives.
27. View tug, barge, and swimmer with kayak from MIF photo archives.
28. Jamie Tout in Harlem River from MIF photo archives.
29. Swimmers south of GW Bridge from MIF photo archives.
30. Viele topological map courtesy of David Rumsey Map Collection, http://www.davidrumsey.com/maps6128.html
31. United Nations photo from MIF photo archives.
32. Tim Johnson, Paul Asmuth, and Drury Gallagher from MIF photo archives.
33. Julie Ridge from MIF photo archives.
34. Drury Gallagher and Sally Friedman from MIF photo archives.

35. Distress Signal, from student manual, US Power Squadron Boating Course booklet.
36. Williamsburg Bridge from MIF photo archives.
37. Harlem River with swimmer, Renken escort boat, and Circle line from MIF photo archives.
38. Riverside Church & Grants Tombs from MIF photo archives.
39. View of the USS Intrepid from MIF photo archives.
40. Tug, barge, & swimmer under GW Bridge from MIF photo archives.
41. View of Lower Manhattan at East River from MIF photo archives.
42. View of Hell Gate from the south from MIF photo archives.
43. Fishing pier at 106th Street and the Harlem River from MIF photo archives.
44. Swimmer congestion at start of Harlem River from MIF photo archives.
45. Approaching Circle Line boat in Harlem from MIF photo archives.
46. Swimmer and Circle Line safely thru the bridge from MIF photo archives.
47. Photo of John van Wisse and Bronwen Whitehead from MIF photo archives.
48. John van Wisse and Richard Clifford in Harlem from MIF photo archives.
49. Spuyten Duyvil shortcut from MIF photo archives.
50. 2000 MIMS finish with tower in view from MIF photo archives.
51. 2000 MIMS finish closeup from MIF photo archives.
52. 2000 MIMS finish final 50 yards from MIF photo archives.
53. 2000 MIMS finish final 10 yards from MIF photo archives.
54. Drury Gallagher and John van Wisse from MIF photo archives.

55. John and Tammy with Commissioner Henry Stern from MIF photo archives.
56. John with Comm. Stern and Lewandowski from MIF photo archives.
57. Kris Rutford from MIF photo archives in 2000.
58. Manhattan Island: from Visible Earth, NASA website.
59. Drury Gallagher and Diddo Clark from MIF photo archives.
60. Richard Marks at the Water Club from MIF photo archives.
61. Shelley Taylor after another win from MIF photo archives.
62. Gail Rice swimming by Columbia C from MIF photo archives.
63. Gail Rice having lunch from MIF photo archives.
64. Morty Berger, Rob Copeland, Tobie Smith, and Drury Gallagher from MIF photo archives.
65. Tobie Smith closeup from MIF photo archives.
66. John and Tammy van Wisse from Reuthers News Photo Service.
67. Julius Carallo, Tim Johnson, Jane Katz, and Dale Petranech from MIF photo archives.
68. Drury Gallagher and Joe Coplan from MIF photo archives.
69. Statue of Liberty and kayaker from MIF photo archives.
70. Gail Rice with Tom Golden boat in background from MIF photo archives.
71. Aerial view of the East River from MIF photo archives.
72. Manhattan Bridge footing with swimmers from MIF photo archives.
73. Spuyten Duyvil Bridge open from MIF photo archives.

74. World Trade Center bulkhead wall from MIF photo archives.
75. A view of the 79th Street boat basin from MIF photo archives.
76. Celebrity Cruise Line's Zenith blocking swim from MIF photo archives.
77. Battery swim start from MIF photo archives.
78. Spectators at Battery for swim finish from MIF photo archives.
79. Staten Island Ferry terminals from MIF photo archives.
80. Light ship at anchor in Hudson River from MIF photo archives.
81. Self, Harold Washington, and Ben Huggard from Tim Johnson photo archives.
82. Julie Ridge from MIF photo archives.
83. USMMA Mariner with Sue Peterson-Lubow from MIF photo archives.
84. MIF pre-race briefing showing Marcia Cleveland, Kris Rutford, and Morty Berger from MIF photo archives .
85. Morty Berger and Paul Lewandowski at finish from MIF photo archives.
86. Boston Whaler lightning rod from MIF photo archives.
87. South Cove approach from MIF photo archives.
88. Harlem River bridges from MIF photo archives.
89. South Cove finish from MIF photo archives.
90. Skip Storch in cage from Tim Johnson photo archives.
91. Skip Storch, Jane Katz, and self from photocopy of front page of The Advocated, 7/14/1990. The newspaper lost the original image.
92. Cage being towed viewed from behind from Skip Storch's photo archives.

93. Cage being towed viewed from the side from Skip Storch's photo archives.
94. Side view of the swim cage from Tim Johnson photo archives.
95. Ibid.
96. Havana aerial view from Tim Johnson archives.
97. Graphics accompanying Suzy Maroney press releases on BBC Online Network: http://news.bbc.co.uk/1/low/world/americas/447999.stm, published 9/15/1999, accessed 10/31/2004.
98. Jamie Tout eating banana from MIF photo archives.
99. Aussie support boat from MIF photo archives.
100. Jelly fish photo from Flickr.com by Kevin Liang.
101. Ibid.
102. Chart of the English Channel from Ron Collins web page, www.distancematters.com.
103. Ibid.
104. Chart 12327 courtesy of Tim Johnson's photo archives.
105. Ibid.
106. Photo courtesy of Tammy van Wisse.
107. Photo courtesy of Tammy van Wisse.
108. Swim start at Bonaire from Randy Nutt's web page, photographer Carolyn Kiper.
109. Boston Lighthouse view courtesy of Boston Light Swim.
110. Straits of Gibraltar courtesy of NASA Earth Observatory:
111. Christof from his website: www.wandratsch.de.
112. Tom Hetzel from MIF photo archives.
113. Photo courtesy of Shelley Taylor-Smith.
114. Rear cover photo courtesy of Bill and Donna Hill taken after I emerged from my leg of a record setting relay around Manhattan in August of 1990.

Index

9/11 238
AAU 76, 170
Abo-Heif, Abdel-Latif 125
accident, swimming/boating 194
accidental swim 416
Achmet Pacha 405
Adam, John Quincy 21
Adam's Bridge 141
Adelaide City Baths 87
Adelaide, Australia 416
Adirondacks 96, 116
Africa 383
age-group swimming 87
Alaska 390, 396
Albany 153
Albany Yacht Club 155
Alcatraz 121, 126
Algeria 40
Allen, Katie 63
Amateur Athletic Union 77
Amateur Champion 56
Ambletense, France 25
American crawl 101
American Indian 45
American Red Cross 336
Anacapa Island 396
Anacostia River 93
Anderle, Alois 98, 359
Andersen, Greta 125
Anderson, Denise 386
Anderson, Greta 369
animals
    dog, *Lucky* 157
    elephant 407

449

horses 406
   shark.........106, 129, 281, 339, 370, 371, 390, 393, 394, 406
   starving..285
Annapolis, Maryland..381
Annisquam Canal..363
Antonick, Gary...230
Appendix...111
April Fool's...80
Aquatic Park...391
Arafet, Nasin..341
Aran Islands...137
Argentina...117, 127
Armstrong, Elizabeth...356
Armstrong, Lance 140
Arne, Charlotte..362
Arranzaso, Lt. Alberto 410
Arsenal 93
Asmuth, Paul...185, 192, 227, 236
Asphalt Green 183, 225, 243
Athletic Club
   Baltimore..70
   Cleveland 108
   Downtown..297, 412
   Hoosier..107
   Illinois...103
   Listing from 1900's..88
   Manhattan 76
   New York..68, 88, 173, 176, 243
   Pastime...76
Atlantic City.................................110, 148, 151, 294, 381, 438
Atlantic City Marahton Swim..382
Austice, Edmund..40
Australia...84, 90, 95, 140, 160, 211, 282, 376
Australian crawl..84, 101
Austria..54, 56, 360
Automatic Position Reporting System....................................263

Auxiliary Coast Guard	276, 423
Aykroyd, Alsie	360
Babe Ruth	108
Bachmayr, Emanuel	56
Bahamas	11
Baia Mare	84
Bala	366
Bali Straits	381
Balmoral	35
Baltic Sea	115, 119, 123
Bangladesh	15
Baptiste, Warren	409
Barber, Jim	230, 231, 232, 341
Barrett, Clarebelle	374
Barton, Clara	58, 336
Barwick, Roger	332
Bass Straits	160
Bath, England	22
bathing	22
Bathing Beach, Washington, DC	89
baths	3, 42, 58, 59, 67
Battan, Philippines	409
Battery	93, 97, 103, 108, 132, 155, 168, 182, 198, 205, 251
Batterysea	44, 52
Bauer, Sybil	107
Bay of Zea	82
Bayles, Jim	365
Bayonne	102, 117
Bayshore, Long Island	117
Beckwith, Agnes	51
Beckwith, Clara	81
Beckwith, Professor	46, 51
Belfast, Ireland	156
Bell, Alan	393
Bell, Marilyn	128, 160
Benner, Jay	234

Benoit, Anne Priller 174
Berg, Ida Mae...120
Berger, Morty 197, 232, 348
Bering Straits 135
Berkeley 184
Bermuda 131
Bethnal 43
Bible 10
bicyclist...55
Big Diomede, USSR 135
Billings, Montana..122, 131
Billingsley, Julie 226
Bimini 133
bioluminescence..286
Bixler, Jim..271
Black Death..15
Black Sea 39, 119, 122, 129
Blackhurst, William H. 76
Blackman, Noel...282
Blackwall 47, 51, 52
Blatch, Nora Stanton...96
Block Island 125, 365
Block Island Sound 338
Blower, Tom 372
boat basin, 79th Street..213, 221
boat breakdowns 228
Bonaire, Netherlands Antilles..356
Bondi...380
boot camp...417
Borg, Arne..111
Bosco, Lori...355
Bosporus 119, 127, 128, 129, 404
Boston 69
Boston Athletic Association 83
Boston Harbor 106
Boston Light..358

Boulogne, France 25, 27
Bowen Island 397
Bowery 73
Boyle, Raymond 103
Boyton, Paul 27, 29, 30, 36, 67, 71, 154, 291, 317
Brammer, Cody 230
Braun, Herman 76, 77
Bray, John 360
Bridgeport 375, 376
Briggs, Harry 364
Bristol Channel 128, 386
British Columbia, Canada 396
Brodie, Steve 72, 77, 78, 80, 154
Bronx River 74
Bronx, Clason Point 99
Bronx, New York 74
Brooklyn Bridge 72, 80, 94
Brous, Nancy 271
Brown, Alfred 97, 99, 102, 359
Brown, H. T. 56
Bruwer, Carina 144, 389
Bryant, Todd 184, 225
Bryon, Lord 21
Buccaneer Hotel, St. Croix 356
Budapest 56
Buffels Bay 389
Burlington, Vermont 365
Burnett, Julie 364
Burton, Karen 400
Butler, Dennis 66
Butler, Dennis T. 76
Buttenwiser, Ann L, ... 60
butterfly 160
Buzzards Bay 364
Cabcaben, Philippines 409
cage 281, 290, 291, 297

Cain, James 143
Calcutta, India 159
Caldwell, Fran 397
California 121, 125, 172, 226
Cameron, Perry 386
Canadian 125
Canadian Ocean Marathon Swimming Association 397
canals
   Grand 39
   Panama 159
   Regent 42
   Surrey 44
Candiotti 117, 122
canoe 25
Cape Agulhas 389
Cape Ann 363
Cape Cod 73, 364
Cape Grisnez 27, 34
Cape Henry 104
Cape of Good Hope 389
Cape Porpoise 363
Cape Town 135, 389
Capelle, Ruble 99
Capps, Bert 126
Capt. Ayer 72
Captain 23
Casanueva, Emilio 395
Castro, Fidel 283
Catalina Channel 141
Catalina Island 172, 394
Catalina Swimming Federation 395
Cavill
   Charles 84
   Fred 14, 47, 50, 84
   Percy 96
   Richard 88, 89, 92, 101

Sydney	89
Cayuga Lake	96
Cerberus Shoal	339
Chadwick, Florence	127, 128, 394
Chambers	404
Champion of Champions	366
Champion of England	48
Champion of the World	69
Champion, Long Distance Swimming	66
Championship of America	65, 66, 67, 75, 77
Amateur	70
Championship of the World	74
Championship, AAU	76
Chanin, Stacy	219
Channel	
Ambrose	347
Buttermilk	103
Catalina	126, 400
English	25, 27, 36, 400
Hawaiian	369
San Pedro	115
Channel Islands	367
Channel Crossing Association	337
Channel Islands	394
Channel Swimming and Piloting Federation	335
Channel Swimming Association	171, 335
Charles Dickens restaurant	332
Charles River	106, 358
Charlestown Bridge	360
Charlton, Andrew	111
Chase, George	93
cheating	291
Cheboygan, Michigan	128
Chelsea	44
Chelsea Piers	220
Cherriman, Leslie	377

Chesapeake Bay 104, 120
Chesapeake Bay Swim.. 381, 415
Chesapeake Bridge/Tunnel swim 104
Cheshire, England 136
Chester, PA 65
Chicago Athletic Association 82
China 139
Chiow, Khoo Swee 140
Chowdhury, Bula 141
Christopherson, Erline 129
Cincinnati, Ohio 103, 107
Circle Line 210
Clark, David S. 395
Clark, Diddo 193
Clark, Shelley 376
Cleveland, Cindy 394, 395, 396
Cleveland, Marcia 199, 232, 233
Clifford, Richard 212, 271, 345
Coast Guard 249, 412
   British.. 334
   regatta permit 244
Cocos Crossing 399
Cojimar, Cuba 285
Cole, G. 48
Coleman, Arthur 272, 343
Collard, J. 50
Collette family 342
Collins, Debbie 397
Collins, Ron 238, 353
Collins, Shane 397
Colorado River.. 143
Columbia River... 315
Columbia University boathouse.............................. 70, 106, 222
Columbus, Christopher 11
computer model 185
computer projection 188

Coney Island 93, 145, 292
Congressional Medal of Honor 54
Connecticut River 120
Constantinople 404
Cook Strait 141, 160, 385
Coolidge, Calvin 109
Copeland, Rob 235
Coplan, Joe 193
Copley, John Singleton 406
Coral Relief Peace Swim 282
Corlears Hook 187, 197, 218
Corregidor Island 409
Corrientes 118
Corrigador, Philippines 124
Corryong, Victoria 160
Corsan, George 61
Corson, Cleminton 171
Corson, Millie Gade 155
Costin, RoAnn 362
Cotswold Water Park 40
Councilman, James "Doc" 130
Cox, Lynne 135, 385, 389
Coyle, Thomas 65
Crabbe, Buster 111
Craven, Terry 117
crawl stroke
   development 13
Crean, Denis 353
Creegan, George 156, 157
Crutchlow, Kenneth 126
Cuba 182, 219, 281, 406
Cuban National Cathedral 284
Cullen, James 361
Cunningham, Hazel 122
Cunningham, Melissa 308
current 166, 218

Currey, Miss Dorothy 382
Currier, Grace 361
Cutler, Barry 135
Cuttyhunk 364
Cyalume 127
cyanide waste water 84
Cyclades 399
Daily, W. H. 68
Daland, Dr. Judson 85
Dalkin, Don 130
Dalton, David 23, 292
Dalton, Millie 410
Daniels, Charlie 88, 101, 248, 440
Danube 54, 56, 84, 117
Danube River 317
Darauche, John 232
Dardanelles 129
Dassen Island 135
Davenport, Horace 53
Davids, Tice 287
Davidson, Michelle 349
Dawson, Henry 93
Deal 40
Dean, Penny 400
debugging 186, 187
Dedale, Dr. 42
DeJesus, Foster 196
Del Orto, Mingie 174
Delage, Guy 313
Delaware River 65, 75, 104, 116, 118, 120
Denison, Ned 396
Denmark 123
Departure Bay 396
Derks, Chris 238, 353
DeRose, Loretta 338
deSouza, Igor 232, 238

Detroit 75, 129, 403
Devenport, Barrie..385
Diamond, Lucy 116
Dianabad 56
Diaz, Ralph 271
Digby, Everard...17
Dimmers, Kunno...66
distances..4
diving 45, 46, 48
Dockrell, George...90
Dohmstreich, Olga..75
Dolphin Swimming and Boating Club...................86
Doncoes, Virginia 120
Donnelly, Palmer 128
Dooley, Tom 412
Doty, Jim...125, 358, 437
Doucette, Russel 362
Dover...25, 325
Dowling, Robert...........................103, 106, 168, 220
Downtown Athletic Club 248
drafting............................290, 292, 296, 308, 309, 311
   FINA rule 291
Drake, Aaron...232
Dreyer, Jim..318
Driffeld, Kelley...401
drown 23, 57
Dublin, Ireland..137
Due, Ethel 100
Duimaras Strait 143
Duke of Edinburgh...51
Dumoulin, Richard.......................................134, 281
Dundee, Scotland 126
Dunn, Walter...103
Durborow, Charles......................99, 102, 103, 104, 360
Dutch..181
Dyas, Maggie..81

459

Dynamo 114
Earley, Brian 381
East 89th Street 210
East 96th Street 227, 244
East River 63, 65, 80, 136, 164, 296, 335, 406, 418
eddy 214, 218
Ederle, Gertrude36, 66, 108, 114, 132, 172, 175, 345, 381, 395, 402
Egg Rock 363
Egypt 9
Elionsky, Ida 178
Ellercamp, Paul 380
Elliott, Duncan 118
Ellis, Paul 315
Ellis, Richard 248
Emergency Control Organization 377
Emich, Gary 392
Empire State College 185
England 22
English Channel 40, 54, 126, 141, 159, 171, 175, 297
environmental swimmer 318
epidemic 429
Erickson, William 116, 172, 383
Escape from Alcatraz 392
Esselborn, George F. 103
Estonia 119
Europe 21, 22
European Champion 82
European Championships 56
Evans, Stewart 130
False Bay 390
false pretenses 293
Farallon Island 130
Farley, Joe 113
Farnsworth, Karen 194, 199
Fay, Philip 93
Filler, Morgan 238, 275

film documentary
  The Big Swim 270
FINA 77, 148, 194, 290
Finlay, Brian 398
Fire Island 117
Fissier, George 115
Fitzgerald, Anna 97
Fitzgerald, Roy G. 119
Florence Chadwick 128
Florida 134, 157, 174
Florida Keys 282
Florida Straits 281, 296
Flying Gull 45
Folkstone 35
footbridge 207
formula to calculate Manattan Island finishing time 190
formula to calculate world record over any distance 401
formulas, mathematical 423
Fort Meyers 137
Forvass, Anders 401
Fosberg, Gerald 366
Foveaux Strait 386
Frances, Shirley 125
Francis, Steve 416
Frank, Ruth 97
Franklin, Benjamin 21
Freedman, Max 361
Freeman, Lucy 106
Freitas, Jose 384
Friedland, Stephen 313
Friedman, Sally 192, 338
Fugger, Johann 56
Fugina-Pennella, Anna 353
Fuiggi 22
Fuller, Edward 93
Fulton Ferry 58

Funston, Colonel Frederick 54
Gade, Amelia 171
Gallagher, Drury 183, 185, 241
Gallagher, Jr., Drury 241
Galway 137
gambling 23, 66, 67, 68
Garabaldi, Mike 126
Garrick, Lillian 174
Gates of Ade 9
Gates, Charles 406
Gateway National Recreation Area 349
Gatti, John 234
Gauss, Lt. Damon "Rocky" 124, 409
Gauthier, Henry 120
Gedser, Denmark 123
GEMS 348
Genesee Falls 74
Geneva, Switzerland 118
Genter, Steve 411
GeoCuba 284
George Pawling Trophy 122
George Washington Bridge 156, 184, 220, 408
Germany 21
Gibraltar Strait 40, 127, 141, 302, 383
Giles, Clarence 122
Gippsland Lakes 140
Gleitze, Mercedes 119, 383
Glen Cove, NY 374
Glendale, California 115
Glendive, Montana 122, 131
Gloucester 364
Gloucester, NJ 65
Gohegan, Jack 322
Golden Amateur 56
Golden Gate 84
Golden, Tommy 185, 219, 249

Golding, Elaine ... 99
Gomez, Stephane ... 383
Goodwin Sands ... 30, 35
Goodwin, Bud ... 90, 98, 106
Governors Island ... 95, 205
GPS receivers ... 263
Gracie Mansion ... 210
Graham, Carlisle ... 312
Grand Museum Natatorium ... 81
Grange-over-Sands ... 367
Grapham, James ... 40
Graves Light ... 363
Gravesend ... 47, 51
Gravesend Bay ... 67
Great Britain ... 83
Great Lakes ... 129, 398
Great Neck Public Library ... 5
Great Salt Lakes ... 122
Great South Bay ... 117
Greece ... 83, 399
Green, Chris ... 136, 205, 221, 249, 366
Green, Wendel ... 158
Greenwich ... 40, 51, 52
Grew, Anita ... 118
Griffith, Ray ... 375
Guam ... 399
Gublemann ... 63
Guernsey ... 368
Gulf of Finland ... 119
Gulf of Tonkin ... 139
Gulf Stream ... 134, 157, 281, 286
Gunn, Joe ... 371
Gunnerson, Edward ... 360
Gupta, Dr. Modaduga ... 143
Gurr, Henry ... 48, 49
Hackett, Grant ... 401

Hagan, Louis 360
Hajos, Alfred 82, 83
Halassy, Oliver 112
Halk, Bob 356
Hallenbad 56
Halliburton, Richard 159
ham radio operators 261
Hanauma Bay, Hawaii 356
Hancox, Keith 385
handicapped 68
Hanks, Fletcher 381
Hanley, Bill 361
Hannekamp, J. H. 57
Hansen, Kenneth 418
Harlem 168, 171
Harlem Navy 89
Harlem River 57, 66, 68, 70, 153, 164, 172, 210
Harley 68
Harper, Ashby 126, 396
Harris, Sarah 120
Hart, David 128
Hartford 120, 374
Hartigan, Bea 345
Hartley, Karen 193
Harvard 184
Harvey, Adam 367
Hastings-on-Hudson 100
Havana 156, 284, 286, 290, 406
   riot 287
Havana Harbor 285
Hearst, William Randolph 121
Hell Gate 100, 136, 173, 182, 207, 212, 252, 296
Heller, Becca 144
Hellespont 21, 39, 119, 129
Hemingway 285
Hemingway Marina 281

Hero...39, 442
Herschmann, Otto 82
Hesenius, Irene..361
Hetzel, Tom...183, 219, 241
Hiland, Amy..128
Hill, Bill and Donna..199, 248
Hines, Patricia..229
Hobie Beach...141
Hoffman, Ricardo 401
Hohai Straits..314
Holbein..54
Holborn..45, 46
Hole, Hans..93
Holt, Jr., Charles 120
Hooper, John 154
Horning, Dave...183, 225, 243
Horseshoe Bay 398
House of Refuge 407
Howe Island 398
Howe Sound..397
Hownslow, T...45
Huddleson, Myrtle 121
Hudson River ..74, 97, 106, 153, 164, 168, 218, 277, 408, 419
Huffaker, Harry..369
Huggard, Ben 130, 200, 219, 252, 265, 302
Hughes, Mimi 317
Hunderby, Chad 400
Hurwitz, Jack 360
Hyde Park..41
Hyman, Jay 283
Ibiza..316
Iglesias, Horacio 125
indexing..5
Indritsanov 107
Inland Passage 396
insurance 265, 291

International Maritime Organization 437
International Professional Swimmers' Association 173
Intrepid 221
invitation 5
IOC 77
Iraq 10
Irish Sea 137, 371
Isaac, Yekhezkiel 126
Ischia 399
Isle of Wight 53
Isles of Shoals 364
Jacot, Louis 359
Jakarta 139
James, F. H. 98
Januski, Leo 375
Japan 10, 22, 113, 137, 139, 399
Jarosh, John 361
Jason's Cradle 437
jellyfish 281
Jersey 368
Jersey City 66
Jian, Zhang 314
John Birch Society 283
Johnson, Harold 226
Johnson, J. B. 26, 27, 30, 36, 50, 51, 64, 65
Johnson, Tim 185
Jones, Ian 368
Juan de Fuca 396
Juno Beach, Florida 133
Kaiser, Linda 369
Kammersgaard, Jenny 115, 123
Kamrau-Corestein, Britta 151
Kanaar, Dr. Adrian 228
Kansas Regiment 54
Katz, Jane, Ed. D. 14, 157, 192, 242, 339
Kauffmann, George 132, 183, 200, 219

Kawauchi, Carl 369, 371
kayaks 271
Keansburg, NJ 132
Keating, Edward 116
Keenam, Ted 372
Keith, Vicki 147, 159
Kellar, F. P. 97
Keller, Steve 271
Kellerman, Annette 95
Kellerman, Fred 95
Kemmerich, Otto 115
Kendall, William 312
Kenney, Arthur 87
Kenney, Nell 103
Kenworthy, Harold 46
Kerschner 117
Key West 156, 353
Kidd, Margaret 373
Kieran, B. B. 87, 90
King Point swim team 267
Kings College 406
Kingston, Ontario 147, 159
Kinsella, John 131
kite swimming 86
Klugman, Steve 389
knot 153
Kole Jr., Stephen A 408
Kostich, Alex 356
Koudinov, Yury 140
Krack 60
Kramer, Benn 229
Krueger, Harold 107
Kuhn, Philip 141
L Street Brownies 358
Laas, Alexander 119
Laban, Josh 357

Ladoga Lake..120
Lagrange, Missouri 123
LaGuardia Airport..296
LaJolla Cove 140, 394
Lake Alexandrina...160
Lake Argyle 316
Lake Champlain 365
Lake Coniston 366
Lake Erie 159
Lake Geneva 118
Lake George..116, 155
Lake Huron 128, 159
Lake Ijsselmeer, Holland 140
Lake Michigan 121, 128, 159
Lake Ohrid 149
Lake Okanagan 398
Lake Ontario 126, 131, 147, 159, 160
Lake Skaha..398
Lake Superior..160
Lake Tahoe..121, 126, 129
Lake Taupo 386
Lake Washington 147
Lake Windermere..366
Lake Winnipesaukee 364
Lakes, Great 159
LaLanne, Jack 392
Lambert, Jenna..147
Landemeters, Annemie 390
Lane, Freddy 88
Langenour, Hazel..84
Laskowitz, Warren 107
Laufer, Walter 107
Laurer, Helen 205
Lawrence, Lt. Col. Tim..368
le Pennec, Denize 368
Leach, Jerry 304

Leander	39, 46
Learn to Swim	11, 47, 121, 270
learning to swim	49
Learn-to-Swim	61
Leary, J. Scott	89
LeComte, Ben	314
Ledger, John	78
Lemberger, Emil	56
LeMoyne, Harry	89
Lewandowski, Paul	204, 248
Lewis, Paul	373, 396
Lewis, Rebecca	367
Liberty State Park	136, 413
Liberty Swim	294
Liberty-to-Liberty Triathlon	413
Lido	39
Liebbrand, Corry	118
lifeguards	62
lifejacket	39
life-saving dress	29
light stick	127
lightning	276
Lima, Antonio	346
Lindstrom, Alex	374
Lininger, Ed	182, 194, 201, 203
Lister, Dr. Joseph	406
Little Baguio, Bataan Peninsula	409
Little Diomede, Alaska	135
Little Duck Key, Florida	290
Liverpool	41, 42, 51, 303
Llewellyn, Dee	367
Lloreda, Carlos	342
Lloyd, Peter	176, 411
LMSC	291
Local Master Swim Committee	291
Loch Lomond	366

Locke, Kieran...356
Logan, John..175
London 19, 44
London Bridge 19, 26, 52, 72
Long Beach, California...179
Long Beach, NY 108, 110, 113
Long Branch..64
Long Island Sound 208, 373
Long, Bill 126
Long, Joe 403
Long, Senator Russell B. 128
Longfellow, Wilbur...58
Lord Byron..39
Lord, Alice 374
Louis XIV 22
Lourmais, Louis 313
Lt. Young 371
Lucason, Adam 374
Lucayans 11
Lunsden, Cliff 128
Macaig, Joe 131
MacArthur, General Douglas..411
MacDonald, Marcella 232
Maciel, Romeo 107
Maciotti, Daniel 384
Mack, P. F..77
MacKenzie, Meda...386
Mackinac Straits..128
Magee, Robert P..70, 76
Magnetic Island...377
Main, Kyle 141
Malacca Strait 140
Malin, Nicolai 122
Mallorca 316
Malta 40, 404
Manes, George 155

Manhasset Bay 114
Manhasset, NY 241
Manhattan 99, 181
   Braun Swimming School 63
Manhattan Bridge..211, 253
Manhattan Island Foundation 121, 268
Manhattan Plaza 242
Manhattan record
   Clark, Diddo 193
   course 194
   Friedman, Sally 192
   Gallagher, Drury 192
   listings 239
   Rutford. Kris 196
   Summers, Byron 172
   Taylor, Shelley 193
Manhattan swim start 258, 278
Manila Bay 409
Manly Cove 144
Mantle, Mickey 110
Mantrell, J. B. 99
Marathon Swimming World Cup 149
Marblehead 364
Mariel Harbor 285
Marine Science 423
marine traffic 335
maritime distress signal 195
Markley, Chris 354
Maroney, Suzy 231, 232, 236, 282, 287, 296, 401
Martha's Vineyard 139, 364
Martineau, Miss 47
Matalene, Henry 111
Maury, Ron 369
Maxey, Brian 271
Mayo, Zachary 417
McCarthy, Jimmy 242

McCullum, Chris..386
McCusker, John 96
McDermott, Michael..103
McDonald, Harry..407
McElwee, Richard...229
McGee, Fibber 284, 298, 302
McGhee, Ambassador George C. 128
McGill, Linda..228, 275
McGillivray, Perry 101
McGinn, Charles J. 159
McMahon, Marty 340
McPhee, N. H..174
Meca, David..316
Mecklenburger Bay..115, 123
Mediterranean Sea 384, 398
Meehan, George R. 103
Meeks Bay 126
Mefferia, A...76
Meffert, Alex..91
Meharg, Brian 372
Melbourne, Australia 87, 403
memorial swim...183
Meraw, Mundigel...398
Mersey River..41, 42
Messina Straits...85
Mexico 10, 311
Middleburgh, Hilton 127
Middleton, Graham 160
Middletown Yacht Club..120
Midtown North Precinct 413
MIF, Board of Advisors...268
Milford...375
Military swims..53
Mill Rock 194, 197, 207, 211, 227, 252
Millennium Relay Team 238
Millie Gade Corson..155

Mindanao	143
Miren, Henry	360
MISA members	245
Mishimura, Setsu	113
Mississippi River	123, 408
Missouri River	124
Mitz, Hilda	117
Miyazaki, Yasuji	114
Moffett, Erica	389
Molokai Straits	179
Monfore, Monte	381
Montagu Bay	123
Montauk	338
Montauk Point	130
Monterey	394
Montgomery, Robert B.	57
Montreal, Canada	87
Morecambe Bay	366
Moreno, Fausta	335
Moser, Lieutenant	54
Moses	440
Moses, Robert	60, 440
Mott Street	59
mudflat	414
Mullen, John	361
Munich, German	61
Murphy, Kevin	130, 372
Murray River	160
Nabit, Chuck	381
Nakama, Keo	116, 369
Nakamura, T.	104
Nance, Matt	199, 231
Nantasket Beach	106
Nantucket	139, 365
Naples	399
Nassau, Bahamas	123

natation 23
National Swimming Association 58
National Swimming School 49
National Swimming Society 44
Naval Academy 111
NCAA 77, 112
Nebraska 196, 232
necropolis 9
Neidrauer, Lisa 365
Neilson, Valeska 81
Nelson Mandella Bay 141
Nelson, Marvin 121
Netherlands 21
Neumann, Dr. Paul 82
Neva River 120
Nevada 121
New Caledonia 403
New Delhi, India 141
New Jersey 234
New Rochelle 111, 178, 374
New South Wales Amateur Swimming Association 87
New York City 59
New York City Police 412
New York Swimming Academy 59
New York Times 5, 23, 70, 80, 109, 114, 121, 270, 320
New York Tribune 132, 170, 178
New Zealand 385
Newark Bay 117
Newport, Rhode Island 67, 86, 96
newspapers 5
Niagara Falls 69, 77
Nicholson, Don 398
Niegenhagen, Germany 123
night swims 127
NOAA 165
Norman's Woe Rock 363

North Beach, Sandy Hook 349
North Mole, Fremantle..376
North River 204
Nortje, Barend...144
Notice to Mariners 229, 249
nternational Swimming Hall of Fame............................130
Nunan, Joe...361
Nutt, Randy 355
Nuttall, Joey 96
Nyad, Diana 131, 133, 242, 281
NYC Parks Department 182, 243
O'Connell, Sean..131
O'Hara, Donald...176, 411
O'Keefe, Dan..400
O'Maolain, Feilim...137
O'Neill, Colm 373
Oak Point, Bronx 74, 75
Obright, Max..64
Odium, Robert Emmett..71
Ohio River..103, 107, 287
Ohio State University...122
Okeanos River..9
Old Field Pt., Long Island..375
Old Orchard Beach 363
Oldham, Ruth..368
Olympic Club..89, 357, 391
Olympics 45, 56, 82, 110, 148, 149, 172, 310, 411
Opdycke, Rendy..238
Opdyke, Randy 272
open water competition
  first mention 49
Oram, Michael 335
Orient Point...374
Ortlip, Glenda 126
Outside Magazine 290
Oxford...44

475

pace	186, 188
Paestum, Italy	9
pain	428
Palk Strait	141, 231
Pamphlio, David	48
Pamplona, Spain	413
Pan American Exposition	89
Panama Canal	158
Pandanaram	364
Pankina, Natalia	152
Papa	285
Parana River	117
parasites	429
Parcells, Dave	353
Park, Tom	125
Parker, Emily	52
Parker, Harry	52
Parker, Henry	48
Passaic Falls	73
Patch, Jumping Sam	73
Patchogue	117
Paterson, New Jersey	73
Patterson, Max	361
Patterson, Tyler	147
Patterson, Walter	374
Pawling Marathon Swim	112
Pearson, Anna	361
Penarth, Wales	128
Pennock Island Challenge	390
Penquin Swim Club	147
Penticton, BC	398
Pepanos, Antonio	82
Percey, William	17
Pereira, Baptista	127
Perth Amboy	128
Perth, Australia	376

Peter the Great..119
Peterson-Lubow, Susan..267
Pewtress 45
Phidippides..21
Philadelphia...65, 75, 116, 118, 120
Philippines...54, 143
Piantidosi, Tina 341
pier dangers...253, 256
Pier-to-Pier..393
Pillars of Hercules...41
Piraeus, Greece 82
Pitonoff, Rose 98, 360
Pittar, James 139, 236
Pittsburgh...103
Placak, Bob 370
Pleasure Bay...64
Plymouth...40, 48
Poenisch, Walter 282, 289
Point Bonita, California 130
Point Marroqui, Spain..127
Point Vincente..115
police...46, 174, 175, 177, 182, 243, 412
Police Harbor Patrol unit 418
politics...281
pollution 102
Pompeii..9
pool swims, 24 hours 308
Porkkala, Finland 120
porpoise oil...177
Port Angeles, Washington 127
Port Washington..114
Portingale, Lee 367
PORTS 166
Portsmouth 53
Portugal..384
Potomac River...21, 93, 109

477

Poughkeepsie 409
Pouilley 107
Power Squadron 230, 265, 276, 423
Power Swim 357
Powers, Dr. John 241
Powley, Mike 396
President's Cup 109
Price, Stephen 373
prisoner 25
Pritchard, Frank 121
professional swimming 48
Professional Swims 148
Professor 23
propaganda 282
prostitution 284
Provincetown 106
publicity 36
Pugh, Gordon 135, 161, 389
Punta Leona, Morocco 383
Putney 47
Qiongzhou Strait 139
Quartemain, John 234
Queen of Hell Gate 99
Queen Victoria 28, 29, 33, 35, 42, 95
Queens, North Beach 100
Quinn, Thomas 361
Radamacker, Frank 98
Raft, George 79
rafts 287
Rague, Suzanne 193
Rahman, Fazlur 15
Ramsgate 40, 51
Randalls Island 63, 407
Raritan Bay 347
Rarotonga 386
Ravenhall, Judge Peter 292

478

Rayburn, Ray 61
Red Cross 58
Red Hook, Brooklyn 346
Reeder, Harry 91
Reid, Ogden 103
Renaissance artist
    Cesio, Carlo 14
    Gatti, Oliviero 11
Renear, D. B. 90
Reval, Estonia 119
Revell, Mary Margaret 129
Rhine 313
Rhode Island 125
Rice, Gail 137, 232, 234, 353
Richards, Samuel 102, 103, 359
Ricks, Carl 89
Ridge, Julie 176, 219, 243, 265
Riis Park, Belle Harbor 113
Rikers Island 136
Riley, Thomas 69, 77
Rio Grande de Pampanga River 54
Ripley, Ohio 287
Ritter, Carlos 128
River Severn 128
Robartes, Marion 117
Robben Island 389
Roberts, Courtney 229
Robinson, John 74
Robinson's Baths 87
Rochester, New York 74
Rockaway, Queens 183
Rogers, Fred 126
Romer Shoal 346
Roosevelt Island 197
Ross, Clarence 109, 114, 175, 177
Ross, Norman 107, 120

Rostock, Germany..115, 123
Roth, Dick...111
Rotterdam...313
Rottnest Channel...376
Rottnest Channel Swimming Association 377
rowing...174
Royal Cinque Ports Yacht Club...30
Royal Humane Society 51
Royall, Lucy..21
Ruberi, Charles 89
Ruddy, Joe...248
Ruddy, Ray 110
Rush, Philip...386, 401
Rutford, Kris 196, 218, 221, 232, 240, 401
Rye, Connecticut...374
Sachner, Antonio...107
Saco River...363
Sadlo, William 119, 173, 174
Safety Pack..437
Salamini, Ambrose..338
Saliba, Mark..377
Salton Sea..142
San Diego, California..128
San Francisco...84, 126, 130
San Jose, California 185
San Luis Obispo..394
San Salvador 11
Sanatchev, Anton...140
sanction...290
Sand Point Bath Club..115
Sanderland Bridge...45
Sandvik, Earl...348
Sandy Hook...103, 108, 132, 345, 365
Sandy Hook Lightship 292
Sanguilly, Manny..220
Sanibel Island..137

Santa Barbara Channel Swimming Association 395
Santa Catalina 115
Santa Cruz 393
Santa Cruz Island 396
Santa Monica 119
Sarangani Bay 143
sarcophagus 9
Saronic Gulf 82
Sasayama 104
Sau, George 261
Saugerties 156
Savannah River 118
Savaros, Gus 229
Schaefer Brewing Company 181
Schaefer, Caprice 128, 145
Schaeffer, E. C. 88, 89
Schlossberg, Ben 313
Schnarr, Fran 246
Schnarr, Nancy 346
Schoemmell, Lottie 116, 155, 157, 172
Schuylkill River 90
Schwartz, Marquand 90, 91
Schwartz, Sadie 118
Schweighart, John 157
Scott, Anastasia 121
scratch swimmer 23
sea bathing 47, 58
Sea Cliff, Long Island 374
Sea Gate 22
Sea Lice 429
Sea of Galilee 126
Sea of Marmara 129
Seacomb Point, England 41
Seaver, Sean 390
Sen, Mihir 159
Seneca Lake 96

Serigne, Michael 403
Serpentine 41, 44, 45, 49, 58
   description 41
Shakespeare Beach 30
shark cage 281, 305, 370
Shark Shield 144, 390
Shenoy, Taranath 231
Shields, Sam 174
Shu-Chou, Tsai 402
Shultz, William 390
Siebecker, Ben 132
Sigmund, John 124
Sills, Jr., F. H. 118
Singapore Strait 140
slavery 287
Smith, Edwin 120
Smith, Michael 45
Smith, Tobie 235
Snowlton, Clifford 126
Snug Harbor 340
Sognefjord, Norway 161
Solitaire, Eddie 383
Solomon Islands 85
Solvent 53
Sombrero Key 302
South Africa 135, 389
South Cove 278
South End Rowing Club 86
South Street Seaport 253
Spanish 11
Spanish-American War 54
Spence, Celia 398
Spence, Walter 114
Spitz 130
Spitz, Mark 82, 130, 411
Sprawson, Charles 297

Spring Valley, New York 282
Spuyten Duyvil 106, 168, 187, 198, 213, 220, 255, 272
Squamish Harbour 398
St. Croix, Virgin Islands 356
St. John, Virgin Island 357
St. Kilda, Australia 87
St. Louis 408
St. Paul 10
St. Vincent's Medical Center 375
stakes race 75
Stanton, David 378
Staten Island 100, 128
Staten Island ferry 199, 251
Staten Island ferry timing 259
Statue of Liberty 75, 136, 157, 294
Staub, Ueli 335
Steadman-Martin, Nancy 349
Stedman 46
Stern 63
Stetser, Eddie 383
Stewart Island 386
Storch, Skip 157, 160, 282, 294, 298, 318, 419
Stoychev, Peter 149
Strait of Georgia 396
Straits of Juan de Fuca 127
Streeter, Alison 335, 368, 372
Strel, Martin 314
stroke development 92
Struble, Diane 181, 252
Sugden, Jorge 127
Sullivan, Denis 335
Sullivan, Frank 101
Sullivan, Henry 105
Sullivan, State Senator Tim 80
Sumatra 140
Sumatra Straits 139

Summers, Byron 115, 172
Sun Moon Lake, Taiwan..402
Sundstrom, Gus..74, 75, 91, 101, 176
Sunshine Coast..396
survival suit..437
Suter, H. F. 83
Suzuki, Takeshi..400
Swain, Christopher...315
Sweden, Linkoping 401
Swim Across America 220
Swim Across the Sound 375
swim cage...299, 302, 311
swim cancellations 64
Swim Club
    Brighton 47, 50, 84
    L Street..360
    Leeds 48, 50
    London 48
    North London..48
    Serpentine 49, 50
    Surrey..46
swim communications 263
swim count 415
swim drag...226
swim mismanagement......................................48, 106, 114, 275
swim optimization...185
swim rescues 413
swim standards...270
swim start change...230
swim, head starts 23, 68
Swimmer's Itch..430
swimmer's shoulder 428
Swimming Association
    Amateur...47
    British Long Distant BLDSA.....................................366
    Gibraltar Strait 383

Metropolitan ... 49
swimming machine ... 43
swimming tubs ... 59
swims gone bad ... 413
swims, 24 hour ... 401
swimsuits ... 317
Switzerland ... 313
Sydney ... 143
Sydney, Australia ... 87
Szekrenyessy, Ungar ... 56
Tahoe City, California ... 121
Tammany Hall ... 80
Tampa Bay ... 353
Tappan Zee Bridge ... 220
Tarifa, Spain ... 383
Tarrytown ... 74, 220
Tasmania ... 160
Tatarskiy Proliv Channel ... 139
Taylor, Annie ... 78
Taylor, Debra ... 139
Taylor, Shelley ... 194, 197, 227, 228, 234, 401
Tenthoff, Edward ... 97
Tenzing Norgay Award ... 141
Texeira, Gene ... 157
Thames ... 19, 39, 66, 95, 325
Thayres, J. H. ... 88
The Race ... 339
The Spider ... 418
The Water Club ... 229
Thomas, Bert ... 127
Thomas, Ross ... 382
Throgsneck Bridge ... 374
ticker tape parade ... 36
tilapia ... 143
timing ... 184
Tobacco ... 45

Tokyo 399
Tomales Bay 393
Tompkins, Barbara 119
Toner, Gary 376
Toomey, Jim 383
Torbay 366
Toth, Charles 105, 106, 116, 360
Toussaint, H. E. 70
Trainor, Ed 340
Trans-Tahoe swim 392
Trapp, Adeline 99
Trautz, Alexander 64
Travers Island 76, 88, 90
Trembly, Bill 54
Tresnack, Harry 122
triathlon 126, 413
Troy 153
trudgen stroke 85
Trudgen, John Arthur 14, 85
Tse-tung, Mao 130
Tsugaru Channel 137
Tuelff, Hans 66
Turkish Swimming Federation 129
Turkish Water Sports Federation 119
Turner, George 76
Tybee Island, Georgia 118
U Thant Island 197
UCLA 371
ukulele 109
Underground Railroad 288
United States Volunteer Life Saving Corps 94
Urquhart, Don 416
US Long Distance Swimming 177
US Master Swimming 266, 290
US Merchant Marine Academy 232, 249, 267
US Power Squadron 266

USAF Academy 368
USMS 177, 290
van den Hoogenband, Peter 401
van der Weijden, Maarten 140
van Dijk, Edith 149
van Rutten, Vincent 357
Van Schoening, Ernest 68
Van Skike, Anna 119
van Wisse, John 211, 236
van Wisse, Tammy 140, 160, 211, 215, 234, 236, 345
Vancouver Island 396
Varnes 32
Venezuela 11
Venice 39
Venice Pier 119
Verrazano Narrows 164
Verrazano Narrows Bridge 100, 346
VHF 275
Victoria Island, Canada 127
Vienna 56, 82, 117
Vierkotter, Ernest 116
Vipond, M. 42
Vladivostok, Russia 139
Volunteer Life Saving Corps 23
volunteers 249, 250, 267, 271
von Dincklage-Schulenburg, Gerd 376
von Isacescu, Countess Walburga 294
Wade, George H. 68
wager 22
Wainwright, Gen. 410
Walker, Carbis 108
Wallace, William 373
Walton Lake 104
Wandratsch, Christof 389, 400
Warnemunde, Germany 115
Warre, Rev. E. 48

Washington Heights, New York 97
Washington, DC 60, 89, 93, 226, 407
Watch Hill 294, 338, 339
water quality 320
Watson, Lord Mayor Brook 406
Watts, Emily 238
wave pool 61
Webb, Matthew 36, 47, 51, 52, 66, 67, 69, 289
Weber, Eleanor 94
Weehawken Police 412
Weir, Bob 364
Weissenborn, W. R. 66
Weissmuller, Johnny 110, 114
Welfare Island 408
Wennerberg, Conrad 125, 148
Werner, John 358
West Point 159
West, Florence 94
Westminister 52
Westminster Bridge 19
Westnedge, Susan 416
Weston-Super-Mare, England 128
Westport, MA 157
wet suit 287, 318
Whirlpool Rapids 69
White, Ed 54
Whitehead, Bronwen 211, 216, 236
Whitehead, John 377
Whiteside, Samantha 147
Williams, Ester 96
Williams, Gardiner 83
Williamsburg Bridge 187, 193, 197, 218
Wilmington, Delaware 118
Wilson, F. 48
Windermere 205, 367
Woerhan, George 68

Wolfe, Ira	342
Wolfe, Jabez	109
Wood, Matt	199
Woodford, Dextor	232
Woodling, Elwood	122
Woods, Jim	313
Woodside, England	41
Woody, Scott	222, 266, 269
World Professional Marathon Swimmer	185
World Trade Center	204, 221
Worth, Mary	346
Wozniak, Steve	122
Wrigley	116, 172
Yale	440
Yamaguchi, Tomomi	400
Yangtze River	114, 130
Yao-sheng, Yao	130
Yellow Sea	314
Yellowstone National Park	122
Yellowstone River	122, 131
YMCA	60, 98, 365
York, John	395
Young, George	116, 172
Young, Paul	395
Yudovin, David	137, 139, 396
YWCA	171
Zegger, Paul	374
Zerganos, Jason	175
Zimmerman, Deke	143
Zimmy, Charles	156, 281
Zitenfield, Bernice and Phylis	155
Zorilla, Albert	110
Zornig, Scott	396

Endnotes

[1] Visit Aquatics International web site: www.aquaticsintl.com click on The History of Aquatics.

[2] Visit the Proquest home page for more information: http://www.il.proquest.com/proquest/.

[3] The Lathrop Report on Newpaper Indexes by Norman and Mary Lou Lathrop or Newspaper Indexes: A location and Subject Guide for Researchers by Anita Milner both date from the late 1970's and show the extend of what indexing there is of newspapers in the country.

[4] The Diver's Tomb, National Museum of Paestum, pamphlet distributed by the Archeological Superintendence for local tourism offices. The scene is so popular it is reproduced on postcards for sale to tourists.

[5] Lloyd, Seton. The Art of the ANCIENT NEAR EAST. New York:Praeger Publishers, 1961:page 198.

[6] The Manchester 2002 XVII Commonwealth Games, Sports> Aquatics> History: http://213.131.178.162/SPORTS/Aquatics/History/default.asp.

[7] A timeline called The History of Aquatics has been posted on the Internet by the Aquatics International staff that is a great visual reference. It can be accessed at www.aquaticsintl.com. Most of the information discussed within the preceding two paragraphs is but a summary of this information. A revision 11/2004 of their web site has dropped this feature.

[8] Visit the Medieval Sourcebook at: http://www.fordham.edu/halsall/source/columbus1.html , October 11, 1492.

[9] Visit Keith A. Pickering's Columbus Navigation homepage: http://www1.minn.net/~keithp/, select *How Long Was Columbus' League?* for the discussion.

[10] Email from Keith Pickering, 11/5/2004, citing Spanish cleric and historian Bartoleme de las Casas records.

[11] Tuchman, Barbara. A Distant Mirrow. New York: Ballantine Books, 1978: page 94.

[12] Buerk, Roland. "Bangladesh Stops Women Swimmers." Home of the BBC on the Internet. http://news.bbc.co.uk/1/hi/world/south_asia/4055857.stm. Published November 30, 2004.

[13] Information from a Kristine in a blog on Serendipities, http://earmarks.org/archives/2005/12/05/30 accessed 3/12/2007.

[14] From featured items in the library collection of the Mariner's Museum website: http://www.mariner.org/library/new/items.php accessed 3/11/2007.

[15] London Times, 9/19/1791

[16] One guinea represents one pound and one shilling (1.05). In today's US dollars, 8 guineas is about $13.

[17] Visit http://midtown.net/dragonwing/col9802.htm for more details.

[18] Rennie's bridge is now located in Lake Havasu, Arizona, having been replaced in 1973.
[19] Port of London Authority, www.pola.co.uk
[20] Phidippides was the runner who ran 26 miles to Athens to announce victory over the Persians, dying shortly afterwards due to exhaustion having completed a 280-mile roundtrip run to Sparta prior to the battle.
[21] Aquatics International, The History of Aquatics, www.aquaticsintl.com from Franklin on Franklin edited by P. M. Zall, accessed 9/14/2004.
[22] Visit an online history of John Quincy Adam at: www.americanpresident.org.
[23] Visit Explore DC at www.exploredc.com and click on US Presidents, Profiles, John Quincy Adams.
[24] Visit the History Section found on Rapscallion No.1, Jan. ,1998, at www.grayson.edu/rrseries/rrseries/rap.htm, 12/06/2004.
[25] Royall, Anne N. *Sketches of History, Life and Manners in the United States, by a Traveler*. New Haven, CT, 1826.
[26] Aquatics International, The History of Aquatics, www.aquaticsintl.com, accessed 9/20/2004
[27] How difficult would it be for a swimmer to emerge from ritual bathing? I happen to live near the Massachusetts Maritime Academy. Their pool is open to the public 3 days a week for two hours to senior citizens. It's nearly impossible to swim laps (no lanes are set up) because of all the people standing about talking and casually strolling about. Every once in a while one of the seniors tears off and breaststrokes up to the deep end only to hang onto the wall for a period of time before returning. I gave up going to this pool but my wife hangs in there mainly because she is stubborn. But she developed the desire to swim distance elsewhere. This is an example of the difficulty this type of bathing would have in promoting a swimming culture.
[28] Bernard Barber, <u>Water—A View from Japan</u>, NY:John Weatherhill, Inc., 1974.
[29] NY Times, 8/17/1906, *New American Record For Swimmer Daniels*.
[30] Visit Anecdotage.com web site: www.anecdotage.com/index.php?aid=8325 , 11/24/2004.
[31] NY Times, 7/1/1899, Book Review:*Gambling in England*, <u>The History of Gambling in England</u> by John Ashton.
[32] NYTimes, 7/1/1899, Book Review, untitled, <u>How to Swim</u> by Captain Davis Dalton. More information about Captain Dalton will be covered later in this book.
[33] *The Random House College Dictionary, The Unabridged Edition,* Jeff Stein, Random House, 1980.
[34] London Times, 8/23/1867
[35] NY Times, 9/8/1872, *A New Leander*, by London Times correspondence.

[36] Willoughby, David. <u>The Super-Athletes</u>. New York: A. S. Barnes and Company, 1970, page 482.
[37] Wennerberg, Conrad. <u>Wind, Waves and Sunburn</u>. New York: A. S. Barnes and Company, 1974, page 46. Gerald Forsberg's book adds the first name.
[38] London Time, 8/26/1872
[39] NY Times, *Swimming Extraordinary*, 9/8/1872
[40] NY Times 9/8/1872
[41] *A long-distance swimmer becomes a national hero, briefly*, Bruce Heydt, British Heritage magazine, September 2004.
[42] London Times, 4/7/1875
[43] Ibid
[44] London Times, 4/8/1875
[45] London Times, 4/10/1875
[46] London Times, 4/12/1875
[47] Ibid.
[48] London Times, 5/28/1875
[49] London Time, 4/8/1875
[50] The yacht club was in Dover, one of the Royal Cinque ports. The Crown has designated only five ports in England as Royal ports (port where Royal goods could be imported), the purpose having since seen its demise but the distinctive label remains.
[51] London Time, 4/9/1875
[52] London Times, 4/10/1875
[53] Ibid
[54] first published record of an escort pilot's name.
[55] This swim is well documented in numerous books and I would encourage the readers to indulge themselves.
[56] Ms. Magazine, July/August 1989
[57] "Lord George Gordon Byron" <u>The Literature Network</u>. http://www.online-literature.com/byron/

> If, in the month of dark December,
> Leander, who was nightly wont
> (What maid will not the tale remember?)
> To cross thy stream, broad Hellespont!
>
> If, when the wintry tempest roared,
> He sped to Hero, nothing loath,
> And thus of old thy current poured,
> Fair Venus! how I pity both!
>
> For me, degenerate modern wretch,

> Though in the genial month of May,
> My dripping limbs I faintly stretch,
> And think I've done a feat today.
>
> But since he crossed the rapid tide,
> According to the doubtful story,
> To woo -and -Lord knows what beside,
> And swam for Love, as I for Glory;
>
> 'Twere hard to say who fared the best:
> Sad mortals! thus the gods still plague you!
> He lost his labour, I my jest;
> For he was drowned, and I've the ague.

[58] Sports Illustrated, 5/25/1987
[59] London Times, 8/31/1804
[60] Robinson, Tony. *The Worst Jobs in History:The Victorians.* A six part video documentary for The History Channel. Shown in the US on 12/27/2004.
[61] Evironmental Agency web page, www.visitthames.co.uk, FAQs, 10/7/2004.
[62] London Times, 9/24/1805
[63] London Times, 9/7/1810
[64] London Times, 9/7/1821
[65] A 3-D view from space is seen at http://earthobservatory.nasa.gov/Newsroom/NewImages/images.php3?img_id=16350
[66] Queensway Tunnel was built under George's Pier and is located on the Liverpool side.
[67] London Times, 8/7/1822 from the Liverpool Mercury
[68] London Times, 7/20/1824
[69] Located south of Queensway Tunnel on the Liverpool side. Liverpool is located on the east side of the Mersey River.
[70] London Times, 7/16/1827 from the Liverpool Courier.
[71] This same race was reported in an essay *The Rise of Competitive Swimming 1840 to 1878* by Claire Parker published in the Journal of Sports History. Two variations about the swim arose between the London Times (my source) and the Manchester Guardian (Claire Parker's source): the spelling of the name of Dr. Dedale was changed to Dr. Bedale and the date of the swim. The variation in the spelling of the name is understandable given the typeset of the day. The date variance most likely occurred in the Manchester Guardian given that Ms. Parker's source for the information was fifty years after the fact.
[72] London Times, 8/20/1829

[73] On a reasonable large sized map of England, if you put your finger on the center of the city, Bethanl-green is under the tip of your fingernail. If you were at Victoria Station, you'd take the N8 bus and ½ hour later you'd be there and it'd only cost you one pound. From London Bridge, it's only 3 subway stops. Of course, they didn't have such transportation in 1838 but the transgressors were undoubtedly city dwellers.
[74] Bathing suit or swim trunks are referred to in English as a costume.
[75] A neighborhood of London located east of Trafalgar Square for about a mile known for its hotels, theatres, and shops.
[76] London Times, 7/17/1838
[77] About Swimming website: http://swimming.about.com from USS SwimFactPact ISHOF.
[78] *The Rise of Competitive Swimming 1840 to 1878*, Claire Parker, The Sports Historian, November 2001, Vol. 21, No. 2, page 63.
[79] London Times, 9/21/1838
[80] Kennington-reach is a part of the Thames that runs along the eastern border of the town of Kennington southwest of Oxford. Oxford is to the east of the Thames and Kennington is on the western bank of the Thames. The appeal of Kennington is the meadow that serves as that border and as such provided opportunities for swimming. The whole of the Thames through here is a small river, a bit wider than a canal but controlled by a series of locks.
[81] London Times, 8/31/1840. The information contained in the London Times is somewhat at variance with the information contained in Claire Parker's *The Rise of Competitive Swimming 1840 to 1878* whose source is T. Terret's *Professional Swimming in England before the rise of Amateurism, 1837-75*. That they agree upon is the time for the distance. The London Times was specific about the school boys competing and the Mr. Hounslow is seen in the next report of 1844 of being in his late thirties given the age difference specified by the reporter.
[82] Holborn is a neighborhood in London, just north of the Thames near the turn of the river upstream from the London Bridge. The baths would have most likely been in the Thames.
[83] London Times, 9/18/1844. See endnote #78.
[84] Summersaults.
[85] London Times, 9/18/1844.
[86] Visit Backyard Agora web site: www.backyardagora.com click on glossary, then S, look for swimming, history of.
[87] 130/30=4.33 feet per second, 150 feet/4.33=34.6 seconds, assuming he doesn't tire over the final 7 yards.
[88] London Times, 9/18/1842 source from the Northern Times
[89] Ibid.
[90] Ibid.
[91] Ibid

[92] Other later performers were Harry Elionsky around the turn of the 20th century and Jack Lalanne in the later part of the 20th century.

[93] Mr. Beckwith would enter this history again when his daughter swam the Thames in 1875. By this time he had become a professor but that is a title that swimming instructors were commonly called. This use of Professor is an example of how high in regard the ability to swim was held.

[94] London Times, 8/6/1851

[95] London Times, 9/27/1859, *Swimming For Ladies*.

[96] The Brighton Swim Club web site points out that the Maidstone Swim Club was in existence as earlier as 1844 but not necessarily continuously. The Maidstone SC used a raft on the River Medway for club sessions. Other swim clubs were the Huddersfield and Lockwood SC in 1825 and a swim club at the St. George Baths at the Pier Head in Liverpool in 1828. Neither of these clubs could claim continuous existence.

[97] Brighton SC website: http://www.brightonsc.co.uk/clubhistory.htm, accessed 9/20/2004.

[98] Ibid. Claire Parker's essay The Rise of Competitive Swimming 1840 to 1878 has the date of formation of the Amateur Swimming Association as 1886. The ASA website: www.britishswimming.org, confirms this date.

[99] NY Times, 7/22/1876, *A Long Swim in the River Thames*, from the London Telegraph, 7/7/1876

[100] London Times, 8/4/1865

[101] London Times, 8/14/1867

[102] London Times, 7/24/1871

[103] The ASA website: www.britishswimming.org, history link confirms that the Metropolitan Swimming Association was formed in 1869 which after a two-year schism from 1884 to 1886 lead to the formation of the ASA .

[104] London Times, 7/26/1871

[105] London Times, 8/26/1871

[106] London Times, 8/28/1871

[107] Ibid.

[108] London Times, 9/15/1873

[109] Ibid.

[110] NY Times, 7/18/1872 from the London Daily News 7/5/1872

[111] NY Times, 8/5/1857, by a special correspondent of the Daily Telegraph.

[112] NY Times, 9/18/1875 from the London papers of Sept. 1.

[113] Harry Parker is the H. Parker, winner of the Amateur Championship of 1871who had participated in the professions swim. See events of 1871 for the discussion.

[114] NY Times, Sept 30, 1875 from the London Standard of Sept. 6th

[115] NY Times, 10/4/`875 from the News of London, 9/20/1875.

[116] NY Times, 10/14/1900, *Channel and Other Swims*.

[117] Now known as Swimming New Zealand.
[118] Swimming New Zealand website: http://www.swimmingnz.org.nz/about/history.php.
[119] Washington Post, 1/2/1892, *Swimming in Uniform*.
[120] Adam, Norbert. Schwimmania 1899/1999 (Swim Mania1899/1999). Horn:Druckerei Ferdinand Berger & Söhne, 1999.
[121] NY Times, 3/6/1898, *Feat of an Austrian Officer*.
[122] Visit the Medal of Honor web site: www.army.mil/cmh/
[123] NY Times, 7/17/1899, *He Swam the Rio Grande*.
[124] Monty Holbein was 2nd in the inaugural Bordeaux-Paris 600 km bicycle race in 1891.
[125] NY Times, 7/26/1899, Bicyclist Holbein Swims 43 Miles, the report erroneously identifies the starting point as Blackwell. There is no Blackwell on the Thames but there is a Blackwall.
[126] NY Times, 8/26/1901, *Holbein's Swimming Feat*.
[127] NY Times, 8/2/1902, *Holbein Unable To Swim From France To England*.
[128] NY Times, 8/29/1902, *Swimmers Fail in Long Test*.
[129] NY Times, 9/3/1903, *Holbein Fails to Swim the Channel*.
[130] NY Times, 8/13/1909, *Fails to Swim Channel*.
[131] Adam, Norbert. Schwimmania 1899/1999 (Swim Mania1899/1999). Horn:Druckerei Ferdinand Berger & Söhne, 1999.
[132] "Fugger." *LoveToKnow 1911 Online Encyclopedia* ©2003, 2004. http://65.1911encyclopedia.org/F/FU/FUGGER.htm. Accessed 12/29/04.
[133] NY Times, 7/19/1858
[134] NY Times, 8/19/1872
[135] NY Times, 7/5/1875
[136] NY Times, 10/18/1874
[137] NY Times, 7/3/1872
[138] NY Times, 6/28/1872
[139] NY Times, 6/28/1872
[140] NY Times, 7/2/1870
[141] NY Times, 8/25/1872, the article erroneously calls the 1872 National Swimming Association annual meet the *first* annual exhibition. The Association had by this time been hosting swimming meets for 34 years.
[142] American Red Cross Museum Timeline: www.redcross.org/museum/timemach.html.
[143] NY Times, 5/27/1900, *Cherry Hill Swimmers, What Spring Means to Pier-Haunting East Side Boys, How They Learned the Art*.
[144] You see these kinds of swimmers even today at public pools, they've never learned to swim and have taught themselves the rudiments. They can't even put their heads in the water. You just hope and pray they don't get in your lane when you are doing a workout. More than once, I've offered a hint or two to

improve their swimming but most are too proud to listen; but those that do are quite thankful. It's a shame that lifeguards are reticent to offer instructions to someone obviously in need.

[145] NY Times, 7/14/1927, *Keating Alone Ends Lake George Swim.*

[146] *A Raid on Nude Swimmers*, NY Times, 7/16/1877.

[147] NY Times, 7/27/1853, *Washing and Bathing.*

[148] The Gazette of the United States, 9/25/1801, p3. In an ad for the Central boarding School in the cityof Bordeaux, France, swimming was listed along with fencing and riding.

[149] NY Times, 7/12/1968, *Public Baths.*

[150] NY Times, 7/11/1867

[151] Wilbert Longfellow who was hired by the Red Cross had been teaching swimming and crusading for water safety programs for some time before he was hired in 1914. He comes from a cadre of swimming masters (as they were called) of whom Mr. Krack is the first mention of a person that I could find whom taught professionally this skill.

[152] NY Times, 7/2/1870

[153] Washington Post, 1/25/1903, *Public Floating Bath.*

[154] New York Daily Tribune, June 26, 1882

[155] Visit www.floatingpool.org and click on their history link. There is mention of two portable baths located at the Battery as early as 1817.

[156] *A Brief History of the YMCA Movement*, from the YMCA website: www.ymca.net/index.jsp.

[157] NY Times, 6/5/1904, *A Century of Free Education in New York.*

[158] The South Boston Inquirer, 7/29/1905, page 3.

[159] NY Times, 6/4/1876, *Opening of the Swimming Baths.*

[160] Randalls Island is on the Bronx side of Hell Gate, separating the Harlem River from the East River. The Triboro bridge collection booths are physically located above the Island. The island has a large mental hospital facility with a spacious lawn coming down to the Harlem River's edge.

[161] NY Times, 8/11/1872

[162] NY Times, 8/14/1875

[163] NY Times, 8/23/1874

[164] NY Times, 8/26/1874

[165] NY Times, 8/29/1874

[166] NY Times, 9/25/1874

[167] NY Times, 7/7/1875

[168] New York Tribune, 7/23/1975

[169] New York Tribune, 8/25/1875

[170] NY Times, 7/7/1875

[171] NY Times, 7/24,1925

[172] by Yankee Stadium.

[173] New York Times, 8/18/1878
[174] New York Times, 8/3/1878
[175] New York Times, 8/31/1878
[176] This bridge is located where Madison Ave runs into the Harlem River, across from Mott Haven section of the Bronx.
[177] New York Times, 8/13/1878
[178] New York Tribune, 8/14/1879
[179] New York Tribune, 8/23/1879
[180] NY Times, 9/15/1879
[181] NY Times, 7/16/1897, *Swimming the English Channel*.
[182] NY Times, 8/23/1882
[183] I once took a workout with Drury Gallagher of Manhasset, the one time record holder for the Manhattan Marathon Swim (twice), a Master's All-American designee, and holder of numerous Master titles and records. He was resting his left shoulder having come back from a National championship. Once again he had blown out his shoulder in a National championship. I was swimming next to him and he's only using his one good arm to stoke laps with. I'm not that bad but I'm not that fast either plus Drury is 2 age groups ahead of me. This was an easy workout for Drury where he stretches out and relaxes, keeping his body tuned and in the groove. He's using one arm and he's beating me. I'd probably have to tie both arms and one leg together before I could take him in a race.
[184] New York Tribune, 8/24/1882.
[185] Washington Post, 7/16/1883, *Over Niagara in a Rubber Ball*.
[186] NY Times, 7/26/1883, Capt. Webb Missing Yet.
[187] Ibid.
[188] NY Times, 7/29/1883, *Capt. Webb's Body Found*.
[189] NY Times, 7/26/1883, *Capt. Webb Missing Yet*.
[190] NY Times, 7/25/1883, *Capt. Webb Drowned*.
[191] Ibid.
[192] NY Times, 7/26/1883, *Capt. Webb Missing Yet*.
[193] NY Times, 7/29/1883, *Capt. Webb's Manager*.
[194] NY Times, 7/29/1883, *Capt. Webb's Body Found*.
[195] Credit for the acute observations of New Yorkers goes to the unnamed writer of the NY Times article, *In and About the City*, 8/31/1884.
[196] Visit the Brooklyn Bridge website: www.endex.com/gf/buildings/bbridge/bbridge.html, maintained by Gary Feuerstein, accessed 12/4/04.
[197] NY Times, 6/20/1885, *Odlum's Leap to Death*.
[198] Washington Post, 8/3/1878, *The Swimming School*.
[199] Washington Post, 10/16/1879, *Sale of the Natatorium Property*.
[200] Washington Post, 5/1/1881, *Opening Exercises at the Natatorium*.

[201] NY Times, 5/20/1885, *Boyton's Story*.
[202] NY Times, 5/22/1885, *Prof. Odlum's Body*. Odium was misidentified by the papers because of the font used for the letter "i" looked very much like an "l".
[203] NY Times editorial, 5/22/1885, *Wasted*.
[204] NY Times, 7/24/1886, *A Leap From The Bridge*.
[205] NY Times, 2/1/1901, *"Steve" Brodie Dead*.
[206] NY Times, 7/25/1886, *Brodie's Path to Wealth*.
[207] NY Times, 7/26/1886, *Wanted to Beat Brodie*; 8/19/1886, *A Bold Man From Boston*; 8/29/1886, *Jumped Off The Bridge*; 8/30/1886, *His Plans Went Amiss*; 9/1/1886, *Says He Made The Jump*.
[208] NY Times, 8/2/1886, *Sunday By The Sea*.
[209] NY Times, 8/19/1886, *A Bold Man From Boston; To Meet Odlum's Fate or Share Brodie's Fame. He Will Jump From The Brooklyn Bridge Unless He Can Be Dropped From a Balloon*.
[210] NY Times, 7/2/1888, *Jumping Sam Patch*.
[211] "Has anyone really gone over Niagara Falls in a barrel?" The Straight Dope. Cecil Adams, Chicago Reader, Inc., 2003. http://www.straightdope.com , 12/20/2004.
[212] NY Times, 8/24/1886, *Swimming The Hudson*.
[213] Point Morris is just east from where the Bruckner Boulevard and Major Deegan divide after the tolls on the Triboro bridge.
[214] The Oak Point marina was located just south of the Randall Ave. Bridge over the Bronx River.
[215] NY Times, 8/29/1886, *Swimmers Racing*.
[216] Visit the Embassy of France web site: www.ambafrance-us.org click on French-American Relations, History, Statue of Liberty.
[217] NY Times, 8/30/1886, *A Daring Lady Swimmer*, from the Detroit Free Press.
[218] NY Times, 8/26/1887, *A Ten-Mile Swim*.
[219] A gale is officially a wind in excess of 39 knots (43 mph); however, this much wind would generate small boat warnings so it's likely the use of gale was more descriptive than factual.
[220] This is the same Braun who competed against the Austrian swimmer mentioned earlier.
[221] NY Times, 8/24/1887, *Swimming Records Broken*.
[222] NY Times, 8/26/1988, *Good Swimming Races*.
[223] Visit the Amateur Athlete Union home page: www.aausports.org click on *About the AAU*.
[224] Visit the Olympic Movement: www.olympics.org click on Passion, Museum, Permanent Exhibitions, Pierre de Coubertin.
[225] Visit the NCAA web site: www.ncaa.org , hover over *About* and select *Overview*, scroll down to click on *History of the NCAA*. Direct link: www.ncaa.org/about/history.html

[226] Visit FINA (Federation Internationale De Natation) web site: www.fina.org/history_officers.html this location is not visible from their main site.

[227] The AAU was the very first sporting organization I ever joined. The Fontana High School swimming coach, Al Zamsky, wanted his swimmers to stay in shape over the summer so he had us join a summer Water Polo league that included teams throughout Southern California. It was great competition, lots of fun, and you had to join the AAU to play. I filled out the paperwork, sent in the fee, and back came this card signed by a fellow named Harry Barr. I joked with my teammates about the name that summer. You can't imagine my surprise when 20 years later at a local Master Swimming Awards Dinner in Hicksville, Long Island, I realized that the Harry Barr I was sitting next to on the podium and that I worked with on the Manhattan Island Swimming Association was the same Harry Barr that had signed my AAU card. Harry got into swimming after his wrestling career ended. What a great guy. I still have that card.

[228] Washington Post, 7/12/1888, *A Big Swimming Match*.

[229] NY Times, 7/11/1888, *The Australian Beaten*.

[230] Yates Country Chronicle, 9/11/1889, p. 2, quoted by Ranji Sanhu in "Buffalo's Forgotten Theatres" on the History of Buffalo website: http://ah.bfn.org/h/movie/sandhu/.

[231] NY Times, 7/19/1883, *Tales About "The Falls"*. This article was published at the time of Capt. Webb's death relates everything known about the falls up until that time. It includes information about suicides, accidents, and near misses (those fortunate individuals who escaped the river). Nothing was mentioned about anyone living after having gone over.

[232] NY Times, 0/8/1889, *Over Niagara Falls*.

[233] Ibid.

[234] Visit Niagara Falls web site: www.niagarafallslive.com and click on daredevils.

[235] From *Brooklyn Bridge Historic Overview* at http://www.nycroads.com/crossings/brooklyn/ "...Contrary to popular belief, Steve Brodie did not jump off the bridge. He merely pulled off a publicity stunt in order to attain fame...".

From Merriam-Webster OnLine: "...The truth of his allegation was never established, but "pulling a Brodie" first became slang for a suicidal leap and then for a fall, failure, or flop. " at: http://www.merriam-webster.com/cgi-bin/wftwarch.pl?052404.

[236] From the Buffalo Free-Net community web site, A History of Buffalo website, *Buffalo's Forgotton Theaters A Few Notes by Ranjit Sandhu*, at: http://at.bfn.org/h/movie/sandhu/.
Internet Movie Database confirms George Raft in 1933 played Steve Brodie, found at http://us.imdb.com/name/nm0706368/#actor1930.

[237] The Columbia Encyclopedia, 6th Ed., Columbia University Press viewable at: http://www.bartleby.com/65/e-/E-Brodie-S.html.
[238] From ENDEX Engineering, Inc., *Brooklyn Bridge Names, Steve Brodie* at http://www.endex.com/gf/buildings/bbridge/BBnames.htm.
[239] From the University of Texas public web site: http://farside.ph.utexas.edu/teaching/301/lectures/node22.html a rate of fall calculation by Richard Fitzpatrick posted on 4/26/2004.
[240] NY Times, 4/1/1898, *Steve Brodie is Dead.*; NY Times, 4/2/1989, *Steve Brodie Very Much Alive.*
[241] From the Buffalo Free-Net community web site, A History of Buffalo website, *Buffalo's Forgotton Theaters A Few Notes by Ranjit Sandhu*, at: http://at.bfn.org/h/movie/sandhu/.
[242] NY Times, 2/7/1901, *"Steve" Brodie's Funeral.*
[243] NY Times, 2/19/1889, *Steve Brodie's Cold Swim.*
[244] Washington Post, 9/28/1889, *A Six-Day's Swimming Match*; Boston Globe, 10/1/1889, *Short Laps, Long Swim*; Boston Globe, 10/2/1889, *Beckwith in the Swim*; Boston Globe, 10/3/1889, *Dyas Gaining in the Swim*; Boston Globe, 10/4/1889, *Swimming Record in Danger*; Boston Globe, 10/5/1889, *Beckwith Increases Her Lead*; Boston Globe, 10/6/1889, *Six Days in the Swim*; NY Times, 9/28/1889, *To Swim For $1000.*
[245] Visit the Olympic Movement: www.olympics.org click on Olympic Games.
[246] Visit Aquatics International web site: www.aquaticsintl.com click on The History of Aquatics.
[247] His 100 yard time based on his 100 meter time would have been 1:15.2. This is comparable to the record for the 100 yards in the early 1880's in London.
[248] Mallon, Bill and Ture Williams. The 1896 Olympic Games. North Carolina:McFarland and Company, Inc., 1998.
[249] Visit the official Olympic web site: www.olympic.org click on Olympic Games, Athens 1896, All the heros from these Games, then select Alfred Hajos Aquatics (Hungary).
[250] Mallon, Bill and Ture Williams. The 1896 Olympic Games. North Carolina:McFarland and Company, Inc., 1998.
[251] NY Times, 7/13/1898, *Dr. Neuman to Swim Abroad*, also: International Swimming Hall of Fame biography seen at http://www.ishof.org/86pneumann.html.
[252] NY Times, 5/7/1896, *Boston Athletes Arrive.*
[253] Mallon, Bill and Ture Williams. The 1896 Olympic Games. North Carolina:McFarland and Company, Inc., 1998.
[254] Olympic Games official web site, www.olympic.org under About Aquatics.
[255] Email from Secr. Gen. Thomas Gangel of the Austrian Swimming Federation, 11/16/2004, asserts that swimmers would swim between the two

cities, a distance of over 120 miles. The veracity of this claim could not be ascertained by the publication date. Such a swim would take over 30 hours.

[256] Created as a leachate (runoff) from a mining operation in Baia Mare. The reservoir holding this leachate broke dumping 100,000 cubic meters of this toxin into the Lapus River and subsequently flowed into the Somes and Tisza and then finally, the Danube. Source found at http://www.public.asu.edu/~goutam/gcu325/danube.htm, accessed 12/17/2004.

[257] Rivers of Europe, at www.public.asu.edu/~goutam/gcu325 and Danube Research web site, www.danube-research.com/danube.html, both accessed 11/3/2004.

[258] NY Times, 9/22/1896,

[259] "The Golden Gate Strait is the entrance to the San Francisco Bay from the Pacific Ocean. The strait is approximately three-miles long by one-mile wide with currents ranging from 4.5 to 7.5 knots. It is generally accepted that the strait was named "Chrysopylae", or Golden Gate, by John C. Fremont, Captain, topographical Engineers of the U.S. Army circa 1846. It reminded him of a harbor in Instanbul named Chrysoceras or Golden Horn." Information from: http://www.goldengatebridge.org/research/facts.html

[260] Dolphin Club web site: www.dolphinclub.org/history.html.

[261] Visit the ISHOF web site: www.ishof.org/70cavillfamily.html.

[262] International Swimming Hall of Fame Honoree, contributor.

[263] NY Times, 10/28/1893, *From Charybdis to Scylla.*

[264] See "Swims" of Boyton in the Appendix.

[265] NY Times, 4/27/1988, *For the Hardy, A San Francisco Swim.*

[266] "Dolphin Club History", Dolphin Club web site: http://www.dolphinclub.org.

[267] Wennerberg, Conrad. Wind, Waves and Sunburn. New York:AS Barnes and Co. 1974. Page 289.

[268] NY Times, 8/19/1899, *Box Kite Swims are the Fad.*

[269] *A Decent and Proper Exertion,* Veronica Raszeja, Australian Society for Sports History, 1992.

[270] Ibid.

[271] NY Times, 9/13/1893, *A Great Swimming Record.*

[272] NY Times, 2/4/1906, *Swimming Year in England.*

[273] Visit Backyard Agora web site: www.backyardagora.com click on glossary, then S, look for swimming, history of.

[274] NY Times, 6/28/1903, *Comparison of Swimmers.*

[275] Visit Backyard Agora web site: www.backyardagora.com click on glossary, then S, look for swimming, history of.

[276] NY Times, 9/21/1902, *Swimming Championships.*

[277] A little known fact about the NYAC tank is that the swimmers, all men, would swim nude except when in competition and public visitors were invited. The author visited the pool and took a swim in the famous tank in the 1980's

and found this custom rather odd never having swam nude before. But then again, the author had never swum at a pool whose history dates all the way back to 1885. This was also customary at YMCA pools.

[278] NY Times, 6/28/1903, *Comparison of Swimmers*.

[279] Unpublished manuscript, *American Style Water Polo, A History* by Bruce Wigo, 1987.

[280] Partial listing from NY Times, 7/30/1900, *Amateur Swimming Races*, NY Times, 9/12/1897, *Aquatics at Bath Beach*.

[281] Sydney Cavill became the swimming/water polo coach some time after 1900.

[282] NY Times, 7/30/1900, *Amateur Swimming Races*.

[283] NY Times, 6/28/1903, *Comparison of Swimmers*.

[284] Unpublished manuscript, *American Style Water Polo, A History* by Bruce Wigo, 1987.

[285] Washington Post, 8/31/1902, *Fast Work in Water*.

[286] NY Times, 8/20/1903, *Daniels's Swimming Record*.

[287] NY Times, 8/21/1904, *World's Swimming Record*.

[288] NY Times, 8/9/1903, *New York Swimmer Wins*.

[289] NY Times, 7/13/1902, *New Swimming Records*.

[290] NY Times, 12/22/1905, *Swimmers Break Records*.

[291] NY Times, 1/14/1906, *New Swimming Records in New York A.C. Tank*.

[292] NY Times, 3/24/2906, *World's Swimming Record*.

[293] Visit ISHOF website: http://www.ishof.org/65cdaniels.html

[294] New York Sun, 2/23/1906, reported "Professor Gus Sundstrom, the NYAC Instructor is the man primarily responsible for the work of Daniels and the others…".

[295] NY Times, 1/13/1907, *New Swimming Records Made by C. M. Daniels*.

[296] NY Times, 7/24/1976, *Better Training is Key to Swim Records*.

[297] NY Times, 4/22/1902, *New Records by Australian Swimmer*.

[298] NY Times, 8/18/1900, *Severe Test for a Swimmer*.

[299] The present day name of this location is Fort Lesley J. McNair. This was the location where Abraham Lincoln's conspirators meet their fate in a remarkably short period of time. Visit American Forts Networks at: http://www.geocities.com/naforts/dc.html#mcnair.

[300] Washington Post, 8/13/1900, *Previous Record Broken*.

[301] The dispute was probably about who was the better swimmer.

[302] NY Times, 8/22/1903, *Swam to Coney Island from the Battery*.

[303] NY Times, 8/29/1904, *Two Girls Make Swim from Bridge to Coney*.

[304] Australia Swimming web site, www.ausswim.telstra.com.au/history/index.cfm, 10/3/2004

[305] NY Times, 11/6/1975, Orbituary, *Annette Kellerman Sullivan, 87, "Million Dollar Mermaid", Dead*

[306] NY Times, 8/26/1904, *Girl Swims Cayuga Lake*.

[307] NY Times, 9/4/1904, *Nuttall First in Swim.*
[308] Boston Globe, 9/3/1904, *Nuttall Wins in RI.* This article had slightly different amount for the cash prizes. The swim stroke was discussed in another article two weeks earlier when they raced in the Charles River over ¼ and ½ mile distances.
[309] NY Times, 9/21/1906
[310] NY Times, 9/9/1907, *Swept by Tide, Brown Wins Race.*
[311] NY Times, 9/16/1907, *Four Swimmers Go Through Hell Gate.*
[312] NY Times, 8/31/1908, *Bud Goodwin Wins Long-Distance Swim.*
[313] NY Times, 7/25/1910, *Swimmers in Peril in Race to Coney.*
[314] NY Times, 8/14/1911, *Girl in Long Swim to Coney Island.*
[315] NY Times, 9/19/1910, *Girl Makes Long Swim to Coney.*
[316] NY Times, 8/24/1914, *Girls Do The Long Coney Island Swim.* The report of Alfred Brown's time of 4:23 for the course is questionable.
[317] NY Times, 9/9/1909, *Amateur's Long Swim in the Delaware.*
[318] NY Times, 3/22/1913, *Americans Will Try To Swim Channel.*
[319] NY Times, 1/25/1914, *Long-Distance Swim.*
[320] Ms. Magazine, July/August 1989
[321] NY Times, 9/4/1911, *Girl Swimmer Makes New Record.*
[322] NY Times, 8/30/1909, *Girls Swim the Narrows.*
[323] NY Times, 2/26/1911, *Criticises Our Swimming.*
[324] NY Times, 4/2/1911, *Swimming Strokes Show Differences.*
[325] NY Times, 8/29/1913, *Life Saver Brown Swims to the Hook.*
[326] NY Times, 9/4/1913, *Brown Fails in Swim.*
[327] NY Times, 8/29/1913, *Life Saver Brown Swims to the Hook.*
[328] NY Times, 9/15/1913, *Richards Succeeds in Sandy Hook Swim.*
[329] NY Times, 1/25/1914, *Long-Distance Swim.*
[330] The records for this particular swim are difficult to come by as the New York Tribune newspapers stopped having their papers indexed in 1905, so the only way to find records for this swim is to read every paper published from 1914 to 1924 when the paper went out of business. Since a competitor sponsored the swim, the NY Times ignored this swim and only occasionally referenced it when reporting a swim resume as background on a swimmer.
[331] Unpublished manuscript, *American Style Water Polo, A History* by Bruce Wigo, 1987.
[332] NY Tribune, 7/20/1914
[333] NY Times, 2/11/1914, *Richards and Durborow Match.*
[334] NY Times, 9/21/1914, *Woman Swims 22 Miles To Hook.*
[335] NY Times, 8/25/1914, *McDermott Best in Long Swim.*
[336] New York Tribune, 9/6/1915
[337] NY Times, 2/12/1914, *Big Japanese Outing.*
[338] NY Times, 6/25/1916, *Great Ocean Swim Made By Amateur.*

339 NY Times, 9/11/1916, *Sets New Swimming Mark.*
340 Charles Toth would swim the English Channel in 1923 in 16:58, one of the men's times that Ederle would beat.
341 NY Times, 8/21/1916
342 New York Tribune, 9/10/1916
343 NY Times, 9/13/1916
344 New York Tribune, 9/13/1916
345 NY Times, 9/3/1917
346 Current was calculated by Tides and Currents, Version 2.0c from Nautical Software, Inc. Ebb started at 1pm at Spuyten Duyvil.
347 NY Times, 9/10/1917
348 NY Times, 7/21/1919, *Ross Seine Race Victor.*
349 NY Times, 8/23/1921, *Makes Record Swim.*
350 NY Times, 6/26/1922, *Pouilley in Trial Swim.*
351 NY Times, 9/20/1922, *Russain Swimmer Fails.*
352 NY Times, 6/7/1922, *To Try Channel Swim.*
353 NY Times, 10/9/1922, *Woman Breaks Man's Record For First Time in Swim History.*
354 NY Times, 8/24/1924
355 NY Time, 6/15/1925, *Miss Ederle Set World Swim Mark.*
356 NY Times, 6/16/1925, *Girls Swims To Hook From The Battery.*
357 NY Times, 7/26/1925, *Coolidge Sponsors a Titled Swim Race.*
358 NY Times, 9/19/1925, *Made to Quit Swim, Miss Ederle Says.*
359 NY Times, 9/20/1925, *Ederle Charges denied by Wolfe.*
360 NY Times, 8/30/1932, *Photo Standalone 8—No Title.*
361 Unpublished manuscript, *American Style Water Polo, A History* by Bruce Wigo, 1987.
362 NY Times, 8/9/1926, *Spence Wins Title in Distance Swim.*
363 NY Times, 6/27/1 927, *Young Ray Ruddy Wins Title Swim.*
364 NY Times, 7/2/1927, *Ray Ruddy, 15, First in 4 ½ Mile Swim.*
365 NY Times, 9/11/1927, *Ruddy Home First in One-Mile Swim.* The information contained in this article points to an earlier beginning to the Atlantic City pageant swim than presently known by the organizers in Atlantic City. Their website and information is reached via the Atlantic City Beach Patrol: www.acbp.org.
366 NY Times, 7/3/1928, *Ray Ruddy Captures One-Mile Swim Title.*
367 NY Times, 7/4/1928, *New York AC Wins at Water polo, 35-20.*

368 NY Times, 8/5/1928, *Miss Norelius Sets World Swim Mark.*
369 NY Times, 8/7/1928, *Miss Norelius and Borg Set World's Records in Winning Olympic Swimming Titles.*
370 NY Times, 8/1 0/1 928, *Zorilla Wins Great Race.*
371 NY Times, 9/22/1 928, *Ray Ruddy is Operated On.*

[372] ISHOF website for Honorees: www.ishof.org/87droth.html.
[373] NY Times, 7/24/1932, *Los Angeles A. C. Wins Final at Water Polo* and NY Times, 7/6/1936, *Los Angeles A. C. Water Polo Victor.*
[374] NY Times, 7/10/1932, *New York A. C. Four Takes Swim Race.*
[375] His leg was amputated below the knee. He was also the European 1500 meters champion. Information from ISHOF website.
[376] NY Times, 8/14/1932, *Water Polo Title Goes to Hungary.*
[377] NY Times, 9/4//1932, *Ray Ruddy Victor for the Sixth Time.*
[378] NY Times, 9/9/1928, *Ruddy Wins Marathon Swim on Schuylkill; Lee is Second.*
[379] NY Times, 7/29/1929, *Ray Ruddy Regains A. A. U. Swim Title.*
[380] NY Times, 8/19/1929, *Ray Ruddy Breaks Five Swim Records.*
[381] NY Times, 4/29/1930, *Ray Ruddy Elected Captain of Columbia Swimming Team.*
[382] NY Times, 3/3/1931, *Ruddy Leaves Columbia.*
[383] NY Times, 3/7/1929, *Ruddy Establishes 3 World Records.*
[384] NY Times, 4/29/1930, *Ray Ruddy Elected Captain of Columbia Swimming Team.*
[385] NY Times, 6/2/1931, *Farley, Swimmer, Stabbed in a Fight.*
[386] NY Times, 9/15/1930, Ray *Ruddy Retains Mile Senior Title.*
[387] NY Times, 9/6/1931, *Title Swim Annexed by Ruddy at Toronto* and *NY* Times, 8/29/1932, *Ruddy Again Annexes 2-Mile Toronto Swim.*
[388] NY Times, 1/7/1932, *Ray Ruddy Topped NYAC Athletes.*
[389] NY Times, 1/4/1933, *NYAC Athletes had Record Year.*
[390] NY Times, 8/14/1933, *Swimming Title Retained by Ruddy.*
[391] NY Times, 7/29/1934, *Ruddy Takes Swim Eighth Time in Row.*
[392] NY Times, 12/5/1938, *Ray Ruddy, Olympic Swim Star, Killed By Plunge Down a Flight of Stairs.*
[393] NY Times, 8/29/1925, *Japanese Swimmer Gives Up in Channel.*
[394] NY Times, 1/20/1926, *Japanese to Try Channel.*
[395] NY Times, 11/27/1927, *Laufer Big Scorer in Trip to Orient.*
[396] NY Times, 8/8/1932, *Japan's Natators Impress Observers.*
[397] NY Times, 8/31/1930, *Athletics Rising Greatly in Soviet.*
[398] NY Times, 8/30/1925, *Finish Line Drifts As Swimmers Race.*
[399] NY Times, 8/28/1925, *German Swims 22 Hours.*
[400] NY Times, 4/25/1927
[401] Ernest Vierkotter swam the channel a month after Gertrude Ederle and took two hours off her time. See www.soloswims.com for complete list of channel swimmers.
[402] NY Times, 7/4/1927, *Channel Stars Enter Lake George Swim.*
[403] NY Times, 7/14/1927, *Keating Alone Ends Lake George Swim.*
[404] NY Times, 9/8/1948 *127 Entered Today in Marathon Swim.*

[405] NY Times, 9/9/1948, *Kerschner Wins Marathon Swimming Race At Lake George.*
[406] NY Times, 7/10/1927, *Women in Long Swim.*
[407] NY Times, 8/26/1928, *Girl Lowers Mark in Bayshore Swim.*
[408] NY Times, 8/26/1929, *Lee Finishes First in Nine Mile Swim*
[409] NY Times, 7/24/1 927, *Gains Grease Coat in Jersey Swim.*
[410] NY Times, 5/24/1928
[411] NY Times, 3/17/1930
[412] Better known as Zarate, about 51 miles from Buenos Aires.
[413] NY Times, 2/25/1935
[414] NY Times, 7/31/1929, *Girl Swims 20 Miles.*
[415] NY Times, 8/6/1929, *20 Mile Savannah Swim.*
[416] NY Times, 8/16/1929, *Girl Swims 37¼ Miles.*
[417] NY Times, 9/25/1929, *Americans Swim Bosporus.*
[418] NY Times, 8/19/1931, *Anita Grew, 22, Swims Length of Bosporus; Estonian Crosses Gulf of Finland, 40 Miles.*
[419] NY Times, 8/5/1930, *American Girl, Age 8, Swims the Bosporus, Asia to Europe.*
[420] NY Times, 8/11/1930, *California Woman Swims 20 Miles on 70th Birthday.*
[421] NY Times, 8/17/1930, *Woman Swims Hellespont.*
[422] Soloswim of Ontario, http://soloswims.com/sadlo.htm, 12/27/05.
[423] "Reval." LoveToKnow 1911 Online Encyclopedia. 2003, http://2.1911encyclopedia.org/R/Reval.htm
[424] NY Times, 8/19/1931, *Anita Grew, 22, Swims Length of Bosporus; Estonian Crosses Gulf of Finland, 40 Miles.*
[425] NY Times, 8/17, 1931, *Sets 18-Mile Swim Record.*
[426] NY Times, 7/30/1931, *Girl Cripple, 14, Swims 10 Miles in 3½ Hours.*
[427] NY Times, 8/15/1931, *Boy, 12, Sets Mark in Swim.*
[428] NY Times, 8/31/1931, *Two Swim Chesapeake Bay.*
[429] NY Times, 10/18/1933, *Girl Swims to Shore From Alcatraz Island.*
[430] NY Times, 7/23/1934
[431] NY Times, 9/3/1934, *Pritchard First in Swim.*
[432] Las Vegas Review Journal, *THIS WAS NEVADA: Phillip I. Earl*, Phillip I Earl, 2/14/1997. We're happy to report that there was no backup at the fruit inspection station when she crossed the state line.
[433] NY Times, 8/18/1935, *Everybody Goes Swimming, These Days.*
[434] NY Times, 8/21/1935, *Russia Acclaims Swimming Exploit.*
[435] NY Times, 8/25/1935, *Potomac Swim to Tresnack.*
[436] NY Times, 7/15/1936
[437] NY Times, 8/15/1937, *Woodling Wins Swim.*
[438] NY Times, 8/29/1937, *Wozniak Takes Capital Swim.*
[439] NY Times, 7/2/1939, 7/3/1939, 7/4/1939

[440] The reasons for leaving the water and the time vary depending on which account is read.
[441] Dawson County Review, 7/6/1939, the Dawson County Review eventually became the Ranger Review, a local Glendive, Montana, newspaper.
[442] NY Times, 6/23/1940, *Swim Race At Nassau.*
[443] NY Times, 8/11/1940, *Chouteau Wins 10-Mile Swim.*
[444] NY Times, 7/30/1938, *Danish Girl, 19, Swims Baltic Sea, 37 Miles in 40 Hours 9 Minutes.*
[445] NY Times, 8/12/1939, *Danish Girl Again Swim Baltic.*
[446] Wennerberg, Conrad. Wind, Waves and Sunburn. New York:AS Barnes and Co. 1974. Page 334-5.
[447] Wennerberg, Conrad. Wind, Waves and Sunburn. New York:AS Barnes and Co. 1974. Page 281. Nor could I find any record of this swim in the NY Times.
[448] NY Times, 7/11/1949, *Schoolgirl Swim 14 Miles to Coney.*
[449] NY Times, 7/3/1950, *Canadian Victor in Swim.*
[450] The New England swims recounted in this section were elicited during an interview with Jim Doty on 1/5/2005.
[451] NY Times, 10/6/1958
[452] NY Times, 12/11/1972
[453] Las Vegas Review Journal, *THIS WAS NEVADA: Phillip I. Earl*, Phillip I Earl, 2/14/1997.
[454] Ashby Harper family source, Margie Harper Reber.
[455] NY Times, 8/1/1988, *Sports World Specials.*
[456] NY Times, 9/19/1955, *Ontario Swimmer Lost: Canadian Vanishes in Darkness on Distance Effort.*
[457] Presently, light sticks are marketed under multiple names for purchase. Look for the one guaranteed 8-12 hours with a 3-year guarantee. For an article discussing how they work visit: http://www.sas.upenn.edu/~mtc/Lightstick.html.
[458] NY Times, 9/21/1953
[459] Visit the web site for Straits of Gibraltar: www.acneg.com, for the complete swimmer's list, click on ida.
[460] Ibid.
[461] Wennerberg, Conrad. Wind, Waves and Sunburn. New York:AS Barnes and Co. 1974. Page 283-285.
[462] NY Times, 8/19/1956, *Woman Swims Strait.* Ms. Hiland would in 1958 swim from Catalina Island to Long Beach, California, a distance of 26 miles instead of the usual distance of 21 miles over the shortest course.
[463] Wennerberg, Conrad. Wind, Waves and Sunburn. New York:AS Barnes and Co. 1974. Page 285-6.
[464] NY Times, 8/19/1956
[465] NY Times, 08/05/1957

[466] NY Times, 7/21/1962, *Miss Revell Swims Bosporus Length*, background information included in the article.
[467] Ibid.
[468] NY Times, 8/29/1961
[469] NY Times, 7/17/1961, *Coast Girl Swims Ten Miles*. Sports Illustrated Magazine reported her Mackinac Straits swim distance at 7.5 miles. This distance was reported first swum in 1955 by Barbara Leonard in 2:36 in Joe Grossman's unpublished manuscript circa 1970.
[470] NY Times, 7/21/1962, *Miss Revell Swims Bosporus Length*. This swim is disputed by Greta Anderson in Joe Grossman's unpublished manuscript circa 1970.
[471] Time Magazine, 5/3/1963, *Queen of the World's Marathoners* and in Willoughby, David. The Super-Athletes. New York:A. S. Barnes and Company, 1970, page 486.
[472] Las Vegas Review Journal, *THIS WAS NEVADA: Phillip I. Earl*, Phillip I Earl, 2/14/1997.
[473] Brian Finlay's website, www.soloswim.com, *Kevin Murphy 2003 Round-up*.
[474] ISHOF Yearbook, 2006.
[475] NY Times, 7/17/1976, *Mao's 1966 River Swim Repeated Across China*.
[476] NY Times, 7/21/1966, *Mao Seems in Good Health, Japanese Visitor Reports*.
[477] NY Times, 7/31/1966, *See the Chairman Swim*.
[478] NY Times, 7/25/1966, *Peking Say Mao Swam 8 Miles in the Yangtze*.
[479] NY Times, 7/18/1973, *Photo Standalone 1--No Title*
[480] NY Times, 7/29/1966, *Chinese Urged to Swim*.
[481] NY Times, 8/9/1967, *Chinese Swims to Quemoy*.
[482] NY Times, 8/29/1967, this swim is covered in detail in Conrad Wennerberg's book, Wind, Waves, and Sunburn.
[483] The other members were Richard Bouillanne, James Olivant, Marty Rea, Ronald Held, George Fecke, and James Wanser.
[484] NY Times, 8/9/1972, *Six-Men Start Montauk-to-Coney Island Relay Swim*.
[485] Quest, May-June 1978, *Beyond All Limits,* by Diana Nyad, p50.
[486] Sports Illustrated, August 1978, *The Machine Cranks Up,* by Ron Reid, p24.
[487] Ranger Review, 7/1/1976 and 7/8/1976.
[488] The Netherland Open Water Web, post 7/6/2006 from The Royal Gazette in Bermuda by Sam Stevens.
[489] NY Times, 7/25/1978
[490] NY Times, 8/21/1979
[491] One of the inkind sponsors of this swim was Raytheon. There were a few Raytheon people on board the escort boat.
[492] Cape Swimming website: www.capeswim.com. Click on Dassen Island.
[493] Ms. Magazine, July/August 1989
[494] Personal records, Tim Johnson, 1988

[495] Information obtained from his swim resume on file with the IMSHOF in Ft. Lauderdale, FL.
[496] From the Greece Now website: http://greecenow.criticalpublics.com/CULTURE/CulturalHeritage/marathonswimforacause.stm, accessed 3/16/2007.
[497] Visit Feilim O'Maolain web site: http://www.soulswimmer.com.
[498] Cambria conquers Hokkaido-Honshu Channel, Margot Smith, The Cambrian, 7/19/1990. Posted on www.DavidYudovinChannelSwimmer.com. Viewed 3/18/2007.
[499] Details from Gail Rice's IMSHOF application for swim certification.
[500] NY Times, 7/24/2000
[501] James Pittar web site: www.freestyleman.com
[502] *Not the easiest way to Sumatra*, Kathe Tanner, The Tribune, 7/15/2000. post on www.DavidYudovinChannelSwimmer.com. Viewed 3/18/2007.
[503] Netherlands Open Water Web, www.noww.com, the link was broken otherwise more information would have been included.
[504] Visit FINA (Federation Internationale De Natation) web site: www.fina.org click on Open Water Swimming then Results.
[505] Details of this swim were elicted during a conversation with William Schulz, swim director of the Pennock Island Challenge.
[506] Stubbs, Dave. "From athlete to cancer patient." The Montreal Gazette. 7/23/2005.
[507] Swee Chiow personal webpage: www.daretodream.com.sg.
[508] Cape Swimming website: www.capeswim.com. Click on Nelson Mandella Bay.
[509] Netherlands Open Water Web www.noww.nl, news channel and solo swims link, 9/15/2004, The Telegraph, Calcutta, India,*Tenzing Norgay Award for Bula*, accessed 10/22/04.
[510] Times courtesy www.channelswimmingassociation.com Sucessful Swims link to www.soloswims.com.
[511] Web site for Straits of Gibraltar: www.acneg.com, for complete swimmer's list, click on ida.
[512] Monday, July 22, 2002, Chandigarh, India, The Tribune online edition, accessed 10/23/2004.
[513] Saturday, August 21, 2004, The Telegraph, Calcutta, India, *Bula in seventh heaven*, www.telegraphindia.com, accessed 10/24/2004.
[514] For an opposing view, read Gautam Kaul opinions: www.gisdevelopment.net/magazine/years/2004/feb/fmab.shtml.
[515] Biswas, Ranotta. "The Call of the Sea." The Hindu. 5/29/2005.
[516] From the Netherlands Open Water Web, via News Long Beach by Bob Keisser. This article also repeats the false claim that Greta Andersen did a double in the Moloki channel.

[517] Visit the Salton Sea web site: http://www.sci.sdsu.edu/salton/SaltonSeaHomePage.html.
[518] From the Netherlands Open Water Web via The Desert Sun of Palm Springs, CA, posted 8/14/06 by Nicole Brambila and Crystal Chatham.
[519] From the American Tilapia Association, click on Tilapia biologist wins... http://ag.arizona.edu/azaqua/ata.html, viewed on 3/15/2007.
[520] From the Netherland Open Water Web via the Phillippines Information Service: www.pia.gov.ph, posted May 23, 2007.
[521] Wikipedia, http://en.wikipedia.org/wiki/Manly,_New_South_Wales, accessed 3/16/07.
[522] The Netherlands Open Water Web, story from The Citizen.co.za, article posted 3/16/06, viewed 3/25/07.
[523] The Netherlands Open Water Web, story from IOL the Cape Times online news, www.iol.co.za, written by a staff writer 3/6/2007. Viewed 3/16/2007.
[524] The Netherland Open Water Web, from the South Florida Sun-Sentinel written by Sharon Robb, posted 6/28/07.
[525] Solo Swims of Canada website: www.soloswims.com. Accessed April 15, 2007.
[526] CBC News story online: www.cbc.ca/story/canada/national/2006/07/19/lake-swim.html?ref=rss. 3/17/2007.
[527] *Man about to turn 40 swims 55 miles around Lake Washington*, AP, 8/28/2006.
[528] See the section that covers sanctions to learn how Master swimming has rescued long distance swims.
[529] FINA website: www.fina.org.
[530] Meuret, Jean-Louis. "HistoFINA Volume X, edition 2005." Copy located on the FINA website.
[531] Dean, Penny. Open Water Swimming. Champaign, Illinois:Human Kinetics. 1998. p. 205.
[532] Visit the Lake Ohrid region web site: www.ohrid.org.mk/eng/maraton/maraton.htm.
[533] From: http://www.fina.org/events/OWS/MSWC/2006/rankings.php.
[534] One Statue mile equals 1.15 times a nautical mile thus 40 nautical miles equals approximately 45 Statue miles.
[535] In quote of his in a NY Times article recounting Boyton's recently completed 4-year odyssey around the world "swimming" published on 12/23/1878, he said the following, "You know that I often take sudden notions into my head and act on them and you needn't wonder if tomorrow, for instance, I ran up to Albany, jumped into the river and paddled down here again. It's never safe to say for certainty just what I will do." This quote was taken at a dinner in his honor after returning from Europe.
[536] NY Times, 4/11/1887, *Capt. Boyton's Welcome*.

[537] NY Times, 6/28/1888, *Brodie Sick of His Task.*
[538] NY Times, 6/27/1888, *Steve Brodie's Long Swim.*
[539] The Albany Yacht Club originally was located on the Albany side of the Hudson River and is now located on the Reneaslear side. Regardless, their club has and still remains the starting location for all swims down the Hudson River.
[540] NY Times, 7/1/1888, *Steve Brodie's Trip.*
[541] NY Times, 9/4/1897, *Swimmer Hooper at Hudson,* 9/9/1897, *Swimmer Hooper Reaches Peekskill,* 9/12/1897 *Hooper's Swim from Albany,* 9/13/1897 *Rev. Dr. Van de Water at Westminster*(3rd article down).
[542] The World, 6/19/1927
[543] NY Times, 8/31/1926
[544] NY Times, 10/21/1926
[545] The World, 7/1/1927
[546] NY Times, 10/29/1927, *50-Hour Record is Set in Swim from Albany.*
[547] NY Times, 8/30/1937
[548] Ibid
[549] NY Times, 8/31/1937
[550] NY Times, 7/16/1952
[551] Newsday, 8/4/1988
[552] Newsday, 8/4/1988
[553] NY Times, 9/26/1928, *Dog In Albany Swim Beats Man's Time.*
[554] NY Post, 8/26/2005, *Water Way to go for Albany-NYC Swimmer*, page 29. This report includes the unofficial time of 41:57 given out by the author at the time who later totaled the accumulated time correctly at 41:30:40.
[555] The author was the Swim Director for this attempt and was witness to all twenty swims. The stage locations were waypointed in the author's GPS and subsequent starts were north of the previous stages finishing point so that the swimmer completed 123.65 nautical miles of the documented route.
[556] Conrad Wennerberg in his book mentions a Captain Alfred Baron as the first swimmer but I can find no record of it.
[557] Halliburton, Richard. New Worlds to Conquer. Indianapolis:The Bobbs-Merrill Co., 1929
[558] NY Times, 6/28/1950
[559] NY Times, 11/1/1966
[560] Website: http://soloswims.com and choose Swimmer Bios, Vicki Keith
[561] The course Vicky Bell swam was from Niagara-on-the-Lake to the Canadian National Exhibition grounds in Toronto.
[562] Website: http://soloswims.com and choose Solo Swims of Ontario
[563] Ibid
[564] The Weekend Australian, 2/19/01.
[565] Tammy van Wisse personal website, www.tammyvanwisse.com, 8/24/2004. The direction was North Island to South Island.

[566] Information gathered from the IMSHOF application for the swim certificate.
[567] Website: http://www.extreme-planet.com then search on explorers selection for Gordon Lewis Pugh.
[568] News release dated 10/14/2006 from CHN, the Iranian Cultural Heritage News Agency, about a planned swim of the Persian Gulf that included information about the Caspian Sea swim.
[569] Flotsam abounds in Manhattan, pick any semi-submersed object as your marker.
[570] NY Times 8/15/1915
[571] Information from the Washington Heights & Inwood Online website: http://www.washington-heights.us/history/archives/marble_hill_116.html. This action separated Marble Hill, the tip of Manhattan from the rest of Manhattan. This work went on for years, 1888-1895 according to S. Berliner per his website: http://home.att.net/~Berliner-Ultrasonics/history.html#manhbrnx who also references an industrial archaeologist, Thomas Flagg.
[572] The Harlem River when it floods flows south and flows north when it ebbs. The ebb current spills out into the Hudson River and the flood current joins the East River as it flows out to Long Island through Hell Gate.
[573] Section of Egbert Viele's Sanitary & Topological Map of NY, recorded 1855. No major bridges are shown on this map as the Brooklyn Bridge would not be built until 25 years hence.
[574] NY Tribune, 8/16/1915
[575] New York Tribune, 9/5/1915, this course is the normal sequence for the marathon swim presently but was not the course taken by the swimmer. One can only wonders what was the source of the erroneous information that was to become the standard.
[576] New York Tribune, 9/6/1915
[577] NY Times, 9/6/1915
[578] NY Times, 6/27/1921
[579] NY Times, 8/31 1926
[580] NY Times, 9/19/1927
[581] NY Times, 9/26/1927
[582] NY Times, 6/18/1928, *Three Swimmers Fail to Circle Manhattan.*
[583] NY Times, 7/2/1928
[584] NY Times, 7/28/1930
[585] NY Times, 10/6/1958, *Greek Fails in Swim Around Manhattan.* Variation of the spelling of the last name is Zirganos.
[586] A visit to the Channel Swimming Association web site listing: www.soloswims.com , finds no listing for Jason Zerganos under the successful solo swim listing. However, he did complete the swim in 1954 during the professional race across the channel coming in fourth according to Joe Grossman in an unpublish manuscript.

[587] Wennerberg, Conrad. Wind, Waves and Sunburn. New York:AS Barnes and Co. 1974. Page 218.
[588] NY Times, 10/6/1958, *Greek Fails in Swim Around Manhattan*. The last line of this article stated that swims "…around Manhattan had been infrequent in recent year but it once was a seasonal challenge for swimmers, singly or in mass contests." This sort of contextual remark in a newspaper article is an attempt by the writer to jog the public memory so that they might have some basis for interpreting the event reported upon.
[589] NY Times, 9/3/1968
[590] Since this time, the Coast Guard has required would be swimmers to notify them by filing for a Marine Event permit.
[591] NY Times, 9/18/1974
[592] A visit to the Channel Swimming Association web site listing: www.soloswims.com , finds no listing for Peter Lloyd.
[593] Gus helped Charlie Daniels develop the stroke that set new records for the 100 yards freestyle in the early 1900's.
[594] The location of the NYAC aquatic center in the 1880's before the opening of their Travers Island location was on the opposite bank of the Harlem River from the present day Yankee Stadium.
[595] NY Times, 7/27/1885, *Swimming Many Miles*.
[596] NY Times, 7/29/1886, *Swimming Sixteen Miles*.
[597] NY Times, 9/22/1926
[598] This was included in his swim biography at the ISHOF as of November, 2004, before I discussed the claim with Preston Levi, Historian at the ISHOF. Visit his page at the International Swimming Hall of Fame: www.ishof.org/88cross.html.
[599] NY Times, 8/13/1927, *Clarence Ross Turns Pro to Enter Swim*.
[600] NY Times, 9/9/1928, *Young and C. Ross win in Lake Swims*.
[601] NY Times, 7/28/1930, *Four Beat Records in Manhattan Swim*.
[602] NY Times, 6/27/1921
[603] NY Times, 7/25/1914, *Aquatic Stunts for Elionsky*.
[604] NY Times, 7/22/1929
[605] New York Tribune, 9/3/1915
[606] Newsday, 7/20/1982, *Strivers: Taking watery way around town*, People column by Al Cohn, background information included in the article. This is the only report of this swim.
[607] Wennerberg, Conrad. Wind, Waves and Sunburn. New York:AS Barnes and Co. 1974. Page 271. Also, NY Times, 8/24/1958, *Mother, 25, First to Swim Length Lake George*.
[608] NY Times, 8/16/1959, *Swimmer Circles Island in 11 Hrs*.
[609] Marathon, Gail Campbell, Sterling Publishing Co., NY 1977

[610] Wennerberg, Conrad. <u>Wind, Waves and Sunburn</u>. New York:AS Barnes and Co. 1974. Page 271.
[611] NY Times, 8/16/1959, *Swimmer Circles Island in 11 Hrs*, photo caption that accompanies the article with picture of the two swimmers.
[612] Larry Muchca, an fellow employee of New York Telephone, related this account to the author in 1984.
[613] NY Times, 8/25/1929, *Swept Under Boats, Youth Dies in River*.
[614] Except for one occasion when we were setting up the swim start at East 96th Street in the early years. Not long after dropping the ladder into the water the night before, a fellow came up to me dressed in a bathrobe and asked if he could go swimming. I told him to go for it. He climbed down, swam around for a little bit, got out and thanked me. His family came along to watch him.
[615] NY Times, 9/25/1975, *Woman Fails in Attempt to Swim Around Manhattan*.
[616] NY Times, 10/7/1975, *Woman Swimmer Circles Manhattan on her 2nd Attempt*.
[617] NY Times, 7/30/1976, *Cramps End Woman's Attempt to Swim 24 Miles Across Sound; Weight-Lifting Blamed*.
[618] Newsday, 7/18/1982, *Around Manhattan in 8-10 Hours*, by Joe Krupinski.
[619] Manhasset Press, 1/6/1983, *Swim marathon is memorial to his son*, by Eileen Byrnes.
[620] NY Times, 9/15/1982, *Another Marathon Arrives in the City*.
[621] Ibid. Asphalt Green was then know as the Fire Boat House Environmental Center.
[622] The computer checkpoint location in the East River: Brooklyn Bridge, Williamsburg Bridge, the southern tip of Roosevelt Island, Mill Rock pier at Hell Gate; Harlem River: footbridge at entrance to the Harlem River, Triboro Bridge, High Bridge (by Yankee Stadium), and Spuyten Duyvil; Hudson River: George Washington Bridge, 79th Street Boat Basin, the Intrepid at 42nd Street, the corner where the World Trade Center bulkhead wall begins, and the Finish at Gangway 5 at the Battery.
[623] These locations were changed to Hell Gate, Spuyten Duyvil, and 79th Street when the swim start location was switched to the Battery.
[624] U.P.I., 10/8/1983
[625] U Thant Island is named after the UN Secretary General (1962-1972), was formerly known as Belmont Island.
[626] email received 9/2/2004
[627] Mill Rock at one time was fortified with cannon during the War of 1812 to guard the Port of New York against the British. The blockhouse burned down in 1821. The island was next owned and occupied by the Gibson family when the Federal government purchased it where upon it passed into the City of New York hands in 1953. From the Big Apple Almanac, Newsday, September 11, 1994.

[628] The FDR Drive roadway raises and becomes an overpass above East 96th Street so this location is easy to spot from the East River as you enter Hell Gate.
[629] NY Times, 7/11/1979
[630] NY Times, 8/28/1980
[631] Personal record in file.
[632] Associated Press, *Woman Swims Around Manhattan Island Three Times*, August 29, 1984.
[633] Tommy Golden was the author's favorite pilot. He chanced upon him one day when another pilot dropped out of a swim. His boat, nicknamed the Julie R was a lobster boat and was a long, broad open stern cockpit with a low freeboard. The boat design was perfect for escorting swimmers as the crew could from within the boat reach out and hand their swimmers their food. Tommy could put the boat right next to the swimmer, so experienced from his years on the water working as a lobster man and hold it there provided the sea state didn't come up. With a red buoy hung over the side of the boat, a swimmer could be paced and directed from the helm. He probably worked over 50 swims over the years.
[634] NY Times, 9/15/1982, *Another Marathon Arrives in the City*.
[635] Gus uttered a memorable line when the 1st NYC Triathlon was about to begin: "No cash, no splash". The organizers of the event found his boat fee money within 15 minutes when I told them they had to remove their camera equipment from his boat.
[636] Visit the Water Club web site: www.thewaterclub.com.
[637] Cody's brother attempted the swim in 1989 and an article appeared in Sports Illustrated for Kids in January 1990. He was four months younger than his sister and he left the swim when he begame cold. Skip Storch was the official observer for this swim.
[638] "MIMS Update: 24th Annual Manhatttan Island Marathon Swim Called Due to Severe Weather." www.nyswim.org. Version 7/9/2005, 7/24/2005. <http://www.nyswim.org/Articles/Article.aspx?Article_ID=1028>.
[639] Conversation with Morty Berger on 7/27/2005.
[640] NY Times, 7/21/1982
[641] Manhasset Press, 1/6/1983, *Swim marathon is memorial to his son*, by Eileen Byrnes.
[642] Interview with Drury Gallagher 11/6/2004.
[643] Letter dated 5/15/1984 from John Lowe, Deputy Chief, to Drury Gallagher.
[644] Special Event Permit #670, dated 423/1984.
[645] USCG Permit #03-NY-028-84. Special Local Regulations required: 1. No rubber rafts as the sole swimmer support, a powered and fully equipped boat will be available, 2. All escort boats equipped with VHF radio, 3. All chase boats equipped with a flag (white background, red stripe for diver in the water),

4. No swimmers allowed without an escort boat, 5. Each escort boat be equipped with a foghorn or other sound device for signaling.

[646] All the major athletic clubs are basically membership-only hotels with a really good athletic facility attached. They all have website and the DAC is no different. Visit their website at www.downtownac.com.

[647] Visit their web site: http://www.arcecs.org for some recent photos of the group.

[648] APRS is also known as Automatic Packet Reporting System.

[649] In fact, Carol Zaleski in a phone conversation with me cited problems from another swim where swimmers were injured by a powerboat. At the time I was flabbergasted that she was using an incident in another swim to pull the insurance for Manhattan and I had nothing to say in response. Now, I suspect that she was telling me about the incident in San Francisco harbor tug accident that occurred over 25 years previously.

[650] Letter of 7/29/1990 from Tom Biglin of the USPS to Drury Gallagher.

[651] Manhattan Island Swimming Association, Inc. letter from Drury Gallagher, president, to Morty Berger representing Manhattan Island Marathon Swimming Foundation, Inc. granting MIF exclusive rights to conduct the Manhattan Island Marathon Swim (MIMS) under that name, dated August 2, 1993.

[652] NY Times, 8/22/1993

[653] Visit the MIF website: www.nycswim.org, click on History or the Learn to Swim links.

[654] One year, long after leaving New York for Massachusetts and a new career, I returned on the day of the swim, unannounced and just handled the lines of the boats as they were tying up to drop off the crew at South Cove. I saw a lot of old friends.

[655] See the chapter on staged swims for this personality.

[656] While swim director for the Skip Storch attempt in 1993, the Cuban's introduced one of the relay swimmers from that attempt to Skip and me. He told us their cage fell apart during the attempt and the swim was aborted.

[657] Outside, September, 1993

[658] I had attended one meeting in San Bernardino, California, with my father while I was in high school and won the door prize. I never really joined the John Birch Society.

[659] Human Rights Watch website: http://www.hrw.org/reports/1995/WR95/AMERICAS-04.htm, accessed 9/19/2004.

[660] US custom regulations forbid the passing of American currency to Cuba.

[661] NY Times, 6/4/1899, *The Underground Railroad*.

[662] Swim Magazine, May/June 1994 by Michael Stott.

[663] Phillip Weiss, "Truth be Told, They Lied." <u>Outside Magazine</u> May 1997.

[664] Visit FINA (Federation Internationale De Natation) web site: www.fina.org/history_officers.html this location is not visible from their main site.

[665] See the section in Manhattan Marathon about the swim organization to learn of the down side of sanctions. This is the problem: the insurance needs to be separated from the sanction. Ergo, the USMS should offer an insurance option to swims so that the sanction only refers to the validity of the swim.

[666] Visit http://bicyclelongisland.org/murphy/murphy.htm for a drawing of the hood and a photo of the bike.

[667] NY Times, 7/1/1899, exact time for the mile was 57.8 second or 62.3 miles per hour.

[668] Visit http://arrts-arrchives.com/mmm.html, accessed 11/10/2004.

[669] NY Times, 8/14/1897, *Swept Away to Sea*.

[670] NY Times, 8/15/1897, *The Swimmer Swims Back*.

[671] David Dalton at age 40 is purported to have swum the English Channel on July 17-18, 1890. The dispute is over the start: he jumped into the water off Boulogne harbor at some point to begin the swim. The Channel Swimming Association doesn't recognize this swim. Information from an unpublished manuscript by Joe Grossman.

[672] NYTimes, 7/1/1899, Book Review, untitled, How to Swim by Captain Davis Dalton.

[673] Ibid.

[674] Washington Post, 11/21/1900, *Swam The English Channel, An Austrian Countess the First Woman to Accomplish that Difficult Feat*.

[675] New York Times, 10/12/1927, *Set's Woman's Mark for Channel Swim*; New York Times, 10/16/1927, *Girl Admits Hoax in Channel Swim*; New York Times, 10/17/1927, *British Criticize Miss Logan's Hoax*; New York Times, 10/17/1927, *Certifying Channel Swimmers*; and New York Times, 10/18/1927, *Paris Laughs at Hoax*.

[676] The Advocate, Stamford, Conn., 7/21/1990

[677] The Philadelphia Inquirer, New Jersey Edition, July 24, 1989

[678] Malcolm Forbes came to the start of the swim in part because Skip Storch had sought his support for the swim. I was busy with loading the press boats at Liberty State Park in New Jersey with the reporters who had grown to a sizeable number (35). They all got aboard the first boat, which dangerously overloaded it. As I tried to move them to different support boats, I noticed a small man sitting quietly on a park bench watching the mayhem. I wondered if he was supposed to go with us but since he looked more like a grandfather waiting for his grandsons to go fishing, I ignored him to attend to the needy reporters. I was told when the reporters returned, he was still there; he was recognized and the reporters mobbed him. I just can't imagine what it must have been like for one

of the richest men in the United States to be ignored, but you can imagine my surprise when I found out who I left sitting on a bench in the park.

[679] New York Times, 7/22/1989

[680] New Haven Register, New Haven, Conn., 7/19/1990

[681] Journal News, *Skip Completes Liberty Trek for Environment,* by Alan Rittner, July 24, 1990.

[682] Ibid.

[683] NY Times, 5/13/1997. Also, CNN web site: http://www.cnn.com/WORLD/9705/12/australian.swimmer/ , posted 5/12/1999, accessed 10/21/2004.

[684] 90/24.5=3.67, 90 nautical miles divided by 24.5 hours results in a speed of 3.67 knots.

[685] Presently held by Grant Hackett, 1500 meter in 14:34.56.

[686] Leader Sport, *Maroney is magnificent in 24-hour record swim*, Brad Forrest, 4/25/1995

[687] Chris's swim is not listed with the Gibraltar Straits Swimming Association, perhaps because he did not know they existed or they were not interested in recording a cage swim.

[688] I had worked on their cage earlier in the week and when I returned to the hotel I had my clothes laundered. Since I was an American, I couldn't spend any money in Cuba due to the US embargo at that time and all my expenses had to be sponsored. They knew this when we went down to Cuba. It was this $4US laundry bill they objected to paying.

[689] 90/24.5=3.67, 90 nautical miles divided by 24.5 hours results in a speed of 3.67 knots.

[690] The Sun-Herald, Australia, 4/23/95, see *Current records of note* for latest data on this event.

[691] 93.6km=102362.2yds, 102362.2/(24*60)=71yds/minute, 1650/71=23.2min/mile or 23 minutes 12 seconds per 1650 mile.

[692] 50.5 nautical miles divided by 24 hours gives 2.06 knots as the speed.

[693] 90 nautical miles=182,283.5 yards, 182,283.5/24.5*60=124yds/minute, 1650/124=13.3min/mile or 13 minutes 18 seconds per 1650 mile.

[694] 13.3 minutes is 57.3% of 23.2minutes, 57.3% of 1650 yards is 945.9 yards, the distance she'd swim in a pool in 13.3 minutes; 1650 yards minus 945.9 yards leave the current to cover 704.1 yards in 13.3 minutes.

[695] Over an hour the current would push her (60/13.3)*704.1=3176.4 yards, 3176.4/2025.4=1.6 knot.

[696] Visit the National Oceanographic Partnership Program through the HYCOM Consortium for Data Assimilative Modeling program (a long name but a great site for ocean current information) at: http://oceancurrents.rsmas.miami.edu/index.html , click on Atlantic, then Gulf Stream (bottom of 2nd column), then find under the title, *Example Plots and*

Links, click on that then slice down to Figure 5. Click on Figure 5 to enlarge it. Notice that all the current between Cuba and the Keys is colored cyan for a current direction of due east. Not northerly as claimed by Suzy Maroney. For current speed, click on Figure 4. The orange-reddish color of the water between Cuba and Florida is for current speed of 40-50 centimeters per second (.8 knots) with strips of black that are over 100 centimeters per second (1.94 knots). This current should cause a drift to the east for a swimmer.

[697] Julius was down in Cuba to view the attempt by Susie and invited Suzy and her Mother to come stay at his home in Oyster Bay after the swim. Since the Maroney's owed me expense money of approximately $600, I joined them for dinner. Julius has a lovely place in Oyster Bay and was a friend of Kate Hayward.

[698] This would be west of where Walter Poenisch landed because Suzy who swims faster would have spent less time in the main portion of the Gulf Stream and not have been carried by the current as far as he was.

[699] At least on Cuba.

[700] BBC news website: http://news.bbc.co.uk/1/hi/world/americas/104664.stm accessed 9/19/2004.

[701] BBC news website: http://news.bbc.co.uk/1/hi/world/americas/447999.stm, accessed 9/19/2004.

[702] Visit BBC Online Network: http://news.bbc.co.uk/1/hi/world/americas/104664.stm published 6/2/1998, accessed 10/31/2004. A graphic associated with this report shows a drawing of the cage with the swimmer inside it attached off the stern of the escorting vessel.

[703] Visit the National Oceanographic Partnership at: http://oceancurrents.rsmas.miami.edu/index.html, click on Atlantic, then Caribbean System. The information there is not as extensive as for the Gulf Stream but the vectors shown under the seasonal plots are evidence enough. Notice the lack of a coherent stream north of Jamaica (Jamaica is the island south of Cuba).

[704] Visit web site: www.cnnsi.com for Associated Press report *Maroney to swim from Jamaica to Cuba* posted 8/17/1999, accessed 10/31/2004. Also, BBC Online Network: http://news.bbc.co.uk/1/low/world/americas/447999.stm, published 9/15/1999, accessed 10/31/2004.

[705] South New website: http://southmovement.alphalink.com.au/southnews/June7.htm#5, accessed 9/19/2004.

[706] Washington Post, 8/23/1886, *The Feat Done At Last. Swimming The Rapids And Living To Tell The Tale*.

[707] Washington Post, 0/1/1902, *Swam The Lower Rapids*. Background information used in an article about his second swim.

[708] NY Times, 9/1/1902, *Swam Niagara Rapids*.

[709] NY Times, 1/21/1902, *Graham Plans a Long Swim*.
[710] NY Times, 8/3/1931, *Girl Swims The Niagara*.
[711] NY Times, 12/7/1958
[712] NY Times, 3/27/1960
[713] 25°43N 79°19W
[714] Swim Magazine, *Shark Cage Swims: Postcards from the Edge, Voices From the Deep*, Michael Stott, May/June 1994.
[715] 26°56N 80°03W
[716] NY Times, 7/23/1968
[717] NY Times, 2/12/1995, *For French, Long Swim Is Not Enough*, by Craig Whitney.
[718] While this amount is disputed, Guy claims to have swum 10 hours a day thereby covering 23 miles each day, not an unreasonable amount and giving a swim speed of 2.0 knots.
[719] Sports Illustrated, by Kostya Kennedy, February, 1995
[720] In 1991, Guy Delage had flown an ultralight airplane from Cape Verde Island to Brazil in 27 hours.
[721] People Weekly, 2/20/1995
[722] $2*6*73=876$; $876/3716=.235$. Even swimming 24 hours a day, it would take 77 days to complete the distance at 2 knots.
[723] The strength of an electromagnetic field is inversely proportional to the distance. Radio signals are common electromagnetic field. It is common knowledge that the further away from a radio station you are; the weaker the signal.
[724] *Zhang Jian Swims Across Bohai Gulf*, Ju Chuanjiang, China Daily, 8/10/2000 from NOWW.
[725] Distance appears to include the river length, 2860 km, and 144km of the estuary at the river's mouth.
[726] Website: http://www.martinstrel.com
[727] Website: http://www.columbiaswim.org
[728] Website: http://www.indystar.com
[729] Website: http://signonsandiego.com the online present of the San Diego Union Tribune, article by Will Weissert, Associated Press, 8/5/2004.
[730] ABC News from their website: http://abclocal.go.com/wpvi/story?section=local&id=4375756. AP source.
[731] The Netherlands Open Water Web from several sources: El Pais, The Spain Hearld, the International Hearld Tribune, and Stuff.co.za. Viewed 3/17/2007. None of the paper's search functions were able to retrieve their articles. Accounts are from the pasted articles in NOWW.
[732] *Six swimmers complete croc marathon*, Jane Hammond, 6/26/06, AAP. Note: no time was included on any report of this swim other than 2 days.
[733] *Down the Danube*, Field Report, Rotarian, March 2007.

[734] Cape Swim website: www.capeswim.com. News article: The saga of the swimsuit." Tony Scalabrino. 2/14/2005.
[735] Visit Jim Dreyer's personal web site: www.swimjimswim.org and look at any of the photos of him swimming.
[736] The Advocate, Stanford Connecticut, 7/21/1990
[737] Visit Surfriders Foundation, Santa Cruz Chapter, Lab Manual Procedures, Test Purpose and Summary at: www.surfridersantacruz.org/labman.htm.
[738] Marriott, Michael. The Lure of Splashes in the Night; With Safety in Mind, Parks Dept. Battles Young Trespassers CITY Parks Agency Battles young Pool Trespassers. NY Times. 8/21/1993.
[739] NYC Dept of Environmental Protection website: http://www.ci.nyc.ny.us/html/dep/html/northri.html
[740] New York Times, 9/9/1992
[741] New York Times, 6/15/1995
[742] NY Times, 7/21/2000, *Time to Swim in the Hudson, State Says.*
[743] Muddy water is best memorialized in Pat Boone's *Moody River* while dirty water is celebrated in *Dirty Water* by the Standells. Water quality is part of the folklore of popular music.
[744] This organization was created at the Channel Swimming Association General Meeting of 2001.
[745] Visit their web site at www.channelcrossingassociation.com for more information.
[746] Information provided by South Carolina Department of Natural Resources web site: http://www.dnr.sc.gov/marine/pub/seascience/jellyfi.html.
[747] Ibid.
[748] Visit their web site at www.channelswimmingassociation.com for more information.
[749] Chart SC1892 covers the Dover Strait Western Part on a scale of 1:75,000. This chart can be purchased In Dover at Sharp & Enright, a Ship Chandler located across the street from the Dover Marina at 133 Snargate Street, (0)1304-206295.
[750] Modern Marathon Swimming, page 149.
[751] Modern Marathon Swimming, page 174.
[752] a fast swimmer's currents in the English Channel are dictated by tidal station J, K, & N.
[753] The error did not exceed a 1/10 of a knot and the current direction vector matched closely with the observed data.
[754] Modern Marathon Swimming, page 146.
[755] Two unescorted swimmers died crossing the Channel, one in 1926 and another in 1954.

[756] UK Gardian Online, 8/21/1999, *Channel swimmer drowns* by Julia Hartley-Brewer   Further background provided from discussion with CSA Secretary Duncan Taylor in August of 2001.
[757] RTE News Online, www.rte.ie/news/2001/0812/drowning.html
[758] Washington Post, 8/2/1897, *Drowned Swimming For A Wager*.
[759] American Red Cross Museum Timeline: www.redcross.org/museum/timemach.html
[760] The issues were about money as could be expected. The Red Cross Society had divided into two hostile camps. One side believed Clara ignored the authority of the executive committee, didn't report her expenditures properly and was lax in observation of services. Appeals were made to the Congress, the President, and the courts. Efforts to remove her failed when a majority of the society sustained her. But she couldn't work with the executive committee. At a meeting to resolve the differences a letter was drafted where she submitted her resignation that was accepted with regrets. NY Times, 5/15/1904, *Miss Barton Retires As Red Cross Head*.
[761] The Providence Journal, 07/28/1990
[762] Latitude is the north-south increment of the grid overlaid on charts that allow one to find a position and compare it with another location. Sailing by latitudes is an ancient sailing technique that allows a vessel to travel first north or south to the correct latitude then sail east or west until one bumped into their destination. Latitude was easier to determine than longitude until accurate clocks were invented. The latitude could easily be determined by the sun's position above the horizon at noon.
[763] Frank Mingus is the legendary shark fisherman who chartered his boat out of Montauk to Donnie Braddick that caught the largest shark every, 3,427 pounds in 1986 by rod and reel.
[764] Florida Sports, December/January 1998-99, *Bill Specht, Gail Rice and St. Croix*, by Swimming in a Nutt-Shell (Randy Nutt's column).
[765] Visit the official St. Croix Coral Reef Swim at www.swimrace.com.
[766] Potter, Michael. "Three athletes smash record in Power Swim." The Virgin Island Daily News. 5/30/2005.
[767] NY Times, 9/15/1913, *Richards Succeeds in Sandy Hook Swim*.
[768] This is the same Alois who placed 3rd in the 1908 Battery to Coney Island swim. The NY Times report spelled the name Aderley.
[769] NY Times, 8/30/1909, *Swims to Boston Light*.
[770] NY Times, 8/7/1911, *Breaks Swimming Record*.
[771] NY Times, 8/21/1911, *Girl Swims to Boston Light*.
[772] NY Times, 9/15/1913, *Richards Succeeds in Sandy Hook Swim*.
[773] NY Times, 9/7/1914, *Fails to Swim to Boston Light*.
[774] NY Times, 8/20/1915, *Boy Beats Richards' Record*.
[775] NY Times, 8/15/1921, *Toth Wins Long Swim*.

[776] Boston Globe, 8/24/1931, *Swims to Glory But Gets Nothing*. Resume of one of the swimmers for 1931 referred to this earlier race.
[777] NY Times, 8/17/1925, *2 Swimmers Reach The Boston Light*.
[778] NY Times, 8/31/1925, *Wins Boston Light Race*.
[779] Boston Globe, 8/13/1928, *Girl Sets Mark Swimming Nude*.
[780] Ibid.
[781] Boston Globe, 8/27/1928, *Cullen Winner, Kid of 16 Next*.
[782] Boston Globe, 8/26/1929, *Prize Winners of Harbor Swims Awarded Cups*. Photo and caption.
[783] NY Times, 8/19/1929, *Miss Pearson, 19, Is First In 11-Mile Boston Light Swim*.
[784] NY Times, 8/11/1930, *Richards is Swim Victor*.
[785] Boston Globe, 8/24/1931, *Swims to Glory But Gets Nothing*.
[786] Boston Globe, 8/15/1932, *Two Break Record for Light Swim*.
[787] Boston Globe, 8/7/1933, *Nunan Once More Wins Light Swim*.
[788] NY Times, 9/3/1934, *Girl Makes Record Swim*.
[789] Boston Globe, 8/1/1938, Doucette Wins Icy Light Swim. The information on 1936 and 1937 races come from this article.
[790] This is an actual reef that exists in Gloucester Harbor that Longfellow uses in his poem *The Wreck of the Hesperus*.
[791] It is interesting that this description of the waters in Salem Sound be described as frothy for that is one description used by Longfellow in his poem *The Wreck of the Hesperus* that occurred in the same waters.
[792] The New England swims recounted in this section were elicited during an interview with Jim Doty on 1/5/2005. Jim was a bit shy on dates but long on details.
[793] The Union Leader, 7/11/1995, *It's a First: Woman Swims Length of Winnipesaukee*. Also, The Citizen, 7/11/1995, *12 Hour Swim Sets Record*.
[794] Detailed swim reports are found on Jim Bayles' web site: www.swimmingforhope.com
[795] YMCA Holds 10th Annual Lake Swim, WCAX Channel 3 News, 8/5/2006.
[796] Forsberg, Gerald. <u>Modern Long Distance Swimming</u>. London:Routledge & Kegan Paul, 1963, page 6.
[797] British Long Distance Swimming Association website: www.bldsa.org.uk. Click on event reports.
[798] Wikipedia: http://en.wikipedia.org/wiki/Channel_islands.
[799] Most of the information on Channel swims comes from www.jerseyseaswims.org. viewed 3/16/2007.
[800] Website: www.hawaiiswim.org/
[801] In 1939, four Hawaiian fishermen in the Molokai Straits swam to Oahu, some 16 miles distance in 15 hours when their boat sank. This incident did not inspire

any swimmer to repeat the swim. Wennerberg, Conrad. <u>Wind, Waves and Sunburn</u>. New York:AS Barnes and Co. 1974. Page 210.

[802] Press Telegram, 1/20/1961. Summary from Bob Keisser of Greta Anderson's press clippings kept by the local Long Beach paper.

[803] Email from Bob Keisser, 12/8/2004. Summary from Bob Keisser of Greta Anderson's press clippings kept by the local Long Beach paper.

[804] Press Telegram, 4/1961. Summary from Bob Keisser of Greta Anderson's press clippings kept by the local Long Beach paper.

[805] The Maui News, 8/31/2003.

[806] Carl Kawauchi in an email dated 9/28/2004,

[807] Kahoolawe was at that time under US Navy control and visitors were required to have a Navy escort.

[808] Visit CNN's travel guide for Hawaiian food at www.cnn.com/TRAVEL/PURSUITS/FOOD/9903/hawaii.food.

[809] Irish Long Distance Swimming Association Records prepared by William Wallace on 12/08/2004.

[810] From the Swim Ireland website: www.swimireland.ie. 8/14/2006.

[811] New York Tribune, 8/13/1915

[812] NY Times, 7/24/1924

[813] NY Times, 9/1/1921, *Swims Sound From Bridgeport to Huntington in 11 Hours.*

[814] NY Times, 8/11/1924. This article included a reference to a swim by Walter Patterson in 1919 however there is no record at the NY Times of a swim in 1919 but the previous sited swim in 1921.

[815] NY Times, 6/21/1926, *Girl Swim Sound for 10½ Hours.*

[816] NY Times, 7/12/1926, *Lucason Annexes Sound Swim Test.*

[817] NY Times, 8/30/1932, *Sound Swimmer Saved.*

[818] NY Times, 9/4/1960, *L. I. Skin Diver Swims The Sound Under Water.*

[819] Featured story at: www.ausswim.telstra.com.au, *Shelley Clark Wins Across the Sound Marathon*, dated 8/16/2001, accessed 10/24/2004.

[820] The Connecticut Post, 8/6/2006 by Marian Gail Brown fron NOWW site.

[821] Visit the web site of the Rottnest Channel Swimming Association: www.rottnestchannelswim.com.au.

[822] The inclusion of the website does not in anyway construe an endorsement of this particular website. I find the gratuitous photos of women swimmers treding water, the method of taking some of the photos, the stories of drunken parties, the ridicule of some swimmers and their bodies wholly disrespectful of the sport and an example of extremely juvenile reporting. They've passed one too many margaritas over their keyboards.

[823] World Food Program press release, www.wfp.org, 6/28/2006.

[824] NY Times, 6/30/1 907, *Long Atlantic City Swim.*

[825] NY Times, 9/11/1927, *Ruddy Home First in One-Mile Swim.*

[826] NY Times, 6/25/1927, *69 Swimmers Ready to Go In 15-Mile Ocean Swim Today.*
[827] NY Times, 6/26/1927, *Ocean Swim Race Won By Erickson.*
[828] Atlantic City swim website history page, *Around The Island in Eight Hours,* www.acswim.org, 1/15/2006.
[829] NY Times, 4/7/1928 report dated 4/6/1928 from Gibraltar. The report states that she swam the day before across the Straits, meaning April 5, 1928 which is slightly at variance with the Associations records.
[830] The Gibraltar Strait Swimming Association web site: www.acneg.com.
[831] Netherlands Open Water Web www.noww.nl, news channel and solo swims link.
[832] Cape Swimming website: www.capeswim.com. News item.
[833] Cape Swimming website: www.capeswim.com. News item. "First Three Capes Swim." Damien du Toit. Swim took place on April 14, 2004 with four swimmers: Gordon Lewis Pugh, Tony Sellmeyer, Kevin Anderson and Gill Strawberry.
[834] Mannak, Miriam. "Swimmer smashes open water record by more than one hour." Cape Times, 2/11/2005.
[835] Robben Island was where Nelson Mandella was imprisoned.
[836] Mannak, Miriam. "Disqualified swimmer breaks record." Cape Times. 2/8/2005.
[837] Open Water Swimming South Africa website: www.openswim.co.za.
[838] Website: www.int.iol.co.za. Sports news item: "Triple swim sinks Robben Island record." Douglas Carew. Weekend Argus. 3/1/2003.
[839] Cape Swim website: www.capeswim.com. News article: The saga of the swimsuit." Tony Scalabrino. 2/14/2005.
[840] Press Release, www.carinabruwer.com.
[841] Cape Swim website: www.capeswim.com. Click on False Bay.
[842] Swim website: www.laskateamada.com. Click on Race Results.
[843] The author's nickname at college was Jazz which was bestowed upon him by his English professor when an attempt to utilized a collogialism, the professor lached upon the suspected verbage and proceeded to skewer the state of English education in California and my speech into hyperbole.
[844] Visit the Olympic Club at www.olyclub.com and click on events.
[845] For the latest update on the quarantine visit California Department of Food and Argriculture at: http://www.cdfa.ca.gov/phpps/pe/summary.htm.
ation provided in the San Francisco and Vicinity section was developed from the Fall 2004 The South Ender and from conversations with Gary Emich, Chris Blakeslee, Nancy Ridout, Herb Barthels, and Wayne Black. Not to be forgotten, the Pacific Masters website was quite handy: http://www.pacificmasters.org/comp/.
[847] Pacific Masters web page, www.pacificmasters.org then select Results.

[848] Conversation with Joel Wilson, race director Pier-to-Pier on 8/12/2005. Email contact: openwatr@got.net or www.cruzswim.org. This information was verified by David S. Clark, in an email received 4/6/07 with the time info.
[849] McHugh, Paul. "Santa Cruz to Monterey the Hard Way." Chronicle. 10/4/2001.
[850] Website: www.avilaswimming.com. Announcement posted 9/28/2003 by race director Dave Van Mouwerik.
[851] Norcross, Don. "Tucson teen easily defends ladies title." Union-Tribune 9/12/2005.
[852] Wrigley mentions turning down swimmers who desired to swim the Catalina Channel in an interview in the New York Times on 8/12/1926. There was a report of a successful swim in 1926 in the *Catalina Islander* on 11/24/1926.
[853] Dean, Penny. A History of the Catalina Channel Swims Since 1927. unpublished, 1980.
[854] Information from David S. Clark in an email received 4/6/2007.
[855] Santa Barbara Channel Swimming Association web site: www.santabarbaraswim.org. 3/17/2007
[856] Information from Xtide, Victoria station in British Columbia hosted by http://www.dairiki.org/tides/monthly.php/vic/2005-08-01.
[857] Information provided by Canadian Ocean Marathon Swimming Association, 5326 Westhaven Wynd, West Vancouver, British Columbia, BC, Canada, V7F3E8.
[858] Ibid.
[859] Email and conversation with Debbie Collins 8/10/2005. Swim witnessed by Debbie Collins and Cameron Calder under COMSA rules.
[860] The Shaka Lake Ultra swim web site: www.ultraswimcanada.com.
[861] Netherland Open Water Web, press article on the release of her new book Marathon Swimmer, Maple Ridge Times, 6/4/04.
[862] Website: www.soloswims.com, in the Solo Swims of Ontario, click on Ratified Swims then pick your lake.
[863] Information provided by Gary Emich, 12/30/05.
[864] Website: www.swimtrek.com.
[865] The information about Japan was for swims occurring in 1998 provided by Mitsuru Fujiwara with a reference to the www.chichibu.ne.jp website.
[866] Pieper, Mark. "O'Keefe nabs fifth title." Pacific Daily News. 5/30/2005.
[867] *Motoyama leads swimmers to Micro Beach*, Brad Ruszala, Saipan Tribune, 5/5/05, from NOWW.
[868] Catalina Channel Swimming Federation information packet circa 1980
[869] This record was set with Kevin Murphy aboard Michael Oram's boat as a witness. Source: news report from Internet sources listing Phil Whitten as author. This swim is not recognized by the CSA.
[870] Brian Finley website www.soloswims.com.

871 101900m/24hrs=4245m/hr,4245m/1852m/nmile=2.29 knots
872 Guinness Book of World Records, 2003.
873 1500 meters is considered the metric mile, one Statue mile is 1609.3 meters.
874 Visit FINA (Federation Internationale De Natation) web site: www.fina.org/wldreckm.html
875 1500/(14*60+34.56)=1.715m/s, 1.715*60*60=6174m/hour, 6174/1852 (1852=meters in nautical mile)=3.33 knots.
876 Visit FINA (Federation Internationale De Natation) web site: www.fina.org/wldreckm.html
877 Based upon present world records.
878 An Excel spreadsheet using trendlines and variance worked up by the author reveals this information.
879 Visit International Swimming Hall of Fame web site: www.ishof.org and look for the news items, *Sun Moon Lake Swimming Festival.*
880 A collier is a barge that carries coal.
881 NY Times, 7/29/1873
882 NY Times, 7/21/1873
883 Chambers's Journal was a weekly paper published by Robert and William Chambers of Scotland beginning in 1832 that dealt with history, religion, language, and science. Many of the articles published were written by Robert. In this case, Robert seems to in the mood for an adventure tale. The veracity of the story was addressed in the last line of the story: "…and she gave our mess a very handsome silver salver, which still remains to bear witness to the truth of this plain unvarnished tale."
884 For the sake of simplicity, let's call him the local governor.
885 NY Times, 9/14/1873, *A Night on the Bosporus* from Chambers's Journal.
886 Washington Post, 8/10/1878, *Bit By A Shark.*
887 NY Times, 8/16/1878, *A Shark Victim.*
888 Visit Brian Gardiner's website: http://web.ukonline.co.uk/b.gardiner/lister.html for a biography of Joseph Lister and his role in promoting the adoption of antiseptics in hospitals.
889 NY Times, 11/1/1885, *The Horse Was A Good Swimmer*, also: NY Times, 7/10/1927, *Horse Takes A Night Swim.*
890 NY Times, 7/27/1940, *Dock Horse Takes A Swim.*
891 Washington Post, 8/20/1900, *Wonderful Diving Horses.*
892 NY Times, 11/14/1975, *Elephant Lands in Jail for Swimming Narrows; Crosses from Coney to New Dorp in Early Dawn.*, this was a reproduction of an orginal report published June 5, 1905.
893 Randalls and Wards Island connected together serve as the point of land that divides the Harlem River flowing north from the East River flowing east out toward Long Island. Today, swimmers in the Manhattan marathon have a lovely

view of Randalls Island's spacious lawn and an imposing edifice of a building surrounded by Weeping Willow trees.

[894] The locations specified in the news report meant he swam across the Harlem River, not the East River as written.

[895] NY Times, 1/17/1899, *Boy's Swim for Freedom*.

[896] NY Times, 9/9/1899, *Chasing boy Prisoners*.

[897] NY Times, 10/2/1931, *3 Boys Swim For Freedom*.

[898] For a history of Randalls and Wards Island visit the Van Alen Institute, an architectural and civil engineering website: www.vanalen.org/workshops/east_river/sites/his09.htm.

[899] NY Times, 9/4/1939

[900] NY Times, 9/2/1940, *Boy Swim Hudson, Balks "Rescue"*.

[901] Other remarkable accounts from this period are recorded in Conrad Wennerberg's Wind, Wave and Sunburn starting at the bottom of page 211.

[902] Lt. Gause actually referred to his jump as "our Steve Brodie act", reminiscence of the Steve Brodie dive from the Brooklyn Bridge in 1886. How he knew of Steve Brodie is an interesting question for which I have no answer.

[903] Amazingly, even though he was determined to get to Corregidor, the driftwood hinted at his opinion of his swimming skills, yet he'd rather face the water than surrender to the Japanese.

[904] The War Journal of Major Damon "Rocky" Gause, Damon "Rocky" Gause deceased with an introduction by Damon L. Gause, Compass Press, 1999

[905] Long Beach Press Telegram, 7/4/2004, *Long Beach's Waterlogged Sports History* by Bob Keisser.

[906] A visit to the Channel Swimming Association web site listing: www.soloswims.com , finds no listing for Peter Lloyd.

[907] The police in outlying boroughs and suburbs around Manhattan are only too willing to provide bus fare or a token for any individual who might pose a problem for their local command. I remember only while in Flushing the officers from the local precinct rousting an individual, homeless for sure, and giving him a token to board the subway whose parting instructions where for the man to give their best to Mayor John Lindsay. And who says you can't get a free ride?

[908] NY Times, 9/18/1974

[909] The Spanish town that features an event called Running with the Bulls during their Festival of San Fermin and featured in Ernest Hemingway's *The Sun Also Rises*. I'm sure that this recounting was edited out in Ernest's *Old Man and The Sea* that has only just surfaced in the New York Times.

[910] A map of the area is seen at www.hudsoncity.net/tubesenglish/1-constructionhistory.html. The terminal build is for the Central Railroad of New Jersey and Baltimore and Ohio Depot next to the Morris Canal.

[911] The swimmers weight amount to about 5 extra tons.

[912] There are actual emergencies with greater numbers of persons in the water: in 1904, an excursion vessel, the General Slocum, caught fire in the East River and burned with 1300 persons aboard resulting in 1021 deaths, mostly by drowning. This was the greatest single disaster prior to 9/11 in New York.

[913] Washington Post, 6/29/1992, *Rough Seas Leave Swimmers Struggling for Shore* by Paul Valentine.

[914] Tides and Current software by Nautical Software, Inc. for 7/28/1992 at Sandy Point, ESE .8 nautical mile, station ID 4891.

[915] Hutchison, Jim. *We're Going Down*. Reader's Digest. August, 1995.

[916] Michelmore, Peter. *Adrift in the Arabian Sea*. Reader's Digest. August 1996.

[917] United States Coastal Pilot 2 Atlantic Coast: Cape Cod, MA to Sandy Hook, NJ, US Dept of Commerce, National Ocean Service, 2003, page 364.

[918] Email correspondence with Nuala Moore after the swim on 9/11/2006.

[919] Times any factor for using a substation.

[920] The swimmer should be tucked away in a cove or behind a pier until the current switches or dies enough to resume their journey. See the discussion on the reverse Manhattan swim.

[921] Krammer, Scott; Young, Craig; Niedfeldt, Mark; Swimming Injuries and Illnesses, American Journal of Sports Medicine, April, 1993

[922] Florida University University website: http://www.fau.edu/safe/sea-lice.html. This site has excellent photos of the dermatitis condition. Accessed 3/26/2007.

[923] The New Zealand Dermatology Network: http://dermnetnz.org/arthropods/swimmers-itch.html.

[924] Center for Disease Control web site: http://www.cdc.gov/ncidod/dpd/parasites/schistosomiasis/factsht_schistosomiasis.htm.

[925] NY Times, 12/23/1878 *Capt. Boyton at Home*.

[926] NY Times, 12/23/1878 *Capt. Boyton at Home*.

[927] NY Times, 12/23/1878 *Capt. Boyton at Home*.

[928] NY Times, 12/23/1878 *Capt. Boyton at Home*.

[929] NY Times, 2/7/1879, *Paul Boyton in the Allegheny*.

[930] NY Times, 2/18/1879, *Paul Boyton's Cold Journey*.

[931] NY Times 3/21/1879, *Boyton in Peril*.

[932] NY Times, 4/28/1879, *Capt. Boyton at New Orleans*.

[933] NY Times, 8/6/1879, *A contest in the water;* NY Times, 9/7/1879, *Mystery about a Swimming Match*.

[934] NY Times, 9/10/1879, *Webb and Boyton to Swim Again*.

[935] NYTimes, 8/31/1879, *The Webb-Boyton Race Arranged*.

[936] NY Times, 9/10/1879, *Webb and Boyton to Swim Again*.

[937] NY Times, 10/15/1879, *Paul Boyton's Swim*.

[938] NY Times, 3/9/1881, *Letter from Paul Boyton*.

[939] NY Times, 5/21/1881, *Notes from Washington*.

[940] NY Times, 6/19/1881, *Swimming Down the Mississippi*.
[941] NY Times 11/1/1881, *Capt. Boyton's Voyage*.
[942] NY Times, 5/7/1885, *Under the Garnet's Keel; Capt. Boyton's Little Joke on the Englishmen. An exploit with an empty torpedo case which startled the cruiser's officers and rejoiced the Irish heart.*
[943] NY Times 5/20/1885 *Capt. Boyton's Story*.
[944] NY Times, 6/29/1885, *Blown Up by Paul Boyton*.
[945] NY TIMES, 1/24/1886, *Selling Out Boyton's Ship*, and NY Times 1/26/1886, *Capt. Boyton's Ship Dismantled*.
[946] NY Times 3/29, 1887, *Paul Boyton Discouraged*.
[947] NY Times, 4/11/1887, *Capt. Boyton's Welcome*.
[948] NY Times, 4/9/1887, *Boyton To Travel With Barnum*.
[949] NY Times, 12/17/1888, *...Boyton's Educated Seals Arrive...*
[950] NY Times, 9/30/1893, *Was It Capt. Paul Boyton; Attempt to Blow Up Insurgents Ships*.
[951] NY Times, 4/20/1924, *Capt. Paul Boyton, Inventor, is Dead*.
[952] Professional Mariner, Dec/Jan 2005, *Correspondance* by 2nd Mate Russel Devaney aboard the *Merlin*.
[953] NY Times, 12/23/1878 *Capt. Boyton at Home*.
[954] Snyder, John. "Industry signals." Professional Mariner. Aug/Sept 2005:14.
[955] The information was elicited during an interview with Jim Doty on 1/5/2005.
[956] Visit http://www.jasonscradle.com/
[957] *Two More Records for C. M..Daniels*, NY Times, 1/21/1908.
[958] Obituary, *Robert Moses, Master Builder, is Dead at 92*, Paul Goldberger, 7/30/1981. Also, Cornelius Armory Pugsley Gold Medal Award, 1936, from http://www.rpts.tamu.edu/pugsley/Moses.htm.
[959] *Comments on a New Yorker Profile and Biography* by Robert Moses, 8/26/1974. Copy of typewritten letter found at The Bridge and Tunnel Club, Robert Moses' Response to Robert Caro's The Power Broker, website: http://www.bridgeandtunnelclub.com/detritus/moses/index.htm

www.ingramcontent.com/pod-product-compliance
Lightning Source LLC
Chambersburg PA
CBHW021824220426
43663CB00005B/119